CALVINISM VS. ARMINIANISM

THE BIBLE ANSWERS

EDWARD D. ANDREWS

CALVINISM VS. ARMINIANISM

THE BIBLE ANSWERS

Edward D. Andrews

Christian Publishing House
Cambridge, Ohio

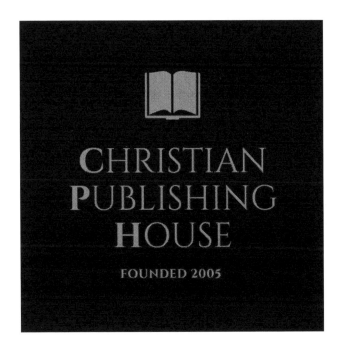

CHRISTIAN
PUBLISHING
HOUSE
FOUNDED 2005

CALVINISM VS. ARMINIANISM: The Bible Answers by Edward D. Andrews

ISBN-13: **978-1-949586-99-2**

ISBN-10: **1-949586-99-5**

Table of Contents

Lost
Lost
Saved
Saved
Lost
Lost
Saved
Saved
Lost
Saved

Preface

To possess "the light of life," one must put faith in Jesus Christ and become his follower. On social media every day, millions of Christians are saying such things as "I am a Calvinist," "I am an Arminian." "I am a Lutheran," "I am a Wesleyan," and so on. They then debate and argue theology as though it is a blood sport. This author is not an Arminian, Calvinist, Wesleyan, Lutheran, Baptist, follower, disciple, or learner of any other denomination; Andrews is non-denominational.

TRUE CHRISTIANS—Are Not followers of Men

Are some chosen (predestined) to eternal salvation, and others to eternal condemnation? Andrews will have entire chapters dealing with this important issue and inform the reader from the Calvinist and Arminian perspectives. In the end, he will answer the following questions.

- Is Total Depravity Biblical?
- Is Unconditional Election Biblical?
- Is Limited Atonement Biblical?
- Is Irresistible Grace Biblical?
- Is Perseverance of the Saints Biblical?

INTRODUCTION The History of the Calvinist-Arminian Debate

The Reformer Who Challenged Calvin's Barbarianism

To some, Calvin was a maverick, to others a menace, and to Sebastian Castellio, a murderer.

Sebastian Castellio (also Sébastien Châteillon, Châtaillon, Castellión, and Castello; 1515 – 29 December 1563) was a French preacher and theologian; and one of the first Reformed Christian proponents of religious toleration, freedom of conscience and thought.

Castellio and Calvin's disagreements grew exponentially when during a public meeting Castellio rose to his feet and claimed that clergy should stop persecuting those who disagree with them on matters of Biblical interpretation, and should be held to the same standards that all other believers were held to. Soon after, Calvin charged Castellio with the offense of "undermining the prestige of the clergy." Castellio was forced to resign from his position of Rector and asked to be dismissed from being a preacher in Vandoeuvres. Anticipating future attacks from Calvin, Castellio asked for a signed letter that outlined in detail the reasons for his departure: "That no one may form a false idea of the reasons for the departure of Sebastian Castellio, we all declare that he has voluntarily resigned his position as rector at the College, and up till now performed his duties in such a way that we regarded him worthy to become one of our preachers. If, in the end, the affair was not thus arranged, this is not because any fault has been found in Castellio's conduct, but merely for the reasons previously indicated."[1]

The man who once was the Rector in Geneva was now homeless and in deep poverty. The next few years were desperate times for him. Though one of the most learned men of his time, his life came down to begging for food from door to door. Living in abject poverty with his eight dependents, Castellio was forced to depend on strangers to stay alive. His plight brought sympathy and admiration from his contemporaries. Montaigne wrote "it was deplorable that a man who had done such good service as Castellio should have fallen upon evil days" and added that "many persons would

[1] Zweig 1951, p. 250.

unquestionably have been glad to help Castellio had they known soon enough that he was in want."[2]

History indicates that many perhaps were afraid to help Castellio for fear of reprisals from Geneva.[3] Castellio's existence ranged from begging and digging ditches for food to proof-reading for the Basel printshop of Johannes Oporinus. He also worked as a private tutor while translating thousands of pages from Greek, Hebrew and Latin into French and German. He was also the designated successor to Desiderius Erasmus in continuing his work of the reconciliation of Christianity in the Protestant, Anabaptist, and Catholic branches, and prophetically predicted[citation needed] the French Wars of Religion, and potentially the destruction of Christianity in Europe, if Christians could not learn to tolerate and reach each other by love and reason rather than by force of arms, and in short become real followers of Christ, rather than of bitter, partisan, and sectarian ideologies.

History of the Calvinist-Arminian Debate

The history of the Calvinist–Arminian debate begins in early 17th century in the Netherlands with a **Christian theological**[4] dispute between the followers of **John Calvin**[5] and **Jacobus Arminius**,[6] and continues today among some **Protestants**,[7] particularly **evangelicals**.[8] The debate centers

[2] Zweig 1951, p. 252.

[3] Zweig 1951, pp. 337ff.

[4] Christian theology is the theology of Christian belief and practice. Such study concentrates primarily upon the texts of the Old Testament and of the New Testament, as well as on Christian tradition.

[5] John Calvin (10 July 1509 – 27 May 1564) was a French theologian, pastor, and reformer in Geneva during the Protestant Reformation. He was a principal figure in the development of the system of Christian theology later called Calvinism, including its doctrines of predestination and of God's absolute sovereignty in the salvation of the human soul from death and eternal damnation.

[6] Jacobus Arminius (10 October 1560 – 19 October 1609), the Latinized name of Jakob Hermanszoon, was a Dutch theologian during the Protestant Reformation period whose views became the basis of Arminianism and the Dutch Remonstrant movement. He served from 1603 as professor in theology at the University of Leiden and wrote many books and treatises on theology.

[7] Protestantism is a form of Christianity that originated with the 16th-century Reformation, a movement against what its followers perceived to be errors in the Catholic Church. Protestants originating in the Reformation reject the Roman Catholic doctrine of papal supremacy, but disagree among themselves regarding the number of sacraments, the real presence of Christ in the Eucharist, and matters of ecclesiastical polity and apostolic succession.

[8] Evangelicalism (), also called evangelical Christianity or evangelical Protestantism, is a worldwide interdenominational movement within Protestant Christianity that affirms the centrality of being "born again", in which an individual experiences personal conversion, the authority of the Bible as God's revelation to humanity (biblical inerrancy), and in spreading the Christian message. The word evangelical comes from the Greek (euangelion) word for "good news".Its origins are usually traced to 1738, with various theological streams contributing to its foundation, including Pietism, Puritanism, Quakerism, Presbyterianism and Moravianism (in particular its bishop Nicolaus Zinzendorf and his community at Herrnhut).

around **soteriology**,[9] or the study of salvation, and includes disputes about **total depravity**,[10] **predestination**,[11] and **atonement**. While the debate was given its Calvinist–Arminian form in the 17th century, issues central to the debate have been discussed in Christianity in some form since **Augustine of Hippo**'s[12] disputes with the **Pelagians**[13] in the 5th century.

Quinquarticular Controversy

The **Quinquarticular Controversy** is a term used to refer to the purely theological Calvinist–Arminian clashes of the period 1609 to 1618, a time in which the debate had serious political overtones in the Netherlands. This controversy is the one that was addressed by the Dutch **Reformed churches** at the **Synod of Dort**[14] in 1618–1619, a meeting to which Protestant representatives from Reformed churches in other countries were invited. Quinquarticular (i.e. "having to do with five points") refers to points of contention raised by the Arminian party in its publication of **five articles of Remonstrance**[15] in 1610. These were rejected by the Synod in the Canons

[9] Soteriology (; Greek: σωτηρία sōtēria "salvation" from σωτήρ sōtēr "savior, preserver" and λόγος logos "study" or "word") is the study of religious doctrines of salvation. Salvation theory occupies a place of special significance in many religions.

[10] Total depravity (also called radical corruption or pervasive depravity) is a Protestant theological doctrine derived from the concept of original sin. It teaches that, as a consequence of man's fall, every person born into the world is enslaved to the service of sin as a result of their fallen nature and, apart from the efficacious (irresistible) or prevenient (enabling) grace of God, is completely unable to choose by themselves to follow God, refrain from evil, or accept the gift of salvation as it is offered.

[11] Predestination, in Christian theology, is the doctrine that all events have been willed by God, usually with reference to the eventual fate of the individual soul. Explanations of predestination often seek to address the paradox of free will, whereby God's omniscience seems incompatible with human free will.

[12] Augustine of Hippo (, also US: ; Latin: Aurelius Augustinus Hipponensis; 13 November 354 – 28 August 430), also known as Saint Augustine, was a theologian and philosopher of Berber origin and the bishop of Hippo Regius in Numidia, Roman North Africa. His writings influenced the development of Western philosophy and Western Christianity, and he is viewed as one of the most important Church Fathers of the Latin Church in the Patristic Period.

[13] Pelagianism is a heretical Christian theological position that holds that the original sin did not taint human nature and that humans by divine grace have free will to achieve human perfection. Pelagius (c. 355 – c. 420 AD), an Irish ascetic and philosopher, taught that God could not command believers to do the impossible, and therefore it must be possible to satisfy all divine commandments.

[14] The Synod of Dort (also known as the Synod of Dordt or the Synod of Dordrecht) was an international Synod held in Dordrecht in 1618–1619, by the Dutch Reformed Church, to settle a divisive controversy caused by the rise of Arminianism. The first meeting was on 13 November 1618 and the final meeting, the 180th, was on 29 May 1619.

[15] The Five Articles of Remonstrance or the Remonstrance were theological propositions advanced in 1610 by followers of Jacobus Arminius who had died in 1609, in disagreement with interpretations of the teaching of John Calvin then current in the Dutch Reformed Church. Those who supported them were called RRemonstrants."

of Dort, the essence of which is commonly referred to as the **Five Points of Calvinism.**[16]

The Controversy marked the transformation of the Arminian movement into a separate, persecuted church organization in the Netherlands. For Arminians it was the start of full persecution after the imposition of an edict, while for Calvinists it resulted in the settling in clear points of doctrine that were initiated by John Calvin and clarified by Theodore Beza. For Lutherans the controversies saw the ending of any possibility of unification with the Calvinists.

Protestant Beliefs about Salvation			
This table summarizes the classical views of three Protestant beliefs about salvation.			
Topic	**Calvinism**	**Lutheranism**	**Arminianism**
Human will	**Total depravity**: Humanity possesses "free will," but it is in bondage to sin, until it is "transformed."	Original Sin: Humanity possesses free will in regard to "goods and possessions," but is sinful by nature and unable to contribute to its own salvation.	Total depravity: Humanity possesses freedom from necessity, but not "freedom from sin" unless enabled by "prevenient grace."
Election	Unconditional election	Unconditional election	Conditional election in view of foreseen faith or unbelief.

[16] The most important Reformed theologians include Calvin, Zwingli, Martin Bucer, William Farel, Heinrich Bullinger, Peter Martyr Vermigli, Theodore Beza, and John Knox. In the twentieth century, Abraham Kuyper, Herman Bavinck, B. B. Warfield, J. Gresham Machen, Louis Berkhof, Karl Barth, Martyn Lloyd-Jones, Cornelius Van Til, R. C. Sproul, and J. I. Packer were influential. Contemporary Reformed theologians include John MacArthur, Timothy J. Keller, David Wells, John Piper, and Michael Horton.

The five points have been summarized under the acrostic TULIP.[72] The five points are popularly said to summarize the Canons of Dort; however, there is no historical relationship between them, and some scholars argue that their language distorts the meaning of the Canons, Calvin's theology, and the theology of 17th-century Calvinistic orthodoxy, particularly in the language of total depravity and limited atonement.[73] The five points were more recently popularized in the 1963 booklet The Five Points of Calvinism Defined, Defended, Documented by David N. Steele and Curtis C. Thomas. The origins of the five points and the acrostic are uncertain, but they appear to be outlined in the Counter Remonstrance of 1611, a lesser-known Reformed reply to the Arminians, which was written prior to the Canons of Dort.[74] The acrostic was used by Cleland Boyd McAfee as early as circa 1905.[75] An early printed appearance of the acrostic can be found in Loraine Boettner's 1932 book, The Reformed Doctrine of Predestination.

Protestant Beliefs about Salvation			
Justification and atonement	Justification by faith alone. Various views regarding the extent of the atonement.	Justification for all men, completed at Christ's death and effective through faith alone.	Justification made possible for all through Christ's death, but only completed upon choosing faith in Jesus.
Conversion	Monergistic, through the means of grace, irresistible.	Monergistic, through the means of grace, resistible.	Synergistic, resistible due to the common grace of free will.
Perseverance and apostasy	Perseverance of the saints: the eternally elect in Christ will certainly persevere in faith.	Falling away is possible, but God gives gospel assurance.	Preservation is conditional upon continued faith in Christ; with the possibility of a final apostasy.

The central assertion of TULIP is that God saves every person upon whom he has mercy, and that his efforts are not frustrated by the unrighteousness or inability of humans.

- **Total depravity** (also called *radical corruption* or *pervasive depravity*) asserts that as a consequence of the **fall of man into sin**,[17] every person is enslaved to sin. People are not by nature inclined to love God, but rather to serve their own interests and to reject the rule of God. Thus, all people by their own faculties are morally unable to choose to trust God for their salvation and be saved (the term "total" in this context refers to sin affecting every part of a person, not that every person is as evil as they could be). This doctrine is derived from Calvin's interpretation of Augustine's explanation about **Original Sin**.[18] While the phrases "totally depraved" and

[17] The fall of man, the fall of Adam, or simply the Fall, is a term used in Christianity to describe the transition of the first man and woman from a state of innocent obedience to God to a state of guilty disobedience. The doctrine of the Fall comes from a biblical interpretation of Genesis, chapters 1-3.

[18] Original sin is the Christian doctrine that holds that humans, through the fact of birth, inherit a tainted nature in need of regeneration and a proclivity to sinful conduct. The biblical bases for the belief are generally found in Genesis 3 (the story of the expulsion of Adam and Eve from the Garden of Eden), in a line in psalm 51:5 ("I was brought forth in iniquity, and in sin did my mother conceive me"), and in Paul's Epistle to the Romans, 5:12-21 ("Therefore, just as sin entered the world through one man, and death through sin, and in this way death came to all people, because all sinned").The belief began to emerge in the 3rd century, but only became fully formed with the writings of Augustine of Hippo (354–430), who was the first author to use the phrase "original sin" (Latin: peccatum originale).

"utterly perverse" were used by Calvin, what was meant was the inability to save oneself from sin rather than being absent of goodness. Phrases like "total depravity" cannot be found in the Canons of Dort, and the Canons as well as later Reformed orthodox theologians arguably offer a more moderate view of the nature of fallen humanity than Calvin.

- **Unconditional election** (also called *sovereign election* or *unconditional grace*) asserts that God has chosen from eternity those whom he will bring to himself not based on foreseen virtue, merit, or faith in those people; rather, his choice is unconditionally grounded in his mercy alone. God has chosen from eternity to extend mercy to those he has chosen and to withhold mercy from those not chosen. Those chosen receive salvation through Christ alone. Those not chosen receive the just wrath that is warranted for their sins against God.[111]
- **Limited atonement** (also called *definite atonement* or *particular redemption*) asserts that Jesus's **substitutionary atonement**[19] was definite and certain in its purpose and in what it accomplished. This implies that only the sins of the elect were **atoned**[20] for by Jesus's death. Calvinists do not believe, however, that the atonement is limited in its value or power, but rather that the atonement is limited in the sense that it is intended for some and not all. Some Calvinists have summarized this as "The atonement is sufficient for all and efficient for the elect."
- **Irresistible grace** (also called *effectual grace*, *effectual calling*, or *efficacious grace*) asserts that the saving grace of God is effectually applied to those whom he has determined to save (that is, the elect) and overcomes their resistance to obeying the call of the gospel, bringing them to a saving faith. This means that when God sovereignly purposes to save someone, that individual certainly will be saved. The doctrine holds that this purposeful influence of God's Holy Spirit cannot be resisted, but that the Holy Spirit, "graciously causes

---

[19] Substitutionary atonement, also called vicarious atonement, is a central concept within Christian theology which asserts that Jesus died "for us", as propagated by the Western classic and objective paradigms of atonement in Christianity, which regard Jesus as dying as a substitute for others, "instead of" them. Substitutionary atonement has been explicated in the "classic paradigm" of the Early Church Fathers, namely the ransom theory, as well as in Gustaf Aulen's demystified reformulation, the Christus Victor theory; and in the "objective paradigm," which includes Anselm of Canterbury's satisfaction theory, the Reformed period's penal substitution theory, and the Governmental theory of atonement.

[20] Penal substitution (sometimes, esp. in older writings, called forensic theory) is a theory of the atonement within Christian theology, which declares that Christ, voluntarily submitting to God the Father's plan, was punished (penalized) in the place of sinners (substitution), thus satisfying the demands of justice so God can justly forgive sins making us at one with God (atonement).

the elect sinner to cooperate, to believe, to repent, to come freely and willingly to Christ." This is not to deny the fact that the Spirit's outward call (through the proclamation of the Gospel) can be, and often is, rejected by sinners; rather, it is that inward call which cannot be rejected.

- **Perseverance of the saints** (also called *preservation of the saints*; the "saints" being those whom God has predestined to salvation) asserts that since God is sovereign and his will cannot be frustrated by humans or anything else, those whom God has called into communion with himself will continue in faith until the end. Those who apparently fall away either never had true faith to begin with (1 John 2:19), or, if they are saved but not presently walking in the Spirit, they will be divinely chastened (Hebrews 12:5–11) and will repent (1 John 3:6–9).

Theological background

Augustine and Pelagius

Pelagius was a British monk who journeyed to Rome around the year 400 A.D. and was appalled at the lax behavior within churches. To combat this lack of holiness, he preached a Gospel that began with justification through faith alone (it was actually Pelagius, not Luther, who first added the word alone to Paul's phrase) but finished through human effort and morality. He had read Augustine's **Confessions**[21] and believed it to be a fatalistic and pessimistic view of human nature. Pelagius' followers, including **Caelestius**,[22] went further than their teacher and removed justification through faith, setting up the morality- and works-based salvation known as Pelagianism. It should be mentioned that the only historical evidence of the teachings of Pelagius or his followers is found through the writings of his two strongest opponents — Augustine and **Jerome**.[23]

In response to Pelagius, Augustine adopted a theological system that included not only original sin (which Pelagius denied), but also a form of

21 Confessions (Latin: Confessiones) is an autobiographical work by Saint Augustine of Hippo, consisting of 13 books written in Latin between AD 397 and 400. The work outlines Saint Augustine's sinful youth and his conversion to Christianity.

22 Caelestius (or Celestius) was the major follower of the Christian teacher Pelagius and the Christian doctrine of Pelagianism, which was opposed to Augustine of Hippo and his doctrine in original sin, and was later declared to be heresy.

23 Jerome (Latin: Eusebius Sophronius Hieronymus; Greek: Εὐσέβιος Σωφρόνιος Ἱερώνυμος; c. 342 – c. 347 – 30 September 420), also known as Jerome of Stridon, was a Christian priest, confessor, theologian, and historian; he is commonly known as Saint Jerome. Jerome was born at Stridon, a village near Emona on the border of Dalmatia and Pannonia.

predestination. Some authors maintain that Augustine taught the doctrines of limited atonement and of irresistible grace, later associated with classic Calvinism; however, others insist that Augustine's writings conflict with these doctrines. Critics maintain that part of Augustine's philosophy might have stemmed from his expertise in Greek philosophy, particularly **Platonism**[24] and **Manichaeism,**[25] which maintained a very high view of a man's spirit and very low view of a man's body.[2] Against the Pelagian notion that man can do everything right, he taught that man could do little right. Thus, he reasoned, man cannot even accept the offer of salvation — it must be God who chooses for himself individuals to bring to salvation.

A group of Italian bishops, led by Julian, defended the Pelagian view against the Augustinian concept of predestination but was rejected by the **Council of Ephesus**[26] in 431. Later a monastic movement in Southern Gaul (modern-day France) also sought to explain predestination in light of God's foreknowledge, but a flurry of writings from Augustine (Grace and Free Will, Correction and Grace, The Predestination of the Saints and The Gift of Perseverance) helped maintain the papal authority of his doctrines.

Semi-Pelagianism and Semi-Augustinianism

After the death of Augustine, a more moderate form of Pelagianism persisted, which claimed that man's faith was an act of **free will**[27] unassisted by previous internal grace. The **Second Council of Orange** (529)[28] was

[24] Platonism is the philosophy of Plato and philosophical systems closely derived from it, though contemporary platonists do not necessarily accept all of the doctrines of Plato. Platonism had a profound effect on Western thought.

[25] Manichaeism (; in New Persian آیینِ مانی Āyīn-e Mānī; Chinese: 摩尼教; pinyin: Mónījiào) was a major religion founded in the 3rd century AD by the Parthian prophet Mani (AD 216–274), in the Sasanian Empire.Manichaeism taught an elaborate dualistic cosmology describing the struggle between a good, spiritual world of light, and an evil, material world of darkness. Through an ongoing process that takes place in human history, light is gradually removed from the world of matter and returned to the world of light, whence it came.

[26] The Council of Ephesus was a council of Christian bishops convened in Ephesus (near present-day Selçuk in Turkey) in AD 431 by the Roman Emperor Theodosius II. This third ecumenical council, an effort to attain consensus in the church through an assembly representing all of Christendom, confirmed the original Nicene Creed, and condemned the teachings of Nestorius, Patriarch of Constantinople, who held that the Virgin Mary may be called the Christotokos, "Christ-bearer" but not the Theotokos, "God-bearer." It met in June and July 431 at the Church of Mary in Ephesus in Anatolia.

[27] Free will in theology is an important part of the debate on free will in general. Religions vary greatly in their response to the standard argument against free will and thus might appeal to any number of responses to the paradox of free will, the claim that omniscience and free will are incompatible.

[28] The Second Council of Orange (or Second Synod of Orange) was held in 529 at Orange, which was then part of the Ostrogothic Kingdom. It affirmed much of the theology of Augustine of Hippo, and made numerous proclamations against what later would come to be known as semi-Pelagian doctrine.

convened to address whether this moderate form of semi-Pelagianism could be affirmed, or if the doctrines of Augustine were to be affirmed.

The determination of the Council could be considered "semi-Augustinian." It defined that faith, though a free act, resulted even in its beginnings from the grace of God, enlightening the human mind and enabling belief. However, it also denied strict predestination, stating, "We not only do not believe that any are foreordained to evil by the power of God, but even state with utter abhorrence that if there are those who want to believe so evil a thing, they are anathema." The document received papal sanction.

Calvinist Reformers used the Council's canons to demonstrate that their formulations of original sin and depravity had already been taught much earlier in the church. Arminian theologians also refer to the Council of Orange as a historical document that strongly affirms man's depravity and God's **prevenient grace**[29] but does not present grace as irresistible or adhere to a strictly Augustinian view of predestination.

Middle Ages

Augustine's teaching on **divine grace**[30] was considered a touchstone of orthodoxy within the western church throughout the **Middle Ages**.[31] Nevertheless, within an Augustinian context, theologians continued to debate the precise nature of God and man's participation in salvation, as well as attempting to work out a place for the church's emerging system of sacraments in the overall scheme of salvation.

Thomas Aquinas,[32] the most influential Catholic theologian of the Middle Ages, taught that, from man's fallen state, there were three steps to salvation:

---

[29] Prevenient grace (or enabling grace) is a Christian theological concept rooted in Arminian theology, though it appeared earlier in Catholic theologies. It is divine grace that precedes human decisions.

[30] Divine grace is a theological term present in many religions. It has been defined as the divine influence which operates in humans to regenerate and sanctify, to inspire virtuous impulses, and to impart strength to endure trial and resist temptation; and as an individual virtue or excellence of divine origin.

[31] In the history of Europe, the Middle Ages or medieval period lasted approximately from the 5th to the late 15th centuries, similar to the post-classical period of global history. It began with the fall of the Western Roman Empire and transitioned into the Renaissance and the Age of Discovery.

[32] Thomas Aquinas (; Italian: Tommaso d'Aquino, lit. 'Thomas of Aquino'; 1225 – 7 March 1274) was an Italian Dominican friar and priest, who was an immensely influential philosopher, theologian, and jurist in the tradition of scholasticism; he is also known within the latter as the Doctor Angelicus, the Doctor Communis, and the Doctor Universalis. The name Aquinas identifies his ancestral origins in the county of Aquino in present-day Lazio, Italy.

Infusion of grace (infusio gratiae)- God infuses grace into the human soul - the Christian now has faith and, with it, the ability to do good - this step is entirely God's work and is not done by man, and once a man has faith, he can never entirely lose it - however, faith alone is not enough for salvation;

Faith formed by charity (fides caritate formata)- with man's free will restored, man must now do his best to do good works in order to have a faith formed by charity; and then

Condign merit[33] (meritum de condigno) - God then judges and awards eternal life on the basis of these good works which Aquinas called man's condign merit.

Aquinas believed that by this system, he had reconciled Ephesians 2:8 ("By grace are ye saved through faith, and that not of yourselves: it is the gift of God") and James 2:20 ("faith without works is dead") and 2:24 ("by works a man is justified and not by faith only"), and had provided an exposition of the Bible's teaching on salvation compatible with Augustine's teachings.

A second stream of medieval thought, commonly referred to as the **Ockhamists**[34] after **William of Ockham**[35] and also including **Duns Scotus**[36] and **Gabriel Biel**[37] rejected Aquinas' system as destroying man's free will. The Ockhamists argued that if a man loved God simply because of "infused grace", then man did not love God freely. They argued that before a man received an infusion of grace, man must do his best in a state of nature (i.e. based on man's reason and inborn moral sense). They argued that just as God awards eternal life on the basis of man's condign merit for doing his

---

[33] Condign merit (meritum de condigno) is an aspect of Catholic theology signifying merit with the dignity of Christ. A person born again in Christ does not merit of his own virtue but the virtues of Christ are applied to his work.

[34] Occamism (or Ockhamism) is the philosophical and theological teaching developed by William of Ockham (1285–1347) and his disciples, which had widespread currency in the 14th century. Occamism differed from the other Scholastic schools on two major points: (1) that only individuals exist, rather than supra-individual metaphysical universals, essences, or forms (universals are the mind's abstract products and have no independent existence), and (2) the reduction of ontology.

[35] William of Ockham (; also Occam, from Latin: Gulielmus Occamus; c. 1287 – 10 April 1347) was an English Franciscan friar, scholastic philosopher, and theologian, who is believed to have been born in Ockham, a small village in Surrey.

[36] John Duns Scotus (c. 1265/66 – 8 November 1308), commonly called Duns Scotus (SKOH-təs; Ecclesiastical Latin: [duns ˈskotus]; "Duns the Scot"), was a Scottish Catholic priest and Franciscan friar, university professor, philosopher, and theologian. He is one of the four most important philosopher-theologians of Western Europe in the High Middle Ages, together with Thomas Aquinas, Bonaventure, and William of Ockham.Scotus has had considerable influence on both Catholic and secular thought.

[37] Gabriel Biel (German: [biːl]; 1420 to 1425 – 7 December 1495) was a German scholastic philosopher and member of the Canons Regular of the Congregation of Windesheim, who were the clerical counterpart to the Brethren of the Common Life. Biel was born in Speyer and died in Einsiedel near Tübingen.

best to do good works after receiving faith as a gift from God, so too, the original infusion of grace was given to man on the basis of "congruent merit", a reward for man's doing his best in a state of nature. (Unlike condign merit, which is fully deserved by man, congruent merit is not fully deserved, and includes a measure of grace on God's part. Congruent merit is therefore also sometimes called "semimerit". According to the Ockhamists, a gracious God awards an individual with congruent merit when he or she does the best that he or she is able to do.)

Aquinas' followers, commonly referred to as the Thomists, accused the Ockhamists of Pelagianism for basing the infusion of grace on man's works. The Ockhamists defended themselves from charges of Pelagianism by arguing that, in the Ockhamist system, God was not bound to award the infusion of grace on the basis of congruent merit; rather, God's decision to award the infusion of grace on the basis of congruent merit was an entirely gracious act on God's part.

Martin Luther's condemnation of "justification by works" clearly condemned Ockhamism. Some proponents of **ecumenism**[38] argue that the Thomist view of salvation is not opposed to Luther's view of grace, and, since Ockhamism was rejected as **Semipelagian**[39] by the Catholic Church at the Council of Trent, theology of salvation need not pose a bar to Protestant-Catholic reunion. (The major streams of modern Catholic thought on the theology of salvation are Thomism and **Molinism,**[40] a theology developed by Jesuit theologian **Luis Molina**[41] in the 16th century and also held today by some Protestants such as William Lane Craig and Alvin Plantinga.)

---

[38] Ecumenism (), also spelled oecumenism, is the concept and principle that Christians who belong to different Christian denominations should work together to develop closer relationships among their churches and promote Christian unity. The adjective ecumenical is thus applied to any interdenominational initiative that encourages greater cooperation between Christians and their churches.

[39] Semi-Pelagianism (or Semipelagianism) is a Christian theological and soteriological school of thought on salvation. Semipelagian thought stands in contrast to the earlier Pelagian teaching about salvation, the Pelagianism (in which people achieve their own salvation by their own means) which had been dismissed as heresy.

[40] Molinism, named after 16th-century Spanish Jesuit priest and Roman Catholic theologian Luis de Molina, is the thesis that God has middle knowledge. It seeks to reconcile the apparent tension of divine providence and human free will.:20 Prominent contemporary Molinists include William Lane Craig, Alfred Freddoso, Thomas Flint, Kenneth Keathley, and Dave Armstrong.

[41] Luis de Molina (29 September 1535 – 12 October 1600) was a Spanish Jesuit priest and scholastic, a staunch defender of free will in the controversy over human liberty and God's grace. His theology is known as Molinism.

However, since the Catholic Church's rejection of **Jansenism**[42] in the bull **Unigenitus**[43] (1713), it has been clear that Calvinism could not be accommodated within Catholicism. Arminianism, on the other hand, while it might not square entirely with Catholic theologies of salvation, probably could be accommodated within the Catholic Church, a fact which Arminianism's Protestant opponents have often pointed out. (**Augustus Toplady,**[44] for example, famously claimed that Arminianism was the "Road to Rome.")

Martin Luther and Erasmus of Rotterdam

Martin Luther was an Augustinian monk in Erfurt. In his Disputation Against Scholastic Theology of 4 September 1517, Luther entered into the medieval debate between the Thomists and the Ockhamists by attacking the Ockhamist position and arguing that man by nature lacks the ability to do good that the Ockhamists asserted he had (and thus denying that man could do anything to deserve congruent merit). Modern scholars disagree about whether Luther in fact intended to criticize all scholastics in this Disputation or if he was concerned only with the Ockhamists. Arguing in favor of a broader interpretation is the fact that Luther went on to criticize the use of Aristotle in theology (Aristotle was the basis of Thomist as well as Ockhamist theology). If this is the case, it is likely that Luther saw Aquinas' fides caritate formata as merely a more cautious form of Pelagianism (or as Semipelagianism).

Luther continued to defend these views. In 1520, Pope Leo X issued the papal bull Exsurge Domine, which condemned a position which Luther had maintained at the 1518 Heidelberg Disputation, namely that "After the Fall free will is something in name only and when it does what is in it, it sins mortally." Luther subsequently defended the proposition in his Defense and Explanation of All the Articles Unjustly Condemned by the Roman Bull of Leo X (1520), in the process stating that "free will is really a fiction...with no reality, because it is in no man's power to plan any evil or good. As the article of Wycliffe, condemned at Constance, correctly teaches: everything takes place by absolute necessity."

---

[42] Jansenism was an early modern theological movement within Catholicism, primarily active in the Kingdom of France, that emphasized original sin, human depravity, the necessity of divine grace, and predestination. It was declared a heresy by the Roman Catholic Church.

[43] Unigenitus (named for its Latin opening words Unigenitus dei filius, or "Only-begotten son of God") is an apostolic constitution in the form of a papal bull promulgated by Pope Clement XI in 1713. It opened the final phase of the Jansenist controversy in France.

[44] Augustus Montague Toplady (4 November 1740 – 11 August 1778) was an Anglican cleric and hymn writer. He was a major Calvinist opponent of John Wesley.

Desiderius Erasmus of Rotterdam, though first sympathetic to Luther, reacted negatively to what he saw as Luther's determinism. In his De libero arbitrio diatribe sive collatio (A Disquisition on Freedom of the Will) (1524), Erasmus caricatures the limitations of free will that he saw Luther espousing. Though at times in the Diatribe, Erasmus sounded like an Ockhamist, for the most part he attempted to espouse a middle course between grace and free will, attempting to avoid on the one hand the errors of the Pelagians and the Ockhamists, and on the other hand, the "Manichaean" error of Luther and other strict Augustinians.

Luther responded with his De Servo Arbitrio (On the Bondage of the Will) (1525) in which he attacked Erasmus vehemently and argued that man was not free to do good. Rather, man's fallen nature is in bondage to sin and to Satan and man can only do evil. The only way an individual can be saved is if God freely chooses to give that person the gift of faith. Luther's position in On the Bondage of the Will became the position adopted by the Protestant movement.

Jacobus Arminius and the Synod of Dort

Jacobus Arminius enrolled at Leiden University, and after five years of education traveled in the early 1580s to study in Geneva. Theodore Beza was the chairman of theology at the university there. Beza later defended Arminius by saying "let it be known to you that from the time Arminius returned to us from Basel, his life and learning both have so approved themselves to us, that we hope the best of him in every respect..." In late 1587, at the age of 28, Arminius returned to Amsterdam to fulfill his desire to be a pastor.

Arminius' entry into the predestination debate in Amsterdam was two years after his return, when he was asked by city officials to refute a modified form of Beza's Lapsarianism. According to historic tradition, Arminius' study of the Scriptures led him to the conclusion that the Bible did not support Calvinism. Other scholars believe that Arminius never accepted Beza's views, even while a student at Geneva. Arminius avoided adding to the controversy apart from two incidents regarding sermons on Romans 7 and Romans 9.

When Arminius received his doctorate and professorship of theology at Leiden in 1603, the debate over Calvinism came back to life. Conflicts over predestination had appeared early in the Dutch Reformed Church, but "these had been of a local nature, occurring between two fellow ministers, for instance, but since the appointment of Jacobus Arminius as a professor at Leyden University (1603) the strife had moved to the place where the education of future ministers took place."

Arminius taught that Calvinist predestination and unconditional election made God the author of evil. Instead, Arminius insisted, God's election was an election of believers and therefore was conditioned on faith. Furthermore, Arminius argued, God's exhaustive foreknowledge did not require a doctrine of determinism.

Arminius and his followers believed that a national synod should confer, to win tolerance for their views. His opponents in the Dutch Reformed Church maintained the authority of local synods and denied the necessity of a national convention. When the States of Holland called together the parties, Arminius's opponents, led by his colleague Franciscus Gomarus, accused him not only of the teaching of the doctrines characteristic of Arminianism as it would become (see below), but also of errors on the authority of Scripture, the Trinity, original sin, and works salvation. These charges Arminius denied, citing agreement with both Calvin and Scripture.

Arminius was acquitted of any doctrinal error. He then accepted an invitation to a "friendly conference" with Gomarus[8] but his health caused the conference to end prematurely. Two months later, on 19 October 1609, Jacobus Arminius died.

The Remonstrants and Calvinist Reaction

After the death of Arminius, the Hague court chaplain, Johannes Wtenbogaert, one of the professor's followers "who dogmatically and theologically was on one line with him, but who in the field of Church politics was a much more radical supporter of state influence championed his cause. This was seen as a betrayal on Gomarus' side, for earlier in his career (as a minister of Utrecht) Wtenbogaert "had resisted state influence with all his might."

Gradually Arminian-minded candidates for ordination into the ministry ran into ever greater difficulties. In their classes examinations, not only was subscription to the Dutch Confession and the Heidelberg Catechism demanded (which most were willing to do), "but they were asked questions that were formulated in such a way that ambiguous answers were no longer possible."

In reaction to this growing pressure Wtenbogaert drew up a petition to the State General, called a Remonstrance in late 1609, early 1610. The "Remonstrants" highlighted five aspects of their theology: (1) election was conditional on foreseen faith; (2) Christ's atonement was unlimited in extent; (3) total depravity; (4) prevenient and resistible grace; and (5) necessity of perseverance and the possibility of apostasy. The Remonstrants first expressed an uncertainty about the possibility of apostasy. They removed it latter in the document they presented officially at the Synod of Dort, The Opinion of The Remonstrants (1618), holding to conditional preservation of the saints.

Forty-four ministers (mostly from the province of Holland) signed onto the Remonstrance, and on 14 January 1610 it was submitted to the Grand Pensionary, Johan van Oldenbarnevelt. (Due to this document the followers of Arminius became known as Remonstrants.) Oldenbarnevelt held onto the Remonstrance for an unusually long period and it was not until June 1610 that it was submitted in an altered form to the States of Holland. "The States sent the five articles to all classes, forbidding them to go 'higher' in their examinations of ordinands than what was expressed in the articles. Needless to say, most classes did not take the slightest notice of this prohibition."

In another attempt to avoid a provincial synod, the States held The Hague Conference which lasted from 11 March to 20 May 1611 (with intermissions). It was at this conference that the delegates of Arminius' opponents submitted a response to the Remonstrance, called the Counter-Remonstrance (from which the name Contra- or Counter-Remonstrants was given them).

Leading influences among Arminius' followers (now called Remonstrants) were Arminius' close friend and Roman Catholic-turned-Reformed pastor Johannes Wtenbogaert, lawyer Hugo Grotius, and a scholar named Simon Episcopius. Due to the Remonstrants' view of the supremacy of civil authorities over church matters, King James I of England came out in support of the Remonstrance (later he would join with their opponents against Conrad Vorstius).

Behind the theological debate lay a political one between Prince Maurice, a strong military leader, and his former mentor Johan van Oldenbarnevelt, Grand Pensionary of Holland and personification of civil power. Maurice, who had Calvinist leanings, desired war with Holland's enemy, Roman Catholic Spain. Oldenbarnevelt, along with Arminius and his followers, desired peace.

Numerous historians hold that many of the civic officials that sided with the Remonstrants did so because of their shared position of State supremacy over the Church and not because of other doctrinal ideas, saying "the alliance between the regents and the Remonstrants during the years of the Truce is merely a coalition suited to the occasion, not the result of principal agreement...the magistracy of Delft was Counter-Remonstrant-minded, but in the States of Holland the city supported Oldenbarnevelt's policy regarding the convocation of a National Synod [to avoid calling one]. Incidentally, suspectedly Calvinistic opinions went together in Oldenbarnevelt's person. "

In the years after Arminius' death, Maurice became convinced that Oldenbarnevelt (and by association, Arminians) had strong Catholic sympathies and were working to deliver Holland to Spain. As insurance, Maurice and his militia systematically and forcibly replaced Remonstrant magistrates with Calvinist ones. Thus, when the State General called for a synod in 1618, its outcome was predetermined. Oldenbarnevelt and Grotius were arrested, and the synod, held at Dordrecht (Dort), was convened.

This Synod of Dort included Calvinist representatives from Great Britain, Switzerland, Germany, and France, though Arminians were denied acceptance. Three Arminian delegates from Utrecht managed to gain seats, but were soon forcibly ejected and replaced with Calvinist alternates.

The Synod was a six versus six style of representation that lasted over six months with 154 meetings. The synod ultimately ruled that Arminius' teachings were heretical, reaffirming the Belgic Confession and Heidelberg Catechism as its orthodox statements of doctrine. One of the results of the synod was the formation of the five points of Calvinism in direct response to the five articles of the Remonstrants.

Robert Picirilli gives this summary of the aftermath of the Synod of Dort:

> "Punishment for the Remonstrants, now officially condemned as heretics and therefore under severe judgement of both church and state, was severe. All Arminian pastors — some 200 of them — were deprived of office; any who would not agree to be silent were banished from the country. Spies were paid to hunt down those suspected of returning to their homeland. Some were imprisoned, among them Grotius; but he escaped and fled the country. Five days after the synod was over, Oldenbarnevelt was beheaded.[45]

Somewhat later, after Maurice died, the Remonstrants were accorded toleration by the state and granted the freedom to follow their religion in peace, to build churches and schools. The Remonstrant Theological Seminary was instituted in Amsterdam, and Episcopius and Grotius were

[45] Picirilli, p. 16.

among its first professors. Today both the seminary and the church have shifted from their founders' theology.[46]

Seventeenth-Century English Politics

Early Stuart society was religious, and religion at that time was political. King James I managed religious conflicts for most of the 1610s, but most Protestants maintained a fear of Catholicism. Though Arminians were Protestant, they were perceived as being less antagonistic to Catholicism than the Calvinists were. James I initially moved to keep them out of his realm, and supported the official position of the Synod of Dort.

In 1618, the Thirty Years' War began. It was a religious war, and many of James's subjects (particularly in Parliament) wanted his kingdom to go to war on the side of the king's son-in-law, Frederick V, Elector Palatine. James, however, preferred diplomacy. The loudest of the supporters for war were Puritans, a term presenting difficulties of definition but who doctrinally were in general orthodox Calvinists. Some scholars believe that the Arminians' support for the king's efforts to prevent war led to him promoting a number of them in order to balance out the Puritans.[citation needed] Others argue that these promotions were simply the result of meritocratic considerations: 'James promoted Arminians because they were scholarly, diligent and able men in their diocese.' In 1625, James I died, leaving the throne to his son, Charles I.

Charles I supported the Arminians, and continued the trend of promoting them; Charles tended to promote only Arminians. The religious changes which Charles imposed on his subjects, in the form of Laudianism, were identified (rightly or wrongly) with Arminian theology.[citation needed] They brought him into direct conflict with the Scottish Presbyterian Calvinists of the Church of Scotland. The resulting Bishops' Wars were a trigger for the English Civil War, both of them part of the larger Wars of the Three Kingdoms which had complex roots, among which religious beliefs were a major factor.

---

[46] Platt, Frederic "Arminianism", Encyclopaedia of Religion and Ethics, ed. James Hastings (New York: Charles Scribner's Sons, n.d.) 1:811.

Four-point Calvinists

The so-called "four-point Calvinists" claim that the doctrine of **limited atonement**[47] is non-scriptural and that it was never endorsed by Calvin or the Synod of Dort.

The four-point Calvinists, like five-point Calvinists,[citation needed] accept a distinction initially made by **Peter Lombard**[48] and subsequently adopted by Thomas Aquinas that the atonement was sufficient for the whole world but efficient only to the elect. Put another way, Christ's death atones for the whole world (it is sufficient to atone for the sins of the whole world), but the benefits of Christ's death are applied only to the elect (it is efficient only to atone for the sins of the elect).

The four-point Calvinists argue that Calvin adopted this position when he wrote that "It is also a fact, without controversy, that Christ came to atone for the sins 'of the whole world.'" They also believe that the four-point position was endorsed by the Synod of Dort under Article 3 of the Second Main Point of Doctrine where the synod proclaimed that "This death of God's Son is the only and entirely complete sacrifice and satisfaction for sins; it is of infinite value and worth, more than sufficient to atone for the sins of the whole world."

---

[47] Limited atonement (also called definite atonement or particular redemption) is a doctrine accepted in some Christian theological traditions. It is particularly associated with the Reformed tradition and is one of the five points of Calvinism.

[48] Peter Lombard (also Peter the Lombard, Pierre Lombard or Petrus Lombardus; c. 1096, Novara – 21/22 July 1160, Paris), was a scholastic theologian, Bishop of Paris, and author of Four Books of Sentences which became the standard textbook of theology, for which he earned the accolade Magister Sententiarum.

This is the position which the leader of the English **Presbyterians,**[49] **Richard Baxter,**[50] asserted in his famous controversy with the leader of the English **Congregationalists,**[51] **John Owen**.[52]

Early Methodism

These theological issues played a divisive part in the early history of **Methodism**[53] in the 18th century. Heated discussions on Arminianism took place between Methodist ministers **John Wesley**[54] and **George Whitefield**.[55] From 1740 Wesley broke with Calvinism. His position caused initially the rupture with the Welsh **Calvinistic Methodists**[56] under **Howell Harris**[57] in 1742–3; and then the creation of the **Countess of Huntingdon's**

[49] Presbyterianism is a part of the Reformed tradition within Protestantism that traces its origin to the Church of Scotland. Presbyterian churches derive their name from the presbyterian form of church government by representative assemblies of elders.

[50] Richard Baxter (12 November 1615 – 8 December 1691) was an English Puritan church leader, poet, hymnodist, theologian, and controversialist. Dean Stanley called him "the chief of English Protestant Schoolmen."

[51] Congregational churches (also Congregationalist churches; Congregationalism) are Protestant churches in the Calvinist tradition practising congregationalist church governance, in which each congregation independently and autonomously runs its own affairs. Congregationalism, as defined by the Pew Research Center, is estimated to represent 0.5 percent of the worldwide Protestant population; though their organizational customs and other ideas influenced significant parts of Protestantism, as well as other Christian congregations.

[52] John Owen (1616 – 24 August 1683) was an English Nonconformist church leader, theologian, and academic administrator at the University of Oxford. He was briefly a member of parliament for the University's constituency, sitting in the First Protectorate Parliament of 1654 to 1655.

[53] Methodism, also called the Methodist movement, is a group of historically related denominations of Protestant Christianity whose origins, doctrine and practice derive from the life and teachings of John Wesley. George Whitefield and John's brother Charles Wesley were also significant early leaders in the movement.

[54] John Wesley (; 28 June [O.S. 17 June] 1703 – 2 March 1791) was an English cleric, theologian, and evangelist, who was a leader of a revival movement within the Church of England known as Methodism. The societies he founded became the dominant form of the independent Methodist movement that continues to this day.

[55] George Whitefield (; 27 December [O.S. 16 December] 1714 – 30 September 1770), also known as George Whitfield, was an Anglican cleric and evangelist who was one of the founders of Methodism and the evangelical movement.Born in Gloucester, he matriculated at Pembroke College at the University of Oxford in 1732. There he joined the "Holy Club" and was introduced to the Wesley brothers, John and Charles, with whom he would work closely in his later ministry.

[56] Calvinistic Methodists were born out of the 18th-century Welsh Methodist revival and survive as a body of Christians now forming the Presbyterian Church of Wales. Calvinistic Methodism became a major denomination in Wales, growing rapidly in the 19th century, and taking a leadership role in the Welsh Religious Revival of 1904-5.Calvinistic Methodism claims to be the only denomination in Wales to be of purely Welsh origin, owing no influence in its formation to Scottish Presbyterianism.

[57] Howell Harris (Welsh: Howel Harris; 23 January 1714 – 21 July 1773) was a Calvinistic Methodist evangelist. He was one of the main leaders of the Welsh Methodist revival in the 18th century, along with Daniel Rowland and William Williams Pantycelyn.

Connexion[58] in 1756, about the same time when Wesley broke with **James Hervey.**[59] In the 1770s a very sharp debate occurred between Wesley and **Augustus Montague Toplady.**[60]

Wesley was a champion of the teaching of Arminius, defending his soteriology in a periodical entitled The Arminian and writing articles such as Predestination Calmly Considered. He defended Arminius against charges of semi-Pelaganism, holding strongly to beliefs in original sin and total depravity. At the same time, Wesley attacked the **determinism**[61] that he claimed characterized unconditional election and maintained a belief in the **ability to lose salvation.**[62] Whitefield debated Wesley on every point (except for their agreement on total depravity) but did not introduce any additional elements into the Calvinists' conclusions set forth at Westminster.[citation needed]

Denominational Views

Protestant Denominations

[58] The Countess of Huntingdon's Connexion is a small society of evangelical churches, founded in 1783 by Selina Hastings, Countess of Huntingdon, as a result of the Evangelical Revival. For many years it was strongly associated with the Calvinist Methodist movement of George Whitefield.

[59] James Hervey (26 February 1714 – 25 December 1758) was an English clergyman and writer.

[60] Augustus Montague Toplady (4 November 1740 – 11 August 1778) was an Anglican cleric and hymn writer. He was a major Calvinist opponent of John Wesley.

[61] Determinism is the philosophical view that all events are determined completely by previously existing causes. Deterministic theories throughout the history of philosophy have sprung from diverse and sometimes overlapping motives and considerations.

[62] The conditional preservation of the saints, or conditional perseverance of the saints, or commonly conditional security, is the Arminian Christian belief that believers are kept safe by God in their saving relationship with him upon the condition of a persevering faith in Christ. Arminians find the Scriptures describing both the initial act of faith in Christ, "whereby the relationship is effected", and the persevering faith in him "whereby the relationship is sustained." The relationship of "the believer to Christ is never a static relationship existing as the irrevocable consequence of a past decision, act, or experience." Rather, it is a living union "proceeding upon a living faith in a living Savior." This living union is captured in the simple command by Christ, "Remain in me, and I in you" (John 15:4).According to Arminians, biblical saving faith expresses itself in love and obedience to God (Galatians 5:6; Hebrews 5:8–9).

To this day, Methodism and offshoots of the denomination: **Pentecostals,**[63] and **Third Wave,**[64] along with **General Baptists,**[65] usually are the ones to subscribe to Arminianism, while **Presbyterians,**[66] **Reformed Churches,**[67] **Reformed Baptists,**[68] and others subscribe to Calvinism. Largely because of its origins in Germany and Scandinavia rather than the British Isles or Holland, **Lutheranism**[69] was uninvolved in the dispute, and official Lutheran doctrine does not fully support either group, preferring instead its own doctrinal formulations about the relation of human freedom to divine sovereignty. This is also true of **Primitive Baptist**[70] belief.

Restorationist[71] fellowships are customarily free will in their soteriology. Within this trend, Churches of Christ are prone to cite Biblical

---

[63] Pentecostalism or classical Pentecostalism is a Protestant Charismatic Christian movement that emphasizes direct personal experience of God through baptism with the Holy Spirit. The term Pentecostal is derived from Pentecost, an event that commemorates the descent of the Holy Spirit upon the followers of Jesus Christ, and the speaking in "foreign" tongues as described in the second chapter of the Acts of the Apostles.

[64] Signs and wonders refers to experiences that are perceived to be miraculous as being normative in the modern Christian experience, and is a phrase associated with groups that are a part of modern charismatic movements and Pentecostalism. This phrase is seen multiple times throughout the Bible to describe the activities of the early church, and is historically recorded as continuing, at least in practice, since the time of Christ.

[65] General Baptists are Baptists who hold the general or unlimited atonement view, the belief that Jesus Christ died for the entire world and not just for the chosen elect. General Baptists are theologically Arminian, which distinguishes them from Reformed Baptists (also known as "Particular Baptists" for their belief in particular redemption).Free Will Baptists are General Baptists; opponents of the English General Baptists in North Carolina dubbed them "Freewillers" and they later assumed the name.General Baptist denominations have explicated their faith in two major confessions of faith, "The Standard Confession" (1660), and "The Orthodox Creed" (1678).

[66] Presbyterianism is a part of the Reformed tradition within Protestantism that traces its origin to the Church of Scotland. Presbyterian churches derive their name from the presbyterian form of church government by representative assemblies of elders.

[67] Calvinism (also called the Reformed Tradition, Reformed Protestantism or Reformed Christianity) is a major branch of Protestantism that follows the theological tradition and forms of Christian practice set down by John Calvin and other Reformation-era theologians. It emphasises the sovereignty of God and the authority of the Bible.

[68] Reformed Baptists (sometimes known as Particular Baptists or Calvinistic Baptists) are Baptists that hold to a Calvinist soteriology, (salvation). They can trace their history through the early modern Particular Baptists of England.

[69] Lutheranism is one of the largest branches of Protestantism, identifying with the theology of Martin Luther, a 16th-century German monk and reformer whose efforts to reform the theology and practice of the Roman Catholic Church launched the Protestant Reformation. The reaction of the government and church authorities to the international spread of his writings, beginning with the Ninety-five Theses, divided Western Christianity.

[70] Primitive Baptists – also known as Hard Shell Baptists, Foot Washing Baptists or Old School Baptists – are conservative Baptists adhering to a degree of Calvinist beliefs who coalesced out of the controversy among Baptists in the early 19th century over the appropriateness of mission boards, tract societies, and temperance societies. The adjective "primitive" in the name is used in the sense of "original."

[71] The Restoration Movement (also known as the American Restoration Movement or the Stone–Campbell Movement, and pejoratively as Campbellism) is a Christian movement that began on the United

passages in support of the view while often intensely locked in contention with Presbyterians and (usually Calvinistic) Baptists. The doctrinal components, in small towns particularly in the United States, often ally the **Churches of Christ**[72] with their Methodist neighbors on opposition to "once-saved-always-saved" doctrine despite the similarity between Churches of Christ and Baptists on immersion.

Roman Catholic Views

Post-reformation Roman Catholicism has remained largely outside the debate, although Thomist and Molinist views continue within the church. Augustinian theodicy, including those elements wherein Calvin was influenced by Augustine of Hippo, continues to be the prevalent soteriology in Roman Catholicism. Also, Jansenism has been seen by many as very similar to Calvinist doctrine, and was condemned as such by the Catholic Church in the late 17th century.

Eastern Orthodox Views

A Synod of Eastern Orthodox Churches was called in Jerusalem in 1672 to refute attempted encroachments of Protestant Calvinism. The Synod of Jerusalem (1672) also referred to as The Confession of Dositheus in 1672, strongly rejected Calvinistic formulations and named them heresy. In part, it stated,

> We believe the most good God to have from eternity predestinated unto glory those whom He hath chosen, and to have consigned unto condemnation those whom He hath rejected; but not so that He would justify the one, and consign and condemn the other without cause....since He foreknew the one would make a right use of their free-will, and the other a wrong, He predestinated the one, or condemned the other.[73]

States frontier during the Second Great Awakening (1790–1840) of the early 19th century. The pioneers of this movement were seeking to reform the church from within and sought "the unification of all Christians in a single body patterned after the church of the New Testament.":54The Restoration Movement developed from several independent strands of religious revival that idealized early Christianity.

[72] The Churches of Christ are autonomous Christian congregations associated with one another through distinct beliefs and practices based on their interpretation of the Bible. Represented in the United States and one of several branches across the world, they believe in using only Bible texts for their doctrine and practices, citing examples from the early Christian church as described in the New Testament.

[73] Synod of Jerusalem: Sometimes Called the Council of Bethlehem, Holden Under Dositheus, Patriarch of Jerusalem in 1672, (Baker), 1899

In the same document, the synod renounced Calvin by name and pronounced an anathema upon anyone teaching that God predestined anyone to evil or Hell.

Hyper-Calvinism

Hyper-Calvinism is a branch of Protestant theology that denies the universal duty of human beings to believe in Christ for the salvation of their souls. It is at times regarded as a variation of Calvinism, but critics emphasize its differences from traditional Calvinistic beliefs. Hyper-Calvinism distinguishes itself from traditional Calvinism as regards the "sufficiency and efficiency" of Christ's atonement. Predestination in Calvinism traditionally argues that only the elect are able to understand Christ's atonement, but that the sufficiency of the atonement stretches to all humanity, while Hyper-Calvinism argues the atonement is sufficient only to the elect.

The term originated in the 19th century as a sometimes-pejorative descriptor predated by terms such as "false Calvinism" and "High Calvinism". The term can be used vaguely, and its distinction from traditional Calvinism is not always clear; writers such as Jim Ellis have suggested that Hyper-Calvinism as a concept is sometimes applied broadly to denominations more theologically conservative than the speaker's, rather than to a consistent theological stance. Nonetheless, Hyper-Calvinism is still distinguished as a distinct theological branch, associated with figures such as the 18th-century theologian John Gill.

Biblical support for Hyper-Calvinism is controversial. Writers such as Gill, Richard Baxter, Daniel Whitby, and Arthur Pink have debated the support or opposition of various Biblical verses for the stance.

Definitions

Peter Toon notes that the expression "Hyper-Calvinism" came to be generally used in the 19th century while the terms "False Calvinism" and "High Calvinism" were used near the end of the 18th century to define the same doctrinal views. "High Calvinism" has sometimes been used as a synonym for Hyper-Calvinism, and at other times as a synonym for the Calvinism of the Canons of Dort (1619). Although the doctrine of limited atonement is taught in the Canons of Dort, the term "Hyper-Calvinism" in previous generations has been used to define those who reject the view that the atonement is sufficient for all mankind or that there is a general design in the death of Christ.

Historic Definitions of the Term

In his publication from 1825, George Croft defined Hyper-Calvinism as holding to a particular design of Christ's death and denying a general design. He also notes that Hyper-Calvinists were generally styled High-Calvinists because they had views above genuine Calvinism: denying that the death of Christ was "in any respect" intended for the salvation of all, not inviting all to believe in Christ for salvation, contending that invitations should only be given to the "willing", and holding to antinomian doctrines, which tend to discourage holiness.[6] In a Protestant Dictionary from 1904, Charles Neil defined Hyper-Calvinism as a view that maintains the theory of limited atonement and limits the scope of gospel invitations to the elect.

Modern Definitions of the Term

Modern definitions of Hyper-Calvinism usually distinguish it from points of Calvinism, such as limited atonement or supralapsarianism. There is not, however, unanimity regarding the definition.

Curt Daniel defines Hyper-Calvinism as "that school of supralapsarian Five Point Calvinism which so stresses the sovereignty of God by overemphasizing the secret [will of God] over the revealed will [of God] and eternity over time, that it minimizes the responsibility of Man, notably with respect to the denial of the word 'offer' in relation to the preaching of the Gospel of a finished and limited atonement, thus undermining the universal duty of sinners to believe savingly with assurance that the Lord Jesus Christ died for them." Daniel goes on to suggest that the real difference between "High" and "Hyper-" Calvinism is the word "offer."]

Iain Murray adopts a different approach, putting the emphasis on the denial of a "universal command to repent and believe" and the assertion "that we have only warrant to invite to Christ those who are conscious of a sense of sin and need."

Jim Ellis argues that "adequately defining what constitutes the fundamental error of hyper-Calvinism" is problematic because many definitions "blur the distinction between it and legitimate Calvinism", and most of them include an apparent bias against Five Point Calvinism. Ellis goes on to say that Hyper-Calvinism "consists of two fundamental errors: a denial of duty-faith and a resultant denial of the universal call of the gospel."

Adherents

The term "Hyper-Calvinist" is sometimes used as a pejorative; Jim Ellis suggests that "it seems as if anyone to the right of one's own theological position is fair game to be labeled a hyper-Calvinist." Notwithstanding this, people who have been described as Hyper-Calvinists include John Skepp (d. 1721), Lewis Wayman (d. 1764), John Brine (d. 1765), and John Gill (d. 1771).

David Engelsma notes that his own denomination, the Protestant Reformed Churches in America, has been labelled as "Hyper-Calvinist" for its rejection of the "well-meant offer of the gospel." Engelsma disputes this label, and says that Hyper-Calvinism is instead "the denial that God in the preaching of the gospel calls everyone who hears the preaching to repent and believe... that the church should call everyone in the preaching... that the unregenerated have a duty to repent and believe."

Differences from Orthodox Calvinism

Hyper-Calvinism Doctrine

The beliefs which have been termed "Hyper-Calvinism" may be seen in historic writings of numerous Calvinistic ministers and clearly in the Gospel Standard Articles of Faith (See Articles 24, 26, 27, 28 and 29). The Hyper-Calvinism of these articles arose in part as a reaction to the Amyraldism of men like Richard Baxter. According to J. I. Packer, Baxter "devised an eclectic middle route between Reformed, Arminian, and Roman doctrines of grace: interpreting the kingdom of God in terms of contemporary political ideas, he explained Christ's death as an act of universal redemption (penal and vicarious, but not substitutionary), in virtue of which God has made a new law offering pardon and amnesty to the penitent. Repentance and faith, being obedience to this law, are the believer's personal saving righteousness."

The Gospel Standard Articles of Faith and statements by ministers

Denial of sufficient grace in the atonement for all persons

Article 28 states a rejection of the general redemption view of Richard Baxter and a denial that there is a residue of grace in Christ for non-elect persons if they will only accept it. The Baptist minister Daniel Whitaker reasoned against "Baxterianism" and defined it as the teaching that Christ died intentionally for the elect only, but sufficiently for the rest. He believed that the Baxterian view allowed a possible and probable salvation for non-elect persons from the sufficiency of the death of Christ. John Stevens, also a Baptist minister, affirmed that the atonement is "insufficient" to save those whom Christ never intended to save. He reasoned that Christ has never benefited any person "unintentionally" and that his meritorious worth should not be divided or confounded.

Denial of indiscriminate offers of the gospel to all persons

Article 24 states a confession that invitations of the gospel are only for sensible sinners who are made aware of their need for Christ, article 27 states a denial that the non-elect are ever enlightened by the Holy Spirit to receive grace and article 29 states a confession that the gospel is to be preached in all the world without indiscriminate offers of the gospel to all. The English Baptist pastor John Gill denied that there are universal offers of grace made to any, but that grace and salvation are published and revealed in the gospel. The English Anglican Church pastor Robert Hawker contended that Jesus only invited the weary and heavy laden. He believed that it is in "direct contradiction to scripture" to invite all. He also reasoned that an attempt to offer Christ is "little short of blasphemy" and those who make invitations to allure the carnal world to faith and repentance know not the scriptures nor the power of God.

Denial of Duty-Faith

Article 26 states a confession that the natural man should not be given exhortation or duties to "spiritually and savingly" repent and believe. Article 26 has been a subject of controversy concerning what was intended. In his book "What Gospel Standard Baptists Believe," J.H. Gosden clarifies that this article is not meant to minimize the sin of unbelief. He understood this article to be a denial that man is duty bound to believe "each individual is himself" included in the redemption work of Christ and he affirmed that man is "inexcusable in his unbelief" against God's revealed word and works. The Baptist pastor William Styles reasoned that duty-faith blends the covenant of works with the covenant of grace and makes faith a work of the law. W. Kitchen reasoned in a Strict Baptists magazine that duty-faith would imply a universal design in the atonement by calling on all persons to exercise a faith which grants them to believe Jesus gave himself for them.

Orthodox Calvinistic Doctrine

While "Hyper Calvinism" reasons that the sufficiency of the atonement extends no further than its efficiency, "Orthodox Calvinism" reasons that Christ suffered sufficiently for the whole world, but efficiently only for the elect.

John Calvin

John Calvin denied that the sins of the reprobate have been expiated, but he maintained that Christ died sufficiently for the whole world and only efficiently for the elect. He affirmed that Jesus makes his favor "common to all" and offered "indiscriminately to all", though not "extended to all;" for all do not receive him. He also stated that it is their unbelief which prevents anyone from receiving benefit from the death of Christ. With reference to God's desire concerning the reprobate wicked, Calvin condemns the view of Georgius the Sicilian that "God Would have all men to be saved" and continues by saying "It follows, therefore, according to his understanding of that passage, either that God is disappointed in His wishes, or that all men without exception must be saved ... why, if such be the case, God did not command the Gospel to be preached to all men indiscriminately from the beginning of the world? why [did] He [suffer] so many generations of men to wander for so many ages in all the darkness of death?"

Confessions and Catechisms

The Canons of Dort affirm an abundant sufficiency in the death of Christ of "infinite worth and value" for the whole world. The word offer or free offer was used in the Westminster Standards and the Westminster Larger Catechism leaves no room for doubt that the phrase "grace offered" is used in reference to persons who "never truly come" to Christ. In his "Question & Answers on the Shorter Catechism", John Brown addressed and answered questions concerning the free offer of the gospel; he reasoned that God commands every person that hears the gospel to "take his gift Christ out of his hand", that Christ offers himself "Fully, freely, earnestly, and indefinitely" to all persons that hear the gospel "without exception", that this offer is for every person's case "as if he was named in it" and that to embrace the offer of Christ is to be persuaded that "Christ in the promise is mine."

Opposition to the Doctrine

Both Calvinistic and non-Calvinistic ministers have expounded on several Bible passages as contradicting the doctrines which are considered to be Hyper-Calvinism. Verification that such scripture citations were a matter of doctrinal controversy may be seen in William Styles' A Manual of Faith and Practice, Andrew Fuller's The Gospel Worthy of All Acceptation, John Gill's The Cause of God and Truth, Richard Baxter's Universal Redemption, Daniel Whitby's A Discourse Concerning Election and Reprobation and William Button's The Nature of Special Faith in Christ Considered. Arthur Pink wrote an article arguing for the doctrine of faith as the bounden duty of every person who hears the gospel.

Biblical References Used in Favor of Orthodox Calvinism

Matthew 23:37 "...how often would I have gathered thy children together, even as a hen gathereth her chickens under her wings, and ye would not!" Adam Clarke believed that here it is evident that there were persons whom Jesus "wished to save, and bled to save" who perished because they would not come unto him. Richard Baxter referred to this scripture as teaching that the cause of persons perishing is not "for want of an expiatory Sacrifice", but "for want of Faith" to receive Christ and his benefits. John Calvin reasoned from this scripture that God "calls all men indiscriminately to salvation", that he "wills to gather all to himself" and that this is distinct from his secret purpose to efficaciously gather whomsoever he wills. John Gill understood that Christ here expresses his "will for their temporal good" that they may be gathered under the ministry of his word and acknowledge him as the Messiah in order to preserve them from the "temporal ruin" threatened upon their city. He concludes that this scripture does not prove men resist the operations of God's grace, but rather reveals the "obstructions and discouragements" that were "thrown in the way" of attendance to the ministry of his word.

John 1:7 "...that all men through him might believe." Albert Barnes noted on this scripture that John and Jesus came that "we may all" trust in Christ for salvation. John Calvin commented here that John came to prepare a church for Christ by "inviting all" to him. John Gill reasoned that the faith here required was not to believe Jesus died for them, but to acknowledge him as the Messiah. He also contended that souls who are made sensible of their lost state and "need of a Savior" ought to believe that Jesus died for them and "none but such."

John 3:16-17 "...that the world through him might be saved." On this scripture, Richard Baxter interpreted the world which Jesus came to save to be divided into believers who will eventually be saved and unbelievers who will eventually be condemned. John Calvin stated that the word "world" is repeated here so that no man may consider himself "wholly excluded," if he only "keep the road of faith." John Gill commented here that the "world" is referring to the elect in general and in particular God's people among the gentiles.

Romans 3:22-23 "...unto all and upon all them that believe: for there is no difference: For all have sinned..." Adam Clarke commented here that all human creatures are "equally helpless and guilty" and therefore God's "endless mercy has embraced all." John Calvin stated here that Christ "is offered to all" and becomes an advantage only to believers. He also commented that the apostle Paul here "urges on all, without exception" concerning the "necessity of seeking righteousness in Christ." John Gill understood these scriptures to refer to "not all men," but to persons who "believe in Christ for salvation" and that there is no room here for any person to "despair of the grace and righteousness of Christ" on account of viewing themselves as the worst of sinners.

Revelation 3:20 "...if any man hear my voice, and open the door..." Albert Barnes reasoned that this scripture is "applicable to all persons" and is the method by which Jesus seeks to come into the heart of a sinner. William Styles commented that this scripture is not referring to the unconverted, but rather regenerated persons of the church at Laodicea who were in "a low and lukewarm state" showing little regard for Christ. He understood the purpose of this appeal to be "not salvation from the punishment of sin," but of communion with Christ.

Additional Scriptures

John 5:34 is addressed by William Styles (A Manual of Faith and Practice, pg. 274). John 10:31 is addressed by William Styles (A Manual of Faith and Practice, pg. 245).

Biblical References Used in Favor of the Concept of Duty-Faith

Psalm 2:12 "Kiss the Son, lest he be angry..." Andrew Fuller concluded from this scripture that "unconverted sinners are commanded to believe in Christ for salvation" and that "believing in Christ for salvation is their duty."[58] William Button understood the phrase "Kiss the Son" as a duty to reverence Christ and the phrase "Blessed are they" to be an encouragement to those who are privileged to "believe in him for pardon."

John 12:36 "While ye have light, believe in the light, that ye may be the children of light..." Andrew Fuller stated that the belief which was required of these "unbelievers" would have "issued in their salvation." William Styles understood "believe in the light" to mean "receive my testimony concerning Myself and My mission" and that the title "children of light" intends "Jews whose minds were informed by the teaching of Jesus" and not "spiritually illuminated persons."

2 Corinthians 5:17-21 "...we pray you in Christ's stead, be ye reconciled to God." Andrew Fuller reasoned that this scripture is spoken to "rebellious subjects" and to not "submit" to this mercy is to maintain "the war." Albert Barnes, on this scripture, stated that "ministers of reconciliation" are to "urge this duty on their fellow-men." John Calvin commented here that the phrase "be reconciled" is addressed to believers as a daily embassy "sounded forth in the Church." John Gill commented on this scripture as referring to "new creatures" that Christ died for.

2 Thessalonians 1:8 "...them that know not God, and that obey not the gospel of our Lord Jesus Christ."

1 John 3:23 "...this is his commandment, That we should believe on the name of his Son Jesus Christ..."

Additional Scriptures

Isaiah 55:6-7 is addressed by William Button (The Nature of Special Faith in Christ Considered, pg. 30). Acts 16:30-31 is addressed by John Gill (The Cause of God and Truth, pg. 574).

Support for the Doctrine

Several bible passages are urged as supporting the doctrines which are considered to be Hyper-Calvinism. Verification that such scripture citations were a matter of doctrinal controversy may be seen in William Styles' Baptist Manual Complete, Andrew Fuller's The Gospel Worthy of All Acceptation, John Gill's The Cause of God and Truth,[68] Richard Baxter's Universal Redemption, Daniel Whitby's A Discourse Concerning Election and Reprobation and William Button's The Nature of Special Faith in Christ Considered.

Biblical References Used to Support the Position of Gospel Invitations Going to Certain Persons Only

Isaiah 55:1 "Ho, every one that thirsteth, come ye to the waters..." John Gill taught that the persons here under the description of "thirsty" are spiritual persons "thirsting after forgiveness of sin by the blood of Christ" and to such is the gospel invitation given. Andrew Fuller believed that "thirst" here does not mean "holy desire after spiritual blessings" but rather a "natural desire of happiness" which God places in every bosom.

Matthew 11:25-28 "...Come unto me, all ye that labour and are heavy laden..." John Gill reasoned from this scripture that the persons invited here are "not all the individuals of mankind," but those who are "burdened with the guilt of sin upon their consciences." John Calvin commented here that "it would be in vain" for Christ to invite those who are "devoted to the world" or those who are "intoxicated with their own righteousness." On this verse, he also stated that Christ is "ready to reveal the Father to all" though the greater part is careless of coming to him.

Mark 2:15-17 "...I came not to call the righteous, but sinners to repentance." John Gill noted here that Christ "attended the one, and not the other." He also stated that this scripture refers to the "usefulness of Christ to one sort, and not another."

Luke 4:18 "...he hath anointed me to preach the gospel to the poor; he hath sent me to heal the brokenhearted..."

Revelation 22:17 "...let him that is athirst come. And whosoever will, let him take the water of life freely."

Biblical References Used against Duty-Faith

Romans 4:13 "...the promise, that he should be the heir of the world, was not to Abraham, or to his seed, through the law, but through the righteousness of faith." The Baptist pastor Job Hupton concluded from this scripture that "the eternal inheritance" is not by "the law and its duty," but through "the gospel and its promises."

Romans 4:16 "...it is of faith, that it might be by grace; to the end the promise might be sure..." William Button made the argument here that "if faith is a duty (and so a work)" the apostle Paul should have rather said "It is of faith that it might be by works." He concluded that there is a "beauty" here in the apostles words because faith is rather a "blessing of the covenant of grace" and a "fruit of electing grace."

Galatians 3:11-12 "...the law is not of faith..." The Baptist minister William Wales Horne asserted from this scripture that because faith is a grace of the Spirit, it is therefore not a duty of the law. He also reasoned that faith is not "a duty which God requires of his people," but rather "a grace which he gives them."

Ephesians 2:8-9 "...by grace are ye saved through faith; and that not of yourselves..." The English Baptist John Foreman made an argument here that their faith was not a "duty produced of themselves" or of a "divine requirement," for God determined that his gift should "not be of works, and so not of duty."

2 Timothy 1:9 "...not according to our works, but according to his own purpose and grace..." John Foreman reasoned from this scripture that grace is "sovereign and particular only" and that here is the reason why all men are not called and saved by God's purpose and grace given before the world began. In light of this, he contended against the view that persons are "damned for not coming" to Christ for salvation.

Neo-Calvinism

Neo-Calvinism, a form of Dutch Calvinism, is a theological movement initiated by the theologian and former Dutch prime minister Abraham Kuyper. James Bratt has identified a number of different types of Dutch Calvinism: The Seceders, split into the Reformed Church "West" and the Confessionalists; the neo-Calvinists; and the Positives and the Antithetical Calvinists. The Seceders were largely infralapsarian and the neo-Calvinists usually supralapsarian.

Kuyper wanted to awaken the church from what he viewed as its pietistic slumber. He declared:

> No single piece of our mental world is to be sealed off from the rest and there is not a square inch in the whole domain of human existence over which Christ, who is sovereign over all, does not cry: 'Mine!'

This refrain has become something of a rallying call for neo-Calvinists.

Emphases of neo-Calvinism

Source:

- *Jesus is Lord over all of creation.* Jesus' Lordship extends through every area and aspect of life – it is not restricted to the sphere of church or of personal piety.
- *The idea that all of life is to be redeemed.* The work of Jesus on the cross extends over all of life – no area is exempt from its impact. All knowledge is affected by the true knowledge of God through redemption in Christ.
- *Cultural Mandate.* Genesis 1:26–28 has been described as a cultural mandate. It is the mandate to cultivate and develop the creation. There is a historical development and cultural unfolding. Some neo-Calvinists hold that the Cultural Mandate is as important as the Great Commission.
- *Creation, fall and redemption.* God's good creation has been disrupted by the fall. Redemption is a restoration of creation.
- *Sphere sovereignty (Soevereiniteit in eigen kring).* Each sphere (or sector) of life has its own distinct responsibilities and authority as designed by God – for instance, communities dedicated to worship, civil justice, agriculture, family, etc. – and no one area of life is sovereign over

another. Hence, neither faith-institutions nor an institution of civil justice (that is, the state) should seek totalitarian control or any regulation of human activity outside their limited competence.

- *A rejection of dualism.* Dualisms are (purportedly false) bifurcations, dichotomies, contrasts, or oppositions, such as the dualism between nature and grace that [allegedly] dominated much of Scholasticism. In the neo-Calvinist view, nature is the God-created and sustained cosmic order, not a "non-supernatural" category, and grace is God's means of renewing the cosmic order, it is not something "non-creational" added onto nature (albeit eschatological in consummated glorification of bodily resurrection to eternal life and cosmic transformation of the new heavens and earth).

- *Structure and direction.* Structure denotes created laws and norms for (other) created things. Direction denotes relative deviation or conformity to norms; primarily regarding the central orientation of the human heart toward or away from God in Christ.

- *Common grace.* God providentially sustains the created order, restraining of possible evils and giving non-salvific good gifts to all humanity despite their fall into sin, God's curse, and his eventual condemnation of the unredeemed.

- *Presuppositional apologetics.* The only framework in which any fact about the world is intelligible is the Christian worldview in general, and the theologically Reformed worldview in particular. The principles of logic and the use of reason assume the existence of God. Presuppositionalism is a *reductio ad absurdum* approach to Christian apologetics, in that it argues that all non-Christian worldviews are internally inconsistent.

- *The antithesis.* There is a struggle in history and within every person – between submission to and rebellion against God; between the kingdom of light and the kingdom of darkness; between the age to come (already inaugurated in Christ) and this present evil age (of sin).

- *World views.* Neo-Calvinists reject the notion that theoretical thought can be religiously neutral. All thinking and practice is shaped by world views and religious ground motives. For the neo-Calvinist, life in all its aspects can be shaped by a distinctively Christian world view.

- *The role of law.* For neo-Calvinists, "Law" is more than the Mosaic Decalogue, or even the entire abiding moral will of God. Law is, rather, the order for creation (or creation ordinances) established by

God and includes a variety of types of cultural norms including physiological, psychological, logical, historical, linguistic, social, economic, aesthetic, juridical, and faith norms.

Key Individuals Associated with Neo-Calvinism

- Guillaume Groen van Prinsterer
- Abraham Kuyper
- Herman Bavinck
- Klaas Schilder
- Herman Dooyeweerd
- Greg Bahnsen
- D. H. Th. Vollenhoven
- Gerrit Cornelis Berkouwer
- Albert Wolters
- Craig Bartholomew
- R.J. Rushdoony
- Nicholas Wolterstorff
- James K.A. Smith
- Richard Mouw
- George Marsden
- Cornelius Plantinga
- E. L. Hebden Taylor
- H. Evan Runner
- Hans Rookmaaker
- Auguste Lecerf
- Chuck Colson
- Stephanus Jacobus du Toit
- Neo-Calvinist institutions and organizations
- Arrowhead Christian Academy in Redlands, California
- Calvin University, Grand Rapids, MI
- The Center for Public Justice
- Dordt College, Sioux Center, IA, USA.
- Free University in Amsterdam, The Netherlands

Theological University of the Reformed Churches in Kampen, the Netherlands

- Institute for Christian Studies, Toronto, Canada
- Kuyper College

- Geneva College, Beaver Falls, PA
- Covenant College, Lookout Mtn, GA
- Redeemer University College, Ancaster, ON, Canada
- Trinity Christian College, Palos Heights, IL
- The Kings College, Edmonton, Alberta, Canada

Key texts

- Bavinck, Herman, Reformed Dogmatics.
- Kuyper, Abraham, Calvinism: Stone Lectures.
- Wolters, Albert M., Creation Regained: Biblical Basics for a Reformational Worldview.
- Bahnsen, Greg, By This Standard.
- Rushdoony, R.J., The Institutes of Biblical Law.
- Rutherford, Samuel, Lex Rex.

Christian Reconstructionism

Christian reconstructionism is a fundamentalist Calvinist theonomic movement. It developed under the ideas of Rousas Rushdoony, Greg Bahnsen and Gary North and has had an important influence on the Christian right in the United States. In keeping with the cultural mandate, Christian reconstructionists advocate theonomy and the restoration of certain biblical laws said to have continuing applicability. These include the death penalty not only for murder, but also for propagators of all forms of idolatry, open homosexuals, adulterers, practitioners of witchcraft and blasphemers.

The Christian reconstructionism movement became very popular outside the United States after 2000, especially in countries with large Pentecostal populations (Sub-saharan Africa, Central America and Caribbean).[citation needed]

Christian reconstructionists are usually postmillennialists and followers of the presuppositional apologetics of Cornelius Van Til.

A Christian denomination that advocated the view of Christian reconstructionism until its dissolution in 2020 was the Reformed Presbyterian Church in the United States. Most Calvinist Christians, however, disavow Christian reconstructionism and hold to classical covenant theology, the traditional Calvinist view of the relationship between the Old Covenant and Christianity.

Reconstructionist Perspective

Theonomy[74]

Christian reconstructionists advocate a theonomic government and libertarian economic principles. They maintain a distinction of spheres of authority between self, family, church, and state. For example, the enforcement of moral sanctions under theonomy is carried out by the family and church government, and sanctions for moral offenses are outside the authority of civil government (which is limited to criminal matters, courts and national defense). However, some believe these distinctions become blurred, as the application of theonomy implies an increase in the authority of the civil government. Reconstructionists also say that the theonomic government is not an oligarchy or monarchy of man communicating with God, but rather, a national recognition of existing laws. Prominent advocates of Christian reconstructionism have written that according to their understanding, God's law approves of the death penalty not only for murder, but also for propagators of all forms of idolatry, open homosexuality, adulterers, practitioners of witchcraft, blasphemers, and perhaps even recalcitrant youths (see the List of capital crimes in the Bible).

Christian reconstructionism's founder, Rousas Rushdoony, wrote in The Institutes of Biblical Law (the founding document of reconstructionism) that Old Testament law should be applied to modern society, and he advocates the reinstatement of the Mosaic law's penal sanctions such as stoning. Under such a system, the list of civil crimes which carried a death sentence would include murder, homosexuality, adultery, incest, lying about one's virginity, bestiality, witchcraft, idolatry or apostasy, public blasphemy, false prophesying, kidnapping, rape, and bearing false witness in a capital case. However, Greg Bahnsen points out that such a system would only be possible if the culture at large were a Christian culture, and that the force of government could not be used to impose Christianity on a culture that did not want it.

Kayser points out that the Bible advocates justice, and that biblical punishments prescribed for crimes are the maximum allowable to maintain justice and not the only available option, because lesser punishments are authorized as well.

Views on Pluralism

Rousas Rushdoony wrote in The Institutes of Biblical Law: "The heresy of democracy has since [the days of colonial New England] worked havoc in

[74] Theonomy, from theos (god) and nomos (law), is a hypothetical Christian form of government in which society is ruled by divine law. Theonomists hold that divine law, particularly the judicial laws of the Old Testament, should be observed by modern societies.

church and state" and: "Christianity and democracy are inevitably enemies", and he said elsewhere that "Christianity is completely and radically anti-democratic; it is committed to spiritual aristocracy," and characterized democracy as "the great love of the failures and cowards of life." He nevertheless repeatedly expressed his opposition to any sort of violent revolution and advocated instead the gradual reformation (often termed "regeneration" in his writings) of society from the bottom up, beginning with the individual and the family and from there gradually reforming other spheres of authority, including the church and the state.

Rushdoony believed that a republic is a better form of civil government than a democracy. According to Rushdoony, a republic avoided mob rule and the rule of the "51%" of society; in other words "might does not make right" in a republic. Rushdoony wrote that America's separation of powers between 3 branches of government is a far more neutral and better method of civil government than a direct democracy, stating "[t]he [American] Constitution was designed to perpetuate a Christian order". Rushdoony argues that the Constitution's purpose was to protect religion from the federal government and to preserve "states' rights."

Douglas W. Kennard, a Professor Theology and Philosophy at the Houston Graduate School of Theology, wrote with regard to Christian reconstructionism, that Christians of non-Calvinist traditions, such as some "Baptist, Methodist, Catholic, [and] Orthodox", would be "under threat of capital punishment as fostered by the extreme Theonomist." On the other hand, Ligon Duncan has stated that "Roman Catholics to Episcopalians to Presbyterians to Pentecostals", as well as "Arminian and Calvinist, charismatic and non-charismatic, high Church and low Church traditions are all represented in the broader umbrella of Reconstructionism (often in the form of the "Christian America" movement)."

New Calvinism

New Calvinism, also known as the Young, Restless, and Reformed Movement, is a new religious movement within conservative Evangelicalism that reinterprets 16th-century Calvinism under US values and ideologies.

History

The New Calvinist movement began to emerge in the 1960s when Evangelical theologians, seminarians, and pastors rediscovered Puritan Literature. In the 1970s, the movement incorporated religious marketing practices employed by charismatic churches, such as mega-churches, a more contemporary language, expanding to an audience outside their own denominations. Thus, they formed networks of independent leaders and churches in which these ideas flowed. In the 1980s, with lessening of the tensions of the Cold War, the individualist discourse of New Calvinism gained adherents as an alternative to Prosperity Gospel as well as to the former apocalyptic concern that dispensationalists had in the Cold War decades.

The movement gained wider publicity with a conference held in Louisville, Kentucky, in 2006, Together for the Gospel by American pastors John Piper, Mark Driscoll, Matt Chandler, Al Mohler, Mark Dever and CJ Mahaney. In March 2009, Time magazine ranked it as one of the "10 Ideas Changing the World Right Now."

During the campaigns and government of Donald Trump, New Calvinism leaders endorsed and actively supported that president's speeches and policies. Especially with the defeat in the second elections and the invasion of the US Congress, some leaders have distanced themselves from Trumpism.

Networks and ministries

- 9 Marks (Mark Dever)
- Acts 29 church planting network (Mark Driscoll, Matt Chandler)
- Crossway
- Desiring God Ministries (John Piper)
- Ligonier Ministries (R. C. Sproul)
- Redeemer City to City (Tim Keller)
- Sovereign Grace Ministries (C. J. Mahaney)
- The Gospel Coalition
- Together for the Gospel

"Old" and New Calvinism

Rooted in the historical tradition of Calvinist theology, New Calvinists are united by their common doctrine. In a Christianity Today article, Collin Hansen describes the speakers of a Christian conference:

> Each of the seven speakers holds to the five points of Calvinism. Yet none of them spoke of Calvinism unless I asked about it. They did express worry about perceived evangelical accommodation to postmodernism and criticized churches for applying business models to ministry. They mostly joked about their many differences on such historically difficult issues as

baptism, church government, eschatology, and the gifts of the Holy Spirit. They drew unity as Calvinist evangelicals from their concerns: with seeker churches, church-growth marketing, and manipulative revival techniques.

The New Calvinists look to Puritans, like Jonathan Edwards, who taught that sanctification requires a vigorous and vigilant pursuit of holy living, not a passive attitude of mechanical progress[12] (see Lordship salvation); however, as implied by the "New" designation, some differences have been observed between the New and Old schools. Mark Driscoll, for example, has identified what he considers to be four main differences between the two:

New Calvinism is missional and seeks to create and redeem culture.

New Calvinism is flooding into cities.

Old Calvinism was generally cessationist (i.e. believing the gifts of the Holy Spirit such as tongues and prophecy had ceased). New Calvinism is generally continuationist with regard to spiritual gifts.

New Calvinism is open to dialogue with other Christian positions.

This fourth distinctive is what Driscoll considers a vital component in being able to engage with contemporary society.

Criticism

R. Scott Clark, professor of church history and historical theology from Westminster Seminary California, argues that New Calvinists like Driscoll should not be called Calvinists merely because they believe in the five points of Calvinism, but rather he suggests that adherence to the Three Forms of Unity and other Reformed confessions of faith is what qualifies one a Calvinist. Specifically, he suggests that many of the New Calvinists' positions on infant baptism, covenant theology, and continuation of the gifts of the Spirit are out of step with the Reformed tradition.

J. Todd Billings, professor of Reformed Theology at Western Theological Seminary, argues that the New Calvinists "tend to obscure the fact that the Reformed tradition has a deeply catholic heritage, a Christ-centered sacramental practice and a wide-lens, kingdom vision for the Christian's vocation in the world."

Between 2012 and 2013 numerous Southern Baptist Ministers responded to New Calvinism by affirming a "Statement of the Traditional Southern Baptist Understanding." The document was originally endorsed by six former SBC presidents: Morris Chapman, Jimmy Draper, Paige Patterson,

Bailey Smith, Bobby Welch, and Jerry Vines, two seminary presidents Chuck Kelley of New Orleans Baptist Theological Seminary and former SBC president and former Southwestern Baptist Theological Seminary President Paige Patterson, and five state executive directors (Jim Futral of Mississippi, David Hankins of Louisiana, Mike Procter of Alaska, John Sullivan of Florida, and Bob White of Georgia). The statement includes a Preamble and 10 articles of affirmation and denial as it relates to Christian Soteriology.

Theologians and social scientists have raised concerns that the New Calvinist movement and its theology are associated as a source of psychological abuse, sectarian exclusivism, and personality cult.

Traditional Reformed theologians criticize the selective and altered use of texts by Reformed classical authors, like Spurgeon in the publications of the New Calvinists without alerting their readers.[28] Another criticism is that publications of the movement are sold as if they were historical Calvinists with no indication of the ideological bases of New Calvinism. Calvinist theologians also criticize hermeneutical inconsistencies with the grammatical-historical method and the Lordship salvation by works of the New Calvinists.

Protestant Arminianism

Arminianism is a branch of Protestantism based on the theological ideas of the Dutch Reformed theologian Jacobus Arminius (1560–1609) and his historic supporters known as Remonstrants. Dutch Arminianism was originally articulated in the Remonstrance (1610), a theological statement submitted to the States General of the Netherlands. This expressed an attempt to moderate the doctrines of Calvinism related to its interpretation of predestination. The Synod of Dort (1618–19) was called by the States General to consider the Five Articles of Remonstrance.

Classical Arminianism, to which Arminius is the main contributor, and Wesleyan Arminianism, to which John Wesley is the main contributor, are the two main schools of thought.

Many Christian denominations have been influenced by Arminian views on the will of man being freed by grace prior to regeneration, notably the Baptists in 17th century, the Methodists in the 18th century, and the Pentecostals in the 20th century.

History

Precursor movements and theological influences

According to Roger E. Olson, Arminius' beliefs, i.e., Arminianism, did not begin with him. Denominations such as the Waldensians and other groups prior to the Reformation have similarly to Arminianism affirmed that each person may choose the contingent response of either resisting God's grace or yielding to it. Anabaptist theologian Balthasar Hubmaier also promoted much the same view as Arminius nearly a century before him.[1] The soteriological doctrines of Arminianism and Anabaptism are roughly equivalent. In particular, Mennonites have been historically Arminian whether they distinctly espoused the Arminian viewpoint or not, and rejected Calvinism soteriology. Anabaptist theology seems to have influenced Jacobus Arminius. At least, he was "sympathetic to the Anabaptist point of view, and Anabaptists were commonly in attendance on his preaching." Similarly, Arminius mentions Danish Lutheran theologian Niels Hemmingsen as holding the basic view of soteriology he held and Hemmingsen may have influenced him.

Emergence of Arminianism

Portrait of Jacobus Arminius, from Kupferstich aus Theatrum Europaeum by Matthaeus Merian in 1662

Portrait of Jacobus Arminius, from Kupferstich aus Theatrum Europaeum by Matthaeus Merian in 1662

Jacobus Arminius was a Dutch pastor and theologian in the late 16th and early 17th centuries. He was taught by Theodore Beza, Calvin's hand-picked successor, but after examination of the scriptures, he rejected his teacher's theology that it is God who unconditionally elects some for salvation.[7] Instead Arminius proposed that the election of God was of believers, thereby making it conditional on faith. Arminius's views were challenged by the Dutch Calvinists, especially Franciscus Gomarus, but Arminius died before a national synod could occur.

Arminius died before he could satisfy Holland's State General's request for a 14-page paper outlining his views. Arminius's followers replied in his stead crafting the Five articles of Remonstrance (1610), in which they express their points of divergence with the stricter Calvinism of the Belgic Confession. This is how Arminius's followers were called Remonstrants, and following a Counter Remonstrance in 1611, Gomarus' followers were called Counter-Remonstrants.

After some political maneuvering, the Dutch Calvinists were able to convince Prince Maurice of Nassau to deal with the situation. Maurice systematically removed Arminian magistrates from office and called a national synod at Dordrecht. This Synod of Dort was open primarily to Dutch Calvinists (102 people), while the Arminians were excluded (13 people banned from voting), with Calvinist representatives from other countries (28 people), and in 1618 published a condemnation of Arminius and his followers as heretics. Part of this publication was the famous Five points of Calvinism in response to the five articles of Remonstrance.

Arminians across Holland were removed from office, imprisoned, banished, and sworn to silence. Twelve years later Holland officially granted Arminianism protection as a religion, although animosity between Arminians and Calvinists continued. Most of the early Remonstrants followed a classical version of Arminianism. However, some of them such as Philipp van Limborch, moved in the direction of semi-Pelagianism and rationalism.[10]

Arminianism in the Church of England

In England, the so-labelled Arminian doctrines were held, in substance, before and in parallel of Arminius. Actually, the Thirty-nine Articles of Religion (finalised in 1571), were sufficiently ambiguous that they could be interpreted as either Arminian or Calvinistic. Arminianism in the Church of England was fundamentally an expression of negation of Calvinism, and only some theologians held to classical Arminianism, but for the rest they were either semi-Pelagian or Pelagian. In this specific context, contemporary historians prefer to use the term "proto-Arminians" rather than "Arminians" to designate the leanings of divines who didn't follow classical Arminianism. English Arminianism was represented by Arminian Puritans such as John Goodwin or High Anglican Arminians such as Jeremy Taylor and Henry Hammond. Anglican Arminians of the 17th century such as William Laud fought Calvinist Puritans. They actually saw Arminianism in terms of a state church, idea that was completely alien to the views of Arminius. This position became particularly evident under the reign (1625-1649) of Charles I of England. Following the English Civil War (1642–1651) Charles II of England, who tolerated the Presbyterians, re-instituted Arminian thought in the Church of England. It was dominant there for some fifty years.

Baptists

The debate between Calvin's followers and Arminius's followers is characteristic of post-Reformation church history. The emerging Baptist movement in 17th-century England, for example, was a microcosm of the historic debate between Calvinists and Arminians. The first Baptists—called "General Baptists" because of their confession of a "general" or unlimited atonement—were Arminians. The Baptist movement originated with Thomas Helwys, who left his mentor John Smyth (who had moved into shared belief and other distinctives of the Dutch Waterlander Mennonites of Amsterdam) and returned to London to start the first English Baptist Church in 1611. Later General Baptists such as John Griffith, Samuel Loveday, and Thomas Grantham defended a Reformed Arminian theology that reflected the Arminianism of Arminius. The General Baptists encapsulated their Arminian views in numerous confessions, the most influential of which was the Standard Confession of 1660. In the 1640s the Particular Baptists were formed, diverging strongly from Arminian doctrine and embracing the strong Calvinism of the Presbyterians and Independents. Their robust Calvinism was publicized in such confessions as the London Baptist Confession of 1644 and the Second London Confession of 1689. The London Confession of 1689 was later used by Calvinistic Baptists in America (called the Philadelphia Baptist Confession), whereas the Standard Confession of 1660 was used by the American heirs of the English General Baptists, who soon came to be known as Free Will Baptists.

Methodists

This same dynamic between Arminianism and Calvinism can be seen in the heated discussions between friends and fellow Anglican ministers John Wesley and George Whitefield. Wesley was highly influenced by 17th-century English Arminianism and thinkers such as John Goodwin, Jeremy Taylor and Henry Hammond of the Anglican "Holy Living" school, and the Remonstrant Hugo Grotius. Wesley knew very little about the beliefs of Jacobus Arminius and arrived at his religious views independently of Arminius. Wesley acknowledged late in life, with the 1778 publication of a periodical titled The Arminian, that he and Arminius were in general agreement. Theology Professor W. Stephen Gunther concludes he was "a faithful representative" of Arminius' beliefs. Wesley was a champion of Arminian teachings, defending his soteriology in The Arminian and writing articles such as Predestination Calmly Considered. He defended Arminianism against charges of semi-Pelagianism, holding strongly to beliefs in original sin and total depravity. At the same time, Wesley attacked the determinism that he claimed characterized Calvinistic doctrines of unconditional election and reprobation and maintained a belief in the ability to lose salvation. Wesley also clarified the doctrine of prevenient grace and preached the ability of Christians to attain to perfection (fully mature, not "sinlessness"). His system of thought has become known as Wesleyan Arminianism, the foundations of which were laid by Wesley and his fellow preacher John William Fletcher.

Pentecostals

Pentecostalism has its background in the activity of Charles Parham (1873–1929). Its origin as a movement was in the Azusa Street Revival in Los Angeles in 1906. This revival was led by William J. Seymour (1870–1922). Due to the Methodist and Holiness background of many early Pentecostal preachers, the Pentecostal churches usually possessed practices that arose from the Wesleyan Arminianism. During the 20th century, as Pentecostal churches began to settle and incorporate more standard forms, they started to formulate theology that was fully Arminian. Currently, the two largest Pentecostal denominations in the world, the Assemblies of God and the Pentecostal Church of God denominations, hold officially to Arminian views such as resistible grace, conditional election, or conditional security of the believer for the first.

Current Arminian Landscape

Protestant Denominations

Advocates of Arminianism find a home in many Protestant denominations, and sometimes other beliefs such as Calvinism exist within the same denomination. Even though Arminianism is not historically part of the Lutheran theological tradition, there may be some Lutheran churches that are open to it. Faiths leaning at least in part in the Arminian direction include some of high-church Anglicanism. Arminianism is found within the Conservative Mennonites, the Old Order Mennonites and the Amish.[30][28] It is found in the mainline Methodists churches, and especially in the various Holiness denominations such as the Church of the Nazarene, the Free Methodist Church, the Wesleyan Church, and the Salvation Army. It is found within the Restoration movement in the Christian Churches and Churches of Christ. It is found in the Seventh-day Adventist Church. It is found within the General Baptists and the Free Will Baptists. The majority of Southern Baptists accept Arminianism, with an exception allowing for a doctrine of eternal security, though many see Calvinism as growing in acceptance. It is also found in a part of the Charismatics, including the Pentecostals.

Scholarly Support

The current scholarly support for Arminianism is varied: Among Baptist theologians, Roger E. Olson, F. Leroy Forlines, Robert Picirilli, and J. Matthew Pinson are four supporters of a return to the teachings of Arminius. Methodist theologian Thomas Oden, "Evangelical Methodists" Bible scholar Ben Witherington III, and Christian apologist David Pawson are generally Arminian in their theologies. Holiness movement theologians Henry Orton Wiley, Carl O. Bangs and J. Kenneth Grider can also be mentioned among recent proponents of Arminianism. Various other theologians or Bible scholars as B. J. Oropeza, Keith D. Stanglin, Craig S. Keener, Thomas H. McCall, and Grant R. Osborne can be mentioned as well.

Theology of Arminian

The original beliefs of Jacobus Arminius are commonly called Arminianism, but more broadly, the term may embrace the teachings of Simon Episcopius, Hugo Grotius, John Wesley, and others. Arminian theology usually falls into one of two groups: Classical Arminianism, drawn from the teaching of Jacobus Arminius, and Wesleyan Arminian, drawing primarily from Wesley. The two groups overlap substantially.

In 529, at the Second Council of Orange, the question at hand was whether the doctrines of Augustine on God's providence were to be affirmed, or if semi-Pelagianism could be affirmed. Semi-Pelagianism was a moderate form of Pelagianism that teaches that the first step of salvation is by human will and not the grace of God. The determination of the Council could be considered "semi-Augustinian." It defined that faith, though a free act of man, resulted, even in its beginnings, from the grace of God, enlightening the human mind and enabling belief. This describes the operation of prevenient grace allowing the unregenerate to repent in faith. On the other hand, the Council of Orange condemned the Augustinian teaching of predestination to damnation. Since Arminianism is aligned with those characteristic semi-Augustinian views it has been seen by some as a reclamation of early church theological consensus. Moreover, Arminianism can also be seen as a soteriological diversification of Calvinism or as a theological middle ground between Calvinism and semi-Pelagianism.

Classical Arminianism

Classical Arminianism is the theological system that was presented by Jacobus Arminius and maintained by some of the Remonstrants. Theologians as Forlines and Olson have referred to this system as "classical Arminianism," while others as Picirilli and Pinson prefer to term it "Reformation Arminianism" or "Reformed Arminianism."

The teachings of Arminius held to Sola fide and Sola gratia of the Reformation, but they were distinct from particular teachings of Martin Luther, Huldrych Zwingli, John Calvin, and other Protestant Reformers.

Classical Arminianism was originally articulated in the Five Articles of Remonstrance. "These points", note Keith D. Stanglin and Thomas H. McCall, "are consistent with the views of Arminius; indeed, some come verbatim from his Declaration of Sentiments." A list of beliefs of classical Arminianism is given below:

God's Providence and Human Free Will

The majority Arminian view accepts classical theism, which states that God is **omnipresent,**[75] **omnipotent,**[76] and **omniscient.**[77] In that view, God's power, knowledge, and presence have no external limitations, that is, outside of his divine nature and character.

Besides, Arminianism view on God's **sovereignty**[78] is based on postulates stemming from God's character, especially as fully revealed in Jesus Christ. On the first hand, divine election must be defined in such a way that God is not in any case, and even in a secondary way, the author of evil. It would not correspond to the character of God. On the other hand, man's responsibility for evil must be absolutely preserved. Those two postulates require a specific way by which God chooses to manifest his sovereignty when interacting with his creatures:

On one hand, it requires for God to operate according to a limited mode of **providence.**[79] This means that God purposely exercises his sovereignty in ways that do not illustrate the full extent of his omnipotence. On the other hand, it requires for God's **election**[80] to be a "predestination by foreknowledge."

In that respect, God's foreknowledge reconciles with human free will in the following way: Human free will is limited by original sin, though God's prevenient grace restores to humanity the ability to accept God's call of salvation. God's foreknowledge of the future is exhaustive and complete, and therefore the future is certain and not contingent on human action. God does

[75] Omnipresence or ubiquity is the property of being present anywhere and everywhere. The term omnipresence is most often used in a religious context as an attribute of a deity or supreme being, while the term ubiquity is generally used to describe something "existing or being everywhere at the same time, constantly encountered, widespread, common".

[76] Omnipotence is the quality of having unlimited power. Monotheistic religions generally attribute omnipotence only to the deity of their faith.

[77] Omniscience is the capacity to know everything. In monotheistic religions, such as Sikhism and the Abrahamic religions, this is an attribute of God.

[78] Sovereignty of God in Christianity can be defined primarily as the right of God to exercise his ruling power over his creation, and secondarily, but not necessarily, as the exercise of this right. The way God exercises his ruling power is subject to divergences notably related to the concept of God's self-imposed limitations.

[79] In theology, Divine Providence, or simply Providence, is God's intervention in the Universe. The term Divine Providence (usually capitalized) is also used as a title of God.

[80] God's decision in choosing a special group or certain persons for salvation or service. The term is used especially of the predestination of the individual recipients of salvation. – Millard J. Erickson, The Concise Dictionary of Christian Theology (Wheaton, IL: Crossway Books, 2001), 56.

not determine the future, but He does know it. God's certainty and human contingency are compatible.

Roger Olson expressed those defining ideas in a more practical way:

> ""Arminianism," [...] is simply a term we use in theology for the view, held by some people before Arminius and many after him, that sinners who hear the gospel have the free will to accept or reject God's offer of saving grace and that nobody is excluded by God from the possibility of salvation except those who freely exclude themselves. But true, historical, classical Arminianism includes the belief that this free will [to repent and believe unto salvation] is itself a gift of God through prevenient grace."[81]

Condition of Humanity

Depravity is total: Arminius states "In this [fallen] state, the free will of man towards the true good is not only wounded, infirm, bent, and weakened; but it is also imprisoned, destroyed, and lost. And its powers are not only debilitated and useless unless they be assisted by grace, but it has no powers whatever except such as are excited by Divine grace."[82]

Extent and Nature of the Atonement

Atonement is intended for all:[83] Jesus's death was for all people, Jesus draws all people to himself, and all people have opportunity for salvation through faith.[84]

Jesus's death satisfies God's justice:[85] The penalty for the sins of the elect is paid in full through the crucifixion of Christ. Thus Christ's death atones for the sins of all, but requires faith to be effected. Arminius states that "Justification, when used for the act of a Judge, is either purely the imputation of righteousness through mercy [...] or that man is justified before God [...] according to the rigor of justice without any forgiveness." Stephen

---

[81] Olson 2017.

[82] Arminius 1853a, p. 252.

[83] Unlimited atonement (sometimes called general atonement or universal atonement) is a doctrine in Protestant Christianity that is normally associated with Amyraldism (four-point Calvinism), as well as Arminianism and other non-Calvinist traditions. The doctrine states that Jesus died as a propitiation for the benefit of all humans without exception.

[84] Arminius 1853a, p. 316.

[85] The satisfaction theory of atonement is a theory in Catholic theology which holds that Jesus Christ redeemed humanity through making satisfaction for humankind's disobedience through his own supererogatory obedience. The theory draws primarily from the works of Anselm of Canterbury, specifically his Cur Deus Homo ("Why was God a man?").

Ashby clarifies: "Arminius allowed for only two possible ways in which the sinner might be justified: (1) by our absolute and perfect adherence to the law, or (2) purely by God's imputation of Christ's righteousness." W. Stephen Gunter concurs that Arminius would not take a rigid position on the doctrine of **imputed righteousness**[86] (the righteousness of Christ is imputed for righteousness of the believer).[78] For Keith D. Stanglin and Thomas H. McCall, Arminius would not object to saying rather that "the righteousness of Christ is imputed to righteousness." Forlines put it this way: "On the condition of faith, we are placed in **union with Christ**.[87] Based on that union, we receive His death and righteousness."

Christ's atonement has a substitutionary effect which is limited only to the elect. Arminius held that God's justice was satisfied by penal substitution. Hugo Grotius taught that it was satisfied governmentally. According to Roger Olson, historical and contemporary Arminians have held to one of these views.[88]

Conversion of Man

Grace is resistible:[89] God takes initiative in the salvation process and his grace comes to all people. This grace (often called prevenient or pre-regenerating grace) acts on all people to convince them of the Gospel, draw them strongly towards salvation, and enable the possibility of sincere faith. Picirilli states that "indeed this grace is so close to **regeneration**[90] that it inevitably leads to regeneration unless finally resisted." The offer of salvation through grace does not act irresistibly in a purely cause-effect, deterministic method but rather in an influence-and-response fashion that can be both freely accepted and freely denied.

---

[86] Imputed righteousness is a concept in Christian theology proposing that the "righteousness of Christ ... is imputed to [believers] — that is, treated as if it were theirs through faith.": 106 It is on the basis of Jesus' righteousness that God accepts humans.

[87] In its widest sense, the phrase union with Christ refers to the relationship between the believer and Jesus Christ. In this sense, John Murray says, union with Christ is "the central truth of the whole doctrine of salvation." The expression "in Christ" (en Christo, en kyrio, en Christo Iesou, en auto etc.) occurs 216 times in the Pauline letters and 26 times in the Johannine literature.

[88] Olson 2009, p. 224, .

[89] Prevenient grace (or enabling grace) is a Christian theological concept rooted in Arminian theology, though it appeared earlier in Catholic theologies. It is divine grace that precedes human decisions.

[90] Regeneration, while sometimes perceived to be a step in the Ordo salutis ('order of salvation'), is generally understood in Christian theology to be the objective work of God in a believer's life. Spiritually, it means that God brings a person to new life (that they are "born again") from a previous state of separation from God and subjection to the decay of death (Ephesians 2:5). "The work of the Holy Spirit in creating a new life in the sinful person who repents and comes to believe in Christ." Millard J. Erickson, The Concise Dictionary of Christian Theology (Wheaton, IL: Crossway Books, 2001), 168.

Man has a freed will to respond or resist: Free will is granted and limited by God's sovereignty, but God's sovereignty allows all men the choice to accept the Gospel of Jesus through faith, simultaneously allowing all men to resist.

Conversion is synergistic:[91] As Roger Olson put it: "[Arminius]' evangelical synergism reserves all the power, ability and efficacy in salvation to grace, but allows humans the God-granted ability to resist or not resist it. The only "contribution" humans make is nonresistance to grace."

Election of Man

Election is conditional:[92] Arminius defined election as "the decree of God by which, of Himself, from eternity, He decreed to justify in Christ, believers, and to accept them unto eternal life."[93] God alone determines who will be saved and his determination is that all who believe Jesus through faith will be justified. According to Arminius, "God regards no one in Christ unless they are engrafted in him by faith."[94]

God predestines the elect to a glorious future: Predestination is not the predetermination of who will believe, but rather the predetermination of the believer's future inheritance. The elect are therefore predestined to sonship through adoption, glorification, and eternal life.

Preservation of Man

Related to eschatological considerations, Jacobus Arminius and the first Remonstrants, including **Simon Episcopius**[95] believed in everlasting fire where the wicked are thrown by God at judgment day.

Eternal preservation is conditional: All believers have full **assurance of salvation**[96] with the condition that they remain in Christ. Salvation is

---

[91] In Christian theology, synergism is the position of those who hold that salvation involves some form of cooperation between divine grace and human freedom. Synergism is upheld by the Roman Catholic Church, Orthodox Churches, Anabaptist Churches and Methodist Churches.

[92] In Christian theology, conditional election is the belief that God chooses for eternal salvation those whom he foresees will have faith in Christ. This belief emphasizes the importance of a person's free will.

[93] Arminius 1853c, p. 311.

[94] Arminius 1853c, p. 311.

[95] Simon Episcopius (January 8, 1583 – April 4, 1643) was a Dutch theologian and Remonstrant who played a significant role at the Synod of Dort in 1618. His name is the Latinized form of his Dutch name Simon Bisschop.

[96] Assurance, also known as the Witness of the Spirit, is a Protestant Christian doctrine that states that the inner witness of the Holy Spirit allows the Christian disciple to know that he or she is justified. Based on the writings of St. Augustine of Hippo, assurance was historically a very important doctrine in Lutheranism and Calvinism, and remains a distinguishing doctrine of Methodism and Quakerism though

conditioned on faith, therefore perseverance is also conditioned. Arminius believed the Scriptures taught that believers are graciously empowered by Christ and the Holy Spirit "to fight against Satan, sin, the world and their own flesh, and to gain the victory over these enemies." Furthermore, Christ and the Spirit are ever present to aid and assist believers through various temptations. But this security was not unconditional but conditional—"provided they [believers] stand prepared for the battle, implore his help, and be not wanting to themselves, Christ preserves them from **falling**."[97]

Possibility of Apostasy

Arminius believed in the possibility for a believer to commit **apostasy**[98] (i.e., desert Christ by cleaving again to this evil world, losing a good conscience, or by failing to hold on to sound doctrine). However, over the period of time Arminius wrote on this question, he expressed sometimes more prudently. For instance, Arminius declared in 1599 that this matter required further study in the Scriptures. Arminius said also in his "Declaration of Sentiments" (1607), "I never taught that a true believer can, either totally or finally fall away from the faith, and perish; yet I will not conceal, that there are passages of scripture which seem to me to wear this aspect; and those answers to them which I have been permitted to see, are not of such a kind as to approve themselves on all points to my understanding."

But in his other writings he expressed certainty about the possibility of falling away: Arminius wrote in ca. 1602, that "a person who is being 'built' into the church of Christ may resist the continuation of this process." Concerning the believers he said "It may suffice to encourage them, if they know that no power or prudence can dislodge them from the rock, unless

---

there are differences among these Christian traditions. Hymns that celebrate the witness of the Holy Spirit, such as "Blessed Assurance" are sung in Christian liturgies to celebrate the belief in assurance.

[97] Backsliding, also known as falling away or described as "committing apostasy", is a term used within Christianity to describe a process by which an individual who has converted to Christianity reverts to pre-conversion habits and/or lapses or falls into sin, when a person turns from God to pursue their own desire. To revert to sin or wrongdoing, especially in religious practice, someone lapses into previous undesirable patterns of behavior.

Arminius 1853b, pp. 465, 466. "This seems to fit with Arminius' other statements on the need for perseverance in faith. For example: "God resolves to receive into favor those who repent and believe, and to save in Christ, on account of Christ, and through Christ, those who persevere [in faith], but to leave under sin and wrath those who are impenitent and unbelievers, and to condemn them as aliens from Christ." Arminius 1853c, pp. 412, 413. "[God] wills that they, who believe and persevere in faith, shall be saved, but that those, who are unbelieving and impenitent, shall remain under condemnation."

[98] Apostasy in Christianity is the rejection of Christianity by someone who formerly was a Christian and/or who wishes to administratively be removed from a formal registry of church members. The term apostasy comes from the Greek word apostasia ("ἀποστασία") meaning "defection", "departure", "revolt", or "rebellion."

they of their own will forsake their position." He continued by saying that the covenant of God (Jeremiah 23) "does not contain in itself an impossibility of defection from God, but a promise of the gift of fear, whereby they shall be hindered from going away from God so long as that shall flourish in their hearts." He then taught that had King David died in his sins he would have been lost. In 1602, Arminius also wrote: "A believing member of Christ may become slothful, give place to sin, and gradually die altogether, ceasing to be a member."

For Arminius, certain class of sin would cause a believer to fall, especially sin motivated by malice. In 1605 Arminius wrote: "But it is possible for a believer to fall into a mortal sin, as is seen in David. Therefore he can fall at that moment in which if he were to die, he would be condemned." Stanglin, along with McCall, point out that Arminius clearly sets forth two paths to apostasy 1. "rejection", or 2. "malicious sinning." Oropeza gives a general conclusion "If there is any consistency in Arminius' position, he did not seem to deny the possibility of falling away."

After the death of Arminius in 1609, his followers wrote a **Remonstrance**[99] (1610) based quite literally on their leader's "Declaration of Sentiments" (1607) which expressed prudence on the possibility of apostasy. In particular, its fifth article expressed the necessity of further study on the possibility of apostasy. Sometime between 1610 and the official proceeding of the Synod of Dort (1618), the Remonstrants became fully persuaded in their minds that the Scriptures taught that a true believer was capable of falling away from faith and perishing eternally as an unbeliever. They formalized their views in "The Opinion of the Remonstrants" (1618) which was their official stand during the Synod of Dort. Picirilli remarks: "Ever since that early period, then, when the issue was being examined again, Arminians have taught that those who are truly saved need to be warned against apostasy as a real and possible danger." They later expressed this same view in the Remonstrant Confession (1621).

Forgivability of Apostasy

Stanglin points out that Arminius held that if the apostasy came from "malicious" sin, then it was forgivable. If it came from "rejection" it was not. Following Arminius, the Remonstrants believed that, though possible,

[99] The Five Articles of Remonstrance or the Remonstrance were theological propositions advanced in 1610 by followers of Jacobus Arminius who had died in 1609, in disagreement with interpretations of the teaching of John Calvin then current in the Dutch Reformed Church. Those who supported them were called "Remonstrants".

apostasy was not in general irremediable. However, other classical Arminians as the **Free Will Baptists**[100] have taught that apostasy is irremediable.

Wesleyan Arminianism

John Wesley thoroughly agreed with the vast majority of what Arminius himself taught. Wesleyan Arminianism is classical Arminianism with the addition of **Wesleyan perfectionism.**[101] Here are mentioned some positions on specific issues within Wesleyan Arminianism:

Nature of the Atonement

Steven Harper proposed that Wesley's atonement is a hybrid of the penal substitution theory and the governmental theory. However, theologians as Robert Picirilli, Roger Olson and Darren Cushman Wood consider that the view of Wesley concerning atonement is by penal substitution. Wesleyan Arminians have historically adopted either penal or governmental theory of the atonement.

Preservation and Apostasy of Man

Wesley fully accepted the Arminian view that genuine Christians could apostatize and lose their salvation, as his famous sermon "A Call to Backsliders" clearly demonstrates. Harper summarizes as follows: "the act of committing sin is not in itself ground for the loss of salvation [...] the loss of salvation is much more related to experiences that are profound and prolonged. Wesley sees two primary pathways that could result in a permanent fall from grace: unconfessed sin and the actual expression of apostasy." Wesley believed that such apostasy was not irremediable. When talking about those who have made "shipwreck" of their faith,(1 Tim 1:19) Wesley claims that "not one, or a hundred only, but I am persuaded, several thousands [...] innumerable are the instances [...] of those who had fallen but now stand upright."

Christian Perfection

One issue that typify Wesleyan Arminianism is **Christian perfection**. According to Wesley's teaching, Christians could attain a state of practical perfection, meaning a lack of all voluntary sin by the empowerment of the

---

[100] Free Will Baptist is a General Baptist Christian denomination and group of people that believe in free grace, free salvation and free will. The movement can be traced back to the 1600s with the development of General Baptism in England.

[101] Christian perfection is the name given to theological concepts within some sects of Christianity that purport to describe a process of achieving spiritual maturity or perfection. The ultimate goal of this process is union with God characterized by pure love of God and other people as well as personal holiness or sanctification.

Holy Spirit, in this life. Christian perfection (or entire sanctification), according to Wesley, is "purity of intention, dedicating all the life to God" and "the mind which was in Christ, enabling us to walk as Christ walked." It is "loving God with all our heart, and our neighbor as ourselves." It is "a restoration not only to the favour, but likewise to the image of God," our "being filled with the fullness of God." Wesley was clear that Christian perfection did not imply perfection of bodily health or an infallibility of judgment. It also does not mean we no longer violate the will of God, for involuntary transgressions remain. Perfected Christians remain subject to temptation, and have continued need to pray for forgiveness and holiness. It is not an absolute perfection but a perfection in love. Furthermore, Wesley did not teach a salvation by perfection, but rather says that, "Even perfect holiness is acceptable to God only through Jesus Christ."

Other Variations

Some doctrines adhere among other to the Arminian foundation and, while minority views, are highlighted below.

Open Theism

The doctrine of open theism states that God is omnipresent, omnipotent, and omniscient, but differs on the nature of the future. Open theists claim that the future is not completely determined (or "settled") because people have not made their free decisions yet. God therefore knows the future partially in possibilities (human free actions) rather than solely certainties (divinely determined events). Some Arminians, such as professor and theologian Robert Picirilli, reject the doctrine of open theism as a "deformed Arminianism." Joseph Dongell stated that "open theism actually moves beyond classical Arminianism towards process theology." There are also some Arminians, like Roger Olson, who believe Open theism to be an alternative view that a Christian can have.

Corporate View of Election

The majority Arminian view is that election is individual and based on God's foreknowledge of faith, but a second perspective deserves mention. These Arminians reject the concept of individual election entirely, preferring to understand the doctrine in corporate terms. According to this corporate election, God never chose individuals to elect to salvation, but rather He chose to elect the believing church to salvation. Dutch Reformed theologian

Herman Ridderbos[102] says "[The certainty of salvation] does not rest on the fact that the church belongs to a certain "number", but that it belongs to Christ, from before the foundation of the world. Fixity does not lie in a hidden decree, therefore, but in corporate unity of the Church with Christ, whom it has come to know in the gospel and has learned to embrace in faith."

Corporate election draws support from a similar concept of corporate election found in the Old Testament and Jewish law. Indeed most biblical scholarship is in agreement that Judeo-Greco-Roman thought in the 1st century was opposite of the Western world's "individual first" mantra—it was very collectivist or communitarian in nature. Identity stemmed from membership in a group more than individuality. According to Romans 9–11, supporters claim, Jewish election as the chosen people ceased with their national rejection of Jesus as Messiah. As a result of the new covenant, God's chosen people are now the corporate body of Christ, the church (sometimes called spiritual Israel—see also Covenant theology). The pastor and theologian Brian Abasciano claims "What Paul says about Jews, Gentiles, and Christians, whether of their place in God's plan, or their election, or their salvation, or how they should think or behave, he says from a corporate perspective which views the group as primary and those he speaks about as embedded in the group. These individuals act as members of the group to which they belong, and what happens to them happens by virtue of their membership in the group."

These scholars also maintain that Jesus was the only human ever elected and that individuals must be "in Christ" through faith to be part of the elect. This was, in fact, Swiss Reformed theologian, Karl Barth's, understanding of the doctrine of election. Joseph Dongell, professor at Asbury Theological Seminary, states "the most conspicuous feature of Ephesians 1:3–2:10 is the phrase 'in Christ', which occurs twelve times in Ephesians 1:3–14 alone [...] this means that Jesus Christ himself is the chosen one, the predestined one. Whenever one is incorporated into him by grace through faith, one comes to share in Jesus' special status as chosen of God." Markus Barth illustrates the inter-connectedness: "Election in Christ must be understood as the election of God's people. Only as members of that community do individuals share in the benefits of God's gracious choice."

---

[102] Herman Nicolaas Ridderbos (13 February 1909 – 8 March 2007) was a Dutch theologian and biblical scholar. He was an important New Testament theologian, having worked extensively on the history of salvation (Heilsgeschichte) and biblical theology.

Arminianism and Other Views

Divergence with Pelagianism

Pelagianism is a doctrine denying original sin and total depravity. No system of Arminianism founded on Arminius or Wesley denies original sin or total depravity; both Arminius and Wesley *strongly* affirmed that man's basic condition is one in which he cannot be righteous, understand God, or seek God. Arminius referred to Pelagianism as "the grand falsehood" and stated that he "must confess that I detest, from my heart, the consequences [of that theology]." David Pawson, a British pastor, decries this association as "libelous" when attributed to Arminius' or Wesley's doctrine. Indeed, most Arminians reject all accusations of Pelagianism.

Divergence with Semi-Pelagianism

Some schools of thought, notably semi-Pelagianism, which teaches that the first step of Salvation is by human will, are confused as being Arminian in nature. But classical Arminianism and Wesleyan Arminianism hold that the first step of Salvation is through the prevenient grace of God, though "the subsequent grace entails a cooperative relationship."

Divergence with Calvinism

The two systems of Calvinism and Arminianism share both history and many doctrines, and the history of Christian theology. However, because of their differences over the doctrines of divine predestination and election, many people view these schools of thought as opposed to each other. The distinction is whether God desires to save all yet allows individuals to resist the grace offered (in the Arminian doctrine) or if God desires to save only some and grace is irresistible to those chosen (in the Calvinist doctrine). Many consider the theological differences to be crucial differences in doctrine, while others find them to be relatively minor.

Similarities

- Total depravity – Arminians agree with Calvinists over the doctrine of total depravity. The differences come in the understanding of how God remedies this human depravity.

Differences

- Nature of election – Arminians hold that election to eternal salvation has the condition of faith attached. The Calvinist doctrine of unconditional election states that salvation cannot be earned or achieved and is therefore not conditional upon any human effort, so faith is not a condition of salvation but the divinely apportioned means to it. In other words, Arminians believe that they owe their election to their faith, whereas Calvinists believe that they owe their faith to their election.

- Nature of grace – Arminians believe that, through grace, God restores free will concerning salvation to all humanity, and each individual, therefore, is able either to accept the Gospel call through faith or resist it through unbelief. Calvinists hold that God's grace to enable salvation is given only to the elect and irresistibly leads to salvation.
- Extent of the atonement – Arminians, along with four-point Calvinists or Amyraldians, hold to a universal atonement instead of the Calvinist doctrine that atonement is limited to the elect only, which many Calvinists prefer to call *particular redemption*. Both sides (with the exception of hyper-Calvinists) believe the invitation of the gospel is universal and "must be presented to everyone [they] can reach without any distinction."
- Perseverance in faith – Arminians believe that future salvation and eternal life is secured in Christ and protected from all external forces but is conditional on remaining in Christ and can be lost through apostasy. Traditional Calvinists believe in the doctrine of the perseverance of the saints, which says that because God chose some unto salvation and actually paid for their particular sins, he keeps them from apostasy and that those who do apostatize were never truly regenerated (that is, born again) or saved. Non-traditional Calvinists and other evangelicals advocate the similar but distinct doctrine of eternal security that teaches if a person was once saved, his or her salvation can never be in jeopardy, even if the person completely apostatizes.[103]

[103] **Attribution**: This article incorporates some text from the public domain: Wikipedia, the free encyclopedia, and Edward D. Andrews

CHAPTER 1 EPHESIANS 1:4: Are Some Chosen (Predestined) to Eternal Salvation, and Others to Eternal Condemnation?

Ephesians 1:4 Updated American standard Version (UASV)

4 even as he chose us in him before the foundation of the world, that we should be holy and blameless before him.[104] In love

EPHESIANS 1:4: How is it that Adam and Eve were blamed for their actions before the foundation of the world (predestination) when they had not been created yet? Doesn't that violate God's principle of justice?

This is not a case of predestination, as the doctrine of predestination is unbiblical. Scriptures like that speak of certain ones as being "chosen according to the **foreknowledge** of God," 'chosen before the founding of the world,' '**foreordained** us to **adoption** as sons through Jesus Christ'? (1 Pet. 1:1, 2; Eph. 1:3-5, 11) Because of Scriptures such as these, Christian leaders such as Augustine, Martin Luther, and John Calvin taught that Adam and Eve were predestined to disobey God before being created. Therefore, all their future generations were chosen beforehand, making them destined for either salvation or eternal torment. We will take a moment to define the key terms in this order adoption, foreordain, and finally foreknowledge.

Adoption: (υἱοθεσία huiothesia) The Greek noun is a legal term that literally means "adoption as a son," which means to take or accept a son or daughter who is not naturally such by relationship, including full inheritance rights. The apostle Paul mentions adoption several times about those with a new status as called and chosen by God. These ones were born as offspring of the imperfect Adam, were formerly in slavery to sin. Through purchase through Jesus' life as a ransom, many have received the adoption as sons and daughters becoming heirs with the only-begotten Son of God, Jesus Christ. – Rom. 8:15, 23; 9:4; Gal. 4:5; Eph. 1:5.

Foreordain: (προορίζω proorizō) The Greek noun has the sense of deciding beforehand, determining something ahead of time or before its occurrence. God's ability to foreknow and foreordain is plainly stated in the Bible. For how God can decide beforehand, determine something ahead of

[104] Or h*im, having in love foreordained us*

time or before its occurrence, see footnotes on foreknowledge in Acts 2:23 and 1 Pet. 1:2. – Ac 4:28; Ro 8:29-30; 1Co 2:7; Eph 1:5, 11.

Foreknowledge: (πρόγνωσις prognōsis) The Greek noun simply means to plan in advance, **have knowledge beforehand**, **what is known beforehand**, that which is known ahead of time or before a particular temporal reference. (Acts 2:23; 1 Pet. 1:2) If we accept the equation that foreknowledge equals foreordain, sin is the result, not the result of Adam's choice, but of God's choosing, which should make us feel uncomfortable. Foreknowledge does not equal foreordain. It is better to understand that God knows in advance what choice people will freely make. The free decisions of human beings determine what foreknowledge God has of them, as opposed to the reverse. The foreknowledge does not determine the free decision; it is the free decisions that determine the foreknowledge. In this, we can distinguish what we might call **Chronological Priority and Logical Priority**. Chronological priority would mean that Event "A" [God's knowledge], as it relates to time, would come before Event "B" [the event God foreknows]. Thus, God's knowledge is chronologically prior to the event that he foreknows. However, logically speaking, the event is prior to God's foreknowledge. In other words, the event does not happen because God foreknows it, but God foreknows the event because it will happen. The event is logically prior to the foreknowledge, so he foreknows it because it will happen, even though the foreknowledge is chronologically prior to the event.

We can see foreknowledge in this as the foreshadowing of something. When you see the shadow of someone coming around the corner of the building, you see their shadow on the ground before you see the person. You know that person is about to come around the corner because of their shadow, but the shadow does not determine the person; the person determines the shadow.

God's foreknowledge is like the foreshadowing of a future event. By seeing this foreshadowing, you know the events will happen, But the shadow does not determine the reality; the reality determines the shadow. Therefore, we should think of God's foreknowledge as the foreshadowing of things to come. Therefore, just because God will know something will happen, this does not prejudice or remove the freedom of that happening.

In fact, if the events were to happen differently, God's foreknowledge would be different as well. An illustration of this is as an infallible barometer of the weather. Whatever the barometer says, you know what the weather will be like because it is infallible. However, the barometer does not determine the temperature; the weather determines the barometer's findings.

Thus, God's foreknowledge is like an infallible barometer of the future. It lets him know what the future will be, but it does not constrain the future in any way. The future will happen anyway the free moral agent wants it to happen. However, the barometer will track whatever direction the future will take.

Suppose this is the timeline **. . . . .** Let us place an event "**E**" on the timeline, i.e., Judas' betrayal of Jesus. Let us suppose **God** is back here in time, and by his foreknowledge (the dotted line), he knows that "**E**" will happen (Judas will betray Jesus). How does God's knowledge about "E" constrain "E" from happening? How can God's knowing "**E**" will occur make "**E**" occur?

If you were to erase the line and say **God** does not have foreknowledge of the future, how has anything changed? How would "**E**" (Judas' betrayal) be affected if you erased God's foreknowledge of it? "**E**" (Judas' betrayal) would occur just the same; it would not affect anything at all.

Therefore, the presence of God's foreknowledge really does not prejudice anything about whether "**E**" will occur or not. What we need to understand is this, if Judas ("**E**") were not to betray Jesus, then God would **not** have foreknown Judas' betrayal **("E")** of Jesus because it would not have been on the timeline. In addition, as long as that statement is true, "**E**" being able to occur and not occur, God's foreknowledge does not prejudice anything concerning "**E**'s" occurrence. – **Attribution**: Much of this information is borrowed from a Dr. William Lane Craig video.

EPHESIANS 1:4: Are some chosen (predestined) to eternal salvation, and others to eternal condemnation?

Are some chosen (predestined) to eternal salvation and others to eternal condemnation? The 16th-century Reformer John Calvin wrote: "We define predestination as the eternal design of God, whereby he determined what he wanted to do with each man. For he did not create them all in the same condition but foreordains some to everlasting life and others to eternal damnation." Does God really ordain each of us individually ahead of time as to what our actions and our final destiny are going to be? What does the Bible really teach?

We know that God can foretell the future. He describes himself as "declaring the end from the beginning and from ancient times things not yet done, saying, 'My counsel shall stand, and I will accomplish all my purpose.'" (Isaiah 46:10) There are many examples of God having used his foreknowledge to foretell events before they were to take place in the Scriptures. In many cases, this was centuries before they were to take place.

(Daniel 8:20, 21; Micah 5:2)And they came true just as he had prophesied. God had chosen the Israelite nation and Christians before the founding of the earth as his chosen ones. In ancient times Israel became the typical holy nation, for to it, Jehovah said: "And you shall be to me a kingdom of priests and a holy nation. These are the words that you shall speak to the sons of Israel. For you are a holy people to Jehovah your God: Jehovah your God has chosen you to be a people for his own possession, out of all the peoples that are on the face of the earth." (Ex. 19:6; Deut. 7:6) When we look at the Greek New Testament, it speaks of predestination or foreordination relative to those who will receive eternal life and those who will receive eternal destruction.

The words generally translated as "foreknow," "foreknowledge," and "foreordain" (i.e., predestine) are found in the Greek New Testament; the same basic views are conveyed in the Hebrew Scriptures. God indeed has the power of predestination and the faculty of foreknowledge. However, we need to understand foreknowledge and foreordination as they relate to God, grasping certain aspects. There are certain situations and events that take place because God has foreordained that they will (no creature in the universe can hinder these things), but it is not the case that **every event** must take place as it does because God has predetermined it; removing all free will. What God foreknows is because of the infallibility of his power of perception into the future, as though it were a timeline (more on this later). However, as we will see, this in no way violates our free will. In most cases, predestination has to do with groups like the Israelites and events, like the Exodus from Egypt, without foreordaining the specific individuals who will be involved in these groups or events. On the other hand, God's foreknowledge is not limited to groups and events, as he can see the future of every living creature.

God knows in advance what choice people will freely make. The free decisions of human beings determine what foreknowledge God has of them, as opposed to the reverse. The foreknowledge does not determine the free decision; it is the free decisions that determine the foreknowledge. Judas Iscariot betraying Jesus does not happen because God foreknows it, but God foreknows the event because it will happen. The event is logically prior to the foreknowledge, so he foreknows it because it will happen, even though the foreknowledge is chronologically before the event. We can see foreknowledge in this as the foreshadowing of something. When you see the shadow of someone coming around the corner of the building, you see his or her shadow on the ground before you see the person. You know that person is about to come around the corner because of their shadow, but the shadow does not determine the person; the person determines the shadow. God's foreknowledge is like the foreshadowing of a future event. By seeing this foreshadowing, you know the events will happen, But the shadow does not determine the reality; the reality determines the shadow. Therefore, we should think of God's foreknowledge as the foreshadowing of things to come. Therefore, just because God will know something will happen, this does not prejudice or remove the freedom of that happening. Thus, those who believe that God's foreknowledge removes the freedom of the person are mistaken. They posit a constraint upon human choices, which is really quite unintelligible.

God can step into the timeline and tweak anything to create a different outcome if he chooses to do so, which will then alter many future events because it will create a ripple effect in the timeline. If God were to alter anything that was already going to happen, making different choices outside of what was already going to occur in the present, it would have a ripple effect on future events. Let us use Willian Tyndale, which I believe God did step in to the timeline to protect Tyndale from the Catholic Church that was hunting him down for translating the Bible from the original languages of Hebrew (OT) and Greek (NT) into English. Let us say that God did step in to alter things, allowing Tyndale to survive to the point of bringing us the first printed translation in 1526; it would have had an impact on all English translations that lay ahead in the future: the Coverdale translation of 1535, the Matthew's Bible of 1537, The Great Bible of 1539, Cranmer's Bible of 1540, the Geneva Bible of 1560, and, of course, the King James Version of 1611, and all others down to the Revised Version of 1881, the 1801 American Standard Version, the 1952 Revised Standard Version, the 1960-1995 New American Standard Bible, the 2001 English Standard Version, and 2022 Updated American Standard Version. Think of the impact of the English translations had the Catholic Church executed Tyndale in 1523.

Earlier, we said that those who believe that God's foreknowledge removes a person's freedom are mistaken. They posit a constraint upon human choices, which is really quite unintelligible. How so? Those who God chose must persevere if they are to receive the reward of eternal life. In fact, Jesus said, "the one who endures to the end will be saved." (Matt. 24:13) Why are we told this, if the ones chosen thousands of years ago were final? "God created man in his own image." (Genesis 1:27) When creating man, free will was imperative if he was to love and honor God, serving him faithfully. God did not create robots with every moment predetermined beforehand. Our free-willed love is how God can refute Satan's false accusations. God says: "Be wise, my son, and make my heart glad, that I may return a word to my reproacher." (Proverbs 27:11) That is, 'that I may reply to him who reproaches me.'

If God's foreknowledge **does** determine our free decisions, those chosen by God would note freely love God; their love for their Creator could never be genuine. This is why Satan called man's love for God into question in the book of Job. Also, the Bible says that God is impartial, but how can that be so if foreknowledge determines those who are chosen for salvation irrespective of their individual merits? In addition, if these ones are receiving such privileged and favored positions, while others are fated to eternal punishment, how could anyone expect genuine and heartfelt feelings of appreciation and thankfulness in the "elect," or "chosen ones"? – Genesis 1:27; Job 1:8; Acts 10:34-35.

The greatest difficulty is the Great Commission that Jesus Christ gave to his "elect" or "chosen ones." He said, "this gospel of the kingdom will be proclaimed throughout the whole world as a testimony to all nations, and then the end will come." (Matt. 24:14) Why, this would be pointless work because some are supposedly predestined to eternal salvation, and others to eternal condemnation. Jesus later said, "Go therefore and **make disciples** of all nations, baptizing them … teaching them …" Why if some are supposedly predestined to eternal salvation and others to eternal condemnation. Jesus said before his ascension back to heaven, "you will be my witnesses in Jerusalem and in all Judea and Samaria, and to the end of the earth." If God's foreknowledge does determine their free decisions, the preaching work essentially pointless? Persuading, persuading, and persuasion, as well as explaining, proving, and defending, are used in regards to Paul's preaching work many times. Notice the meaning of persuasion and how it is meaningless when the outcome is already predetermined.

Persuasion: (Gr. πεισμονή peismonē, πείθω peithō) The Greek word literally means to **1.) persuade**, convince (Matt. 27:20; Ac 12:20; 18:4; 19:8, 26; 23:28; 26:28). It means "to be assured of" or "to be convinced and certain of the truth of something." Through the art of persuasion, one can cause another to adopt a certain position, view, belief, or course of action. Someone convinces or persuades another by bringing about a change of mind by means of sound, logical reasoning. Someone convinces or persuades another to adopt a new belief and to act on that belief. It also means to **2.) trust**, rely (Lu 11:22; 2 Cor. 1:9); **3.) be assured** (1 John 3:19); **4.) obey** (Heb. 13:17); **5.) be a follower**, be a disciple (Ac 5:36, 37); **6.) be certain**, be sure (Heb. 13:18).

Predestine? Paul told the Christians in Rome, "For those whom he **foreknew** he also **predestined** to be conformed to the image of his Son, in order that he might be the firstborn among many brothers. And those whom he predestined he also called, and those whom he called he also justified, and those whom he justified he also glorified." (Romans 8:29-30, ESV, CSB, LEB, NASB, similar) How should we understand the term "predestined" used by Paul? The Greek word (προορίζω proorizō) has the sense of **predetermining**, which means to **determine** something ahead of time or before its occurrence, **decide beforehand**, predestine (Ac 4:28; Ro 8:29, 30; 1Co 2:7; Eph 1:5, 11) Paul's words here cannot be used as a dogmatic argument for individual predetermined predestination. If we are going to understand this in context, we must look at the last two verses Romans 8:38-39, "For I am sure that neither death nor life, nor angels nor rulers, nor things present nor things to come, nor powers, nor height nor depth, nor anything else in all creation, **will be able to separate us from <u>the love of God</u>** in Christ Jesus our Lord." *Nothing* can separate the believer from God's love. This does not mean that a believer cannot choose to abandon the love of God.

Jude 5 Updated American Standard Version (UASV)

5 Now I want to remind you, though you know all things once for all, that the Lord, after saving a people out of the land of Egypt, *afterward destroyed* those who did not believe.

Matthew 24:13 Updated American Standard Version (UASV)

13 But the one who endures to the end will be saved.

Here, Jesus clearly states that a person's salvation is not guaranteed at the moment that they accept him, have faith in him, and dedicate their lives to him.

Philippians 2:12 Updated American Standard Version (UASV)

12 So then, my beloved, just as you have always obeyed, not as in my presence only, but now much more in my absence, work out your own salvation with fear and trembling;

Paul, here was writing to born-again Christians, "the saints" or "holy ones" at Philippi, for Philippians 1:1 state, "Paul and Timothy, servants pledged to Christ Jesus, to all the holy ones in Christ Jesus that are in Philippi …" Paul in 2:12 is urging them not to be overly confident, as their final salvation was not assured as Jesus had stated, only those who survived to the end. (Matthew 24:13) True, God is at work in us, enabling us to carry out his will and purposes, but we must cooperate with the Holy Spirit by, as Paul said, working out our salvation.

Hebrews 6:4-6 Updated American Standard Version (UASV)

[4] For in the case of **those who have** once been enlightened and have tasted of the heavenly gift and have been made partakers of the Holy Spirit, [5] and have tasted the good word of God and the powers of the age to come, [6] **and then** [after that] have **fallen away**, it is impossible to **renew** them again to repentance, since they again crucify to themselves the Son of God and put him to public shame.

Fall Away, Forsake, or Turn Away: (Gr. *parapiptō*) The sense of *parapiptō* is to fall away or forsake the truth.–Heb. 6:6.

Renew, Restore, or Bring Back: (Gr. *anakainizō*) The sense of *anakainizō* is to cause change to a previous state, to start anew.–Heb. 6:6.

On this text M. R. De Haan in *Studies in Hebrews* correctly observes,

If that is not a description of true, born-again believers, then language means nothing, and we cannot understand anything in the Word of God anymore. Five marks of the believer are given:

1. They were once enlightened.
2. They had tasted the heavenly gift.
3. They were partakers of the Holy Ghost.
4. They had tasted the good Word of God.
5. They had knowledge of prophecy.[105]

Hebrews 10:26-27 Updated American Standard Version (UASV)

[26] For if **we** [Paul and the born-again Jewish Christians] **go on sinning** deliberately **after receiving** the **accurate knowledge** of the truth, there no longer remains a sacrifice for sins, [27] but a fearful expectation of judgment, and a fury of fire that will consume the adversaries.

This clearly states that one can lose salvation. Paul says "we," meaning that he includes himself and the born again Jewish Christians that he is writing to, both needing to remain faithful, which suggests that they have the free will to be unfaithful.

Albert Barnes on Hebrews 6:4-6

Hebrews 4:4. For it is impossible. It is needless to say that the passage here (Hebrews 4:4–6), has given occasion to much controversy, and that the

---

[105] M. R. De Haan, *Studies in Hebrews* (Grand Rapids, MI: Kregel Publications, 1996), 104–105.

opinions of commentators and of the Christian world are yet greatly divided in regard to its meaning. On the one hand, it is held that the passage is not intended to describe those who are true Christians, but only those who have been awakened and enlightened, and who then fall back; and on the other it is maintained that it refers to those who *are* true Christians, and who then apostatize. The contending parties have been Calvinists and Arminians; each party, in general, interpreting it according to the views which are held on the question about falling from grace. I shall endeavor, as well as I may be able, to state the true meaning of the passage, by an examination of the words and phrases in detail, observing here, in general, that it seems to me that it refers to true Christians; that the object is to keep them from apostasy, and that it teaches that if they should apostatize, it would be impossible to renew them again or to save them. That it refers to true Christians will be apparent from these considerations. (1.) Such is the sense which would strike the great mass of readers. Unless there were some theory to defend, the great body of readers of the New Testament would consider the expression here used as describing true Christians. (2.) The connection demands such an interpretation. The apostle was addressing Christians. He was endeavoring to keep them from apostasy. The object was not to keep those who were awakened and enlightened from apostasy, but it was to preserve those who were already in the Church of Christ, from going back to perdition. The kind of exhortation appropriate to those who were awakened and convicted, but who were not truly converted, would be *to become converted;* not to warn them of the danger of *falling away*. Besides, the apostle would not have said of such persons that they *could not* be converted and saved. But of sincere Christians it might be said with the utmost propriety, that they *could not* be renewed again and be saved if they should fall away—because they rejected the only plan of salvation after they had tried it, and renounced the only scheme of redemption after they had tasted its benefits. If that plan could not save them, what could? If they neglected that, by what other means could they be brought to God? (3.) This interpretation accords, as I suppose, with the exact meaning of the phrases which the apostle uses. An examination of those phrases will show that he refers to those who are sincere believers. The phrase "it is impossible" obviously and properly denotes absolute impossibility. It has been contended, by Storr and others, that it denotes only great difficulty. But the meaning which would at first strike all readers would be that *the thing could not be done;* that it was not merely very difficult, but absolutely impracticable. The word—ἀδύνατον—occurs only in the New Testament in the following places, in all which it denotes that the thing could not be done; Matt. 19:26; Mark 10:27, "With men this is impossible;" that is, men could not save one who was rich, implying that the thing was wholly beyond human power. Luke 18:27, "The things which are impossible with men are possible with God"—referring to the same case; Acts 14:8, "A man of Lystra, *impotent* in his feet;" that is, who was wholly *unable* to walk; Rom. 8:3, "For what the law could not do;" what was absolutely *impossible* for the law to accomplish; that is, to save men; Heb. 6:18, "In which it was *impossible* for God to lie; Heb. 10:4, "It is not *possible* for the blood of bulls and of goats to take away sin;" and Heb. 11:6, "Without faith it is *impossible* to please God;" in all of these instances denoting absolute impossibility. These passages show that it is not merely a great difficulty to which the apostle refers, but that he meant to say that the thing was wholly impracticable; that it could not be done. And if this be the meaning, then it proves that *if* those referred to should fall away, they could never be renewed. Their case was hopeless, and they must perish:—that is, if a true Christian should apostatize, or fall from grace, *he never could be renewed again*, and could not be saved. Paul did not teach that he might fall away and be renewed again as often as he pleased. He had other views of the grace of God than this; and he meant to teach, that if a man should once cast off true religion, his case was hopeless, and he must perish; and by this solemn consideration—the only one that would be effectual in such a case—he meant to guard them against the danger of apostasy.

For those who were once enlightened. The phrase "to be enlightened" is one that is often used in the Scriptures, and may be applied either to one whose understanding has been enlightened to discern his duty, though he is not converted (comp. Note John 1:9); or more commonly to one who is truly converted; see Note on Eph. 1:18. It does not of necessity refer to true Christians, though it cannot be denied that it more obviously suggests the idea that the heart is truly changed, and that it is more commonly used in that sense; comp. Ps. 19:8. Light, in the Scriptures, is the emblem of knowledge, holiness, and happiness, and there is no impropriety here in understanding it in accordance with the more decisive phrases which follow, as referring to true Christians.

And have tasted. To *taste* of a thing means, according to the usage in the Scriptures, to *experience*, or to *understand* it. The expression is derived from the fact that the *taste* is one of the means by which we ascertain the nature or quality of an object; comp. Matt. 16:28; John 8:51; Heb. 2:9. The proper idea here is, that they had *experienced* the heavenly gift, or had learned its nature.

The heavenly gift. The gift from heaven, or which pertains to heaven; comp. Note John 4:10. The expression properly means some favor or gift which has descended from heaven and may refer to any of the benefits which God has conferred on man in the work of redemption. It might include the plan of salvation; the forgiveness of sins; the enlightening, renewing, and sanctifying influences of the Holy Spirit, or any one of the graces which that Spirit imparts. The use of the article, however—"*the* heavenly gift,"—limits it to something special, as being conferred directly from heaven, and the connection would seem to demand that we understand it of some *peculiar* favor which could be conferred only on the children of God. It is an expression which *may* be applied to sincere Christians; it is at least doubtful whether it can with propriety be applied to any other.

And were made partakers of the Holy Spirit. Partakers of the influences of the Holy Spirit—for it is only in this sense that we can partake of the Holy Spirit. We *partake* of food when we share it with others; we *partake* of pleasure when we enjoy it with others; we *partake* of spoils in war when they are divided between us and others. So we partake of the influences of the Holy Spirit when we share these influences conferred on his people. This is not language which can properly be applied to anyone but a true Christian; and though it is true that an unpardoned sinner may be enlightened and awakened by the Holy Spirit, yet the language here used is not such as would be likely to be employed to describe his state. It is too clearly expressive of those influences which renew and sanctify the soul. It is as elevated language as can be used to describe the joy of the Christian and is undoubtedly used in that sense here. If it is not, it would be difficult to find any language which would properly express the condition of a renewed heart. Grotius, Bloomfield, and some others, understood this of the miraculous gifts of the Holy Spirit. But this is not necessary and does not accord well with the general description here, which evidently pertains to the mass of those whom the apostle addressed.

Hebrews 4:5. **And have tasted the good word of God**. That is, either the doctrines which he teaches, and which are good, or pleasant to the soul; or the word of God which is connected with *good*, that is, which promises good. The former seems to me to the correct meaning—that the word of God, or the truth which he taught, was itself a good. It was that which the soul desired, and in which it found comfort and peace; comp. Ps. 119:103; 141:6. The meaning here is, that they had experienced the excellency of the truth of God; they had seen and enjoyed its beauty. This is language which cannot be applied to an impenitent sinner. He has no *relish* for the truth of God; sees no beauty in it; derives no comfort from it. It is only the true Christian who has pleasure in its contemplation, and who can be said to "taste" and enjoy it. This language describes a state of mind of which every sincere Christian is conscious. It is that of pleasure in the word of God. He loves the Bible; he loves the truth of God that is preached. He sees an exquisite beauty in that truth. It is not merely in its poetry; in its sublimity; in its argument; but he has now a *taste* or *relish* for the truth itself, which he had not before his conversion. Then he might have admired the Bible for its beauty of language or for its poetry; he might have been interested in preaching for its eloquence or power of argument; but now his love is for *the truth;* comp. Ps. 19:10. There is no book that he so much delights in as the Bible; and no pleasure is so pure as that which he has in contemplating the truth; comp. Josh. 21:45; 23:15.

And the powers of the world to come. Or of the "coming age." "The age to come" was a phrase in common use among the Hebrews, to denote the future dispensation, the times of the Messiah. The same idea was expressed by the phrases "the last times," "the end of the world," &c. which are of so frequent occurrence in the Scriptures. They all denoted an age which was to succeed the old dispensation; the time of the Messiah; or the period in which the affairs of the world would be wound up; see Notes on Isa. 2:2. Here it evidently refers to that period, and the meaning is, that they had participated in the peculiar blessings to be expected in that dispensation—to wit, in the clear views of the way of salvation, and the influences of the Holy Spirit on the soul. The word "powers" here implies that in that time there would be some extraordinary manifestation of the *power* of God. An unusual energy would be put forth to save men, particularly as evinced by the agency of the Holy Spirit on the heart. Of this "power" the apostle here says they of whom he spoke had partaken. They had been brought under the awakening and renewing energy which God put forth under the Messiah, in saving the soul. They had experienced the promised blessings of the new and last dispensation; and the language here is such as appropriately describes Christians, and as indeed can be applicable to no other. It may be remarked respecting the various expressions used here (Heb. 4:4-5), (1.) that they are such as properly denote a renewed state. They obviously describe the condition of a Christian; and though it may be not certain that any *one* of them if taken by itself would *prove* that the person to whom it was applied was truly converted, yet taken together it is clear that they are designed to describe such a state. If they are not, it would be difficult to find any language which would be properly descriptive of the character of a sincere Christian. I regard the description here, therefore, as that which is clearly designed to denote the state of those who were born again and were the true children of God; and it seems plain to me that no other interpretation would have ever been thought of if this view had not seemed to conflict with the doctrine of the "perseverance of the saints." (2.) There is a regular gradation here from the first elements of piety in the soul to its highest developments; and, whether the apostle so designed it or not, the language describes the successive steps by which a true Christian advance to the highest stage of Christian experience. The mind is (*a*) enlightened; then (*b*) *tastes* the gift of heaven, or has some experience of it; then (*c*) it is made to partake of the influences of the Holy Ghost; then (*d*) there is experience of the excellence and loveliness of the word of God; and (*e*) finally there is a participation of the full "powers" of the new dispensation; of the extraordinary energy which God puts forth in the gospel to sanctify and save the soul.

Hebrews 4:6. If they shall fall away. Literally, "and having fallen away." "There is no *if* in the Greek in this place—"having fallen away." *Dr. J. P. Wilson*. It is not an affirmation that any *had* actually fallen away, or that in fact they *would* do it; but the statement is, that *on the supposition that they had fallen away*, it would be impossible to renew them again. It is the same as supposing a case which in fact might never occur:—as if we should say, "had a man fallen down a precipice it would be impossible to save him;" or "had the child fallen into the stream, he would certainly have been drowned." But though this literally means, "having fallen away," yet the sense in the connection in which it stands is not improperly expressed by our common translation. The Syriac has given a version which is remarkable, not as a correct translation, but as showing what was the prevailing belief in the time in which it was made, (probably, the first or second century), in regard to the doctrine of the perseverance of the saints. "For it is impossible that they who have been baptized, and who have tasted the gift, which is from heaven, and have received the spirit of holiness, and have tasted the good word of God, and the power of the coming age, should again sin, so that they should be renewed again to repentance, and again crucify the Son of God and put him to ignominy." The word rendered "fall away" means properly "to fall near by anyone;" "to fall in with or meet;" and thus to fall aside from, to swerve or deviate from; and here means undoubtedly to *apostatize from*, and implies an entire renunciation of Christianity, or a going back to a state of Judaism, heathenism, or sin. The Greek word occurs nowhere else in the New Testament. It is material to remark here that the apostle does not say that any true Christian ever had fallen away. He makes a statement of what would occur on the supposition that such a thing should happen—but a statement may be made of what *would* occur on the supposition that a certain thing should take place, and yet it be morally certain that the event never would happen. It would be easy to suppose what would happen if the ocean should overflow a continent, or if the sun should cease to rise, and still there be entire certainty that such an event never would occur.

To renew them again. Implying that they had been before renewed or had been true Christians. The word "*again*"—πάλιν—supposes this; and this passage, therefore, confirms the considerations suggested above, showing that they were true Christians who were referred to. They had once repented, but it would be impossible to bring them to this state *again*. This declaration of course to be read in connection with the first clause of ver. 4, "It is impossible to renew again to repentance those who once were true Christians should they fall away." I know of no declaration more unambiguous than this. It is a positive declaration. It is not that it would be very difficult to do it; or that it would be impossible for *man* to do it, though it might be done by God; it is an unequivocal and absolute declaration that it would be utterly impracticable that it should be done by anyone, or by any means; and this, I have no doubt, is the meaning of the apostle. Should a Christian fall from grace, he *must perish*. He never could be saved. The *reason* of this the apostle immediately adds.

Seeing. This word is not in the Greek, though the sense is expressed. The Greek literally is, "having again crucified to themselves the Son of God." The *reason* here given is, that the crime would be so great, and they would so effectually exclude themselves from the only plan of salvation, that they could not be saved. There is but one way of salvation. Having tried that, and then renounced it, how could they then be saved? The case is like that of a drowning man. If there was but one plank by which he could be saved, and he should get on that and then push it away and plunge into the deep, he must die. Or if there was but one rope by which the shore could be reached from a wreck, and he should cut that and cast it off, he must die. Or if a man were sick, and there was but one kind of medicine that could possibly restore him, and he should deliberately dash that away, he must die. So in religion. There is *but one* way of salvation. If a man deliberately rejects that, he must perish.

They crucify to themselves the Son of God afresh. Our translators have rendered this as if the Greek were—ἀνασταυροῦντας πάλιν—*crucify again*, and so it is rendered by Chrysostom, by Tindal, Coverdale, Beza, Luther, and others. But this is not properly the meaning of the Greek. The word ἀνασταυρόω—is an *intensive* word and is employed instead of the usual word "to crucify" only to denote *emphasis*. It means that such an act of apostasy would be equivalent to crucifying him in an aggravated manner. Of course this is to be taken *figuratively*. It could not be literally true that they would thus crucify the Redeemer. The meaning is, that their conduct would be *as if* they had crucified him; it would bear a strong resemblance to the act by which the Lord Jesus was publicly rejected and condemned to die. The act of crucifying the Son of God was the great crime which outweighs any other deed of human guilt. Yet the apostle says that should they who had been true Christians fall away and reject him, they would be guilty of a similar crime. It would be a public and solemn act of rejecting him. It would show that if they had been there, they would have joined in the cry "crucify him, crucify him."

The *intensity* and *aggravation* of such a crime perhaps the apostle meant to indicate by the intensive or emphatic ἀνὰ in the word ἀνασταυροῦντας. Such an act would render their salvation impossible, because (1.) the crime would be aggravated beyond that of those who rejected him and put him to death—for they knew not what they did; and (2.) because it would be a rejection of the only possible plan of salvation after they had had experience of its power and known its efficacy. The phrase "to themselves," Tindal renders, "as concerning themselves." Others, "as far as in them lies," or as far as they have ability to do. Others, "to their own heart." Probably Grotius has suggested the true sense. "They do it *for themselves*. They make the act their own. It is as if they did it themselves; and they are to be regarded as having done the deed." So we make the act of another our own when we authorize it beforehand or approve of it after it is done.

And put him to an open shame. Make him a public example; or hold him up as worthy of death on the cross; see the same word explained in the Notes on Matt. 1:19, in the phrase "make her a public example." The word occurs nowhere else in the New Testament. Their apostasy and rejection of the Savior would be like holding him up publicly as deserving the infamy and ignominy of the cross. A great part of the crime attending the crucifixion of the Lord Jesus, consisted in exhibiting him to the passing multitude as deserving the death of a malefactor. Of that sin they would partake who should reject him, for they would thus show that they regarded his religion as an imposture and would in a public manner hold him up as worthy only of rejection and contempt. Such, it seems to me, is the fair meaning of this much-disputed passage—a passage which would never have given so much perplexity if it had not been supposed that the obvious interpretation would interfere with some prevalent articles of theology. The passage *proves* that if true Christians should apostatize, it would be impossible to renew and save them. If then it should be asked whether I believe that any true Christian ever did, or ever will fall from grace, and wholly lose his religion, I would answer unhesitatingly, *no;* comp. Notes on John 10:27, 28; Rom. 8:38, 39; Gal. 6:4. If then it be asked what the *use* of a warning like this was, I answer, (1.) It would show the great *sin* of apostasy from God if it were to occur. It is proper to state the greatness of an act of sin, though it might never occur, in order to show how it would be regarded by God. (2.) Such a statement might be one of the most effectual means of preserving from apostasy. To state that a fall from a precipice would cause certain death, would be one of the most certain means of preserving one from falling; to affirm that arsenic would be certainly fatal, is one of the most effectual means of preventing its being taken; to know that fire certainly destroys, is one of the most sure checks from the danger. Thousands have been preserved from going over the Falls of Niagara by knowing that there would be no possibility of escape; and so effectual has been this knowledge that it has preserved all from such a catastrophe, except the very few who have gone over by accident. So in religion. The knowledge that apostasy would be fatal, and there could be no hope of being saved should it once occur would be a more effectual preventive of the danger than all the other means that could be used. If a man believed that it would be an easy matter to be restored again, should he apostatize, he would feel little solicitude in regard to it; and it has occurred in fact, that they who suppose that this may occur, have manifested little of the care to walk in the paths of strict religion, which should have been evinced. (3.) It may be added that the means used by God to preserve his people from apostasy, have been entirely effectual. There is no evidence that one has ever fallen away who was a true Christian, (comp. John 10:27, 28, and 1 John 2:19); and to the end of the world it will be true that the means which he uses to keep his people from apostasy will not in a single instance fail.

Edward D. Andrews Note: If I were to stop there it would be theological bias on my part because Albert Barnes just laid out the best case that the author of Hebrews, Paul, said of Hebrews 6:4-6 that these verses are explicitly referring to true Christians, not those who are awakened and enlightened, then fall back. However, it is Albert Barnes that goes on to commit theological bias. If one state what a verse is referring to, what it is saying and then that jeopardizes a favored doctrinal view, such as eternal security (the holy one's perseverance), so they go on to say, how can we interpret this so that it still supports my favored doctrinal view. The apostle Peter had this to say about Paul's letters, "And count the patience of our Lord as salvation, just as **our beloved brother Paul** also wrote to you according to the wisdom given him, as he does in all his letters **when he speaks in them of these matters**. There are **some things in them that are hard to understand**, which the ignorant and unstable **twist to their own destruction, as they do the other Scriptures**." (2 Peter 3:15-16) So, Albert Barnes started the next section of our excursion by saying aloud that his intention is to reign in what Hebrews 6:4-6 is saying and twist it until he gets it to support his doctrinal view.

[**This view seems not opposed to the doctrine of the holy one's perseverance**. It professes indeed, to meet the objection usually raised from the passage, if not in a new mode, yet in a mode different from that commonly adopted by orthodox expositors. Admitting that *true* Christians are intended, it is asserted only, that if they *should* fall, their recovery would be impossible. It is not said that they ever *have* fallen or *will* fall. "The apostle in thus giving judgment on the case, if it should happen, does not declare that it actually does." And as to the use of supposing a case which never can occur, it is argued that *means* are constantly used to bring about that which the decree or determination of God had before rendered certain. These exhortations are the means by which perseverance is secured.

Yet it may be doubted, whether there be any thing in the passage to convince us, that the apostle has introduced an *impossible* case. He seems rather to speak of that which *might* happen, of which there was *danger*. If the reader incline to this view, he will apply the description to professors, and learn from it how far these may go, and yet fall short of the mark. But how would this suit the apostle's design? Well. If *professors* may go *so far*, how much is this fact fitted to arouse all to vigilance and inquiry. We, notwithstanding our gifts and *apparent* graces, may not be *true* Christians, may, therefore, not be *secure*, may fall away and sink, under the doom of him whom it is impossible to renew. And he must be a very exalted Christian indeed, who does not occasionally find need of inquiry, and examination of evidences. Certainly, the whole passage may be explained in perfect consistency with this application of it. Men may be enlightened, *i.e.* well acquainted with the doctrines and duties of the Christian faith; may have tasted of the heavenly gift, and been made partakers of the Holy Ghost in his miraculous influences, which many in primitive times enjoyed, without any sanctifying virtue; may have tasted the good word of God, or experienced impressions of affection and joy under it, as in the case of the stony ground hearers; may have tasted the powers of the world to come, or been influenced by the doctrine of a future state, with its accompanying rewards and punishments;—and yet not be *true* Christians. "All these things, except miraculous gifts, often take place in the hearts and consciences of men in these days, who yet continue unregenerate. They have knowledge, convictions, fears, hope, joys, and seasons of apparent earnestness, and deep concern about eternal things; and they are endued with such gifts, as often make them acceptable and useful to others, but they are not truly *humbled;* they are not *spiritually minded;* religion is not their element and delight."—*Scott.*

It should be observed, moreover, that while there are many *infallible* marks of the true Christian, none of these are mentioned in this place. The persons described are not said to have been elected, to have been regenerated, to have believed, or to have been sanctified. The apostle writes very differently when describing the character and privileges of the saints, Rom. 8:27, 30. The succeeding context, too, is supposed to favour this opinion. "They (the characters in question) are, in the following verses, compared to the ground on which the rain often falls, and beareth nothing but thorns and briars. But this is not so with true believers, for faith itself is an herb peculiar to the inclosed garden of Christ. And the apostle afterwards, discoursing of true believers, doth in many particulars distinguish them from such as may be apostates, which is supposed of the persons here intended. He ascribeth to them, in general, better things and such as accompany salvation. He ascribes a work and labour of love, asserts their preservation, &c."—*Owen.* Our author, however, fortifies himself against the objection in the first part of this quotation, by repeating and applying at verse 7. his *principle* of exposition. "The design," says he, "is to show, that if Christians should become like the barren earth, they would be cast away and lost." Yet the attentive reader of this very ingenious exposition will observe, that the author has difficulty in carrying out his principles, and finds it necessary to introduce the *mere professor* ere he has done with the passage. "It is not supposed," says he, commenting on the 8th verse, "that a true Christian will fall away and be lost, but we may remark, that there are many *professed* Christians who seem to be in danger of such ruin. Corrupt desires are as certainly seen in their lives, as thorns on a bad soil. Such are nigh unto cursing. *Unsanctified*, &c., there is nothing else which can be done for them, and they must be lost. What a thought!" Yet that the case of the professor in danger cannot very consistently be introduced by him, appears from the fact, that such ruin as is here described is suspended on a condition which never occurs. It happens *only if* the *Christian* should fall. According to the author, it is not *here* denounced *on any other supposition.* As then true Christians cannot fall, the ruin never can occur *in any case whatever.* From these premises we *dare not* draw the conclusion, that any class of professors will be given over *to* final impenitence.

As to what may be alleged concerning the *apparent* sense of the passage, or the sense which would strike "the mass of readers;" every one will judge according to the sense which himself thinks most obvious. Few perhaps would imagine that the apostle was introducing an impossible case. Nor does the "connection" stand much in the way of the application to professors. In addition to what has already been stated, let it be farther observed, that although the appropriate exhortation to awakened, yet unconverted persons would be, "to become converted; not to warn them of the danger of falling away;" yet the apostle is writing to the Hebrews at large, is addressing a body of professing Christians, concerning whom he could have no infallible assurance that *all of them* were true Christians. Therefore, it was right that they should be warned in the way the apostle has adopted. The objection leaves out of sight the important fact that *the exhortations and warnings addressed to the saints in Scripture are addressed to mixed societies, in which there may be hypocrites as well as believers.* Those who profess the faith, and associate with the church, are addressed without any decision regarding *state.* But the very existence of the warnings implies a fear that there may be some whose state is not safe. And *all*, therefore, have need to inquire whether this be their condition. How appropriate then such warnings. This consideration, too, will furnish an answer to what has been alleged by another celebrated transatlantic writer, viz. "that whatever may be true in the divine purposes us to the final salvation of all those who are once truly regenerated, and this doctrine I feel constrained to admit, yet nothing can be plainer, than that the sacred writers have every where addressed saints in the same manner as they would address those whom they considered as constantly exposed to fall away and to perish for ever." Lastly. The phraseology of the passage does not appear to remove it out of all possible application to *mere* professors It has already been briefly explained in consistency with such application. There is difficulty, indeed, connected with the phrase, παλιν ανακαινιζειν εις μετανοιαν, *again* to renew to repentance; implying, as is said, that they, to whom reference is made, had been renewed *before*. But what should hinder this being understood of *reinstating in former condition*, or in possession of former privilege? Bloomfield supposes, there may be an allusion to the non-reiteration of baptism, and Owen explains the phrase of bringing them again into a state of profession by a second renovation, and a second baptism, as a pledge thereof. The renewing he understands here *externally* of a solemn confession of faith and repentance, followed by baptism. This, says he, was their ανακαινισμος, their renovation. It would seem then that there is nothing in the phrase to prevent its interpretation on the same principle that above has been applied to the passage generally.][106]

End of Excursion

2 Peter 2:20-21 Updated American Standard Version (UASV)

20 For if, after they **[born-again believers]** have escaped the defilements of the world by the accurate knowledge of the Lord and Savior Jesus Christ, **they are again entangled in them and are overcome**, the last state has become worse for them than the first. 21 For it would have been **better for them never to have known** the way of righteousness than after knowing it to **turn back from the holy** commandment delivered to them.

If the born-again believer who has been made righteous through "the accurate knowledge the Lord and Savior Jesus Christ" cannot lose their salvation, why are there so many warnings about their **falling away** or **turning back**? Again, many Bible verses show that those who have been saved; are still obligated to endure faithfully. (Matthew 24:13; Hebrews 10:36; 12:2, 3; Revelation 2:10) The Christians in the First-century showed joy when they saw that fellow born-again believers were enduring in their faith. (1 Thessalonians 1:2, 3; 3 John 3-4) So, does it seem logical that God,

---

106 Albert Barnes, *Notes on the New Testament: Hebrews*, ed. Robert Frew (London: Blackie & Son, 1884–1885), 126–133.

through the Bible, would emphasize **faithful endurance** and warn of **falling away** (leaving the faith, leaving Christ) if those who did not endure and fell away would be saved anyway?

Ephesians 2:8-9 Updated American Standard Version (UASV) [8] For by grace you have been **saved through faith**; and that not of yourselves, it is the gift of God; [9] not from works, so that no man may boast.

The complete provision for salvation for a born-again Christian is God's grace. There is no way that any human can gain salvation on their own, regardless of how man good Christian works they may do. Salvation is an undeserved gift from God to all who put faith in the sin-atoning sacrifice of Jesus Christ. Let's look a little deeper at Ephesians 2:8-9.

For by grace, you have been saved – By an undeserved gift from God. It is not by your Own merit; it is not because we have any claim.

Through faith – Grace bestowed the underserved gift of salvation through faith or with believing **into** Jesus Christ.

And that not of yourselves – Salvation does not proceed from yourself. The word rendered "that" - τοῦτο touto - is in the neuter gender, and the word "faith" - πίστις pistis - is in the feminine. Therefore, the word "that," does not refer particularly to faith as being the gift of God but to "the salvation by grace" of which he had been speaking.

It is the gift of God – Salvation by grace is his gift. It is not of merit; it is wholly by favor.

Not from works – The entire provision for salvation is an expression of God's undeserved kindness. There is no way that a descendant of Adam can gain salvation on his own, no matter how noble his works are. Salvation is a gift from God given to those who put faith in the sin-atoning value of the ransom sacrifice of the Son, Jesus Christ.

James 2:14-26 is no contradiction with Paul here in Ephesians 2:8-9, it is a compliment. James makes it clear that faith is not just some head knowledge alone, but true faith is manifested in producing appropriate actions consistent with what one claims to profess. James here asks the question for his audience to ponder and think about to come to their conclusion as he states, **can such faith save him**?

Faith does not just begin and end at a mere profession of Christ. Good works in one's life then must evidence it. These works are not done as a way to earn salvation but rather out of gratitude for a heart that has been changed by the power of Christ that made one a new creation in Christ. Good works are to be done out of the overflow of the heart that the power of God has redeemed through Christ. As he explains in verses 15-26, the answer to James' question is that faith without works is not true saving faith.

Therefore, the fact that one does not act according to his words proves his words to be dead and false. It is dead in itself to just claim to have faith but have no works. The word that James uses for dead is *nekros* which means "*inactive, inoperative*." (Vine 1996, 148) This believer's mere lip service to faith without the outward expression of faith through works is inactive. James is making it clear that without works, his faith is dormant and dead and, therefore, proves that he truly does not have faith. Jesus himself said that many would be judged for the supposed claim of faith without works on judgment day with the parable of the sheep and the goats. – Matthew 25:31-46.

For the body apart from the spirit is dead, so also faith apart from works is dead. (James 2:26)

For the body apart from the spirit is dead. The Greek word (πνεῦμα pneuma) is commonly used to denote *spirit*, *wind*, *breath*, and *life force*. The meaning here is the obvious one, that the body is animated or kept alive by the presence of the (spirit) life force and that when that is withdrawn, hope departs. The body has no life independent of the presence of the spirit. The Greek *pneuma* represents the life force from God that was given to Adam and Eve, which is introduced into every child thereafter, and animates the human soul or person. As James 2:26 states: "The body apart from the spirit [*pneumatos*] is dead."

So also, faith without works is dead. It is just as essential that faith and that works should be animated by faith as there is that the body and spirit should be united to form a living man. If good works do not result from faith, there is no true faith. No justification does not put a person on the path to salvation. There is no being declared righteous by God. If faith does not generate works, a truly Christian life, it is dead. It has no power, and it is worthless. James was not making some argument against real and genuine faith. In addition, he was not making an argument against its significance in justification. He was arguing against the idea Christians only needed faith alone to be on the path of salvation, and it need not come with good works. James argues that if there is genuine faith, it will always follow that good works are there. Just as you cannot have a body without the breath of life, you cannot have faith without works. It is *only* faith that can justify and save. But if that faith does not have works, it is not really faith. It is pseudo-faith, so there is no justification, no salvation. If the faith does not result in genuine

Christian life, it is like the body without the spirit (breath of life). It is meaningless.

James and Paul are not at odds with each other, as they both agree that the person needs true faith to be justified, declared righteous, and enter the path of salvation. Both James and Paul agree that to have genuine faith; one must have works as well that evidence a holy Christian life. Both believe the opposite of that is true too. If a Christian does not have a holy life, their faith is a mere facade. The entire New Testament makes these things clear. If we do not believe in Jesus Christ, we cannot be justified before God, and if our faith is not genuine, it is impossible to lead a holy life. Claiming that no works are necessary for having faith is like saying a dead body of a living man. It is just ridiculous.

When a person (a soul) dies (beyond clinical death), there is no longer any animating force or "spirit" within any single cell out of the body's one hundred trillion cells. Many of us have seen the animation video in science classes at school, where the cell is shown to be like a microscopic factory with an enormous amount of work taking place. Therefore, no work is taking place within the lifeless body, as all of the cells animated by the spirit are dead. The body is not good for anything. This is the similarity that James is trying to draw our attention to, as a faith that lacks works is just as lifeless, producing no results and of no use as a corpse. The literal eye cannot see faith; however, works demonstrate that faith can be seen. When one is not moved to good works, it is clear that this one has no real faith. Alternatively, any Christian that is motivated to do good works, possesses a genuine faith.

We have spoken about works for many pages now. So, the next question is, what are some examples of works that should be evident in Christian life? The works are the fruitage of the Spirit (Gal. 5:22-23), the will of the Father (Matt. 7:21-23), and the Great Commission (Matt. 24:14; 28;19-20; Acts 1:8), as well as obeying such things as love your neighbor, helping those who need it if it is within your power, living a holy life, etc.

What about the Following Bible Verse?

John 6:37, 39 Updated American Standard Version (UASV)

37 All that the Father gives me will come to me, and the one who comes to me I will never cast out. 39 And this is the will of him who sent me, that I should **lose nothing of all that he has given me**, but raise it up on the last day.

This verse does nothing to undo the fact that born-again Christians have free will and can choose to reject Jesus Christ. It only says, Jesus will never cast the born-again believer out and that he will not lose any believers but it does not say that believers are unable to exercise their free will, choosing to leave him.

The argument that some make is that true born-again believers in Christ cannot lose their salvation. Their argument is that if anyone professing Christian rejects Jesus Christ, he simply was not truly a born-again believer in the first place. Their verse to support this is,

1 John 2:19 Updated American Standard Version (UASV)

19 They went out from us, but **they were not of us**; for if they had been of us, they would have continued with us; but they went out, so that they would be revealed that they all are not of us.

This is not dealing with born-again believers as to whether they can lose their salvation or not; it is dealing with the antichrist.

1 John 2:18 Updated American Standard Version (UASV)

18 Little children, it is the last hour; and just as you heard that antichrist is coming, even now many antichrists have arisen; whereby we know that it is the last hour.

The context for 1 John 2;19 is 1 John 2:8, which talks about the antichrist, not whether true believers can or cannot lose their salvation. It is not about whether believers were really believers at all; it is about the antichrist.[107]

[107] **Antichrist**: (ἀντίχριστος antichristos) The term "Antichrist," occurs in the NT five times. From those five times, we gather this entity is "against" (i.e., denies Christ) or "instead of" (i.e., false Christs) Jesus Christ. *Many antichrists* began back in the apostle John's day and will continue up unto Jesus' second coming. (1 John 2:18) The antichrist is referred to as a number of individuals taken together, i.e., collectively. (2 John 1;7) Persons who deny Jesus Christ are the antichrist. (1 John 2:22) All who deny the divinity of Jesus Christ as the One and Only Son of God is the antichrist. (1 John 2:22; John 10:36; Lu 9:35) Some antichrists are apostates who left the faith and are now in opposition to the truth. (1 John 2:18-19) Those who oppose the true followers of Jesus are the antichrist. (John 15:20-21) Antichrists are individuals or nations opposing Jesus or trying to supplant his kingly authority. – Ps. 2:2; Matt. 24:24; Rev. 17:3, 12-14; 19:11-21.

CHAPTER 2 What the Bible Authors Really Meant by Atonement

The English word "atonement" "is derived from Anglo-Saxon words meaning, "making at one," hence "at-one-ment." It presupposes a separation or alienation that needs to be overcome if human beings are to know God and have fellowship with him. As a term expressing relationship, atonement is tied closely to such terms as reconciliation and forgiveness."[108] The *Baker Encyclopedia of the Bible* goes on to add "The word "atonement" occurs many times in the OT but only once in the NT (Rom 5:11 KJV). Modern translations generally, and more correctly, render the word "reconciliation." The idea of atonement is ever present in the NT, however, and is one of the fundamental concepts of Scripture."[109] Biblically, it is referring to the covering of sins. On this Norman L. Geisler writes,

> One of the most important expressions of salvation is the word *atonement*, translated from the Hebrew *kaphar*. Literally, *kaphar* means "to cover," but it also carries a broader meaning of "expiation," "condoning," "wiping away," "placating," or "canceling." The Authorized Version translates *kaphar* as "to appease," "to disannul," "to forgive," "to be merciful," "to pacify," "to pardon," "to purge," "to put off," and "to reconcile." The key thoughts are "to cover over in God's eyes" and/or "to wipe away." *Kaphar* is used around one hundred times in the Old Testament (in verbal form).

The Greek term for *atonement* is *hiloskomai*, meaning "to propitiate," "to expiate," or "to conciliate." It is used twice; once in Luke 18:13, when the penitent sinner asks God to "be merciful" to him,[110] and once in Hebrews 2:17, where again we read:

> Therefore, he had to be made like his brethren in every respect, so that he might become a merciful and faithful high priest in the service of God, to make expiation for the sins of the people, (RSV)[111]

The Need for Atonement

Humanity is in need of atonement or the covering over of their sins because as Paul put it, "sin came into the world through one man [Adam], and death through

---

[108] Walter A. Elwell and Barry J. Beitzel, *Baker Encyclopedia of the Bible* (Grand Rapids, MI: Baker Book House, 1988), 231.

[109] Ibid., 231

[110] NKJV, hearkening back to the Old Testament image of God meeting the sinner at the mercy seat and blood atonement being made for his sins.

[111] Norman L. Geisler, *Systematic Theology, Volume Three: Sin, Salvation* (Minneapolis, MN: Bethany House Publishers, 2004), 230–231.

sin, and so death spread to all men because all sinned." (Rom. 5:12) Earlier on in the same letter, he had written of our imperfect condition, "For all have sinned and fall short of the glory of God." (Rom. 3:23) Wise King Solomon was inspired to pen the same, saying, "Surely there is not a righteous man on earth who does good and never sins." (Eccl. 7:20) King David under inspiration penned, "Behold, I was brought forth in iniquity [sin], and in sin did my mother conceive me." (Ps 51:5) Jeremiah in 1 Kings 8:46 wrote similarly, saying, "there is no man who does not sin." (1 Ki 8:46) As we can see from Paul's words at Romans 5:12, it is man's fault that he finds himself in need of an atonement, not God. (Deut. 32:4-5) Adam rebelled, evidencing more love for himself and his newly created wife. Thus, he threw away perfection and the possibility of eternal life, giving sin and death to all of his descendants, placing each of us under the condemnation of death. How God chose to handle this based on perfect justice (the principle of equivalence, or balance, in matters of justice)[112] is also laid out in Romans chapter 5,

Romans 5:16-19 Updated American Standard Version (UASV)

16 And it is not the same with the free gift as with the way things worked through the one man who sinned. For the judgment after one trespass was condemnation, but the gift after many trespasses was justification.[113] 17 For if by the trespass of the one, death reigned through the one, much more those who receive the abundance of grace and of the gift of righteousness will reign in life through the one, Jesus Christ.

One Act of Justification

18 So, then, as through one trespass there was condemnation to all men, so too through one act of righteousness there was justification of life to all men. 19 For as through the one man's disobedience the many were made sinners, so also through the obedience of the one the many will be made righteous.

Thus, we can see that the word and concept of atonement in the Bible carry the essential meaning of "cover over" or "exchange." Therefore, that, which is given in exchange for, or as a "cover" for something else, it must be its equal. Hence, if something is to satisfy justly for something that has been lost, it has to be "at one," or equal with whatever was lost, completely satisfying because it is an exact equivalent. In other words, the replacement cannot be worth more or less, than what had been lost. Thus, no imperfect human life could cover over or be used as an exchange for, i.e., atone for the perfect life that was lost. (Ps. 49:7-8) Therefore, if God were going to atone for what the one perfect man Adam had lost, he was going to need a sin offering that carried the same equal value of a perfect human life. Paul tells us this at 1 Corinthians 15:21-22, "For as by a man came death, by a man has come also the resurrection of the dead. For as in Adam all die, so also in Christ shall all be made alive."

---

112 See Deuteronomy 19:21

113 Lit a declaring of righteous

However, before God offered his Son, He had established a procedure for atonement among the Israelites in the 16th century B.C.E., which symbolized this greater atonement that would be provided some 1600 years later in 33 C.E. Therefore, it is God himself and not man who is to be recognized for providing the perfect sacrifice, later revealing this means of atoning for or covering over Adamic sin,[114] removing the consequential condemnation to death.

Atonement Sacrifices

At the direction of God, the Israelites were commanded to offer a sacrifice as a sin offering for atonement. (Ex. 29:36; Lev. 4:20) Atonement Day was of special importance when the high priest of Israel had to offer an animal sacrifice for the sin offering which was for himself, in order that he may make atonement for himself and his household, as well as the other Levites and the non-priestly tribes of Israel. (Lev. 16) The animals used in these sacrifices were to be a perfect and complete specimen, just as was to be true of the later antitype.

The cost for us to atone for our sins is evidenced in that the animal sacrifice is that of a life, meaning that the animal must give its life. Leviticus 17:11, reads, "The life of the flesh is in the blood, and I have given it for you on the altar to make atonement for your souls, for it is the blood that makes atonement by the life." With all that went into the sin offerings and the various features of the Day of Atonement, it must have made very clear to the Israelite minds the significance of their sinful condition and their great need of a thorough and complete atonement. Nevertheless, the need to do this from year after year also made it clear that the animal sacrifices would never completely atone for Adamic inherited sin because of their being inferior to humans (dominion over the animals), it could never satisfy justice. – Genesis 1:28; Psalm 8:4-8; Hebrews 10:1-4.

[114] Adamic sin is not a reference to the Calvinistic Total Depravity. Calvin is right in that we have a sin nature, we are "by nature children of wrath" (Eph. 2:3), we are "slaves to sin" (Rom. 6:16, 19-20), we are 'mentally bent toward evil" (Gen 6:5; 8:210, 'our heart is deceitful above all things, and desperately sick; which we cannot understand" (J Adamic sin is not a reference to the Calvinistic Total Depravity. Calvin is right in that we have a sin nature, we are "by nature children of wrath" (Eph. 2:3), we are "slaves to sin" (Rom. 6:16, 19-20), we are 'mentally bent toward evil" (Gen 6:5; 8:210, 'our heart is deceitful above all things, and desperately sick; which we cannot understand" (Jer. 17:3). John Calvin is right when he says that without the help of God, we are totally lost. However, Calvin is **wrong** when he says that God picks and chooses winners and losers, and that we are unable to choose God. Calvin is **wrong** when he says salvation is not a choice, as we with our freewill have the choice of choosing Christ or not. (Deut. 30:19; Josh 24:15; Ac 17:30-31) Repeatedly, we read the call for people to 'believe in Jesus Christ' and 'they will be saved.' (Ac 16:31; John 3:16) Moreover, the same is said of Jehovah the Father, "call on the name of Jehovah and be delivered." (Joel 2:32; Ac 2:21; Rom. 10:13) It makes no sense for God to ask everyone to make a decision to call on Jehovah or Jesus to be saved, and then it is God who chooses and we have no real choice. Lastly, why send hundreds of millions of people out to preach and teach God's Word, if the elect are already chosen?

Atonement for Sin in Christ Jesus

It is not until we get to the Greek New Testament of the first century C.E., where we find complete atonement for the death that had spread to all men by the inherited Adamic sin, complete atonement coming only with the ransom sacrifice of Christ Jesus. It is in him that the New Testament authors convey that we find the types and shadows formerly of the Mosaic Law. The constant and continual animal sacrifices for the Israelite nation over a 1,500-year period pointed to Jesus. The apostle Paul writes, "He made him who knew no sin to be sin on our behalf, so that we might become the righteousness of God in him." (2 Cor. 5:21) Yes, Christ, "when he had offered one sacrifice for sins for all time, sat down at the right hand of God" (Heb. 10:12), and he is categorically "the Lamb of God who takes away the sin of the world!" (John 1:29, 36; 1 Cor. 5:7; Rev. 5:12; 13:8; Isa 53:7) Without Jesus, having 'shed his blood there is no forgiveness of sins' (Heb. 4:12), and if "we walk in the light, as he is in the light, we have fellowship with one another, and the blood of Jesus his Son cleanses us from all sin." – 1 John 1:7; Hebrews 9:13-14; Revelation 1:5.

Jesus' perfect human life offered in sacrifice is the antitypical sin offering, (i.e., foreshadowed by earlier animal sacrifices). His life purchased humankind from condemnation to death because of Adam's rebellious rejection of God's sovereignty, namely, we were freed from sin and death. (Tit 2:13-14; Heb. 2:9) Christ himself stated, "Just as the Son of Man did not come to be served, but to serve, and to give his soul a ransom [Gr., *lutron*][115] for many." Jesus' ransom sacrifice atoned or covered over exactly what was given up by Adam when he chose to sin of his own free will. Adam was a perfect human and Jesus was a perfect human. Paul told Timothy that 'Christ Jesus gave himself as a ransom for all.' (1 Tim 2:5) To the Ephesian congregation, Paul stated, "In him we have redemption through his blood, the forgiveness of our trespasses." – Ephesians 1:7.

Reconciliation

The sin of Adam marred man's relationship with God, causing a separation between humanity and God, for sin, is contrary to God's personality and standards. Isaiah makes this separation all too clear when he writes, "But your iniquities have made a separation between you and your God, and your sins have hidden his face from you so that he does not hear." (Isa 59:2, ESV) This was true of the sins of the imperfect Israelites, how much more so of Adam when he was in perfection. Habakkuk wrote of God, "Your eyes are too pure to see evil, and you are not able to look at wrongdoing. …" (Hab. 1:13, LEB) The apostle Paul says of the imperfect human condition, "Among them we too all formerly lived in the lusts of our flesh,

---

[115] The means or instrument by which release or deliverance is made possible–'means of release, ransom. – Johannes P. Louw and Eugene Albert Nida, *Greek-English Lexicon of the New Testament: Based on Semantic Domains* (New York: United Bible Societies, 1996), 487.

indulging the desires of the flesh and of the mind, and were by nature children of wrath, even as the rest." (Eph. 2:3, NASB)

However, God took action the moment Adam sinned, stating that he would provide a means to reconcile imperfect, sinful humanity back into a righteous standing before him, through the perfect man, Christ Jesus. (Gen. 3:15, ESV) Therefore, the apostle Paul wrote, "And not only this, but we also exult in God through our Lord Jesus Christ, through whom we have now received the reconciliation." (Rom. 5:11, NASB; see the chapter Explaining Reconciliation) Nevertheless, if we are to be reconciled, we must accept the provision that God has made for reconciliation through Jesus Christ. It is only through this that we may be declared righteous in the eyes of God while still in imperfection, regaining the relationship that Adam forfeited prior to his willful sin. God is love, and it is that love, which is evident in his making such reconciliation possible. (1 John 4; Rom. 5:6-10) In discussing how sinners are reconciled to God Boyd and Eddy write,

> The penal substitution view of the atonement is the only view that takes at face value and with full seriousness; the Bible's teaching that Jesus died in our place. For this reason, it is the only view that makes clear how an all-holy God could reconcile sinners with himself. Neither the Christus Victor[116] nor the moral government view[117] of the atonement addresses this issue adequately.[118]

God Put forward a Propitiation that Satisfied Justice

God is a God of love; nevertheless, one of his other major attributes is justice, which needed to be satisfied. Although Adam began life in perfection, he fell from that state through willful and knowing sin and thus he was condemned to death, along with all of his future descendants. – Genesis 2:17; 3:6.

It is the principles of righteousness (i.e., justice and fidelity), which necessitated that God; carry out the sentence of death that he stated at 2:17, applying it to disobedient Adam. However, his love for humanity moved him to offer a substitutional arrangement so that justice would still be satisfied. As a result, of this substitution, any offspring of Adam, who repentantly accepted this substitution, would be forgiven, removing the division that has been brought about by Adam's

[116] "The early church emphasized how Jesus' death and resurrection defeated Satan and thus set humankind free from his oppressive rule." Boyd and Eddy

[117] "In the seventeenth century, a Reformer named Hugo Grotius found this view objectionable on a number of grounds. He argued that Jesus did not literally take on the sin of the world and suffer God's punishment on behalf of humanity. Jesus did indeed suffer the wrath of God, in Grotius's view, but as a demonstration of God's wrath against sin. This act was done to teach humanity the consquences of sin and to inspire us to holy living. The cross thus preserves God's moral government of the world." Boyd and Eddy

[118] Boyd, Gregory A.; Eddy, Paul R. (2002-06-01). Across the Spectrum: Understanding Issues in Evangelical Theology (Kindle Locations 2533-2535). Baker Publishing Group. Kindle Edition.

sin, restoring peace between God and man. (Col. 1:19-23) Therefore, the Father "sent his Son to be the propitiation[119] (i.e., "to appease") for our sins." (1 John 4:10) In other words, Jesus' death "appeased" God's wrath toward the sin that had entered the world because Christ received the punishment that God's justice required. Paul spells out this truth, when he said although "all have sinned and fall short of the glory of God (Rom. 3:23, ESV), we are declared righteous by God "by his grace as a gift, through the redemption that is in Christ Jesus, whom God put forward as a propitiation by his blood, to be received by faith." – Romans 3:24-25, ESV.

John, in his first epistle also made this point, saying, "In this is love, not that we have loved God but that he loved us and sent his Son to be the propitiation for our sins." (1 John 4:10, ESV) Paul further wrote, "[Jesus] had to be made like his brothers in every respect, so that he might become a merciful and faithful high priest in the service of God, to make propitiation for the sins of the people." (Heb. 2:17, ESV) Numerous times, the New Testament authors make it clear that humanity had the punishment of condemnation of death coming, and God took that punishment and place it on his Son in our place, as justice required satisfaction by propitiation, "appeasing" God.

Propitiation is the atoning, the reconciling, the covering over Adamic sin, our human weaknesses, restoring us to a favorable relationship with God. Jesus propitiatory sacrifice removed the charge of Adamic sin from his case against us, removing any reason that we are condemned to death, we now have the choice of a restored relationship because of God's mercy. Again, this propitiation expunges the charge of sin, which had us condemned to death, but only if we avail ourselves to it. – 1 John 2:1-2; Romans 6:23.

The idea of substitution is found in the Old Testament sacrificial practices and is declared throughout the New Testament. For instance, Jesus himself said that his death would be a substitution for others. He said to his disciples, "Greater love has no one than this, that someone lay down his life for his friends." (John 15:13, ESV) In another example, Paul stated, "Christ died for our sins in accordance with the Scriptures." (1 Cor. 15:3, ESV, NASB) Elsewhere Paul wrote, "Christ redeemed us from the curse of the Law, having become a curse for us [i.e., Jews]—for it is written, 'Cursed is everyone who hangs on a tree.'" (Gal. 3:13; Deut. 21:23, ASV, NASB) Paul also said, "For our sake he [God] made him [Jesus] to be sin who knew no sin, so that in him we might become the righteousness of God." (2 Cor. 5:21, ESV) This is how "in Christ God was reconciling the world to himself." (2 Cor. 5:19, ESV) Think of it, God placed our sin on Jesus Christ, so that he might place Jesus righteousness on us. In other words, Jesus became our sin. Peter stated, "He himself bore our sins in his body on the tree, that we might die to sin[120] and live to righteousness. By his wounds you have been healed." (1 Pet. 2:24; Isa. 53:5) Peter also wrote, Christ also

---

[119] **appeasement necessitated by sin, *expiation*** – William Arndt, Frederick W. Danker, and Walter Bauer, *A Greek-English Lexicon of the New Testament and Other Early Christian Literature* (Chicago: University of Chicago Press, 2000), 474.

[120] Or *be finished with sin*

died for sins once for all, *the* just for *the* unjust, so that He might bring us to God, having been put to death in the flesh, but made alive in the spirit." – 1 Peter 3:18.

God's Provision Requires Faith

God has offered all of humankind the provision of complete atonement, reconciliation for our inherited sin. (John 3:16; Rom. 8:32; 1 John 3:16) However, if this is to be applied to us, we must truly be repentant and trusting[121] in Jesus, so as to not be destroyed but have eternal life." (John 3:16, UASV) God was not pleased with the sacrifices of Judah, as they were carried out with the wrong attitude. (Isa. 1:10-17) The Father sent for his Son, Jesus Christ "as a propitiation in his blood through faith." (Rom. 3:21-26) It is only those alone, who accept this provision for atonement through Jesus Christ, perhaps they may gain salvation; however, those who reject it cannot. "And there is salvation in no one else, for there is no other name under heaven given among men by which we must be saved." (Ac 4:12) Moreover, any who "go on sinning deliberately after receiving the knowledge of the truth, there no longer remains a sacrifice for sins, but a fearful expectation of judgment …" – Hebrews 10:26-31.

The Penal Substitution View

When Jesus offered his life as a ransom for us, the Father placed Adamic sin, our inherited sin, and our human weakness sin, even our practice of sin (if we truly repent before our death or the return of Christ), **upon Jesus Christ and accepted him in our place**. The Father Accepted Jesus in the place of us as he provided for our atonement, redeeming us from inherited sin and death. (Tit 2:13, 14; Heb. 2:9, ESV) Paul wrote, "For our sake he made him to be sin who knew no sin, so that in him we might become the righteousness of God." (2 Cor. 5:21, ESV). Paul also told the Christians in Rome, "God shows his love for us in that while we were still sinners, Christ died for us." (Rom 5:8, ESV) The Bible is clear that Jesus' sacrifice atoned for the whole of all of humanity, which was a ransom price paid in our behalf. (Matt.20:28) This is known as the Penal Substitution View. On this Boyd and Eddy write, "In the sixteenth century, John Calvin and Martin Luther advocated a view of the atonement that was somewhat different from all these. They believed that Jesus bore the punishment humanity deserved. Only in this way, they argued, could humanity be reconciled to an all-holy God. This view has similarities to Anselm's view, but it differs in stressing that Jesus actually bore the sin of humanity and actually took the punishment humanity deserved."[122]

We arrive at the Penal Substitution View by our going back to the original language Greek words that are rendered in English as "for," because they are found in the phrase "Christ died for our sins." We begin with the Greek word "anti," which

---

[121] The grammatical construction of pisteuo "believe" followed by *eis* "into" plus the accusative causing a different shade of meaning, having faith into Jesus.

[122] Boyd, Gregory A.; Eddy, Paul R. (2002-06-01). *Across the Spectrum: Understanding Issues in Evangelical Theology* (Kindle Locations 2453-2456). Baker Publishing Group. Kindle Edition.

indicates, "that one person or thing is, or is to be, replaced by another, *instead of, in place of.*"[123] Another Greek-English lexicon offers, "a marker of a participant who is benefited by an event, usually with the implication of some type of exchange or substitution involved–'for, on behalf of.'"[124] In other words, "Christ died **instead of us** for our sins." The other Greek word is "*huper*," which is "a marker indicating that an activity or event is in some entity's interest, *for, in behalf of, for the sake of someone.*"[125] Another Greek-English lexicon offers, a marker of a participant who is benefited by an event or on whose behalf an event takes place–'for, on behalf of, for the sake of.'"[126] Thus, we would say, "Christ died **in behalf of** us for our sins."

The fact that "Christ died **instead of us [anti]** for our sins," is found in Matthew 20:28 and Mark 10:45. The fact that "Christ died **in behalf of [huper]** us for our sins," is found John 10:11, 15; 11:50; Romans 5:8; 8:32; 1 Corinthians 15:3; 2 Corinthians 5:14; Galatians 2:20; 3:13; Titus 2:4. William Greenough Thayer Shedd in his *Dogmatic Theology* makes an important observation:

> The ... preposition [anti] excludes the idea of benefit or advantage and specifies only the idea of substitution. The former [*huper*] may include both ideas. Whenever, therefore, the sacred writer would express both together and at once, he selects the preposition *hyper*.[127] In so doing, he teaches both that Christ died in the sinner's place and for the sinner's benefit.[128]

If someone says,

The Penal Substitution View limits God.

They argue this view takes away God's freedom to forgive sin freely, but rather God must punish all sin, which dictates that God had to sacrifice his Son if humans were to be reconciled. First, we need to make the point that nothing or no one can limit God. The only way God could be "limited" is if that limitation came outside of himself. In other words, if someone or something outside of God required that God forgive all sin for the sake of justice being satisfied when God actually wanted to forgive all sin freely, this would limit God. However, this is not the case, but rather it is God's own character, which moves him to satisfy his own attribute, justice,

123 William Arndt, Frederick W. Danker, and Walter Bauer, *A Greek-English Lexicon of the New Testament and Other Early Christian Literature* (Chicago: University of Chicago Press, 2000), 87.

124 Johannes P. Louw and Eugene Albert Nida, *Greek-English Lexicon of the New Testament: Based on Semantic Domains* (New York: United Bible Societies, 1996), 802.

125 William Arndt, Frederick W. Danker, and Walter Bauer, *A Greek-English Lexicon of the New Testament and Other Early Christian Literature* (Chicago: University of Chicago Press, 2000), 1030.

126 Johannes P. Louw and Eugene Albert Nida, *Greek-English Lexicon of the New Testament: Based on Semantic Domains* (New York: United Bible Societies, 1996), 801–802.

127 ὑπέρ

128 William Greenough Thayer Shedd, *Dogmatic Theology*, ed. Alan W. Gomes, 3rd ed. (Phillipsburg, NJ: P & R Pub., 2003), 692.

appeasing himself. There is the common misconception that nothing is impossible for God. This actually is not true. God cannot lie. Paul tells us, "It is impossible for God to lie." (Heb. 6:13-18 See Num. 23:19, ESV) Moreover, God "cannot deny himself." (2 Tim. 2:13, ESV) It is not limiting God by our admitting "God cannot lie," because we are not making that stipulation about him, he is telling us about his own character, his own attributes. We are not placing the requirement that he does not lie on him; this is God informing us that it is impossible for him to lie. The same is true of God not being able to forgive sin freely because his own justice must be satisfied. It is God telling us about himself, not us placing this stipulation, this requirement on him. Therefore, nothing is limiting him.

If someone says,

The Penal Substitution View conflicts with texts that state God forgives sin based on the repentance of the person. (e.g., Lu 15:11-32, ESV)

There is no doubt that God forgives all who repent, which is clear from Scripture. Repentance alone is not what covers over the sin, nor is it alone what moves God to cover the sin, but rather it is informing us **how**, on what basis God will forgive sin, still satisfying justice. It is specifically said, "The blood of Jesus his Son cleanses us from all sin." (1 John 1:7) We are also told in the book of Revelation that Jesus "loosed us from our sins by means of his own blood."[129] (Rev. 1:5) The apostle Paul wrote, "In him we have redemption through his blood, the forgiveness of our trespasses." (Eph. 1:7, ESV) He also wrote, "How much more will the blood of Christ, who through the eternal Spirit offered himself without blemish to God, purify our conscience from dead works to serve the living God." (Heb. 9:14) The apostle Peter wrote, "You were ransomed from the futile ways inherited from your forefathers, not with perishable things such as silver or gold, but with the precious blood of Christ." Again, God forgives all who repent, but it is based on the blood of Jesus Christ. Thus, repentance is but one aspect of the blood of Christ, just as faith is also required if we are to be forgiven. If one repents from a sin, turns around and changes his ways, his sin will be forgiven based on the blood of Christ.

If someone says,

The Penal Substitution View encourages sinful living.

Remember, it is specifically said, "The blood of Jesus his Son cleanses us from all sin." (1 John 1:7) John actually qualifies this point by stating, "My little children,

---

[129] **Leviticus 16:30** American Standard Version (ASV)

for on this day shall atonement be made for you, to cleanse you; from all your sins shall ye be clean before Jehovah.

I am writing these things to you so that you may not commit a sin.[130] But if anyone does sin, we have an advocate with the Father, Jesus Christ the righteous." (1 John 2:1) In other words, the blood of Jesus Christ that cleanses us from all sin is applied to commissions of sin based on human weakness, and does not cover the practice of sin, or living in sin. John went on to say, "No one who abides in him keeps on sinning; no one who keeps on sinning has either seen him or known him." (3:6) John also said a few verses later, "No one born of God makes a practice of sinning, for God's seed abides in him, and he cannot keep on sinning because he has been born of God. By this it is evident who are the children of God, and who are the children of the devil: whoever does not practice righteousness is not of God, nor is the one who does not love his brother." (3:9-10) Therefore, the idea that the Penal Substitution View encourages sinful living is just false. More will be said about this under the heading below, God's Propitiation Requires Faith.

If someone says,

The Penal Substitution View cannot work because guilt cannot be transferred.

The argument here is that it seems to be an injustice that Jesus would receive our guilt when he is sinless, and we would be sinful, yet handing off our guilt to him, seeming to sidestep our liability. Guilt in the modern day western world appears to be associated only with the person responsible for it. We will not attempt to argue away the entirety of this argument against the Penal Substitution View because as Boyd and Eddy put it, "there is an element of mystery to the penal substitution view of the atonement, but it is a mystery we must accept because it is rooted in Scripture."[131]

We would first begin with the concept that somehow humans are avoiding their accountability for their individual guilt, which is not entirely accurate. Humanity has suffered diseases, crimes, old age and death of self, not to mention loved ones. Maybe up to twenty billion humans have lived on earth at this point, who have lived very difficult lives, grown old and died. We must remember, "The wages of sin is death." (Rom. 6:23) While our death is not enough alone to pay for Adam's sin, we certainly would not view the human condition as not being accountable for what Adam had done. Moreover, the idea of Adam sinning, so that he could choose for himself what is good and bad, in essence, rejecting the sovereignty of God, is an act of total independence from his Creator. We live in a world where individuals have always sought their freedom as opposed to community accountability, viewing guilt as an individualistic matter, not a community thing, not a family (humanity) matter.

---

130 Gr., *hamartete,* a verb in the aorist subjunctive. According to *A Grammar of New Testament Greek,* by James H. Moulton, Vol. I, 1908, p. 109, "the Aorist has a 'punctiliar' action, that is, it regards action as a *point:* it represents the point of entrance . . . or that of completion . . . or it looks at a whole action simply as having occurred, without distinguishing any steps in its progress."

131 Boyd, Gregory A.; Eddy, Paul R. (2002-06-01). *Across the Spectrum: Understanding Issues in Evangelical Theology* (Kindle Locations 2567-2568). Baker Publishing Group. Kindle Edition.

If we look at the Scriptures and the history of some cultures, they do not view accountability of guilt in this way. Before addressing that difference, let us ask the all-important question. If we cannot all be saved by one man's righteous act (Jesus), how could we ever all be condemned by the sinful act of one man (Adam)? (Rom. 5:12-14) Looking through the Bible history, at times, God held all of Israel accountable for the sin of a leader, such as King David, or a few, such as in the time where Saul violated a treaty with the Gibeonites, which had been in place for over four hundred years, since the time of Joshua. Yet, Saul and his family paid for his actions. Then, there was Achan, who kept some spoils of war, robbing God, who had commanded them to keep none of the spoils for themselves, when the Israelites were taking Jericho after forty years in the wilderness. Achan, his family, and even his livestock were put to death because Achan chose to ignore God and keep some of the spoils for himself. – 1 Chronicles 21:1-17; 2 Samuel 21:1-9; Joshua 6:17-7:26

Jesus became a perfect human, one who could account for Adamic sin, which is inherited sin from Adam. It also includes any sins that we may commit due to our human weakness in this imperfect state. An imperfect being could not pay the price for Adam's sin, who was a perfect person. In Scripture, Adam is referred to as though he is a representative of humanity as a whole while all humans who accept the ransom sacrifice of Christ, as though they were individuals. Boyd and Eddy sum it up this way, "We were all one "in Adam." Now we are all one "in Christ" (Rom. 5: 12–21)."[132]

If we look at 1 Timothy 2:5-6, it says in part, "the man Christ Jesus, who gave himself as a ransom [*antilytron*] for all." The Greek word *antilytron* appears nowhere else in the Bible. It is related to the word that Jesus used for ransom (*lytron*) at Mark 10:45. The Greek *antilytron* broken down from *anti* means "against; in correspondence to; "instead of;" "in place of," and *lytron* means "ransom [i.e., price paid]") "The *Greek* implies not merely *ransom,* but a *substituted* or *equivalent ransom:* the *Greek* preposition, '*anti,*' implying reciprocity and vicarious substitution."[133] *The New International Dictionary of New Testament Theology* points out that *antilytron* 'accentuates the notion of exchange.' The reason this is the case is that we are talking about the equivalent price of one perfect human for another perfect human. Thus, this was a means for God's principal attribute justice to be satisfied.

If someone says,

The Penal Substitution View sets the Father against the Son.

Some would argue that the Penal Substitution View does away with the unity between the Father and the Son, as they say; it created a rift between the Father and the Son when the Father had to judge the Son. Not at all, this view puts forward a

---

[132] Boyd, Gregory A.; Eddy, Paul R. (2002-06-01). *Across the Spectrum: Understanding Issues in Evangelical Theology* (Kindle Locations 2576-2577). Baker Publishing Group. Kindle Edition.

[133] Robert Jamieson, A. R. Fausset, and David Brown, *Commentary Critical and Explanatory on the Whole Bible*, vol. 2 (Oak Harbor, WA: Logos Research Systems, Inc., 1997), 408.

basis of an argument for a most deeper and weighty unity between the Father and the Son as they work out the salvation of humanity together. This is no clearer than at the time the Father judges the Son.

If we look at the Scriptures, we see the love of the Father for the Son at every turn, knowing the sacrifice is coming. At Jesus' birth, the Father sends Gabriel, a very high-ranking angel, to announce the newborn king. (Lu 1:18-33) At Jesus baptism, out of the heavens, the Father said, "This is my beloved Son, in whom I am well pleased." (Matt 3:17) A few months later, we have Jesus telling us, "For God [i.e., the Father] so loved the world, that He gave His only begotten Son, that whoever believes in Him shall not perish, but have eternal life." (John 3:16, NASB) However, we learn three very important points from Nisan 13th 33 C.E. (Thursday afternoon), just one day before Jesus' death. In prayer to his Father, in anguish in the garden, where some manuscripts say he actually sweated blood.[134] "And going a little farther he [Jesus] fell on his face and prayed, saying, 'My Father, if it be possible, let this cup pass from me; nevertheless, not as I will, but as you will.'" However, before delving into that, we must discuss a comment from Boyd and Eddy, whom we have been quoting. On this, they close out by saying,

> It declares that the Father and Son were both willing to experience a temporary severance in their eternal relationship for the sake of acquiring eternal unity with humanity. Their unified love for lost humanity and their unified will to save humanity led them to experience willingly a loss of unity in their own relationship. Hence, as paradoxical as it sounds, the perfect unity of heart and purpose between the Father and the Son was manifested precisely at the moment Jesus cried out, "My God, my God, why have you forsaken me?" (Matt. 27:46). This constitutes one of the most profound teachings of the entire Bible.[135]

This author would wholeheartedly disagree that "the Father and Son were both willing to experience a temporary severance in their eternal relationship for the sake of acquiring eternal unity with humanity." The evidence for my disagreement is found in the three important points mentioned above. First, let it be said that a person can have a different desire for something and yet do the will of another out of love, which does not necessitate a severance in a relationship. This is especially true if that different desire is predicated on the fact that they do not want reproach to come on the other, which is why they have a different desire. Consider the entirety of Scripture from Genesis to Revelation, there is a complete unity with the Father and Son on the redemption of humanity, Jesus doing the will of the Father in order to carry this out. Jesus knows exactly what is to take place with his death and exactly what he will be accused of, what he will be convicted of and what he will be executed for, and yet he prays this to his Father one day before his execution,

---

134 See Matthew 26:30, 36-56; Mark 14:26, 32-52; Lu 22:39-53 18:1-12

135 Boyd, Gregory A.; Eddy, Paul R. (2002-06-01). *Across the Spectrum: Understanding Issues in Evangelical Theology* (Kindle Locations 2586-2590). Baker Publishing Group. Kindle Edition.

John 17:20-23 Updated American Standard Version (UASV)

[20] "I do not ask for these only, but also for those who will believe in me through their word; [21] that they may all be one, just as you, Father, are in me, and I in you, that they also may be in us, so that the world may believe that you have sent me. [22] The glory that you have given me I have given to them, that they may be one even as we are one, [23] I in them and you in me, that they may be perfected in unity, so that the world may know that you sent me, and loved them, even as you have loved me."

The **first** important point is that Jesus completely trusted the Father to accomplish his will and purposes. This trust is evidenced here in the Garden of Gethsemane. The **second** important point is that Jesus' love for the Father was so great, while, in the most difficult time of his existence, his thoughts were for his Father. We see the reason for his great anguish was that he knew that he was going to be executed as a blasphemer of his Father, and even then, he fell with his face to the ground and prayed, "My Father, if it is possible, may this cup be taken from me. **Yet not as I will, but as you will**." (Matthew 26:39) This is not a case of Jesus backing out of the execution, the ransom that is, but rather he wanted to be executed for another reason, other than a blasphemer. Jesus was an integrity keeper, which brought great joy to the Father. (Pro. 27:11) The **third** important point is that Jesus's will was to have to not go down as a convicted blasphemer against the Father, even though it was not true, but his love for the Father, his complete trust in the Father came first, as he said, "not as I will, but as you will." Therefore, there was no willingness "to experience a temporary severance in their eternal relationship."

Two years earlier in 31, C.E. Jesus attends a feast, where he heals a man and rebukes the Pharisees. Here he also says of himself and the Father. "I can do nothing on my own. As I hear, I judge, and my judgment is just, because **I seek not my own will but the will of him who sent me**." While this does not mean that Jesus' will was different from the Father on judging, it does make it clear that Jesus' will can be different from the Father, which clearly has never done anything to shake the unity that has existed, nor ever will, but goes to refute the mistaken notion from Boyd and Eddy. Remember, they suggested that the Father and the Son were willing "to experience a temporary severance in their eternal relationship for the sake of acquiring eternal unity with humanity." As great a Bible scholar as Boyd and Eddy may be, they are just missing the mark here in trying to provide an answer for the critics of the Penal Substitution View.

Did Jesus' words found at Matthew 27:46 (ESV), "My God, my God, why have you forsaken me?" point to having a lack of faith? No. While there is no comment within any New Testament book that will specifically tell us what Jesus' motives for saying this were, his words do suggest that Jesus now knew the Father had removed all protection so that his Son could experience the full test of his integrity. In addition, Jesus likely used this opportunity because he was fulfilling the prophetic words of Psalm 22:1, which were a reference to him. It reads,

Psalm 22:1 Updated American Standard Version (UASV)

[1] My God, my God, why have you forsaken me? Why are you so far from saving me, from the words of my groaning?

God's Propitiation Requires Faith

One insight that should be added is that Jesus ransom covers the Adamic inherited sin of every person and all that it entails. Everyone has the opportunity of choosing life over death, the ransom is made available, but it can be rejected.

Hebrews 10:26 Updated American Standard Version (UASV)

[26] For if we go on sinning deliberately after receiving the accurate knowledge[136] of the truth, there no longer remains a sacrifice for sins, [27] but a fearful expectation of judgment, and a fury of fire that will consume the adversaries.

Those who have accepted that "Christ died **instead of us [anti]** for our sins," or that "Christ died **in behalf of [huper]** us for our sins," "know that we have passed over from death into life." (1 John 3:14) However, it is also just as possible to pass over from life to death, if we stray too far from **the truth**. Every Christian has the obligation, not just the elders, to help a brother back to the path of the truth. The apostle Paul tells us, "Brothers, if anyone is caught in any transgression, you who are spiritual should restore him in a spirit of gentleness. Keep watch on yourself, lest you too be tempted." (Gal. 6:1) When we think of James informing us of our obligation of helping those who have stumbled in **the truth**, we think back on the power of prayer. Remember, James had just written, "the prayer of faith will save the one who is sick." (5:15) For there to be success, one must diligently apply God's Word and deep prayer to achieve the regaining of the one who has stumbled from the path of **the truth**. If the erring one does not receive the needed help, he can go beyond repentance. Being beyond repentance refers being beyond the desire to repent, to return to **the truth**. In some cases, he will be lost to Satan's world, and no one will be able to reawaken his former desire. (Heb. 6:4-8; 10:26-29)

---

[136] *Epignosis* is a strengthened or intensified form of *gnosis* (*epi,* meaning "additional"), meaning, "true," "real," "full," "complete" or "accurate," depending upon the context. Paul and Peter alone use *epignosis.*

CHAPTER 3 What the Bible Authors Really Meant by Ransom

A ransom is a sum of money or a price demanded or paid to secure the freedom of a slave. The basic idea of "ransom" is the act of saving somebody from an oppressed condition or dangerous situation through self-sacrifice, such as a price that *covers* or satisfies justice, while the term "redemption" is the *deliverance* that results from the ransom. In the biblical instance, "redemption" would be the *deliverance* from Adamic sin[137] (the inherited sin nature of humanity) by the ransom death of Jesus Christ for many.

Below we will consider various Hebrew terms (*kāpar, koper, pādâ, gā'al*), as well as a number of Greek terms (*lytron, antilytron, lytroo, agorazo*), which are translated "ransom and "redeem." They all carry the idea of a price being given or paid to result in a ransom or redemption. As we will see below, there is the sense of an equal or corresponding, that is, a substitution is common in all of these terms. In other words, the ransom sacrifice of Jesus Christ, for example, was given for Adam, which satisfied justice and set matters straight between God and man.

For our Hebrew terms, we will use the Theological Word Book of the Old Testament (TWOT) extensively. "(*kāpar*) **I, *make an atonement, make reconciliation, purge*.** (Denominative verb.) This root should probably be distinguished from *kāpar* II "to smear with pitch." … The root *kāpar* is used some 150 times. It has been much discussed. There is an equivalent Arabic root meaning "cover," or "conceal." On the strength of this connection, it has been supposed that the Hebrew word means, "to cover over sin" and thus pacify the deity, making an atonement (so BDB). It has been suggested that the OT ritual symbolized a covering over of sin until it was dealt with in fact by the atonement of Christ. There is, however, very little evidence for this view. The connection of the Arabic word is weak and the Hebrew root is not used to mean, "cover." The Hebrew verb is never used in the simple or Qal stem, but only in the derived intensive stems. These

---

137 Adamic sin is not a reference to the Calvinistic Total Depravity. Calvin is right in that we have a sin nature, we are "by nature children of wrath" (Eph. 2:3), we are "slaves to sin" (Rom. 6:16, 19-20), we are 'mentally bent toward evil" (Gen 6:5; 8:210, 'our heart is deceitful above all things, and desperately sick; which we cannot understand" (Jer. 17:3). John Calvin is right when he says that without the help of God, we are totally lost. However, Calvin is **wrong** when he says that God picks and chooses winners and losers, and that we are unable to choose God. Calvin is **wrong** when he says salvation is not a choice, as we with our freewill have the choice of choosing Christ or not. (Deut. 30:19; Josh 24:15; Ac 17:30-31) Repeatedly, we read the call for people to 'believe in Jesus Christ' and 'they will be saved.' (Ac 16:31; John 3:16) Moreover, the same is said of Jehovah the Father, "call on the name of Jehovah and be delivered." (Joel 2:32; Ac 2:21; Rom. 10:13) It makes no sense for God to ask everyone to make a decision to call on Jehovah or Jesus to be saved, and then it is God who chooses and we have no real choice. Lastly, why send hundreds of millions of people out to preach and teach God's Word, if the elect are already chosen?

intensive stems often indicate not emphasis, but merely that the verb is derived from a noun whose meaning is more basic to the root idea."[138]

The TWOT helps us to appreciate that "from the meaning of *kōper* "ransom," the meaning of *kāpar* can be better understood. It means, "to atone by offering a substitute." The great majority of the usages concern the priestly ritual of a sprinkling of the sacrificial blood thus "making an atonement" for the worshipper. There are forty-nine instances of this usage in Leviticus alone and no other meaning is there witnessed. The verb is always used in connection with the removal of sin or defilement, except for Gen 32:20; Prov. 16:14; and Isa 28:18 where the related meaning of "appease by a gift" may be observed. It seems clear that this word aptly illustrates the theology of reconciliation in the OT. The life of the sacrificial animal specifically symbolized by its blood was required in exchange for the life of the worshipper. The sacrifice of animals in OT theology was not merely an expression of thanks to the deity by a cattle raising people. It was the symbolic expression of innocent life given for guilty life. This symbolism is further clarified by the action of the worshipper in placing his hands on the head of the sacrifice and confessing his sins over the animal (cf. Lev 16:21; 1:4; 4:4, etc.) which was then killed or sent out as a scapegoat." (Harris, Archer and Waltke 1999, c1980, p. 453; TWOT Number 1023a)

Kāpar is used is used virtually in every case to describe the satisfying of justice through atoning for sins. The noun *kōper* refers to what is given to satisfy justice, i.e., the ransom price. For example, the Psalmist writes, "When iniquities [great injustices] prevail against me, **you atone** for our transgressions." (Psa. 65:3) The greatest blessing for which David offered praise was God's willingness, actually, eagerness to forgive. (Psa. 65:1) Pondering over past Israelite disobedience, David speaks of when they were overcome with sin; God forgave or atoned for their transgressions. David was referring to Israel's moral rebellion against God's Law. Undeservedly, God atoned for their sinfulness, which set aside the consequences.

Later, the Psalmist writes, "Yet he [God], being compassionate, **atoned for** their iniquity [great injustices] and did not destroy them; he turned away his anger often and did not stir up all his wrath." (Psa. 78:38) Regardless of the Israelites history of unfaithfulness, God showed them mercy when he did not have to, atoning for their iniquity [great injustices]. Repeatedly he restrained his wrath from a full expression, making allowances for human imperfection.

The Psalmist also wrote, "Do not remember against us the iniquities of our forefathers let your compassion come speedily to meet us, for we are brought very low. Help us, O God of our salvation, for the glory of your name; deliver us, and **atone for our sins**, for your name's sake!" (Psa. 79:8-9) Many in Israel had suffered much for the sins of their forefathers. Therefore, the psalmist is praying that God would no longer call to mind the sin of their forefathers, namely, that God would no

[138] R. Laird Harris, "1023 כָּפַר," ed. R. Laird Harris, Gleason L. Archer Jr., and Bruce K. Waltke, *Theological Wordbook of the Old Testament* (Chicago: Moody Press, 1999), 452-3.

longer hold these previous sins against them. The psalmist pleads desperately that God come speedily before all of God's chosen people were no more.

If we are to maintain any kind of integrity, we must appreciate the connection between forgiveness and the honor of God's name. He pled that God might help them from the subjugation and persecution of these invading nations. "Atone for our sins," he begged earnestly, asking God to forgive the transgressions of Israel's past. This plea was based on the glory of God's name. In other words, an act of mercy on the part of God would bring glory to his name.

Law of Atonement

As a way of satisfying justice with Israel, God's people, he, in the Mosaic Law, set up a number of sacrifices and offerings, to atone for sins, which also included those of the priestly Levites and the high priest. (Ex. 29:33-37; Lev. 16:6, 11) The sacrifices also included other individuals or the entire nation of Israel as a whole. (Lev. 1:1-4; 4:20, 26, 31, 35) They too were to "make atonement for the holy place, because of the uncleanness of the sons of Israel and because of their transgressions in regard to all their sins …" (Lev. 16:16-20) As a result, the life of the sacrificial animal went in place of the life of the sinner. As much, as was possible prior to Christ, "the blood of goats and bulls and the ashes of a heifer sprinkling those who have been defiled sanctify for the purifying of the flesh." This fundamental truth was reflected in the Mosaic Law. Leviticus 17:11 reads, "For the soul of the flesh is in the blood, and I have given it for you on the altar to make atonement for your souls, for it is the blood that makes atonement by the soul." In God's Word, blood is considered equivalent to life. Therefore, if an Israelite broke a portion of the Mosaic Law, he did not have to remain condemned, as he could repent and offer an animal sacrifice in his place. However, the atonement from the sacrifice was only an interim until the sacrifice of Jesus Christ. – Leviticus 4:27-31; 17:11; Hebrews 9:13, 14; 10:1-4.

A good example of a redeeming exchange is the law regarding injuries that may be caused by domestic animals. If a bull gored a person, killing him, the owner was obligated to kill the bull for the safety of the people. He was not allowed to sell the bull or eat the meat; he suffers a great financial loss. However, because the owner of the bull did not intentionally or willfully cause the gored person to lose their life, the judges may view it proper to only impose a "ransom [*kōper*]" on him, where he would then be obligated to pay the redemption price. The ransom price that was imposed on the owner was viewed as taking the place of his life, compensating for the life that was lost, redeeming him. (Ex. 21:28-32; Deut. 19:21) Nevertheless, suppose that bull was known to gore people, causing injuries, but the owner failed to keep it safely under his control, and the bull got loose, killing someone, both the bull, and its owner would be put to death (paying for the life of the person that had been killed with his own life). There was no ransom price for a willfully deliberate murder. (Num. 35:31-33) This law would deter anyone from being careless with his animals.

As to k*ōper*, i.e., ransom, Exodus 30:11-12 reads, "Jehovah also spoke to Moses, saying, 'When you take the sum of the sons of Israel to number them, then each one of them shall **give a <u>ransom</u>** for his soul to Jehovah when you number them.'" Because a census involved lives, each time the sum of the sons of Israel were taken, every male that was over 20 had to give a ransom (k*ōper*) of a half shekel for his soul to Jehovah at the service in the sanctuary, regardless of whether he was wealthy or poor.

Redemption and Redeemer

The Hebrew verb *pādâ* means, "ransom, rescue, and deliver" and the derivative *pidyôn* means "ransom money,"[139] or "ransom price," "redemption money," or "price of redemption."[140] (Ex. 21:30) The Hebrew root (*pādâ*) has the basic meaning to exchange the ownership of someone or something from one to another through the payment of a (ransom) price, i.e., a corresponding or equivalent substitute.

These terms clearly stress the *releasing* accomplished by the ransom price or redemption money, i.e., an equivalent or corresponding substitute. In addition, *kāpar* also stresses on the *quality* or *content* of the price of redemption and its *effectiveness* in balancing the scales of justice. A "ransom," "rescue" or "deliverance" (*pādâ*) can be from slavery (Lev. 19:20; Deut. 7:8), from troubling times or overbearing situations (2 Sam 4:9; Job 6:23; Psa. 55:18), or from death and the grave. (Job 33:28; Psa. 49:15) God had redeemed the Israelites, bringing them up out of Egypt with a mighty hand (Deut. 9:26; Psa. 78:42) and later he would ransom and redeem the Israelites from both Assyrian and Babylonian exile seven hundred and nine hundred years later respectively. (Isa 35:10; 51:11; Jer. 31:11-12; Zech. 10:8-10) This redeeming required a "ransom price," an exchange. When God redeemed Israel from Egypt, the price was the firstborn of Pharaoh and all of Egypt, as well the animals, because Pharaoh had hardened his heart against the release of Israel, the "firstborn" of God. – Exodus 4:21-23; 11:4-8.

In the eighth century B.C.E., the prophet Isaiah wrote, "But now thus says Jehovah, your Creator, O Jacob, and he who formed you, O Israel: 'do not fear, for I have redeemed you; I have called you by name; you are mine. … For I am Jehovah your God, the Holy One of Israel, your Savior; I have given Egypt as your ransom [form of k*ōper*], Cush and Seba in exchange for you.'" (Isa. 43:3) All of these exchanges satisfy justice as laid out in Proverbs 21:18, "The wicked is a ransom for the righteous, and the treacherous in the place of the upright."

Another Hebrew term associated with redemption is (*gā'al*), and this conveys primarily the thought of "redeem, avenge, revenge, ransom, do the part of a kinsman." (Jer. 32:7-8) The derivatives of the root are (*gĕ'ûlay*) redemption (Isa 63:4

---

[139] William B. Coker, "1734 פָּדָה," ed. R. Laird Harris, Gleason L. Archer Jr., and Bruce K. Waltke, *Theological Wordbook of the Old Testament* (Chicago: Moody Press, 1999), 716.

[140] Ludwig Koehler et al., *The Hebrew and Aramaic Lexicon of the Old Testament* (Leiden; New York: E.J. Brill, 1999), 913.

only), (*gĕ ʾūllâ*) redemption, and right of redemption, the price of redemption, kindred and (*gōʾēl*) redeemer. On this the *Theological Wordbook of the Old Testament* writes, "The primary meaning of this root is to do the part of a kinsman and thus to redeem his kin from difficulty or danger. It is used with its derivatives 118 times. One difference between this root and the very similar root *pādâ* "redeem," is that there is usually an emphasis in *gāʾal* on the redemption being the privilege or duty of a near relative. The participial form of the Qal stem has indeed been translated by some as 'kinsman-redeemer' or as in KJV merely "kinsman."[141] Nevertheless, the similarity of (*gāʾal*) to (*pādâ*) is seen by its being used alongside (*pādâ*) at Hosea 13:14): Shall I ransom [form of *pādâ*] them from the hand of Sheol? Shall I redeem [form of *gāʾal*] them from Death? O Death, where are your destruction? O Sheol, where is your sting? Compassion will be hidden from my eyes."

Again, Hebrew uses the verb (*gāʾal*) to speak of redemption and a derivative form of the verb (*gōʾēl*) for redeemer. The basic meaning and application of the verb is the thought of reclaiming, recovering, or repurchasing, i.e., buying something back. The right of redemption can be for a house (Lev. 25:33) the selling of a person to pay his debts (Lev. 25:48–49) a sacrificial animal (Lev. 27:13), or a field or other property (27:19–26). The Psalmist asks God to defend, redeem, and preserve him because he keeps his word. (Psa. 119:153-54) Under the Mosaic Law, if a husband died, leaving his wife childless, there was a custom and law whereby a man would marry the deceased's widow (closest relative first, namely, the brother), who was sonless, to produce offspring, to carry on the name of his relative. (Gen. 30:1; 38:8; Deut. 25:5-7; Ruth 4:4-7) The man carrying out what was known as "brother-in-law marriage" was called the redeemer (*gōʾēl*).

Anders and Butler observe, "in criminal law, a person who committed a crime against another person was responsible for paying back the cost of his crime. If the injured party for some reason was not available to receive restitution, then the nearest relative was to receive it and was called the go'el (Num. 5:8). In capital punishment cases, the closest relative was responsible for avenging the death of his relative. This avenger was called a go'el of blood, but to prohibit such a custom from getting out of hand and becoming an uncontrolled vendetta, the cities of refuge were set up to protect the person accused of murder (Num. 35:12; Josh. 20:3–9; cp. 1 Kgs. 16:11). Thus in Israel's law redemption was "to redeem that which belongs to the family from outside jurisdiction" (Stamm, TLOT, 1, p. 291)."[142]

The Mosaic Law had a provision for the Israelites who became victim to poverty (Redemption of Property), wherein he was forced to sell his hereditary lands, his house in the city, or even to sell himself into servitude. It reads, "If your brother becomes poor and sells part of his property, then his nearest redeemer (*gōʾēl*) shall come and redeem [*gāʾal*] what his brother has sold." (Lev. 25:25, ESV) What if the

[141] (Harris, Archer and Waltke 1999, c1980, TWOT Number 300a, page 145)

[142] Anders, Max; Butler, Trent (2002-04-01). *Holman Old Testament Commentary - Isaiah* (pp. 351-352). B&H Publishing. Kindle Edition.

man had no relative to redeem it? Then, if he "himself becomes prosperous and finds sufficient means to redeem it, let him calculate the years since he sold it and pay back the balance to the man to whom he sold it, and then return to his property." (Lev. 25:26-27) First, it should be noted that this man was not to be taken advantage of, nor dealt with in a ruthless way. If he had to sell himself into slavery, he is respected and viewed as hired servant (employee), who can be redeemed or released on the Year of Jubilee. The fact that a poor Israelite could become wealthy while in servitude is evidence that he was treated very well, and this served as a perfect protection against a lifetime of poverty.

In the case of a murder, while he could not seek sanctuary in the six cities of refuge (Num. 35:6-32; Josh. 20:2-9); however, he could receive a judicial hearing, if found guilty, "the avenger [*gō'ēl*] of blood shall himself put the murderer to death." The avenger of blood would be a near relative of the victim. Moreover, there was no ransom [*kōper*] for the life of a murderer, who is guilty of death, so he was to be put to death. In addition, no near relative who had the right of redeemer could reclaim the life of his dead relative; therefore, he justly claimed the life of the one who had murdered his relative. – Numbers 35:9-32; Deuteronomy 19:1-13.

Ransom Not Always a Material Price

As was stated in the above, God "redeemed" (*pādâ*) or 'reclaimed' (*gā'al*) Israel from Egypt. (Ex 6:6; Isa 51:10-11) However, more times than can be counted, the Israelites "sold themselves to do that which was evil in the sight of Jehovah, to provoke him to anger." (2 Ki 17:16-17) Therefore, repeatedly, God sold them into the hands of their enemies. (Deut. 32:30; Judges 2:14; 3:8; 10:7; 1 Sam 12:9) Nevertheless, they would eventually repent and God would ransom and redeem them back (buy them back), reclaiming them from subjugation by their neighboring enemies or exile. (Psa. 107:2-3; Isa. 35:9, 10; Micah 4:10) In this, God was carrying out the work of a redeemer (*gō'ēl*), for the Sons of Israel belonged to him. (Isa. 43:1, 14; 48:20; 49:26; 50:1-2; 54:5-7) God takes no pleasure in gold, silver, or land because it all belongs to him anyway, so this is not what the pagan nations paid him. Rather, his payment came in the satisfying of justice and the carrying out his will and purposes, correcting their rebellious spirit and their lack of respect for the Creator of the heavens and the earth.

Isaiah 48:17-18 Updated American Standard Version (UASV)

17 Thus says Jehovah,
your Redeemer, the Holy One of Israel:
"I am Jehovah your God,
who teaches you to profit,
who leads you in the way you should go.
18 Oh that you had paid attention to my commandments!
Then your peace would have been like a river,
and your righteousness like the waves of the sea;

Again, in the case of God, his redeeming does not necessarily need to involve something physical like property, land, gold and silver. When God redeemed the Israelites, who had been in exile in Babylon, Cyrus the Great of Persia was used to liberate them from captivity. Nevertheless, when God redeemed Israel from Nations that had acted with malevolence and hatred against Israel, he demanded a price from the persecutors themselves, in that they paid with their very lives. (Psa. 106:10-11; Isa. 41:11-14; 49:26) When God sold his people to the pagan nations, the Israelites received nothing in return (benefits or relief), meaning that God received nothing, nor was anything given to the captors to balance out the scales. Rather, by the power of his arm, God redeemed his people, the sons of Jacob. – Psalm 77:14-15.

Isaiah 52:3-10 Updated American Standard Version (UASV)

3 For thus says Jehovah, "You were sold for nothing, and you shall be redeemed
without money." 4 For thus says Jehovah God, "My people went down at the first
into Egypt to sojourn there, and the Assyrian oppressed them without cause. 5 Now
therefore, what do I have here," declares Jehovah, "seeing that my people are taken away without cause? Their rulers wail," declares Jehovah, "and continually all the day my name is despised. 6 Therefore my people shall know my name. Therefore in that
day they shall know that it is I who speak; here I am."

7 How beautiful upon the mountains
are the feet of him who brings good news,
who publishes peace, who brings good news of happiness,
who proclaims salvation,
who says to Zion, "Your God reigns!"
8 Listen! your watchmen lift up their voices;
together they sing for joy;
for eye to eye they see
when Jehovah returns to Zion.
9 Break forth, sing for joy together,
you waste places of Jerusalem,
for Jehovah has comforted his people;
he has redeemed Jerusalem.
10 Jehovah has bared his holy arm
before the eyes of all the nations,
and all the ends of the earth shall see
the salvation of our God.

Therefore, the Father in his role as the *gō'ēl* included the punishing of wrongs done to his servants, ending with his sanctifying, and defending his personal name against those who used Israel's suffering as a justification to reproach him. (Psa. 78:35; Isa 59:15-20; 63:3-6, 9) As the Great Kinsman (NASB) and Redeemer of both the nation of Israel as a whole and each individual making up that nation, he pled for their cause, to satisfy justice. – Psa. 119:153-154; Jer. 50:33-34; Lam. 3:58-60; See also Pro. 23:10, 11.

The man of great faith, the disease-stricken Job said, "As for me, I know that my Kinsman[143] lives, and at the last, he will stand upon the earth.[144] King David sang, "Draw near to my soul, redeem me; ransom me because of my enemies!" (Psa. 69:18) He also sang at Psalm 103:4, "Who redeems your life from the pit, who crowns you with lovingkindness and mercy"? King Saul sought to kill David many times, the Philistines wanted David dead as well, as was true of others. However, God showed David loving kindness by redeeming him from the pit, i.e., the grave. – 1 Samuel 18:9-29; 19:10; 21:10-15; 23:6-29.

The Ransom of Christ Jesus

The Hebrew Old Testament Scriptures are what help us appreciate the ransom that was offered by the Son of God, Jesus Christ. It was Adam's siding with Eve in the rebellion against God's sovereignty (right to rule) that brought about the need of a ransom. Adam evidenced more love for Eve than he did for his Creator, who had given him life. Therefore, he sold his soul (life) so that he could join Eve in her transgression, sharing in her condemnation as well, losing his righteous standing before God. Therefore, he also sold any future descendants into slavery to sin and to death, as God had commanded, "from the tree of the knowledge of good and evil you shall not eat,[145] for in the day that you eat from it you shall surely die."[146]" As Adam was a perfect human, who would never have become sick, or grown old, nor ever died, he sold these things for his own selfish desire of being with Eve, and he sold them for all of his progeny.

Romans 5:12-19 Updated American Standard Version (ASV)

12 Therefore, just as through one man sin entered into the world, and death through sin, and so death spread to all men, because all sinned, **13** or until the law sin was in the world, but sin is not imputed when there is no law. **14** Nevertheless death reigned from Adam until Moses, even over them that had not sinned after the likeness of Adam's transgression, who is a type of the one who is to come.

15 But the free gift is not like the trespass.[147] For if by the trespass of the one the many died, much more did the grace of God and the gift by the grace of the one man, Jesus Christ, abound to the many. **16** And it is not the same with the free gift as with the way things worked through the one man who sinned. For the judgment after one trespass was condemnation, but the gift after many trespasses was justification.[148] **17** For if by the trespass of the one, death reigned through the one, much more those who receive the abundance of grace and of the gift of righteousness will reign in life through the one, Jesus Christ.

---

[143] I.e., *Redeemer*

[144] Lit *dust*

[145] Lit eat from it

[146] Lit., *dying you* [singular] *shall die.* Heb., moth tamuth; the first reference to death in the Scriptures

[147] Lit not as the trespass, so also the free gift

[148] Lit a declaring of righteous

[18] So, then, as through one trespass there was condemnation to all men, so too through one act of righteousness there was justification of life to all men. [19] For as through the one man's disobedience the many were made sinners, so also through the obedience of the one the many will be made righteous.

Paul, later in the same letter to the Romans, speaks on the conflict of the two natures.

Romans 7:14-25 Updated American Standard Version (UASV)

[14] For we know that the law is spiritual, but I am of the flesh, sold under sin. [15] For what I am doing, I do not understand; for I am not practicing what I would like to do, but I am doing the very thing I hate. [16] But if what I am not willing to do, this I am doing, I agree that the law is good. [17] So now I am no longer the one doing it, but sin that dwells in me. [18] For I know that nothing good dwells in me, that is, in my flesh; for the desire is present in me, but the doing of the good is not. [19] For the good that I want, I do not do, but I practice the very evil that I do not want. [20] But if what I do not want to do, this I am doing, I am no longer the one doing it, but sin which dwells in me.

[21] I find then the law in me that when I want to do right, that evil is present in me. [22] For I delight in the law of God according to the inner man, [23] but I see a different law in my members, warring against the law of my mind and taking me captive in the law of sin which is in my members. [24] Wretched man that I am! Who will deliver me from this body of death? [25] Thanks be to God through Jesus Christ our Lord! So then, I myself serve the law of God with my mind, but with my flesh, I serve the law of sin.

The law was but a shadow of the good things to come instead of the true form of these realities, as it atoned in a limited way by offering a substitute, i.e., animal sacrifices. "For it is impossible for the blood of bulls and goats to take away sins." (Heb. 10:1-4) The animal sacrifices were pictorial in yet another way, as 'when anyone offered a sacrifice of peace offerings to Jehovah to fulfill a vow or as a freewill offering from the herd or from the flock, to be accepted it must have been perfect; there was to be no blemish in it.' (Lev. 22:21) The animal sacrifices, therefore, picture, the human sacrifice that was to come, in that, he too would have to be perfect and without blemish. In this, he would actually be an equivalent, a corresponding ransom, as Adam was a perfect human, so too, the ransom to remove sin would have to be a perfect human. This enabled that human sacrifice to pay the price of redemption that would remove Adamic sin, inherited imperfection, from any human placing their trust in the human, who had made such a sacrifice.

Adam had sold his descendants into enslavement to their fallen flesh, as everyone who came after Adam is human imperfection and a slave to sin. (Rom. 7:25) By the human offering paying the price of redemption, he released Adam's offspring from sin and death. The apostle Paul wrote, "In him we have redemption through his blood, the forgiveness of our trespasses, according to the riches of his grace." (Eph. 1:7, ESV) The apostle Paul even said of himself, "For we know that the law is spiritual, but I am of the flesh, sold under sin." (Rom. 7:14) David sang,

"Behold, I was brought forth in iniquity,[149] and in sin did my mother conceive me." Therefore, God's perfect justice had to be satisfied, the one that called for a like for like, as in a "life for life, eye for eye, tooth for tooth, hand for hand, and foot for foot." – Exodus 21:23-25; Deuteronomy 19:21.

God's perfect justice does not allow humankind to provide their own redeemer. "Truly no man can ransom another, or give to God the price of his life, for the ransom of their life is costly and can never suffice." (Psa. 49:6-9, ESV) 'God showed his love for us in that while we were still sinners, he offered his Son for us.' (Rom. 5:6-8) This required the Son coming to earth, to be born as a perfect human, to be the equivalent of Adam, a corresponding ransom. Therefore, the Father, in a way we will never fully understand, placed the Son's life in the womb of Mary, a young Jewish virgin girl. (Lu 1:26-37; John 1:14) Jesus did not have a human father from which imperfection could be carried over into him. Moreover, while Mary was imperfect and could pass on sin to any offspring, in this instance, the Holy Spirit came upon her, and the power of the Most High overshadow her, protecting the baby in her womb.

Therefore, Jesus was born holy and could be called the Son of God. It is "the precious blood of Christ, like that of a lamb without blemish or spot," which redeemed humanity from sin and death. (Lu 1:35; John 1:29; 1 Pet 1:18-19) While David was born into sin (as all of humanity has been), this was not true of Jesus. However, Jesus was fully human, so he could 'sympathize with our weaknesses, and one who in every respect has been tempted as we are, yet without sin.' (Heb. 4:15) Yes, Jesus' entire human life was as a perfect human, just as Adam's had been prior to eating from the forbidden tree. Jesus' human life was 'holy, innocent, unstained, and separated from sinners.' (Heb. 7:26) Humanity had been under another Father, Satan the Devil, after Adam rejected God in the Garden of Eden. (Gen 3:1-6; John 8:44) However, through his ransom 'death, Jesus destroyed the one who has the power of death, that is, the devil, and had delivered all those who through fear of death were subject to lifelong slavery.' (Heb. 2:14-15) This is why Isaiah could refer to him prophetically as "Eternal Father." – Isaiah 9:6.

The New Testament makes it all too clear that Jesus' perfect human life was given as a price to satisfy justice and redeem humankind from sin and death. Paul tells us that we "were bought with a price." (1 Cor. 6:20; 7:23) Paul often begins his letters "Paul, a slave of Christ Jesus," as Jesus bought us from Satan the Devil, from condemnation and death, as Peter states, Jesus is the "the Master who bought" us. (Rom. 1:1; 2 Pet. 2.1) Jesus was 'slain, and by his blood, he ransomed [bought] people for God from every tribe and language and people and nation.' (Rev. 5:9, ESV) In the above texts, we find the Greek word *agorazo*, which means "literally *buy, purchase, do business in the marketplace* (MT 13.44); figuratively, as being no longer controlled by sin *set free*; from the analogy of buying a slave's freedom for a price paid by a

149 Iniquity (*awon*) "signifies an offense, intentional or not, against God's law." This meaning is also most basic to the word [*chattat*], "sin," in the Old Testament, and for this reason the words [*chattat*] and [awon] are virtually synonymous." (VCEDONTW, Volume 1, Page 122) Iniquity is anything not in harmony with God's personality, standards, ways, and will, which mars one's relationship with God.

benefactor *redeem* (1C 6.20)."[150] The related *exagorazo* (to release by purchase) means, "*To buy up,* i.e. *ransom,* fig. *to rescue from loss.*"[151] Paul said that Jesus 'redeemed [*exagorazo*][152] those who were under the law, so that we might receive adoption as sons.' Paul speaks of the curse that the Jews and all of humanity was under, when he says, "Christ redeemed [*exagorazo*][153] us from the curse of the law by becoming a curse for us." (Gal. 4:5; 3:13) However, the Greek word more often used for redemption and ransoming is *lytron*, which more fully expresses the intended meaning as well.

Lytron is "the means or instrument by which release or deliverance is made possible–'means of release, ransom."[154] The *Analytical Lexicon of the Greek New Testament* says of lytron, "as a price paid for release from slavery or captivity *ransom*; figuratively, of the cost to Christ in providing deliverance from sin *price of release, ransom, means of setting free*."[155] (See Heb. 11:35) Lytron describes Christ as "the Son of Man came not to be served but to serve, and to give his soul as a ransom [*lytron*] for many." (Matt 20:28; Mark 10:45) The related word *antilytron* appears at 1 Timothy 2:6.

If we look at 1 Timothy 2:5-6, it says in part, "the man Christ Jesus, who gave himself as a ransom [*antilytron*] for all." The Greek word *antilytron* appears nowhere else in the Bible. It is related to the word that Jesus used for ransom (*lytron*) at Mark 10:45. The Greek *antilytron* broken down from *anti* means "against; in correspondence to; "instead of;" "in place of," and *lytron* means "ransom [i.e., price paid]") "The *Greek* implies not merely *ransom,* but a *substituted* or *equivalent ransom:* the *Greek* preposition, '*anti,*' implying reciprocity and vicarious substitution."[156] *The Interpreters Dictionary of the Bible* in volume 4 states: that of antilytron "The word "ransom" (lutron and antilutron) occurs only three times (Matt. 20:28=Mark 10:45; 1 Tim.2:6), but its occurrence in the first two of these passages is nevertheless of fundamental importance for understanding Jesus' own conception of his death as a redemptive act. He gives a new depth to the concept of redemption by associating with it the idea - derived from Isa. 53:5 - 6, 10 - of a substitutionary sacrifice."[157] The reason this is the case is that we are talking about the equivalent price of one perfect

---

[150] Timothy Friberg, Barbara Friberg, and Neva F. Miller, *Analytical Lexicon of the Greek New Testament*, Baker's Greek New Testament Library (Grand Rapids, MI: Baker Books, 2000), 33.

[151] Robert L. Thomas, New American Standard Hebrew-Aramaic and Greek Dictionaries : Updated Edition (Anaheim: Foundation Publications, Inc., 1998).

[152] Lit he might by out

[153] Lit bought out

[154] Johannes P. Louw and Eugene Albert Nida, *Greek-English Lexicon of the New Testament: Based on Semantic Domains* (New York: United Bible Societies, 1996), 487.

[155] Timothy Friberg, Barbara Friberg, and Neva F. Miller, *Analytical Lexicon of the Greek New Testament*, Baker's Greek New Testament Library (Grand Rapids, MI: Baker Books, 2000), 249.

[156] Robert Jamieson, A. R. Fausset, and David Brown, *Commentary Critical and Explanatory on the Whole Bible*, vol. 2 (Oak Harbor, WA: Logos Research Systems, Inc., 1997), 408.

[157] Dentan, R. C. *The Interpreter's Dictionary of the Bible.* Edited by George Arthur Butrick. Vol. 4. 4 vols. Nashville, TN: Abingdon Press, 1962, Volume 4, page 22.

human for another perfect human. Thus, this was a means for God's principal attribute justice to be satisfied.

Another related word is *lytroomai* to release or set free, with the implied analogy to the process of freeing a slave—'to set free, to liberate, to deliver, liberation, deliverance.'[158] Paul wrote to Titus that Jesus "gave himself for us to redeem [*lytroomai*] us from all lawlessness and to purify for himself a people for his own possession who are zealous for good works." (Tit 2:14, ESV) Peter states that we can know that we were ransomed from the futile ways inherited from our forefathers, not with perishable things such as silver or gold, but with the precious blood of Christ, like that of a lamb without blemish or spot." (1 Pet. 1:18-19) Another related word is *apolytrosis*, which means, "'buying back' a slave or captive, i.e. 'making free' by payment of a ransom."[159] Paul writes of Jesus, "In him we have redemption through his blood, the forgiveness of our trespasses, according to the riches of his grace." (Eph. 1:7, 14; Col. 1:14) The basic fact of both the Hebrew and Greek terms are (1) a redeeming or ransoming, i.e., deliverance, (2) brought about by a payment, (3) consisting of a corresponding equivalency.

Even though the ransom sacrifice of Jesus Christ is made available to anyone who wishes to avail himself or herself to it, not all respond to the invitation. Jesus himself said, "The one trusting[160] in the Son has eternal life, but the one who disobeys the Son will not see life, but the wrath of God remains on him." (John 3:36) The point here is that Jesus' ransom covers the Adamic inherited sin of every person and all that it entails. Everyone has the opportunity of choosing life over death, the ransom is made available, but it can be rejected. Moreover, it can be accepted and later rejected as well. "As sin reigned in death, grace also might reign through righteousness leading to eternal life through Jesus Christ our Lord." – Romans 5:21.

Hebrews 10:26 Updated American Standard Version (USV)

26 For if we go on sinning deliberately[161] after receiving the knowledge of the truth, there no longer remains a sacrifice for sins, 27 but a fearful expectation of judgment, and a fury of fire that will consume the adversaries. 28 Anyone who has set aside the law of Moses dies without mercy on the evidence of two or three witnesses. 29 How much worse punishment, do you think, will be deserved by the one who has trampled underfoot the Son of God, and has profaned the blood of the covenant by which he was sanctified, and has outraged the Spirit of grace?

---

158 Johannes P. Louw and Eugene Albert Nida, *Greek-English Lexicon of the New Testament: Based on Semantic Domains* (New York: United Bible Societies, 1996), 487.

159 William Arndt, Frederick W. Danker, and Walter Bauer, *A Greek-English Lexicon of the New Testament and Other Early Christian Literature* (Chicago: University of Chicago Press, 2000), 117.

160 The grammatical construction of pisteuo "believe" followed by eis "into" plus the accusative causing a different shade of meaning, having faith into Jesus.

161 A willful person acts deliberately, or is "obstinately and often perversely self-willed." (*Webster's New Collegiate Dictionary*)

Contrasted with,

Romans 5:9-10 Updated American Standard Version (ASV)

[9] Much more then, having now been justified by his blood, we shall be saved from the wrath of God through him. [10] For if while we were enemies we were reconciled to God through the death of his Son, much more, having been reconciled, we shall be saved by his life.

Just as one could not ransom a willful murderer under the Mosaic Law, Adam willfully murdered humanity with his rejection of God's sovereignty. (Rom. 5:12) Under this Scriptural point, it would seem that Adam could not be ransomed by the sacrificed life of Jesus. Nevertheless, we can be thankful that every descendant of Adam has an opportunity to be ransomed by Jesus sacrifice. Paul wrote, "So, then, as through one trespass there was condemnation to all men, so too through one act of righteousness there was justification of life to all men. For as through the one man's disobedience the many were made sinners, so also through the obedience of the one the many will be made righteous." (Rom 5:18-19) Thus, it is written, "The first man Adam became a living being"; the last Adam became a life-giving spirit. (1 Cor. 15:45) This arrangement evidences the wisdom of God and his righteously satisfying justice while at the same time showing mercy and grace, in his forgiving our sins.

Romans 3:21-26 Updated American Standard Version (UASV)

[21] But now apart from the Law the righteousness of God has been manifested, being witnessed by the Law and the Prophets, [22] even the righteousness of God through faith in Jesus Christ for all those who believe; for there is no distinction; [23] for all have sinned and fall short of the glory of God, [24] being justified as a gift by his grace through the redemption which is in Christ Jesus; [25] whom God displayed publicly as a propitiation in his blood through faith. This was to demonstrate his righteousness, because in the forbearance of God he passed over the sins previously committed; [26] it was to show his righteousness at the present time, so that he might be just and the justifier of the one who has faith in Jesus.

CHAPTER 4 What the Bible Authors Really Meant by Reconciliation

To reconcile means to "restore to friendship or harmony."[162] The Greek *katallasso* means, "'to reconcile.' It is related to the Greek word, *allasso,* which means, "to change, exchange" (6x in the NT: Acts 6:14; Rom 1:23; 1 Cor. 15:51–52; Gal 4:20; Heb. 1:12)."[163] In the New Testament, *katallasso* "is a theological term describing the removal of enmity between humans and God (Rom. 5:10 [2x], 2 Cor. 5:18, 19, 20); it occurs only once in reference to human relationships (1 Cor. 7:11, husband/wife; it is significant that marriage is the relationship chosen for the use of this word). In biblical thought, God reconciles humans to himself through the death of his Son (Rom 5:10; 2 Cor. 5:18–20)."[164]

Reconciliation to God

The Greek word *katallage* in the New Testament is used "for our 'reconciliation' with God, which has taken place through Christ's blood (Rom. 5:11). It is, therefore, a work of God in that he is the one who removes the enmity between himself and humanity (2 Cor. 5:18–19). This divine act does require a response of faith from the human beings. This is why Paul admonishes his readers to 'be reconciled to God' (2 Cor. 5:20; see reconcile). The majority of Jews made reconciliation available to all people because of their rejection of Christ (Rom. 11:15). Now, this is not to say that non-Jews were never going to benefit from the ransom as that was already part of the will and purposes of God from Genesis 3:15 forward. Such removal of enmity between God and the human race should lead to missionary zeal–to our being Christ's ambassadors (2 Cor. 5:20)."[165]

The apostle Paul tells us why reconciliation to God is needed when he writes, "sin came into the world through one man, and death through sin, and so death spread to all men because all sinned." (Rom. 5:12, ESV) Since Adam and Eve rebelled and were expelled from the Garden of Eden, there has been this alienation between man and God, a separation, a lack of harmony with God's personality, standards, ways, and will. In fact, humanity has been in a state of hostility toward God. Paul wrote, "For the mind that is set on the flesh is hostile to God, for it does not submit to God's law; indeed, it cannot. Those who are in the flesh cannot please God." (Rom. 8:7-8, ESV) When Paul says "those who are in the flesh cannot please God," he is not referring to literal human flesh, as this is the very condition in which he

---

162 Frederick C. Mish, "Preface," *Merriam-Webster's Collegiate Dictionary.* (Springfield, MA: Merriam-Webster, Inc., 2003).

163 William D. Mounce, Mounce's Complete Expository Dictionary of Old & New Testament Words (Grand Rapids, MI: Zondervan, 2006), 565.

164 IBID., 566

165 IBID., 566

created humans. Paul's use of "flesh" here is a reference to our fallen condition as imperfect humans with inherited sinful tendencies.

The *Holman New Testament Commentary* on Romans tells us, "Here, in a different language, is Paul's contrast between the deeds of the flesh and the fruit of the Spirit in Galatians 5:19–23. He lists the deeds and the fruit in Galatians; here he explains from whence they arise. The mind of a human being can be set upon only one thing—either the desires of the flesh or the Spirit. The new way of life in the Spirit makes it possible for the mind of the believer to be set upon **what the Spirit desires**. Here is what Paul states, implicitly and explicitly, about the two kinds of people he is describing:"

	Those Who Live in Accordance with the Flesh	**Those Who Live in Accordance with the Spirit**
What they think about doing	Minds are set on the desires of the flesh	Minds are set on the desires of the Spirit
Ultimate end	Leads to death	Leads to life and peace
Attitude toward God	Hostile toward God	Receptive toward God
Attitude toward God's standards	Does not submit to God's law	Seeks to fulfill God's law
Ability to keep God's standards	Unable to submit to God's law	Able to submit to God's law
Ability to please God	Cannot please God	Able to please God

Boa and Kruidenier go on to say that "Paul is not defining two categories of people here: Christians versus non-Christians, or Spirit-filled Christians versus "carnal" Christians. Rather, he is using the opposite extremes of the spectrum to illustrate two ways of living life in God's world. One way is to live it according to the desires and directives of the flesh, a way that produces hostility toward God and ultimately death. The other way is to live life according to the desires of God as revealed and empowered by his Holy Spirit [a laid out in the Word of God], a way that leads to life and peace."[166]

[166] Kenneth Boa and William Kruidenier, *Romans*, vol. 6, Holman New Testament Commentary (Nashville, TN: Broadman & Holman Publishers, 2000), 250–251.

The enmity that exists is because God is perfect and his standards for his human creation are perfect, and God cannot condone simply because we are now living in imperfection. The Psalmist tells us that the Father 'does not delight in wickedness, and evil cannot dwell with him.' He goes on to state that 'righteousness and justice are the foundation of God's throne. (Psa. 5:4; 89:14) The apostle Paul tells us that the Son has "loved righteousness and hated wickedness." (Heb. 1:9) Yes, it is true that God is love" and 'God so loved the world that he gave his only begotten Son, that whoever believes in him shall not perish, but have eternal life.' (1 John 4:8, 16; John 3:16) Nevertheless, humanity as a whole remains at odds toward God. Moreover, the love of the whole world of humankind alienated from God is a principled love (Gr *agape*) as opposed to affection or friendship (Gr *philia*). – See James 4:4

The author of 2 Samuel tells us, "As for God, his way is **perfect**." (22:31, ASV) Moses tells us, ""The Rock, his work is **perfect**, for all his ways are **justice**. A God of faithfulness and **without iniquity**, just and **upright** is he."' (Deut. 32:4, ESV) King David says, "Jehovah is **merciful**, and merciful; **slow to anger** and of great **lovingkindness**." (Psa. 45:8) The apostle tells us "God, being rich in **mercy**, because of the great **love** with which he **loved us**." (Eph. 2:4, ESV) David further said, "God does not deal with us according to our sins, nor repay us according to our iniquities. For as high as the heavens are above the earth, so great is **his steadfast love** toward those who [have reverential] fear [of] him; as far as the east is from the west, so far does **he remove our transgressions** from us." (Psa. 103:10-12, ESV) One thing that we need to realize is, God does not tolerate or view sin favorably, which is contrary to, his personality, standards, ways, and will. Thus, God does not set aside justice so that he can be merciful. *A Biblical and Theological Dictionary* makes the correct observation, "That [the] relation[ship between God and imperfect man] is a legal one, as that of a sovereign in his judicial capacity, and a criminal who has violated his laws and risen up against his authority, and who is, therefore, treated as an enemy." (Watson 1832, 808) Imperfect man finds himself in this situation because of his inheriting sin and death from his father, Adam. The dictionary further says, "by the infection of sin 'the carnal mind is enmity to God,' that human nature is malignantly hostile to God and to the control of law; but this is far from expressing the whole of that relationship of man in which, in Scripture, he is said to be at enmity with God, and so to need a reconciliation, the making of peace between God and him." (p. 807) The reconciliation is a renewing of peace between God and man but it is man be reconciled to God not God to man.

Foundation for Reconciliation

Again, reconciliation is "to reestablish proper friendly interpersonal relations after these have been disrupted or broken (the componential features of this series of meanings involve (1) disruption of friendly relations because of (2) presumed or real provocation, (3) overt behavior designed to remove hostility, and (4) restoration of original friendly relations)—'to reconcile, to make things right with one another, reconciliation.'"[167] In order for man to be reconciled to God, this is the direct result of the Father offering his Son as a ransom sacrifice, making full reconciliation possible. Jesus said, "I am the way, and the truth, and the life. No one comes to the Father except through me." (John 14:6, ESV) Jesus is "is the propitiation for our sins, and not for ours only but also for the sins of the whole world." (1 John 2:2, ESV) John did not mean that Jesus ransom is going to cover everyone's sin, so all receive salvation but rather his ransom sacrifice is available for all to accept. John goes on to write, "In this is love, not that we have loved God but that he loved us and sent his Son to be the propitiation for our sins." (1 John 4:10, ESV) Jesus death served as a propitiatory sacrifice (*hilasmos*), which means an "**appeasement necessitated by sin, *expiation*** [The cancellation of sin, appeasing divine wrath].[168] **Propitiation** [is a] "reference to the idea that Christ's atonement satisfies the wrath of God."[169] Propitiation "is never used of any act whereby man brings God into a favorable attitude or gracious disposition. It is God who is "propitiated" by the vindication of His holy and righteous character, whereby through the provision He has made in the vicarious and expiatory sacrifice of Christ, He has so dealt with sin that He can show mercy to the believing sinner in the removal of his guilt and the remission of his sins."[170] So, what was appeased or satisfied? The ransom sacrifice of Jesus Christ appeased or satisfied, the legal request of God's perfect justice by making available the just and righteous basis for forgiving sin, so that God might "show his righteousness at the present time, so that he might be just and the justifier of the one who has faith in Jesus." – Romans 3:24-26.

Ephesians 1:7 Updated American Standard Version (UASV)

7 in whom we have our redemption through his blood, the forgiveness of our trespasses, according to the riches of his grace

The *Holman New Testament Commentary* offers the following on Ephesians 1:7, "to be redeemed means to be "bought back." It carries with it the sense of being released from slavery. By being redeemed by Christ, we are freed from sin, both the penalty and the enslaving power. This **redemption** was accomplished by the death of Christ on the cross where he shed his blood and died to secure our redemption. His death paid the price for our release from sin and death. **Forgiveness** goes hand in hand with redemption. We cannot have one without the other. To forgive means to give up the right to punish someone for a transgression. Making forgiveness possible was a major accomplishment in God's eyes, since it required the sacrifice of blood and the death of his Son, Jesus. This magnanimous decision to do this for us

---

[167] Johannes P. Louw and Eugene Albert Nida, *Greek-English Lexicon of the New Testament: Based on Semantic Domains* (New York: United Bible Societies, 1996), 501.

[168] William Arndt, Frederick W. Danker, and Walter Bauer, *A Greek-English Lexicon of the New Testament and Other Early Christian Literature* (Chicago: University of Chicago Press, 2000), 474.

[169] Millard J. Erickson, *The Concise Dictionary of Christian Theology* (Wheaton, IL: Crossway Books, 2001), 162.

[170] W. E. Vine, Merrill F. Unger, and William White Jr., *Vine's Complete Expository Dictionary of Old and New Testament Words* (Nashville, TN: T. Nelson, 1996), 493.

grew out of God's grace which he **lavished on us with all wisdom and understanding**."[171]

Hebrews 2:17 Updated American Standard Version (UASV)

17 Therefore, he was obligated to be made like his brothers in all respects, so that he might become a merciful and faithful high priest in things pertaining to God, to make propitiation for the sins of the people.

Thomas D. Lea tells us "Jesus had a complete, perfect humanity. We read two reasons for the incarnation of Christ. First, the incarnation allowed Christ **to become a merciful and faithful high priest in service to God.** Jesus' own suffering allowed him to be sympathetic to others and thus to show mercy. He demonstrated his faithfulness by remaining steadfast to the end without flinching. Jesus was completely trustworthy in everything God called him to do. A second reason for the incarnation was that Jesus **might make atonement for the sins of the people.** Jesus' death handled the personal sins of all human beings. Jesus did in reality what the Old Testament sacrificial ritual could only do in symbols. It was not that Jesus' death satisfied the angry demands of a peevish God. The truth is that God himself provided the payment for our sins because of his ever-abiding love (Rom. 5:8)."[172] There are at least **two additional reasons** why Jesus came to earth as a man. **(1)** Jesus specifically said, "For this purpose I was born and for this purpose I have come into the world, to testify to the truth." (John 18:37) **(2)** The apostle Peter tells us "Christ also suffered for you, leaving you an example, so that you should follow in his footsteps." – 1 Peter 2:21.

God, through his Son, made it possible "to reconcile all things unto himself, having made peace through the blood of his cross." In doing so, those, 'who once were alienated and enemies in their minds, doing evil works, has now been reconciled in his body of flesh by his death, in order to present them holy and blameless and above reproach before him.' (Col 1:19-22) The apostle Paull tells us, "Through this man forgiveness of sins is proclaimed to you, 39 and by him everyone who believes is freed from everything from which you could not be freed by the law of Moses." (Ac 13:38-39) Paul tells the Christians in Rome,

Romans 5:9-10; 8:32-33 Updated American Standard Version (UASV)

9 Much more then, having now been justified by his blood, we shall be saved from the wrath of God through him. 10 For if while we were enemies we were reconciled to God through the death of his Son, much more, having been reconciled, we shall be saved by his life.

---

171 Max Anders, *Galatians-Colossians*, vol. 8, Holman New Testament Commentary (Nashville, TN: Broadman & Holman Publishers, 1999), 92–93.

172 Thomas D. Lea, *Hebrews, James*, vol. 10, Holman New Testament Commentary (Nashville, TN: Broadman & Holman Publishers, 1999), 30.

[32] He who did not spare his own Son, but delivered him over for us all, how will he not also with him freely give us all things? [33] Who will bring charges against God's chosen ones? God is the one who justifies;

If we are to be truly forgiven of our Adamic sin, namely, our inherited sin, and any sin we make commit while in human imperfection, we must repent and ask for forgiveness. Even, though, it is the Christian, who is repenting, turning to God, he must realize it is not his insight, his goodness but rather God who is drawing him. By the Word of God, the unbeliever will come to recognize that he needs to be forgiven, which can only come by and through Christ's atonement sacrifice. Christians, while they are still in imperfection, suffering from human weaknesses, sin-laden flesh, they can still be declared righteous (namely, credited righteousness) because of the merits of the sacrifice of Jesus Christ being applied on their behalf. They then have a righteous, uncondemned standing before God. The Father has given Christians the most precious gift he could, his own begotten Son for his worshipers. God can declare righteous all who accept his Son, Jesus Christ. They will become new persons, who are at peace with God. (Eph. 4:22-24; Col. 3:9-10) How is it possible for persons such as Abel, Noah, Abraham, Moses, Joshua, David and others from pre-Christian times to be reconciled to God and declared righteous when they died before Jesus' ransom sacrifice? The apostle Paul writes, "By faith Abel offered to God a better sacrifice than Cain, through which he obtained the testimony that **he was righteous**, God testifying about his gifts." (Heb. 11:4-5) James writes, "The Scripture was fulfilled that says, "Abraham believed God, and it was **counted to him as righteousness**,"[173] and he was called a friend of God."' (Jam. 2:23) Even John the Baptist died before Jesus had offered himself as a ransom sacrifice. If God had already dealt with these ones and blessed, why would they need reconciliation by means of Jesus' sacrifice? Let us first take an excursion to look at how they were declared righteous.

Declared Righteous Excursion

The Hebrew verb *tsaddiq*, which is related to *tsede*q; means *just, righteous.*[174] "Jehovah is righteous (*tsaddiq*) in all his ways and loyal in all his works." (Ps 145:17; See Ex. 23:7; Deut. 25:1) The Dictionary of Biblical Languages with Semantic Domains says, "righteous, upright, just, i.e., pertaining to being a person in accordance with a proper standard (Ge 18:23, 24(2×),25(2×),26, 28); 2. LN 88.289–88.318 innocent, guiltless, i.e., pertaining to not having sin or wrongdoing according to a just standard (Ex 23:7).[175] This Biblical expression is characterized by his actions and morals. In the New Testament, we have the Greek verb *dikaioo*, which means,

---

[173] Quoted from Gen. 15:6

[174] Robert L. Thomas, *New American Standard Hebrew-Aramaic and Greek Dictionaries : Updated Edition* (Anaheim: Foundation Publications, Inc., 1998).

[175] James Swanson, Dictionary of Biblical Languages with Semantic Domains: Hebrew (Old Testament) (Oak Harbor: Logos Research Systems, Inc., 1997).

"'to declare righteous, justify.' This word is prominent in Paul's letters, containing 27 of the 39x (about 70%)."[176]

On being righteous, *Vine's Complete Expository Dictionary of Old and New Testament Words* has,

> **A. Verb.**
>
> *tsadaq* (צָדַק, 6663), "to be righteous, be in the right, be justified, be just." This verb, which occurs fewer than 40 times in biblical Hebrew, is derived from the noun *tsedeq*. Nowhere is the issue of righteousness more appropriate than in the problem of the suffering of the righteous presented to us in Job, where the verb occurs 17 times. Apart from the Book of Job the frequency of *tsadaq* in the various books is small. The first occurrence of the verb is in Gen. 38:26, where Judah admits that Tamar was just in her demands: "She hath been more righteous than I; because that I gave her not to Shelah my son."
>
> The basic meaning of *tsadaq* is "to be righteous." It is a legal term which involves the whole process of justice. God "is righteous" in all of His relations, and in comparison with Him man is not righteous: "Shall mortal man be more just [righteous] than God?" (Job 4:17). In a derived sense, the case presented may be characterized as a just cause in that all facts indicate that the person is to be cleared of all charges. Isaiah called upon the nations to produce witnesses who might testify that their case was right: "Let them bring forth their witnesses that they may be justified: or let them hear, and say, It is truth" (43:9). Job was concerned about his case and defended it before his friends: "… Though I were righteous, yet would I not answer, but I would make supplication to my judge" (9:15). *Tsadaq* may also be used to signify the outcome of the verdict, when a man is pronounced "just" and is judicially cleared of all charges. Job believed that the Lord would ultimately vindicate him against his opponents (Job 13:18).
>
> In its causative pattern, the meaning of the verb brings out more clearly the sense of a judicial pronouncement of innocence: "If there be a controversy between men, and they come unto judgment, that the judges may judge them; then they shall justify [*tsadaq*] the righteous [*tsaddiq*], and condemn the wicked" (Deut. 25:1). The Israelites were charged with upholding righteousness in all areas of life. When the court system failed became of corruption, the wicked were falsely "justified" and the poor were robbed of justice because of trumped-up charges. Absalom, thus, gained a large following by promising justice to the landowner (2 Sam. 15:4). God, however, assured Israel that justice would be done in the end: "Thou shalt not wrest the judgment of thy poor in

---

176 William D. Mounce, *Mounce's Complete Expository Dictionary of Old & New Testament Words* (Grand Rapids, MI: Zondervan, 2006), 594.

his cause. Keep thee far from a false matter; and the innocent and righteous slay thou not: for I will not justify the wicked" (Exod. 23:6-7). The righteous person followed God's example. The psalmist exhorts his people to change their judicial system: "Defend the poor and fatherless: do justice to the afflicted and needy" (Ps. 82:3).

Job's ultimate hope was in God's declaration of justification. The Old Testament is in agreement with this hope. When injustice prevails, God is the One who "justifies."

The Septuagint translates the verb by *dikaiao* ("to do justice, justly, to vindicate"). In the English versions a frequent translation is "to justify" (KJV, RSV, NASB, NIV); modern versions also give the additional translations "to be vindicated (RSV, NASB, NIV) and "to acquit" (RSV, NIV).

B. Nouns.

tsedeq (צֶדֶק, 6664); *tsedaqah* (צֶדֶק, 6666), "righteousness." These nouns come from a Semitic root which occurs in Hebrew, Phoenician and Aramaic with a juristic sense. In Phoenician and Old Aramaic it carries the sense of "loyalty" demonstrated by a king or priest as a servant of his own god. In these languages a form of the root is combined with other words or names, particularly with the name of a deity in royal names. In the Old Testament we meet the name Melchizedek ("king of righteousness"). A more limited meaning of the root is found in Arabic (a South Semitic language): "truthfulness" (of propositions). In rabbinic Hebrew the noun *tsedaqah* signifies "alms" or "demonstrations of mercy."

The word *tsedaqah*, which occurs 157 times, is found throughout the Old Testament (except for Exodus, Leviticus, 2 Kings, Ecclesiastes, Lamentations, Habakkuk, and Zephaniah). *Tsedeq*, which occurs 119 times, is found mainly in poetic literature. The first usage of *sedeq* is: "Ye shall do no unrighteousness in judgment: thou shalt not respect the person of the poor, nor honor the person of the mighty: but in righteousness shalt thou judge thy neighbor" (Lev. 19:15); and of *tsedaqah* is: "[Abram] believed in the Lord; and he counted it to him for righteousness" (Gen. 15:6).

Translators have found it difficult to translate these two words. The older translations base their understanding on the Septuagint with the translation *dikaiosune* ("righteousness") and on the Vulgate *iustitia* ("justice"). In these translations, the legal relationship of humans is transferred to God in an absolute sense as the Lawgiver and with the perfections of justice and "righteousness."

Exegetes have spilled much ink in an attempt to understand contextually the words *tsedeq* and *tsedaqah*. The conclusions of the researchers indicate a twofold significance. On the one hand, the relationships among people and of a man to his God can be described as *tsedeq*, supposing the parties are faithful to each other's expectations. It is a relational word. In Jacob's proposal to Laban, Jacob used the word *tsedaqah* to indicate the relationship. The KJV gives the following translation of *tsedaqah:* "So shall my righteousness answer for me in time to come, when it shall come for my hire before thy face ..." (Gen. 30:33). The NASB gives the word "righteousness" in a marginal note, but prefers the word "honesty" in the text itself. The NEB reads "fair offer" instead. Finally, the NIV has: "And my honesty [*tsedaqah*] will testify for me in the future, whenever you check on the wages you have paid me." On the other hand "righteousness" as an abstract or as the legal status of a relationship is also present in the Old Testament. The *locus classicus* is Gen. 15:6: "... And he [the Lord] counted it to him [Abraham] for righteousness."

Regrettably, in a discussion of the dynamic versus the static sense of the word, one or the other wins out, though both elements are present. The books of Psalms and of the prophets particularly use the sense of "righteousness" as a state; cf. "Hearken to me, ye that follow after righteousness, ye that seek the Lord: look unto the rock whence ye are hewn, and to the hole of the pit whence ye are digged" (Isa. 51:1); and "My righteousness is near; my salvation is gone forth, and mine arms shall judge the people; the isles shall wait upon me, and on mine arm shall they trust" (Isa. 51:5). The neb exhibits this tension between dynamic and static in the translation of *tsedeq:* "My victory [instead of righteousness] is near, my deliverance has gone forth and my arm shall rule the nations; for me coasts and islands shall wait and they shall look to me for protection" (Isa. 51:5). Thus, in the discussion of the two nouns below the meanings lie between the dynamic and the static.

Tsedeq and *tsedaqah* are legal terms signifying justice in conformity with the legal corpus (the Law; Deut. 16:20), the judicial process (Jer. 22:3), the justice of the king as judge (1 Kings 10:9; Ps. 119:121; Prov. 8:15), and also the source of justice, God Himself: "Judge me, O Lord my God, according to thy righteousness; and let them not rejoice over me.... And my tongue shall speak of thy righteousness and of thy praise all the day long" (Ps. 35:24, 28).

The word "righteousness" also embodies all that God expects of His people. The verbs associated with "righteousness" indicate the practicality of this concept. One judges, deals, sacrifices, and speaks righteously; and one learns, teaches, and pursues after righteousness. Based upon a special relationship with God, the Old Testament saint asked God to deal righteously with him: "Give the king thy judgments, O God, and thy righteousness unto the king's son" (Ps. 72:1).

The Septuagint gives the following translations: *dikaios* ("those who are upright, just, righteous, conforming to God's laws"); *dikalosune* ("righteousness; uprightness"); and *eleemosune* ("land deed; alms; charitable giving"). The KJV gives the senses "righteousness; justice."

C. Adjective.

tsaddiq (צַדִּיק, 6662), "righteous; just." This adjectival form occurs 206 times in biblical Hebrew. In Old Aramaic the adjective signifies "loyalty" of a king or high priest to his personal god, often represented by a gift to the god. Similarly in Phoenician, the noun and adjective apply to the loyal relationship of the king before the gods. The word is used of God in Exod. 9:27: "I have sinned this time: the Lord is righteous, and I and my people are wicked." *Tsaddiq* is used of a nation in Gen. 20:4: "… And he said, Lord, wilt thou slay also a righteous nation?"[177]

Over 4,000 years before the arrival of Jesus Christ, clear back in the Garden of Eden, Adan was perfect, righteous according to God's standards, in fact, "the son of God" at the time. (Lu 3:38, NASB) Moses was inspired to tell us, "God saw everything that he had made [including Adam], and behold; it was very good." (Gen. 1:31, ESV) Adam was righteous by virtue of the fact that the God had created him. Sadly, Adam willfully chose to rebel against God, failing to maintain his righteous standing, as well as all future offspring. – Genesis 3:17-19; Romans 5:12.

However, not all was lost, as God has allowed time to settle the issues rose in the Garden of Eden by Satan's challenges and Adam's action. Some of Adam's descendants have proven to be great men and women of faith. The first great man of faith was Abel. (Heb. 11:4, ESV) Then, we are told, "Enoch walked with God," (Gen. 5:22, ESV) Moreover, "Noah was a righteous man, blameless in his generation. Noah walked with God." (Gen. 6:9, ESV) God himself said of Noah, "I have seen that you are righteous before me in this generation." (Gen 7:1, ESV) Then, "there was a man in the land of Uz whose name was Job, and that man was blameless and upright, one who feared God and turned away from evil." (Job 1:1, 8, ESV) Of Abraham and Rahab, James, the half-brother of Jesus was inspired to tells us of how both place their trust in God, when few others were, moving God to declare them righteous, although imperfect.

James 2:21-23 Updated American Standard Version (UASV)

21 Was not Abraham our father justified by works when he offered up Isaac his son on the altar? **22** You see that faith was working together with his works, and by the works the faith was perfected;[178] **23** and the Scripture was fulfilled that says, "Abraham believed God, and it was counted to him as righteousness,"[179] and he was called a friend of God.

---

[177] W. E. Vine, Merrill F. Unger, and William White Jr., *Vine's Complete Expository Dictionary of Old and New Testament Words* (Nashville, TN: T. Nelson, 1996), 205–207.

[178] Or "*completed*"

[179] Quoted from Gen. 15:6

James 2:25 Updated American Standard Version (UASV)

[25] And in the same way was not also Rahab the prostitute justified by works when she received the messengers and sent them out by another way?

In Paul's letter to the Romans (quoting Genesis 15:6), he speaks of how Abraham's 'faith was credited to him as righteousness.'

Romans 4:3-5 Updated American Standard Version (UASV)

[3] For what does the Scripture say? "Abraham believed God, and it was **credited to him as righteousness**." [4] Now to the one who works, his wages are not credited as a gift but as his due. [5] But to the one who does not work, but believes in him who justifies the ungodly, his faith is **credited as righteousness**,

Romans 4:9-11 Updated American Standard Version (UASV)

[9] Is this blessing then on the circumcised,[180] or on the uncircumcised[181] also? For we say, "**Faith was credited to Abraham as righteousness**." [10] How then was it credited? While he was circumcised,[182] or uncircumcised?[183] Not while circumcised,[184] but while uncircumcised;[185] [11] and he received the sign of circumcision, a seal of the righteousness of the faith which he had while uncircumcised,[186] so that he might be the father of all who believe without being circumcised, that righteousness might be credited to them,

We can better understand the expression 'faith was credited to him as righteousness.' by considering the sense of the Greek verb *logizomai*, rendered as "credited" (LEB, HCSB, NASB (1995), UASV) or "counted" (KJV, ESV) or "reckoned" (ASV, YLT). It means, "To keep records of commercial accounts, involving both debits and credits–'to put into one's account, to charge one's account, to regard as an account.'"[187]

Logizomai "is used of love in 1 Cor. 13:5, as not taking 'account' of evil, RV (KJV, 'thinketh'). In 2 Cor. 3:5 the apostle uses it in repudiation of the idea that he and fellow-servants of God are so self-sufficient as to 'account anything' (RV) as from themselves (KJV, 'think'), i.e., as to attribute anything to themselves. Cf. 12:6.

---

[180] Lit *the circumcision*

[181] Lit *the uncircumcision*

[182] Lit *in circumcision*

[183] Lit *in uncircumcision*

[184] Lit *in circumcision*

[185] Lit *in uncircumcision*

[186] Lit *was in uncircumcision*

[187] Johannes P. Louw and Eugene Albert Nida, *Greek-English Lexicon of the New Testament: Based on Semantic Domains* (New York: United Bible Societies, 1996), 582.

In 2 Tim. 4:16 it is used of laying to a person's 'account' (RV) as a charge against him (KJV, 'charge')."[188]

Looking at the Bible background, we see that "Paul reads [Genesis 15:6] contextually as dependence on God's promise and stresses the word "reckon" (NASB, [1971]) or "credit" (NIV), a bookkeeping term used in ancient business document for crediting payment to one's account." (Keener 1993, 422) Clinton E. Arnold writes, "In order to capture Abraham for his own teaching about the righteousness of faith, Paul seizes on the crucial text of Genesis 15:6 (see also Gal. 3:6). In the Genesis story, Abraham's faith is specifically his conviction that God would send him a natural descendant (Gen. 15:4–5). But this promise of a son born to him and Sarah represents the whole promise of God to Abraham. Critical to Paul's citation of the passage is the idea of "crediting" (Gk. *logizomai* + *eis*). The Hebrew construction does not indicate that Abraham's faith was itself a righteous deed (as some Jews interpreted the text), but that his faith was the means by which God graciously gave Abraham the status of righteousness. Paul seizes on this notion and plays on it throughout Romans 4. This 'crediting' was on the basis of faith, not works—a matter of pure grace on God's part (4:4–8). The 'crediting' was, moreover, not based on circumcision (4:9–12) or the law (4:13–17). This recurring reference to Genesis 15:6 is somewhat similar to the Jewish interpretational technique called *midrash*, in which a Scripture text becomes the basis for an extended discussion.[189] In Paul's day, the Greek word *logizomai* was used for numerical calculations such as in accounting, used both in reference to entering a debit or a credit into one's account. In the case of Abraham's faith, combined with works, he was "credited, counted, reckoned, or attributed to him as righteousness standing before God.

Of course, this does not mean that Abel, Noah, Abraham, Sarah, Rachel, Rebekah, Moses, and other men and women of pre-Christian times were perfect or granted some kind of perfected status. Rather, they were merely reckoned, counted, or credited a righteous standing before God by virtue of their faith in the promised seed. In addition, they were doing just as God commanded, unlike the rest of the world, who were alienated from God. (Gen. 3:15; Psa. 119:2-3) The Psalmist writes, "Blessed is the one whose transgression is forgiven, whose sin is covered. Blessed is the man against whom Jehovah does not impute iniquity, and in whose spirit there is no deceit." (Psa. 32:1-2, UASV) The apostle Paul wrote that the pagan nations "were at that time separated from Christ, alienated from the commonwealth of Israel and strangers to the covenants of promise, having no hope and without God in the world." (Eph. 2:12, UASV) There, we can see how, a perfect, sinless, righteous, and just, Creator could have a relationship with imperfect men, blessing them for their faith and obedience. While, at the same time, 'He could in His loyal love to those who know him, and his righteousness to the upright in heart!' (Ps 36:10)

[188] W. E. Vine, Merrill F. Unger, and William White Jr., *Vine's Complete Expository Dictionary of Old and New Testament Words* (Nashville, TN: T. Nelson, 1996), 9.

[189] Clinton E. Arnold, *Zondervan Illustrated Bible Backgrounds Commentary: Romans to Philemon.*, vol. 3 (Grand Rapids, MI: Zondervan, 2002), 26.

Nevertheless, these ones were well aware through the Hebrew Old Testament that a complete redemption from sin was yet to come.

Psalm 49:7-9 Updated American Standard Version (UASV)

7 Surely no man can redeem a brother,
Or give to God a ransom for him,[190]
8 (for the redemption of their[191] soul is costly,
and it always fails),
9 that he should live on forever
and not see the pit.[192]

Hebrews 9:26 Updated American Standard Version (UASV)

26 Otherwise, he would have needed to suffer often since the foundation of the world; but now he has appeared once at the end of the ages to put away sin by the sacrifice of himself.[193]

The Precious Blood of Christ

The apostle Peter spoke of Christ's perfection, which Paul says was maintained under test. Peter writes, "Knowing that it was not with perishable things like silver or gold that you were redeemed[194] from your futile way of life inherited from your forefathers, but it was with **precious blood**, as of an unblemished and spotless lamb, that of Christ." (1 Pet. 1:18-19) Paul writes, "For it was fitting for him, for whom are all things and through whom are all things in bringing many sons to glory, should make the founder of their salvation perfect **through suffering**." (Heb. 2:10) Paul goes on to say, "In the days of his flesh [i.e. during Christ's earthly life], who having offered up both supplications and prayers with loud crying and tears to the one able to save him from death, and he was heard because of his godly fear. Although he was a son, he **learned obedience from the things which he suffered**. And having been made perfect, he became to all those who obey him the source of eternal salvation …" (Heb. 5:7-10) In his letter to the Christians in Rome, Paul says, "being justified as a gift by his grace through **the redemption** which is in Christ Jesus; whom God displayed publicly as a **propitiation in his blood through faith**. This was to demonstrate his righteousness because in the forbearance of God he passed over the sins previously committed; it was to show his righteousness at the present time, so that he might be just and the justifier of the one who has **faith in Jesus**." (Rom 3:24-26) He adds that Jesus "was delivered over because of our transgressions, and was raised because of our justification." (Rom. 4:25) Going on, he says, "So, then, as through one trespass there was condemnation to all men, so too through **one act of righteousness** [Gr *dikaiomatos*] there was justification [Gr *dikaiosin*] of life to all men.

190 Lit *his cover*, Heb. *kophroh*

191 *their* MT Syr; LXX Vg *his*

192 Or *grave*

193 Or *by his sacrifice*

194 Or *ransomed*

For as through the one man's disobedience the many were made sinners, so also through the obedience of the one the many will be made righteous." (Rom. 5:17-19) It was Jesus proving himself perfectly through his entire time as a human, especially during his persecution and sacrifice; he gave all of humankind, who evidences their trust in him, the basis for being declared righteous.

End of Excursion

Thus, we can say of those men and women who served God prior to the ransom sacrifice of Jesus Christ, they enjoyed a measure of reconciliation to God. Nevertheless, like all of humankind, were sinners by way of inheriting imperfection from Adam' descendants. They were well aware of this by their carrying out animal sacrifices throughout their lives. 'The Mosaic Law was but a shadow of the good things to come [that is, Jesus Christ] instead of the true form of these realities, **it can never**, by the same **sacrifices** that are continually offered year after year, make perfect those who draw near.' (Heb. 10:1-2) It is true that some have been what Scripture calls "gross sinners," and some's sin was as God stated, they "sinned a great sin." (Gen. 13:13; 18:20; Ex 32:30-31; 2 Ki 17:16, 21; Isa. 1:4, 10; 3:9; Lam. 1:8; 4:6) Thus, Scripture does show that there is a **comparative gravity of wrongdoing**. Certainly, no sane person would argue that lying about one's weight is as grave as murdering another human. All the same, sin is still sin, regardless of the degree or extent. All are under sin, as 'all have sinned and fall short of the glory of God because sin came into the world through one man, and death through sin, and so death spread to all men because all sinned. We know that one trespass led to condemnation for all men, by the one man's disobedience the many were made sinners, as sin ruled by bringing death.' (Rom 3:9, 22-23; 5.12, 18-21) Therefore, all men need reconciliation with God that Jesus Christ's ransom sacrifice has made possible.

The friendship that Enoch, Noah, Abraham, Isaac, Jacob, Sarah, Rachel, Rebekah, Moses, Rahab, Elijah and other had with God was relative to their faith in the promised seed, which they believed would remove sin completely one day. (See Heb. 11:1-2, 39-40; John 1:29; 8:56; Ac 2:29-31.) Therefore, the degree of reconciliation that those ones enjoyed was based upon their faith in the promised seed of Genesis 3:15, namely, the long-awaited Messiah, and his ransom sacrifice. As was stated God, "counted," "reckoned" or credited, their faith as righteousness, which enables those ones an opportunity to be considered a friend of God, who could still maintain his perfect standard of justice in the face of sinners. (Rom. 4:3, 9-10; also see 3:25-26; 4:17) Regardless of these great men and women of faith, it still comes back to the fact that the Father's justice had to be satisfied, so that what was credited would then be paid in full, that is, the ransom price of the Son. Clearly, we can see that the greatest act in the history of man came on Nisan 14th 33 C.E. when Jesus gave up his life for all who would believe in him. It is this 'one act of righteousness, it leads to justification and life for all men, so by the one man's obedience, the many will be made righteous. (Rom. 5:18-19) The righteous standing allows us to stand before God. – See Isaiah 64:6; Romans 7:18, 21-25; 1 Corinthians 1:30-31; 1 John 1:8-10.

Steps to Reconciliation

As Scripture makes all too clear, God was the one who was offended, it is his laws that was and is being violated and it was Adam's one act of disobedience, which brought sin into the world and death through sin, and so death has spread to all men. Therefore, it is man who needs to be reconciled[195] to God, not God to man. (Ps 51:1-4; Rom. 5:12, 18-21) It is impossible for man to meet God on equal terms, nor is God's standards of justice, law, morality, ethics and the like are not conditional, subject to change, to being amended, or modified. (Isa 55:6-11; Mal 3:6; see Jam. 1:17) Therefore, God's conditions for reconciliation are set, unchanging, not in question, the subject of discussion, debate, or negotiation. (See Job 40:1-2, 6-8; Isa. 40:13-14) Some renderings of Isaiah 1:18 have caused confusion, which is often used during the Advent season. All of Isaiah Chapter 1 is about the rebellion of God's people and their need to be reconciled to God.

Isaiah 1:18 (ESV) 18 "**Come now, let us reason together**, says the Lord: though your sins are like scarlet, they shall be as white as snow; though they are red like crimson, they shall become like wool.	**Isaiah 1:18** (HCSB) 18 "**Come, let us discuss this**," says the Lord. "Though your sins are like scarlet, they will be as white as snow; though they are as red as crimson, they will be like wool.	**Isaiah 1:18** (NRSV) 18 **Come now, let us argue it out**, says the Lord: though your sins are like scarlet, they shall be like snow; though they are red like crimson, they shall become like wool.
Isaiah 1:18 (LEB) 18 "**Come now, and let us argue**," says Yahweh. "Even though your	**Isaiah 1:18** (NASB) 18 "**Come now, and let us reason together**," Says the Lord, "Though your	**Isaiah 1:18** (ASV, KJV) 18 **Come now, and let us reason together**, saith Jehovah: though your

195 Reconciliation is the reestablishing of cordial relations

sins are like scarlet, they will be white like snow; even though they are red like crimson, they shall become like wool.	sins are as scarlet, They will be as white as snow; Though they are red like crimson, They will be like wool.	sins be as scarlet, they shall be as white as snow; though they be red like crimson, they shall be as wool.

Isaiah 1:18 New International Version (NIV) 18 **"Come now, let us settle the matter,"** says the Lord. "Though your sins are like scarlet, they shall be as white as snow; though they are red as crimson, they shall be like wool.	**Isaiah 1:18** New American Bible (NABRE)[196] 18 Come now, **let us set things right,** says the Lord: Though your sins be like scarlet, they may become white as snow; Though they be red like crimson, they may become white as wool.	**Isaiah 1:18** Update American Standard Version (UASV) 18 **"Come now, let us set matters straight**, says Jehovah: "though your sins are like scarlet, They will be made as white as snow; Though they are red like crimson, they will become like wool.

The New International Version is right on point with, "let us settle the matter," as is true with the New American Bible (Revised Edition), "let us set things right" but the Updated American Standard Version is the best rendering, with "let us set matters straight." However, the least favorable renderings are the NRSV/NEB has

196 (Revised Edition)

"let us argue it out," the HCSB, has "let us discuss this," the ESV/ASV/KJV "let us reason together," and the NASB has "let us argue it out." These latter translations give the impression that Jehovah is trying to cut a deal with the inhabitants of Jerusalem. This is just not the case, as there is only one party at fault here, the Israelites. They were the people who had rebelled too many times to count. (Deut. 32:4-5) This is not some bargaining between two equals, but a warm and loving setting the record straight, bringing the Israelites before the great theocratic court. In essence, the verse is talking about establishing an environment where justice can take place in which the righteous Judge, Almighty God, gives the Israelites another opportunity to turn around, make adjustments and cleanse themselves.

The Hebrew that is "reason together" by the KJV, ASV and ESV essentially mean, "to decide, prove, convince, judge."[197] It has a legal essence, suggesting more than two persons simply reasoning together, the result is a verdict. (Gen. 31:37, 42; Job 9:33; Ps. 50:21; Isa. 2:4) *Mounce's Complete Expository Dictionary of Old & New Testament Words* offers the meaning "to reason together (in a legal case); to be vindicated; to rebuke, discipline, punish; decide, argue, defend, judge; to be chastened; to lodge a charge against."[198] God was commanding: "Come now, let us set things right" New American Bible (Revised Edition) (NABRE) or, "Let us set matters straight." (UASV) The NABRE has the following footnote on Isaiah 1:18, "**Let us set things right**: the Hebrew word refers to the arbitration of legal disputes (Job 23:7). God offers to settle his case with Israel on the basis of the change of behavior demanded above. For Israel it is a life or death choice; life in conformity with God's will or death for continued disobedience."

While this might appear to be an unnerving idea, we can appreciate that Jehovah is full of mercy and is always ready to forgive, who is a compassionate judge. There is no other with such a capacity for forgiveness. (Ps. 86:5; 103:12; Isa. 38:17; Mic. 7:19) It is only God, who could take the sins of Israel that was "like scarlet" and "make them white as snow." There was no amount of effort, or works, sacrifices, or prayers, which could have removed the stain of their sins. However, this act of mercy, loving kindness in forgiving their sins would have been on God's terms, which meant the Israelites would have had to evidence true, wholehearted repentance.

This truth is so paramount that Jehovah repeats it in poetic variation, "though [their sins] are red like crimson, they will become like wool." Jehovah wanted the Israelites to know that he is justly the Forgiver of sins, even ones that would seem unforgivable. However, for this to be the case, he needed to find them sincerely repentant. If today's reader doubts the level of God's forgiveness, they only need to look to the case of Manasseh. His sin was beyond all comprehension for years. He reestablished the high places for false worship, setting up altars to Baal; he offered his sons in a sacrifice to Molech, practiced magic, employed divination, and promoted spiritistic practices. Manasseh also put the graven image of the sacred pole

---

197 W. E. Vine, Merrill F. Unger and William White, Jr., vol. 1, Vine's Complete Expository Dictionary of Old and New Testament Words (Nashville, TN: T. Nelson, 1996), 203.

198 William D. Mounce, Mounce's Complete Expository Dictionary of Old & New Testament Words (Grand Rapids, MI: Zondervan, 2006), 949.

he had made into the house of Jehovah. Nevertheless, he came to God with a repentant heart and was forgiven. – 2 Chronicles 33:9-16.

Hard work to remove a deep stain from clothing is often pointless. Even with the most valiant effort, the stain is merely dulled but nevertheless visible. God wants each of his servants, even those who have committed very serious sins, to understand that it is not too late to "set matters straight." However, he also wants us to appreciate that our repentance needs to be genuine and from the heart. Returning to man as a whole, this is where the fault lies that leaves us out of harmony with, at odds to God's personality, standards, ways, and will. – See Ezekiel 18:25, 29-32.

Sin and imperfection entering creation have not prevented God from taking the initiative in opening the way for reconciliation. The father made this so through the Son. The apostle Paul writes, "**6** For while we were still helpless, at the right time Christ died for the ungodly. **7** For one will scarcely die for a righteous man; though perhaps for a good man one would dare even to die. **8** But God shows his love for us in that while we were still sinners, Christ died for us. **9** Much more then, having now been justified by his blood, we shall be saved from the wrath of God through him. **10** For if while we were enemies we were reconciled to God through the death of his Son, much more, having been reconciled, we shall be saved by his life. **11** Not only that, but we are also exulting in God through our Lord Jesus Christ, through whom we have now received the reconciliation." (Rom. 5:6-11) Elsewhere Paul writes, "All this is from God, who through Christ reconciled us to himself and gave us the ministry of reconciliation." "For our sake he made him to be sin who knew no sin, so that in him we might become the righteousness of God." – 2 Corinthians 5:18, 21.

Because of God's great love for his creation, humankind, Christians 'are ambassadors for Christ, God making his appeal through us. We implore you [all unbelievers in the world] on behalf of Christ, be reconciled to God." This does not mean that the Creator is somehow weak and beggarly, nor that he is soft on wrongdoing, but rather that his love is great and his mercy runs deep, hoping that offenders will escape the condemnation that awaits them. The prophet Ezekiel lets us know that the Father, has "no pleasure in the death of the wicked, but that the wicked turn from his way and live; turn back, turn back from your evil ways, for why will you die, O house of Israel?" (Eze. 33:11, ESV) Paul warned the Corinthians not to accept the mercy and grace of God and misunderstand its purpose. He said, "Working together with him, then, we appeal to you not to receive the grace of God in vain. For he says, 'In a favorable time I listened to you, and in a day of salvation I have helped you.' [Quote Isa. 49:8] Behold, now is the favorable time; behold, now is the day of salvation."

The Following three are needed, and none of the three can be missing.

(1) Knowledge

(2) Belief

(3) Obedience

To become a well-grounded Christian, one must

(1) Obtain a real, broad knowledge of Bible truth (1 Timothy 2:3-4),

(2) Put faith in the things we have learned (Hebrews 11:6),

(3) Repent of your sins (Acts 17:30-31), and

(4) Turn around in your course of life. (Acts 3:18-19);

(5) Then our love for God should move us to dedicate ourselves to Christ.

If one is missing the knowledge department, he cannot believe in something he has no real in-depth knowledge. Once we are reconciled, we are no longer an enemy under the wrath of God. Jesus said, "Truly, truly, I say to you, whoever hears my word and believes him who sent me has eternal life. He does not come into judgment, but has **passed from death to life**." (John 3:16; 5:24) The Father "is near to all who call on him, to all who call on him in truth." (Psa. 145:18, ESV) The apostle Paul exhorts, "the things which you have learned and received and heard about and seen in me, **practice these things**, **and** the God of peace will be with you." (Php 4:9, LEB) Paul also wrote, "he [Jesus] has now reconciled in his body of flesh by his death, in order to present you holy and blameless and above reproach before him, **if** indeed you **[Christians] continue in the faith**, stable and steadfast, **not shifting from** the hope of the gospel that you heard, which has been proclaimed in all creation under heaven, and of which I, Paul, became a minister." (Col. 1:22-23, ESV) Yes, once one has been reconciled to God, being declared righteous they must remain clean in every way.

How Was God In Christ Reconciling the World to Himself?

The apostle Paul said, "In Christ God was reconciling the world to himself, not counting their trespasses against them, and entrusting to us the message of reconciliation." (2 Cor. 5:19) We should not assume that this means that every human is automatically reconciled to God by Jesus' ransom sacrifice. Why? Because Paul's next words were, "we are ambassadors for Christ, **God making his appeal** through us. **We implore you** on behalf of Christ, **be reconciled** to God." (2 Cor. 5:20, ESV) The truth of the matter is, God has made available a *means* (Jesus' ransom) by which every human can willingly accept Christ, and, thus, gain reconciliation. Hence, "the Son of Man came not to be served but to serve, and to give his life as a ransom for many." (Matt. 20:28, ESV) Therefore, "whoever believes [trusts] in the Son has eternal life; whoever does not obey the Son shall not see life, but the wrath of God remains on him." – John 3:36; See also Romans 5:18-19; 2 Thessalonians 1:7-8.

Nevertheless, the Father purposed "to unite all things in him, things in heaven and things on earth." (Eph. 1:10, ESV) "Come now, let us set things right, says the [the Farther]: Though your sins be like scarlet, they may become white as snow; Though they be red like crimson, they may become white as wool." (Isa 1:18, ESV) The reality is, all, who refuse to "set things right," will face destruction, resulting in a renewed earth that will be in harmony with God. John said, "Then I saw a new heaven and a new earth, for the first heaven and the first earth, had passed away, and the sea was no more. And I saw the holy city, new Jerusalem, coming down out of heaven from God, prepared as a bride adorned for her husband. And I heard a loud voice from the throne saying, 'Behold, the dwelling place of God is with man. He will dwell with them, and they will be his people, and God himself will be with them as their God. He will wipe away every tear from their eyes, and death shall be no more, neither shall there be mourning, nor crying nor pain anymore, for the former things have passed away.'" The father will dwell with humanity after Armageddon representatively by means of The Son, Christ Jesus, who will rule over the earth. "When all things are subjected to him [Jesus], then the Son himself will also be subjected to him [the Father] who put all things in subjection under him [the Sone], that God [the Father] may be all in all." Thus, after the thousand-year reign of Christ over the earth, the Son will hand the kingdom over to the Father. – Revelation 21:1-4; 5:9-10; 1 Corinthians 15:28.

In speaking of the Jewish people being God's chosen people, Jesus said, "I tell you, the kingdom of God will be taken away from you and given to a people producing its fruits." (Matt. 21:43) A short time later, he said, "Jerusalem, Jerusalem, who kills the prophets and stones those who are sent to her! How often I wanted to gather your children together, the way a hen gathers her chicks under her wings, and you were unwilling. Paul said, "For if that first covenant had been faultless, there would have been no occasion to look for a second." (Heb. 8:7-13) Clearly, the apostle was referring to the fact that the Israelites had lost covenant relationship with the father because of 1,500 years of horrendous unfaithfulness. "For if their [the Jewish nation of Israel] rejection means the reconciliation of the world [outside of the Jewish people], what will their acceptance mean but life from the dead?" – Romans 11:15.

In other words, natural Israel lost its favored position as God's chosen people, and this was to be given to another. Who? This new nation proved to be a spiritual Israel, which the apostle Paul referred to as "the Israel of God." It would be made up of Jews, who accepted Jesus Christ and non-Jews. Entry into this "Israel of God" was not dependent on natural descent, but rather on one coming to "know you the only true God, and Jesus Christ whom you have sent." (John 17:3), In other words, it was a matter of 'trusting in Jesus Christ.' (John 3:16) Nevertheless, natural Israel was made up of 12 tribes, so James was simply drawing on the number 12, which carries the connotation of completeness. If a natural Jew or a non-Jew were to become a part of this spiritual Israel, the Israel of God, they would have to acknowledge, "Circumcision is a matter of the heart, by the Spirit, not by the letter." (Rom. 2:29) He must further understand "it depends on faith, in order that the promise may rest on grace and be guaranteed to all …" (Rom. 4:16) There are many verses, which qualify what it means to be a part of this Israel of God. – See also, Romans 4:17; 9:6-8; Galatians 3:7, 29; 4:21-31; Philippians 3:3.

Did this mean that no Jewish person could be a part of the Kingdom? Hardly! The first disciples of that Kingdom for seven years, 29 C.E. to 36 C.E. were only Jewish people. After 36 C.E., and the baptism of the first Gentile, Cornelius, anyone, including the Jews, could be a part of this Kingdom, as long as they accepted the King, Jesus Christ. Jesus said, "I am the way, and the truth, and the life. No one comes to the Father except through me." (John 14:6) At Jesus' Baptism, there was a voice from heaven saying, "This is my beloved Son, with whom I am well pleased." (Matt. 3:16-17) Jesus' teaching, miraculous signs, his ransom sacrifice and resurrection, established him as the truth, having the authority and power of the Father.[199] The Christians in the first century were given the position of being God's chosen people. (Acts 1:8; 2:1-4, 43) It would be through Jesus to the Christian congregation that the truth would now flow. As Paul told the Corinthians, "For to us God has revealed them through the Spirit. For the Spirit searches all things, even the depths of God." (1 Cor. 2:10) It happened just as Jesus had said it would, "I praise you, Father, Lord of heaven and earth, because you have hidden these things from the wise and intelligent, and have revealed them to young children." – Matthew 11:25

This "Israel of God" is not based on the requirements that Abraham had received from God, i.e., all males having to be circumcised. Instead, as was stated in Romans 3:26-29, are neither Jew nor Greek … for you are all one in Christ Jesus. And *if you belong to Christ, then you are Abraham's descendants*, heirs according to promise."

On the Israel of God, The College Press NIV Commentary, says, "The true Israel of God, the true descendants of Abraham, are those who have trusted Jesus for their salvation. Those physically born of Abraham are not necessarily his spiritual heirs (Rom 9:6–8). Instead, those who have put on Christ–whether Jew or Greek, slave or free, male or female–are Abraham's seed, heirs according to promise (Gal 3:27–29). Paul could write in a similar fashion to the Philippians that it is we Christians who are really the 'circumcision,' we who glory in Christ Jesus and put no confidence in the flesh (Phil 3:3)." (Boles 1993, Gal. 6:16)

---

[199] Matt. 15:30-31; 20:28; John 4:34; 5:19, 27, 30; 6:38, 40; 7:16-17; 17:1-2; Acts 2:22

CHAPTER 5 What the Bible Authors Really Meant by Sanctification

Harris Franklin Rall

Updated and Expanded by Edward D. Andrews

In dealing with the original language words, Vine says, *hagiasmos*, "sanctification," is used of (a) separation to God, 1 Cor. 1:30; 2 Thess. 2:13; 1 Pet. 1:2; (b) the course of life befitting those so separated, 1 Thess. 4:3, 4, 7; Rom. 6:19, 22; 1 Tim. 2:15; Heb. 12:14. "Sanctification is that relationship with God into which men enter by faith in Christ, Acts 26:18; 1 Cor. 6:11, and to which their sole title is the death of Christ, Eph. 5:25, 26; Col. 1:22; Heb. 10:10, 29; 13:12.

"Sanctification is also used in NT of the separation of the believer from evil things and ways. This sanctification is God's will for the believer, 1 Thess. 4:3, and His purpose in calling him by the gospel, v. 7; it must be learned from God, v. 4, as He teaches it by His Word, John 17:17, 19, cf. Ps. 17:4; 119:9, and it must be pursued by the believer, earnestly and undeviatingly, 1 Tim. 2:15; Heb. 12:14. For the holy character, *hagiosune,* 1 Thess. 3:13, is not vicarious, i.e., it cannot be transferred or imputed, it is an individual possession, built up, little by little, as the result of obedience to the Word of God, and of following the example of Christ, Matt. 11:29; John 13:15; Eph. 4:20; Phil. 2:5, in the power of the Holy Spirit, Rom. 8:13; Eph. 3:16.

"The Holy Spirit is the Agent in sanctification, Rom. 15:16; 2 Thess. 2:13; 1 Pet. 1:2; cf. 1 Cor. 6:11.... The sanctification of the Spirit is associated with the choice, or election, of God; it is a Divine act preceding the acceptance of the Gospel by the individual."

Hagiazo, "to sanctify," "is used of (a) the gold adorning the Temple and of the gift laid on the altar, Matt. 23:17, 19; (b) food, 1 Tim. 4:5; (c) the unbelieving spouse of a believer, 1 Cor. 7:14; (d) the ceremonial cleansing of the Israelites, Heb. 9:13; (e) the Father's Name, Luke 11:2; (f) the consecration of the Son by the Father, John 10:36; (g) the Lord Jesus devoting Himself to the redemption of His people, John 17:19; (h) the setting apart of the believer for God, Acts 20:32; cf. Rom. 15:16; (i) the effect on the believer of the Death of Christ, Heb. 10:10, said of God, and 2:11; 13:12, said of the Lord Jesus; (j) the separation of the believer from the world in his behavior— by the Father through the Word, John 17:17, 19; (k) the believer who turns away from such things as dishonor God and His gospel, 2 Tim. 2:21; (l) the acknowledgment of the Lordship of Christ, 1 Pet. 3:15.

"Since every believer is sanctified in Christ Jesus, 1 Cor. 1:2, cf. Heb. 10:10, a common NT designation of all believers is 'saints,' *hagioi*, i.e., 'sanctified' or 'holy ones.' Thus sainthood, or sanctification, is not an attainment, it is the state into which

God, in grace, calls sinful men, and in which they begin their course as Christians, Col. 3:12; Heb. 3:1." (Vine 1996, Volume 2, Page 546)

Sanctification is the 'act or process of making holy, separating, or setting apart for the service or use of Jehovah God; the state of being holy, sanctified, or purified.' The Hebrew word *qadosh* and the Greek word *hagios*, rendered "holy," "hallowed," "sanctified," "made sacred," and "set apart," and are applied to certain times which were hallowed, such as the Sabbath and the Hebrew festivals. (Ex. 20:8, 11)[200] The Hebrew *qadosh* and Greek *hagios* are also applied to the things said to be holy, sanctified, such as the sacred incense or perfume (Ex 30:36; Matt. 7:6), as well as the sacred vestments (Ex 28:2,4), the sacred utensils (Ex 30:29; 2 Tim. 2:21), the holy bread (Lev. 21:22; 1 Sam. 21:5), the altar (Ex 29:37; Matt. 23:19), and portions of the sacrifices. – Leviticus 2:3, 10.

So, also, of places said to be holly (Ex. 3:5; Ac 7:33), as the holy city, i.e. Jerusalem (Neh. 11:1; Isa 48:2; Mt 4:5),[201] the holy mountain, i.e. Zion (Ps 2:6), the Tabernacle (Nu 18:10); the Temple (Ps 138:2), the most holy place, the oracle (Ex 26:33; Ex 28:43; Heb. 9:2-3,12; 1Ki 6:16; 1Ki 8:6; Eze 41:23). So, also, men are said to be holy, such as Aaron and his sons (1Ch 23:13; 1Ch 24:5; Isa 43:28), the firstborn (Ex 13:2), and the Hebrew people (Ex 19:10,14; Da 12), also the pious Hebrews, the "holy ones" (Deut. 33:3; Ps 16:3; Da 7:18), like the word חָסִיד, rendered "saint" (Ps 30:4; Ps 31:23; Ps 37:28; Ps 1; Ps 5; Ps 52:9; Ps 79:2; Ps 97:10), and "godly" (Ps 4:3).

The terms are also used of those who were ceremonially purified under the Mosaic law (Nu 6:11; Le 22:16, 32; Heb. 9:13). However, though the external purifications of the Hebrews, when any one had transgressed, had to do with restoration to civil and national privileges, they did not necessarily induce moral and spiritual holiness. They, however, reminded the sincere Hebrew that he was unclean in the sight of God; and that the ceremonial cleansings, by which he had been restored to his civil and political rights, were symbols of those "good things that were to come," spiritual and eternal salvation, which should accrue through the sprinkling of the blood of Christ and the gift of the Holy Spirit. He was thus assured that "without holiness no man shall see the Lord" (Heb. 9:14; Heb. 12:14). Hence, sanctification is used to designate that state of mind induced by the indwelling of the Holy Spirit, thus producing internal and external holiness (John 3:5; 1Co 6:11; Eph. 5:26; 1 Th 4:3-4,7). It is true, sanctification is sometimes spoken of as the work of man himself (Ex 19:22; Le 11:44; Le 20:7-8; 1Pe 3:15). When a person solemnly and unreservedly gives himself to God, he then may be said to sanctify himself. He is then enabled to believe in Christ with his heart unto righteousness, and God instantly, by the communication of his Holy Spirit, sanctifies the believer. Thus the believer gives himself to God, and God, in return, gives himself to the believer (Eze 36:25-29; 1 Cor. 3:16-17; 1 Cor. 6:19; 2 Cor. 6:16-18; Eph. 2:22). This sanctification, which is received by faith, is the work of God within us.

---

200 See also Gen. 2-3; Lev. 23:37; 2 Ki 10:20

201 See also Mt 24:15; Mt 27:53; Ac 6:13; Ac 22:28

In a general sense, "sanctification" encompasses the entire Christian life (Gal. 5:22-23; 1 Pet. 1:15-16, 22; Heb. 12:10; Jam. 4:8). In 1 Thess. 5:23, the apostle prays for the sanctification of the entire congregation in all its various departments. In 1 Cor. 7:14, it is said, the unbelieving husband, or wife, is "sanctified," that is, to be regarded not as unclean, but as specially claiming the attention of the Christian community. The term "sanctified" is also used in the sense of expiation – Hebrews 10:10, 14, and 29.

The Formal Sense

By sanctification is ordinarily meant that hallowing of the Christian believer by which he is freed from sin and enabled to realize the will of God in his life. This is not, however, the first or common meaning in the Scriptures. To sanctify means commonly to make holy, that is, to separate from the world and consecrate to God.

In the Old Testament

To understand this primary meaning we must go back to the word "holy" in the Old Testament. That is holy which belongs to Jehovah. There is nothing implied here as to moral character. It may refer to days and seasons, to places, to objects used for worship, or to persons. Exactly the same usage is shown with the word "sanctify." To sanctify anything is to declare it as belonging to God. "Sanctify unto me all the firstborn .... it is mine" (Ex. 13:2; compare Nu 3:13; 8:17). It applies thus to all that is connected with worship, to the Levites (Num. 3:12), the priests and the tent of meeting (Ex. 29:44), the altar and all that touches it (Ex 29:36 f), and the offering (Ex. 29:27; compare Eccles. 7:29). The feast and holy days are to be sanctified, that is, set apart from ordinary business as belonging to Jehovah (the Sabbath, Ne 13:19-22; a fast, Joe 1:14). Therefore, the nation as a whole is sanctified when Jehovah acknowledges it and receives it as His own, "a kingdom of priests, and a holy nation" (Ex 19:5-6). A man may thus sanctify his house or his field (Lev. 27:14, 16), but not the firstling of the flock, for this is already belongs to Jehovah. – Leviticus 27:26.

It is this formal usage without the moral implication that explains such a passage as Gen. 38:21. The word translated "prostitute" here is from the same root *qadhash*, meaning literally, as elsewhere, the sanctified or consecrated one (*qedheshah*; see margin and compare Deut. 23:18; 1 Ki 14:24; Hos. 4:14). It is the hierodule, the familiar figure of the old pagan temple, the sacred slave consecrated to the temple and the deity for immoral purposes. The practice is protested against in Israel (Deut. 23:17 f), but the use of the term illustrates clearly the absence of anything essentially ethical in its primary meaning (also compare 2 Ki 10:20, " And Jehu ordered, 'Sanctify a solemn assembly for Baal.' So they proclaimed it." – compare Joe 1:14.

Very suggestive is the transitive use of the word in the phrase, "to sanctify Jehovah." To understand this we must note the use of the word "holy" as applied to Jehovah in the Old Testament. Its meaning is not primarily ethical. Jehovah's holiness is His supremacy, His sovereignty, His glory, His essential being as God. To say the Holy One is simply to say God. Jehovah's holiness is seen in His might; His manifested glory; it is that before which peoples tremble, which makes the nations dread (Ex. 15:11-18; compare 1 Sam. 6:20; Ps 68:35; 89:7; 99:2-3). Significant is the way in which "jealous" and "holy" are almost identified (Jos 24:19; Eze. 38:23). It is God asserting His supremacy, His unique claim. To sanctify Jehovah, therefore, to make Him holy, is to assert or acknowledge or bring forth His being as God, His supreme power and glory, His sovereign claim. Ezekiel brings this out most clearly. Jehovah has been profaned in the eyes of the nations through Israel's defeat and captivity. True, it was because of Israel's sins, but the nations thought it was because of Jehovah's weakness. The ethical is not wanting in these passages. The people are to be separated from their sins and given a new heart (Eze. 36:25-26,33). However, the word "sanctify" is not used for this. It is applied to Jehovah, and it means the assertion of Jehovah's power in Israel's triumph and the conquest of her foes (Eze. 20:41; 28:25; 36:23; 38:16; 39:27). The sanctification of Jehovah is thus the assertion of His being and power as God, just as the sanctification of a person or object is the assertion of Jehovah's right and claim in the same.

The story of the waters of Meribah illustrates the same meaning. Moses' failure to sanctify Jehovah is his failure to declare Jehovah's glory and power in the miracle of the waters (Num. 20:12-13; 27:14; De 32:51). The story of Nadab and Abihu points the same way. Here "I will be sanctified" is the same as "I will be glorified" (Le 10:1-3). Not essentially different is the usage in Isa 5:16: "Jehovah of hosts is exalted in justice, and God the Holy One is sanctified in righteousness." Holiness again is the exaltedness of God, His supremacy, which is seen here in the judgment (justice, righteousness) meted out to the disobedient people (compare the recurrent refrain of Isa 5:25; 9:12, 17, 21; 10:4). Isaiah 8:13; 29:23 suggest the same idea by the way, in which they relate, "sanctify" to fear and awe. One New Testament passage brings us the same meaning (1 Pet. 3:15): "Sanctify in your hearts Christ as Lord," that is exalt Him as supreme.

In the New Testament

In a few New Testament passages, the Old Testament ritual sense reappears, as when Jesus speaks of the temple sanctifying the gold, and the altar the gift (Matt. 23:17,19; also compare Heb. 9:13; 1 Tim. 4:5). The prevailing meaning is that which we found in the Old Testament. To sanctify is to consecrate or set apart. We may first take the few passages in the Fourth Gospel. As applied to Jesus in John 10:36; 17:19, sanctify cannot mean to make holy in the ethical sense. As the whole context shows, it means to consecrate for His mission in the world. The reference to the disciples, "that they themselves also may be sanctified in truth," has both meanings: that they may be set apart, (for Jesus sends them, as the Father sends Him), and that they may be made holy in truth.

This same meaning of consecration, or separation, appears when we study the word saint, which is the same as "sanctified one." Aside from its use in the Psalms, the word is found mainly in the New Testament. Outside the Gospels, where the term "disciples" is used, it is the common word to designate the followers of Jesus, occurring some 56 times. By "saint" is not meant the morally perfect, but the one who belongs to Christ, just as the sanctified priest or offering belonged to Jehovah. Thus Paul can salute the disciples at Corinth as saints, and a little later rebuke them as carnal and babes, as those among whom are jealousy and strife, who walk after the manner of men (1Co 1:2; 3:1-3). In the same way the phrase "the sanctified" or "those that are sanctified" is used to designate the believers. By "the inheritance among all them that are sanctified" is meant the heritage of the Christian believer (Ac 20:32; 26:18; compare 1Co 1:2; 6:11; Eph. 1:18; Col 1:12).

This is the meaning in Hebrews, which speaks of the believer as being sanctified by the blood of Christ. In 10:29 the writer speaks of one who has fallen away, who "hath counted the blood of the covenant wherewith he was sanctified an unholy thing." Evidently, it is not the inner and personal holiness of this apostate that is referred to, especially in view of the tense, but that he had been separated unto God by this sacrificial blood and had then counted the holy offering a common thing. The contrast is between sacred and common, not between moral perfection and sin (compare 10:10; 13:12). The formal meaning appears again in 1 Corinthians 7:12-14, where the unbelieving husband is said to be sanctified by the wife, and vice versa. It is not moral character that is meant here, but a certain separation from the profane and unclean and a certain relation to God. This is made plain by the reference to the children: "Else were your children unclean, but now are they holy." The formal sense is less certain in other instances where we have the thought of sanctification in or by the Holy Spirit or in Christ; as in Romans 15:16, "being sanctified by the Holy Spirit;" 1 Corinthians 1:2, to "them that are sanctified in Christ Jesus;" 1 Peter 1:2, "in sanctification of the Spirit." Paul's doctrine of the Spirit as the new life in us seems to enter in here, and yet the reference to 1 Corinthians suggests that the primary meaning is still that of setting apart, the relating to God.

The Ethical Sense

We have been considering so far what has been called the formal meaning of the word; but the chief interest of Christian thought lies in the ethical idea, sanctification considered as the active deed or process by which the life is made holy.

Transformation of Formal to Ethical Idea

Our first question is, "How does the idea of belonging to God become the idea of transformation of life and character?" The change is, indeed, nothing less than a part of the whole movement for which the entire Scriptures stand as a monument. The ethical is not wanting at the beginning, but the supremacy of the moral and spiritual over against the formal, the ritual, the ceremonial, the national, is the clear direction in which the movement as a whole tends. Now the pivot of this movement is the conception of God. As the thought of God grows more ethical, more spiritual, it molds and changes all other conceptions. Thus, what it means to belong to God (holiness, sanctification) depends upon the nature of the God to whom man belongs. The hierodules of Corinth are women of shame because of the nature of the goddess to whose temple they belong. The prophets caught a vision of Jehovah, not jealous for His prerogative, not craving the honor of punctilious and proper ceremonial, but with a gracious love for His people and a passion for righteousness. Their great message is: This now is Jehovah; hear what it means to belong to such a God and to serve Him. "What unto me is the multitude of your sacrifices? ... Wash you, make you clean; ... seek justice, relieve the oppressed" (Isa. 1:11, 16-17). "When Israel was a child, then I loved him ... I desire goodness, and not sacrifice; and the knowledge of God more than bunt-offerings" (Ho 11:1; 6:6).

In this way, the formal idea that we have been considering becomes charged with moral meaning. To belong to God, to be His servant, His son, is no mere external matter. Jesus' teaching as to sonship is in point here. The word "sanctification" does not occur in the Synoptic Gospels at all, but "sonship" with the Jews expressed this same relation of belonging. For them, it meant a certain obedience on the one hand, a privilege on the other. Jesus declares that belonging to God means likeness to Him, sonship is sharing His spirit of loving good will (Matt. 5:43-48). Brother and sister for Jesus are those who do God's will (Mark 3:35). Paul takes up the same thought, but joins it definitely to the words holy one" (saint) and "sanctify." The religious means the ethical, those "sanctified in Christ Jesus, called to be holy ones together with all those who in every place call upon the name of our Lord Jesus Christ ..." (1 Cor. 1:2) The significant latter phrase is the same as in Romans 1:1, "Paul, a bond-servant of Christ Jesus, called as an apostle, **set apart** for the gospel of God." In this light, we read Ephesians 4:1, "walk in a manner worthy of the calling to which you have been called." (Compare 1 Thess. 2:12; Php 1:27) In addition, the end of this calling is that we are "foreordained ["predestinated," KJV, ESV, NASB][202] to be patterned after the image of his Son so that he might be the firstborn among many brothers." (Rom. 8:29) We must not limit ourselves to the words holy one ("saint") or "sanctify" to get this teaching with Paul. It is his constant and compelling moral appeal: You belong to Christ; live with Him, live unto Him. (Col 3:1-4; 1 Thess. 5:10) It is no formal belonging, no external surrender. It is the yielding of the life in its passions and purposes, in its deepest affections and highest powers, to be ruled by a new spirit. – Ephesians 4:13, 10, 23-24, and 32; compare Romans 12:1.

Our Relation to God as Personal: New Testament Idea

However, we do not get the full meaning of this thought of sanctification as consecration, or belonging, until we grasp the New Testament thought of our relation to God as personal. The danger has always been that this consecration should be thought of in a negative or passive way. Now the Christian's surrender is not to an outer authority but to an inner, living fellowship. The sanctified life is thus a life of personal fellowship lived out with the Father in the spirit of Christ in loving trust and obedient service. This positive and significant meaning of sanctification dominates Paul's thought. He speaks of living to God, of living to the Lord, and most expressively of all, of being alive unto God. (Rom 14:8; Rom 6:13; Gal. 2:19) So

202 Yet, to these same ones, 2 Peter 1:10 says: "brothers, be all the more diligent to make certain about His calling and choosing you; for as long as you practice these things, you will never fail." (If the individuals were predestinated to salvation, they could not possibly fail, regardless of what they did.

completely is his life filled by the fellowship that he can say, "It is no longer I who live, but Christ who lives in me." (Gal. 2:20). However, there is no Christian mysticism here. It is a very rich and active life, this life of fellowship to which we are surrendered. It is a life of sonship in trust and love, with the spirit that enables us to say "Abba, Father" (Ro 8:15; Ga 4:6). It is a life of unconquerable kindness and good will (Matt. 5:43-48). It is a life of "faith working through love" (Gal. 5:6); it is having the mind of Christ. (Php 2:5) The sanctified life, then, is the life so fully surrendered to fellowship with Christ day by day that His spirit rules the inner spirit and outward expression.

Sanctification as God's Gift

We come now to that aspect which is central for Christian interest, sanctification as the making holy of life, not by our act, but by God's deed and by God's gift. If holiness represents the state of heart and life in conformity with God's will, then sanctification is the deed or process by which that state is wrought. In addition, this deed we are to consider now as the work of God. Jesus prays that the Father may sanctify His disciples in truth. (John 17:17) So Paul prays for the Thessalonians (1 Thess. 5:23), and declares that Christ is to sanctify His congregation. (Compare Rom. 6:22; 2 Thess. 2:13; 2 Tim. 2:21; 1 Pet. 1:2) Here sanctification means to make clean or holy in the ethical sense, though the idea of consecration is not necessarily lacking. However, aside from special passages, we must take into account the whole New Testament teaching, according to which every part of the Christian life is the gift of God and wrought by His Spirit. "it is God who works in you, both to will and to work for his good pleasure." (Php 2:13; compare Rom. 8:2-4, 9, 14, 16-26; Gal. 5:22f) Significant is the use of the words "new creature" (Gr. *Ktisis*, "creation," ESV, LEB, HCSB) and "workmanship" with Paul (2 Cor. 5:17; Gal. 6:15; Eph. 2:10; 4:24). To be "in" or "in union with" Christ here means to enjoy a oneness with him as a member of his body, his bride. (John 17:21; 1 Cor. 12:27) For this relationship to come into existence, Jehovah God draws the individual to his Son and begets such a one with Holy Spirit.

2 Corinthians 5:17 Updated American Standard Version (UASV)

17 Therefore if anyone is in Christ, he is a **new creation**; the old things have passed away; behold, new things have come.

Galatians 6:15 Updated American Standard Version (UASV)

15 For neither circumcision counts for anything, nor uncircumcision, but a **new creation**.

Ephesians 2:10 Updated American Standard Version (UASV)

10 For we are his **workmanship**, created in Christ Jesus for good works, which God prepared beforehand so that we would walk in them.

Ephesians 4:24 Updated American Standard Version (UASV)

24 and put on the **new man**,[203] the one created according to the likeness of God in righteousness and loyalty of the truth.

Questions of Time and Method

When we ask, however, when and how this work is produced or brought about, there is no such clear answer. What we have on the one hand is an uncompromising ideal and demand, and on the other absolute confidence in God. By adding to these two the evident fact that the Christian believers seen in the New Testament are far from the attainment of such Christian perfection, some writers have assumed to have the foundation here for the doctrine that the state of complete holiness of life is a special experience in the Christian life wrought in a definite moment of time. It is well to realize that no New Testament passages give a specific answer to these questions of time and method, and that our conclusions must be drawn from the general teaching of the New Testament as to the Christian life.

An Element in All Christian Life

First, it must be noted that in the New Testament view sanctification in the ethical sense is an essential element and inevitable result of all Christian life and experience. Looked at from the religious point of view, it follows from the doctrine of regeneration. Regeneration is the implanting of a new life in man. So far as that is a new life from God it is ipso facto holy. The doctrine of the Holy Spirit teaches the same. There is no Christian life, from the very beginning, who is not the work of the Spirit. "No one can say 'Jesus is Lord' except in the Holy Spirit." (1 Cor. 12:3). Nevertheless, this Spirit is the Holy Spirit, whether with Paul we say Spirit of Christ or Spirit of God. (Rom. 8:9) His presence, therefore, in so far forth means holiness of life. From the ethical standpoint, the same thing is constantly declared. Jesus builds here upon the prophets: no religion without righteousness; clean hands, pure hearts, deeds of mercy are not mere conditions of worship but joined to humble hearts are themselves the worship that God desires. (Amos 5:21-25; Mic 6:6-8). Jesus deepened the conception, but did not, change it, and Paul was true to this succession. "You, however, are not in the flesh but in the Spirit, if in fact the Spirit of God dwells in you. Anyone who does not have the Spirit of Christ does not belong to him. But if Christ is in you, although the body is dead because of sin, the Spirit is life because of righteousness." (Rom 8:9-10) There is nothing in Paul's teaching to suggest that sanctification is the special event of a unique experience, or that there are two kinds or qualities of sanctification. All Christian living meant for him clean, pure, right living, and that was sanctification. The simple, practical way in which he attacks the bane of sexual impurity in his pagan congregations shows this. "For this is the will of God, your sanctification: that you abstain from sexual immorality; that each one of you know how to control his own body in holiness and honor. For God has not called us for impurity, but in holiness." (1 Thess. 4:3-4, 7) The strength of Paul's

203 An interpretive translation would have, "put on the new person," because it does mean male or female.

teaching, indeed, lies here in this combination of moral earnestness with absolute dependence upon God.

Follows from Fellowship with God

The second general conclusion that we draw from the New Testament teaching as to the Christian life is this: the sanctification, which is a part of all Christian living, follows from the very nature of that life as fellowship with God. Fundamental here is the fact that the Christian life is personal, that nothing belongs in it, which cannot be stated in personal terms. It is a life with God in which He graciously gives Himself to us, and which we live out with Him and with our brothers in the spirit of Christ, which is His Spirit. The two great facts as to this fellowship are, that it is God's gift, and that its fruit is holiness. First, it is God's gift. What God gives us is nothing less than Himself. The gift is not primarily forgiveness, nor victory over sin, nor peace of soul, nor hope of heaven. It is fellowship with Him, which includes all of these and without which none of these can be. Secondly, the fruit of this fellowship is holiness. The real hallowing of our life can come in no other way. For Christian holiness is personal, not something formal or ritual, and its source and power can be nothing lower than the personal. Such is the fellowship into which God graciously lifts the believer. Whatever its mystical aspects, that fellowship is not magical or sacramental. It is ethical through and through. Its condition on our side is ethical. For Christian faith is the moral surrender of our life to Him in whom truth and right come to us with authority to command. The meaning of that surrender is ethical; it is opening the life to definite moral realities and powers, to love, meekness, gentleness, humility, reverence, purity, the passion for righteousness, to that which words cannot analyze but which we know as the Spirit of Christ. Such a fellowship is the supreme moral force for the molding of life. An intimate human fellowship is an analog of this, and we know with what power it works on life and character. It cannot, however, set forth either the intimacy or the power of this supreme and final relation where our Friend is not another but is our real self. So much we know: this fellowship means a new spirit in us, a renewed and daily renewing life.

It is noteworthy that Paul has no hard-and-fast forms for this life. The reality was too rich and great, and his example should teach us caution in the insistence upon theological forms, which may serve to compress the truth instead of expressing it. Here are some of his expressions for this life in us: to "have the mind of Christ" (1 Cor. 2:16; Php 2:5), "the Spirit of Christ" (Rom. 8:9), "Christ is in you" (Rom. 8:10), "the spirit which is from God" (1 Cor. 2:12), "the Spirit of God" (1 Cor. 3:16), "the Holy Spirit" (1 Cor. 6:19), "the Spirit of the Lord" (2 Cor. 3:17), and "the Lord the Spirit." (2 Cor. 3:18) But in all this one fact stands out, this life is personal, a new spirit in us, and that spirit is one that we have in personal fellowship with God; it is His Spirit. Especially significant is the way in which Paul relates this new life to Christ. We have already noted that Paul uses indifferently "Spirit of God" and "Spirit of Christ," and that in the same passage. (Rom. 8:9) Paul's great contribution to the doctrine of the Holy Spirit lies here. As he states it in 2 Corinthians 3:17, "Now the Lord is the Spirit, and where the Spirit of the Lord is, there is freedom." With that, the whole conception of the Spirit gains moral content and personal character. The Spirit is personal, not something, nor some strange and magical power. The Spirit is ethical; there is a definite moral quality, which is, expressed when we say Christ. He has the Spirit who has the qualities of Christ. Thus, the presence of the Spirit is not evidenced in the unusual, the miraculous, the ecstatic utterance of the enthusiast, or some strange deed of power, but in the workaday qualities of kindness, goodness, love, loyalty, patience, self-restraint (Gal. 5:22 f). With this identification of the Spirit and the Christ in mind, we can better understand the passages in which Paul brings out the relation of Christ to the sanctification of the believer. He is the goal (Rom. 8:29). We are to grow up in Him. (Eph. 4:15) He is to be formed in us (Gal. 4:19). We are to behold Him and be changed into His image (2Co 3:17 f). This deepens into Paul's thought of the mystical relation with Christ. The Christian dies to sin with Him that he may live with Him a new life. Christ is now his real life. He dwells in Christ, Christ dwells in him. He has Christ's thoughts, His mind. – See Romans 6:3-11; 8:9-10; 1 Corinthians 2:16; 15:22; and Galatians 2:20.

This vital and positive conception of the sanctification of the believer must be asserted against some popular interpretations. The symbols of fire and water, as suggesting cleansing, have sometimes been made the basis for a whole superstructure of doctrine. (For the former, note Isa 6:6 f; Lu 3:16; Ac 2:3; for the latter, Ac 2:38; 22:16; 1Co 6:11; Eph. 5:26; Tit 3:5; Heb. 10:22; Re 1:5; 7:14.) There is a two-fold danger here, from which these writers have not escaped. The symbols suggest cleansing, and their over-emphasis has meant first a negative and narrow idea of sanctification as primarily separation from sin or defilement. This is a falling back to certain Old Testament levels. Secondly, these material symbols have been literalized, and the result has been a sort of mechanical or magical conception of the work of the Spirit. But the soul is not a substance for mechanical action, however, sublimated. It is personal life that is to be hallowed, thought, affections, motives, desires, will, and only a personal agent through personal fellowship can work this end.

The Process of Sanctification

If one is to be sanctified as a disciple of Jesus Christ, a process or procedure must be followed. Using the word *sanctify* in the sense of the disciple being *purified* or *cleansed* from his or her sin in the eyes of God, the apostle Paul wrote, "For if the blood of goats and bulls, and the sprinkling of defiled persons with the ashes of a heifer, sanctify for the purification of the flesh, how much more will the blood of Christ, who through the eternal Spirit offered himself without blemish to God, purify our conscience from dead works to serve the living God." – Hebrews 9:13-14.

"The blood of Christ" signifies the value of his perfect human life. It is that person's faith, in that ransom sacrifice, which *cleanses* or *purifies* them from the guilt of sin. This is an actual removal of sin and guilt, a purifying of the believer takes place in the sight of God, in which they are justified/declared righteous and all condemnation is removed from them, leaving them with a clean conscience. (Rom. 8:1, 30) These are referred to as *hagioi*, i.e., "holy ones," "saints" (KJV, ASV, ESV, and NASB), namely, sanctified to God. (Eph. 2:19; Col 1:12) In Acts 20:32, they are referred to as "the ones having been sanctified (Gr *tois hegiasmenois*).

Thus, the process or procedure is as follows. Jesus said, "No one can come to me unless **the Father** who sent me **draws him**. And I will raise him up on the last day.' (John 6:44) Jesus later says to the Father is payer, "**Sanctify them** in the truth; your word is truth." (John 17:17, ESV) The apostle Paul wrote of the holy ones, "But we ought always to give thanks to God for you, brothers beloved by the Lord, because **God chose you** as the firstfruits to be saved, through sanctification by the Spirit and belief in the truth." (2 Thess. 2:13, ESV) Once selected by the Father, Paul says of such ones, "And such were some of you [unrighteous that is]. But you were washed, you were sanctified, you were justified in the name of the Lord Jesus Christ and by the Spirit of our God." (1 Cor. 6:11, ESV) Christ accordingly becomes to them "wisdom from God, righteousness and sanctification and redemption," release by ransom sacrifice. (1 Cor. 1:30, ESV) Elsewhere Paul writes of these, "For the One [Christ] who sanctifies and those who are sanctified all have one Father. That is why Jesus is not ashamed to call them brothers." (Heb. 2:11, HCSB) These become sons of God, children of God, fellow heirs with Christ, who are born of water and the Spirit. – Romans 8:14-17; John 3:5, 8.

Must Be Maintained

Now, the sanctification is not just the Father drawing these ones, sanctifying them in the word and truth, sanctifying them (cleansing and purifying), and declaring them righteous. Part of the process of sanctification comes from the one that the Father is drawing into the process. First, he must accept being drawn in, as he can reject the Father and the Son. Second, the sanctification must be maintained, which means the believer has a part in this process as well, i.e., accepting and maintaining his pure and clean state. In other words, after being declared righteous, he can lose his sanctification by falling back into unrighteous ways or he can hold on to it. Paul tells us in Hebrews 10:14, "For by a single offering he has perfected for all time those who are being sanctified." However, in that same chapter, verses 26-27 (ESV), "For if we [i.e., "holy ones" "saints"] go on sinning deliberately after receiving the knowledge of the truth, there no longer remains a sacrifice for sins, but a fearful expectation of judgment, and a fury of fire that will consume the adversaries." Paul, in speaking of these hole ones, said, "God has not called us for impurity, but in holiness." – 1 Thessalonians 4:3-4, 7.

God's Word and the Spirit

The Word of God plays a major role in sanctification, which must be correctly understood and obeyed, if sanctification is to take place and is to be maintained. (Ac 20:32) These holy ones or "saints," "were chosen according to the purpose of God the Father and were made a holy people by his Spirit, to obey Jesus Christ and be purified by his blood." (1 Pet. 1:2, GNT) It is the guidance of the Holy Spirit that makes it possible for these ones to be sanctified, cleanse, purified, declared righteous, acceptable in the eyes of God. (Eph. 4:30; 1Th 4:8; 5:19) The guidance of the Holy

Spirit is not some mystical direction from within the believer, but rather an understanding and heeding the Spirit inspired, inerrant Word of God. – 1 Timothy 3:16; 2 Peter 1:21.

Sanctification as Man's Task

That conclusion we can reach only as we go back again to the fundamental principle of the personal character of the Christian life and the relation thus given between the ethical and the religious. All Christian life is gift and task alike. Paul tells Christians that they need to "work out your own salvation with fear and trembling ... for it is God who works in you." (Php 2:12 f, ESV) All is from God; we can only live what God gives. However, there is a converse to this: only as we live it out can God give to us the life. This appears in Paul's teaching as to sanctification. It is not only God's gift but also our task. "this is the will of God, your sanctification: that you abstain from sexual immorality. [That is lead a clean and pur life]" (1 Thess. 4:3) God's servants must we be clean in every way. God's servants must be spiritually clean, morally clean, mentally clean, end even physically clean. Paul said, "Having therefore these promises ... let us cleanse ourselves from all defilement of flesh and spirit, perfecting holiness (*hagiosune*) in the fear of God." (2 Cor. 7:1) Significant is Paul's use of the word "walk." We are to "walk in newness of life," "by (or in) the Spirit," "in love," and "in Christ Jesus the Lord." (Rom. 6:4; Gal. 5:16; Eph. 5:2; Col 2:6) The gift in each case becomes the task and indeed becomes real and effective only in this activity.

It is only as we walk by the Spirit that this becomes powerful in overcoming the lusts of the flesh (Gal. 5:16; compare Gal. 5:25). However, the ethical is the task that ends only with life. If God gives only as we live, then He cannot give all at once. Sanctification is then the matter of a life and not of a moment. The life may be consecrated in a moment; the right relation to God assumed, and the man stands in saving fellowship with Him. The life is thus made holy in principle. However, the real making holy is co-extensive with the whole life of man. It is nothing less than the constant in the forming of the life of the inner spirit and outer deed with the Spirit of Christ until we, "speaking truth in love, may grow up in all things into him, who is the head." (Eph. 4:15) Read also Rom. 6:1-23; that the Christian is dead to sin is not some fixed static fact, but is true only as he refuses the lower and yields his members to a higher obedience. Note that in 1 Corinthians 5:7 Paul in the same verse declares "Cleanse out the old leaven that you may be a new lump as you really are unleavened. For Christ, our Passover lamb has been sacrificed." – Compare also 1 Thessalonians 5:5-10.

We may sum up as follows: The word "sanctify" is used with two broad meanings: (1) The first is to devote, to consecrate to God, to recognize as holy, that is, as belonging to God. This is the regular Old Testament usage and is most common in the New Testament. The prophets showed that this belonging to Jehovah demanded righteousness. The New Testament deepens this into a whole-hearted surrender to the fellowship of God and to the rule of His Spirit. (2) Though the word itself appears in but few passages with this sense, the New Testament is full of the thought of the making holy of the Christian's life by the Spirit of God in that fellowship into which God lifts us by His grace and in which He gives Himself to us. This sanctifying, or hallowing, is not mechanical or magical. It is wrought out by God's Spirit in a daily fellowship to which man gives himself in aspiration and trust and obedience, receiving with open heart, living out in obedient life. It is not negative, the mere separation from sin, but the progressive hallowing of a life that constantly grows in capacity, as in character, into the stature of full manhood as it is in Christ. And from this, it's very nature it is not momentary, but the deed and the privilege of a whole life.

CHAPTER 6 What the Bible Authors Really Meant By Salvation

A price paid to buy back or to bring about the release from some obligation or undesirable circumstance. A ransom is a sum of money or a price demanded or paid to secure the freedom of a slave. The basic idea of "ransom" is the act of saving somebody from an oppressed condition or dangerous situation through self-sacrifice, such as a price that *covers* or satisfies justice, while the term "redemption" is the *deliverance* that results from the ransom. In the biblical instance, "redemption" would be the *deliverance* from Adamic sin (the sins of humanity) by the ransom death of Jesus Christ for many.

Below we will consider various Hebrew terms (*kāpar, koper, pādâ, gāʾal*), as well as a number of Greek terms (*lytron, antilytron, lytroo, agorazo*), which are translated "ransom and "redeem." They all carry the idea of a price being given or paid to result in a ransom or redemption. As we will see below, there is the sense of an equal or corresponding, that is, a substitution is common in all of these terms. In other words, the ransom sacrifice of Jesus Christ, for example, was given for Adam, which satisfied justice and set matters straight between God and man.

For our Hebrew terms, we will use the Theological Word Book of the Old Testament (TWOT) extensively. "(*kāpar*) **I, *make an atonement, make reconciliation, purge*.** (Denominative verb.) This root should probably be distinguished from *kāpar* II "to smear with pitch." ... The root *kāpar* is used some 150 times. It has been much discussed. There is an equivalent Arabic root meaning "cover," or "conceal." On the strength of this connection, it has been supposed that the Hebrew word means, "to cover over sin" and thus pacify the deity, making an atonement (so BDB). It has been suggested that the OT ritual symbolized a covering over of sin until it was dealt with in fact by the atonement of Christ. There is, however, very little evidence for this view. The connection of the Arabic word is weak, and the Hebrew root is not used to mean, "cover." The Hebrew verb is never used in the simple or Qal stem, but only in the derived intensive stems. These intensive stems often indicate not emphasis, but merely that the verb is derived from a noun whose meaning is more basic to the root idea."[204]

The TWOT helps us to appreciate that "from the meaning of *kōper* "ransom," the meaning of *kāpar* can be better understood. It means, "to atone by offering a substitute." The great majority of the usages concern the priestly ritual of the sprinkling of the sacrificial blood thus "making an atonement" for the worshipper. There are forty-nine instances of this usage in Leviticus alone and no other meaning is there witnessed. The verb is always used in connection with the removal of sin or

---

[204] R. Laird Harris, "1023 כפר," ed. R. Laird Harris, Gleason L. Archer Jr., and Bruce K. Waltke, *Theological Wordbook of the Old Testament* (Chicago: Moody Press, 1999), 452-3.

defilement, except for Gen 32:20; Prov. 16:14; and Isa 28:18 where the related meaning of "appease by a gift" may be observed. It seems clear that this word aptly illustrates the theology of reconciliation in the OT. The life of the sacrificial animal specifically symbolized by its blood was required in exchange for the life of the worshipper. The Sacrifice of animals in OT theology was not merely an expression of thanks to the deity by cattle-raising people. It was the symbolic expression of innocent life given for guilty life. This symbolism is further clarified by the action of the worshipper in placing his hands on the head of the sacrifice and confessing his sins over the animal (cf. Lev 16:21; 1:4; 4:4, etc.) which was then killed or sent out as a scapegoat." (Harris, Archer and Waltke 1999, c1980, p. 453; TWOT Number 1023a)

K*āpar* is used is used virtually in every case to describe the satisfying of justice through atoning for sins. The noun k*ōper* refers to what is given to satisfy justice, i.e., the ransom price. For example, the Psalmist writes, "When iniquities [great injustices] prevail against me, **you <u>atone</u>** for our transgressions." (Psa. 65:3) The greatest blessing for which David offered praise was God's willingness, actually, eagerness to forgive. (Psa. 65:1) Pondering over past Israelite disobedience, David speaks of when they were overcome with sin; God forgave or atoned for their transgressions. David was referring to Israel's moral rebellion against God's Law. Undeservedly, God atoned for their sinfulness, which set aside the consequences.

Later, the Psalmist writes, "Yet he [God], being compassionate, **<u>atoned</u> for** their iniquity [great injustices] and did not destroy them; he turned away his anger often and did not stir up all his wrath." (Psa. 78:38) Regardless of the Israelites history of unfaithfulness, God showed them mercy when he did not have to, atoning for their iniquity [great injustices]. Repeatedly he restrained his wrath from a full expression, making allowances for human imperfection.

The Psalmist also wrote, "Do not remember against us the iniquities of our forefathers let your compassion come speedily to meet us, for we are brought very low. Help us, O God of our salvation, for the glory of your name; deliver us, and **<u>atone</u> for our sins**, for your name's sake!" (Psa. 79:8-9) Many in Israel had suffered much for the sins of their forefathers. Therefore, the psalmist is praying that God would no longer call to mind the sin of their forefathers, namely, that God would no longer hold these previous sins against them. The psalmist pleads desperately that God comes speedily before all of God's chosen people were no more.

If we are to maintain any kind of integrity, we must appreciate the connection between forgiveness and the honor of God's name. He pled that God might help them from the subjugation and persecution of these invading nations. "Atone for our sins," he begged earnestly, asking God to forgive the transgressions of Israel's past. This plea was based on the glory of God's name. In other words, an act of mercy on the part of God would bring glory to his name.

W. E. Vine writes, "*lutron* (μήτε, 3383), lit., 'a means of loosing' (from *luo*, 'to loose'), occurs frequently in the Sept., where it is always used to signify 'equivalence.' Thus, it is used of the 'ransom' for a life, e.g., Exod. 21:30, of the redemption price of a slave, e.g., Lev. 19:20, of land, 25:24, of the price of a captive, Isa. 45:13. In the NT, it occurs in Matt. 20:28 and Mark 10:45, where it is used of Christ's gift of Himself as 'a ransom for many.' Some interpreters have regarded the "ransom" price as being paid to Satan; others, to an impersonal power such as death, or evil, or 'that ultimate necessity which has made the whole course of things what it has been.' Such ideas are largely conjectural, the result of an attempt to press the details of certain Old Testament illustrations beyond the actual statements of New Testament doctrines.

Vine's dictionary goes onto say "That Christ gave up His life in expiatory sacrifice under God's judgment upon sin and thus provided a 'ransom' whereby those who receive Him on this ground obtain deliverance from the penalty due to sin, is what Scripture teaches. What the Lord states in the two passages mentioned involves this essential character of His death. In these passages the preposition is *anti*, which has a vicarious significance, indicating that the "ransom" holds good for those who, accepting it as such, no longer remain in death since Christ suffered death in their stead. The change of preposition in 1 Tim. 2:6, where the word *antilutron*. a substitutionarv 'ransom,' is used, is significant. There the preposition is *huper*, "on behalf of," and the statement is made that He "gave Himself a ransom for all," indicating that the 'ransom' was provisionally universal while being of a vicarious character. Thus the three passages consistently show that while the provision was universal, for Christ died for all men, yet it is actual for those only who accept God's conditions, and who are described in the Gospel statements as 'the many.' The giving of His life was the giving of His entire person, and while His death under divine judgment was alone expiatory, it cannot be dissociated from the character of His life which, being sinless, gave virtue to His death and was a testimony to the fact that His death must be of a vicarious nature."[205]

As to original languages words for salvation, W. E. Vine write, "*soteria* ... denotes 'deliverance, preservation, salvation.' "Salvation" is used in the NT (a) of material and temporal deliverance from danger and apprehension, (1) national, Luke 1:69, 71; Acts 7:25, RV marg., 'salvation' (text, "deliverance"); (2) personal, as from the sea, Acts 27:34; RV, 'safety' (KJV, 'health'); prison, Phil. 1:19; the flood, Heb. 11:7; (b) of the spiritual and eternal deliverance granted immediately by God to those who accept His conditions of repentance and faith in the Lord Jesus, in whom alone it is to be obtained, Acts 4:12, and upon confession of Him as Lord, Rom. 10:10; for this purpose the gospel is the saving instrument, Rom. 1:16; Eph. 1:13 (see further under save); (c) of the present experience of God's power to deliver from the bondage of sin, e.g., Phil. 2:12, where the special, though not the entire, reference is to the maintenance of peace and harmony; 1 Pet. 1:9; this present experience on the part of believers is virtually equivalent to sanctification; for this purpose, God is able

---

[205] W. E. Vine, Merrill F. Unger, and William White Jr., *Vine's Complete Expository Dictionary of Old and New Testament Words* (Nashville, TN: T. Nelson, 1996), 506–507.

to make them wise, 2 Tim. 3:15; they are not to neglect it, Heb. 2:3; (d) of the future deliverance of believers at the Parousia of Christ for His saints, a salvation which is the object of their confident hope, e.g., Rom. 13:11; 1 Thess. 5:8, and v. 9, where 'salvation' is assured to them, as being deliverance from the wrath of God destined to be executed upon the ungodly at the end of this age (see 1 Thess. 1:10); 2 Thess. 2:13; Heb. 1:14; 9:28; 1 Pet. 1:5; 2 Pet. 3:15; (e) of the deliverance of the nation of Israel at the second advent of Christ at the time of 'the epiphany (or shining forth) of His Parousia [presence]' (2 Thess. 2:8); Luke 1:71; Rev. 12:10; (f) inclusively, to sum up all the blessings bestowed by God on men in Christ through the Holy Spirit, e.g., 2 Cor. 6:2; Heb. 5:9; 1 Pet. 1:9, 10; Jude 3; (g) occasionally, as standing virtually for the Savior, e.g., Luke 19:9; cf. John 4:22 (see savior); (h) in ascriptions of praise to God, Rev. 7:10, and as that which it is His prerogative to bestow, 19:1 (RV)."[206]

Redemption and Redeemer

The Hebrew verb *pādâ* means, "ransom, rescue, and deliver" and the derivative *pidyôn* means "ransom money,"[207] or "ransom price," "redemption money," or "price of redemption."[208] (Ex. 21:30) The Hebrew root (*pādâ*) has the basic meaning to exchange the ownership of someone or something from one to another through the payment of a (ransom) price, i.e., a corresponding or equivalent substitute.

These terms clearly stress the *releasing* accomplished by the ransom price or redemption money, i.e., an equivalent or corresponding substitute. In addition, *kāpar* also stresses on the *quality* or *content* of the price of redemption and its *effectiveness* in balancing the scales of justice. A "ransom," "rescue" or "deliverance" (*pādâ*) can be from slavery (Lev. 19:20; Deut. 7:8), from troubling times or overbearing situations (2 Sam 4:9; Job 6:23; Psa. 55:18), or from death and the grave. (Job 33:28; Psa. 49:15) God had redeemed the Israelites, bringing them up out of Egypt with a mighty hand (Deut. 9:26; Psa. 78:42) and later he would ransom and redeem the Israelites from both Assyrian and Babylonian exile seven hundred and nine hundred years later respectively. (Isa 35:10; 51:11; Jer. 31:11-12; Zech. 10:8-10) This redeeming required a "ransom price," an exchange. When God redeemed Israel from Egypt, the price was the firstborn of Pharaoh and all of Egypt, as well the animals, because Pharaoh had hardened his heart against the release of Israel, the "firstborn" of God. – Exodus 4:21-23; 11:4-8.

In the eighth century B.C.E., the prophet Isaiah wrote, "But now thus says Jehovah, your Creator, O Jacob, and he who formed you, O Israel: 'do not fear, for I have redeemed you; I have called you by name; you are mine. … For I am Jehovah

---

206 W. E. Vine, Merrill F. Unger, and William White Jr., *Vine's Complete Expository Dictionary of Old and New Testament Words* (Nashville, TN: T. Nelson, 1996), 545.

207 William B. Coker, "1734 פָּדָה," ed. R. Laird Harris, Gleason L. Archer Jr., and Bruce K. Waltke, *Theological Wordbook of the Old Testament* (Chicago: Moody Press, 1999), 716.

208 Ludwig Koehler et al., *The Hebrew and Aramaic Lexicon of the Old Testament* (Leiden; New York: E.J. Brill, 1999), 913.

your God, the Holy One of Israel, your Savior; I have given Egypt as your ransom [form of *kōper*], Cush and Seba in exchange for you.'" (Isa. 43:3) All of these exchanges satisfy justice as laid out in Proverbs 21:18, "The wicked is a ransom for the righteous, and the treacherous in the place of the upright."

Another Hebrew term associated with redemption is (*gā'al*), and this conveys primarily the thought of "redeem, avenge, revenge, ransom, do the part of a kinsman." (Jer. 32:7-8) The derivatives of the root are (*gĕ'ûlay*) redemption (Isa 63:4 only), (*gĕ'ūllâ*) redemption, and right of redemption, price of redemption, kindred and (*gō'ēl*) redeemer. On this, the *Theological Wordbook of the Old Testament* writes, "The primary meaning of this root is to do the part of a kinsman and thus to redeem his kin from difficulty or danger. It is used with its derivatives 118 times. One difference between this root and the very similar root *pādâ* "redeem," is that there is usually an emphasis in*gā'al* on the redemption being the privilege or duty of a near relative. The participial form of the Qal stem has indeed been translated by some as 'kinsman-redeemer' or as in KJV merely "kinsman."[209] Nevertheless, the similarity of (*gā'al*) to (*pādâ*) is seen by its being used alongside (*pādâ*) at Hosea 13:14): Shall I ransom [form of *pādâ*] them from the hand of Sheol? Shall I redeem [form of *gā'al*] them from Death? O Death, where are your destruction? O Sheol, where is your sting? Compassion will be hidden from my eyes."

Again, Hebrew uses the verb (*gā'al*) to speak of redemption and a derivative form of the verb (*gō'ēl*) for redeemer. The basic meaning and application of the verb is the thought of reclaiming, recovering, or repurchasing, i.e., buying something back. The right of redemption can be for a house (Lev. 25:33) the selling of a person to pay his debts (Lev. 25:48–49) a sacrificial animal (Lev. 27:13), or a field or other property (27:19–26). The Psalmist asks God to defend, redeem, and preserve him because he keeps his word. (Psa. 119:153-54) Under the Mosaic Law, if a husband died, leaving his wife childless, there was a custom and law whereby a man would marry the deceased's widow (closest relative first, namely, the brother), who was sonless, to produce offspring, to carry on the name of his relative. (Gen. 30:1; 38:8; Deut. 25:5-7; Ruth 4:4-7) The man carrying out what was known as "brother-in-law marriage" was called the redeemer (*gō'ēl*).

Anders and Butler observe, "in criminal law, a person who committed a crime against another person was responsible for paying back the cost of his crime. If the injured party for some reason was not available to receive restitution, then the nearest relative was to receive it and was called the goel (Num. 5:8). In capital punishment cases, the closest relative was responsible for avenging the death of his relative. This avenger was called a goel of blood, but to prohibit such a custom from getting out of hand and becoming an uncontrolled vendetta, the cities of refuge were set up to protect the person accused of murder (Num. 35:12; Josh. 20:3–9; cp. 1 Kgs. 16:11).

---

209 (Harris, Archer and Waltke 1999, c1980, TWOT Number 300a, page 145)

Thus in Israel's law redemption was "to redeem that which belongs to the family from outside jurisdiction" (Stamm, TLOT, 1, p. 291)."[210]

The Mosaic Law had a provision for the Israelites who became victim to poverty (Redemption of Property), wherein he was forced to sell his hereditary lands, his house in the city, or even to sell himself into servitude. It reads, "If your brother becomes poor and sells part of his property, then his nearest redeemer (*gō'ēl*) shall come and redeem [*gā'al*] what his brother has sold." (Lev. 25:25, ESV) What if the man had no relative to redeem it? Then, if he "himself becomes prosperous and finds sufficient means to redeem it, let him calculate the years since he sold it and pay back the balance to the man to whom he sold it, and then return to his property." (Lev. 25:26-27) First, it should be noted that this man was not to be taken advantage of, nor dealt with in a ruthless way. If he had to sell himself into slavery, he is respected and viewed as a hired servant (employee), who can be redeemed or released on the Year of Jubilee. The fact that a poor Israelite could become wealthy while in servitude is evidence that he was treated very well, and this served as a perfect protection against a lifetime of poverty.

In the case of a murder, while he could not seek sanctuary in the six cities of refuge (Num. 35:6-32; Josh. 20:2-9); however, he could receive a judicial hearing, if found guilty, "the avenger [*gō'ēl*] of blood shall himself put the murderer to death." The avenger of blood would be a near relative of the victim. Moreover, there was no ransom [k*ōper*] for the life of a murderer, who is guilty of death, so he was to be put to death. In addition, no near relative who had the right of redeemer could reclaim the life of his dead relative; therefore, he justly claimed the life of the one who had murdered his relative. – Numbers 35:9-32; Deuteronomy 19:1-13.

The Redemption or Releasing

Again, Vine helps us with the original language words. He writes, "*Exagorazo* … [is] a strengthened form of *agorazo*, "to buy," denotes "to buy out" (*ex* for *ek*), especially of purchasing a slave with a view to his freedom. It is used metaphorically (a) in Gal. 3:13 and 4:5, of the deliverance by Christ of Christian Jews from the Law and its curse; what is said of *lutron* is true of this verb and of *agorazo*, as to the death of Christ, that Scripture does not say to whom the price was paid; the various suggestions made are purely speculative; (b) in the middle voice, 'to buy up for oneself,' Eph. 5:16 and Col. 4:5, of 'buying up the opportunity' (RSV marg.; text, "redeeming the time," where 'time' is *kairos*, 'a season,' a time in which something is seasonable), i.e., making the most of every opportunity, turning each to the best advantage since none can be recalled if missed."

"*Note:* In Rev. 5:9; 14:3, 4, KJV, *agorazo*, "to purchase" (rv) is translated "redeemed."

---

[210] Anders, Max; Butler, Trent (2002-04-01). *Holman Old Testament Commentary - Isaiah* (pp. 351-352). B&H Publishing. Kindle Edition.

"*lutroo*, 'to release on receipt of ransom' (akin to *lutron*, 'a ransom'), is used in the middle voice, signifying 'to release by paying a ransom price, to redeem' (a) in the natural sense of delivering, Luke 24:21, of setting Israel free from the Roman yoke; (b) in a spiritual sense, Titus 2:14, of the work of Christ in 'redeeming' men 'from all iniquity' (*anomia*, "lawlessness," the bondage of self-will which rejects the will of God); 1 Pet. 1:18 (passive voice), "ye were redeemed," from a vain manner of life, i.e., from bondage to tradition. In both instances, the death of Christ is stated as the means of 'redemption.'"

'*Note:* While both [*exagorazo*] and [*lutroo*] are translated "to redeem," *exagorazo* does not signify the actual 'redemption,' but the price paid with a view to it, *lutroo* signifies the actual "deliverance," the setting at liberty."[211]

Ransom Not Always a Physical Price

As was stated in the above, God "redeemed" (*pādâ*) or 'reclaimed' (*gā'al*) Israel from Egypt. (Ex 6:6; Isa 51:10-11) However, more times than can be counted, the Israelites "sold themselves to do that which was evil in the sight of Jehovah, to provoke him to anger." (2 Ki 17:16-17) Therefore, repeatedly, God sold them into the hands of their enemies. (Deut. 32:30; Judges 2:14; 3:8; 10:7; 1 Sam 12:9) Nevertheless, they would eventually repent and God would ransom and redeem them back (buy them back), reclaiming them from subjugation by their neighboring enemies or exile. (Psa. 107:2-3; Isa. 35:9, 10; Micah 4:10) In this, God was carrying out the work of a redeemer (*gō'ēl*), for the Sons of Israel belonged to him. (Isa. 43:1, 14; 48:20; 49:26; 50:1-2; 54:5-7) God takes no pleasure in gold, silver, or land because it all belongs to him anyway, so this is not what the pagan nations paid him. Rather, his payment came in the satisfying of justice and the carrying out his will and purposes, correcting their rebellious spirit and their lack of respect for the Creator of the heavens and the earth.

Isaiah 48:17-18 Updated American Standard Version (UASV)

17 Thus says Jehovah,
your Redeemer, the Holy One of Israel:
"I am Jehovah your God,
who teaches you to profit,
who leads you in the way you should go.
18 Oh that you had paid attention to my commandments!
Then your peace would have been like a river,
and your righteousness like the waves of the sea;

Again, in the case of God, his redeeming does not necessarily need to involve something physical like property, land, gold and silver. When God redeemed the Israelites, who had been in exile in Babylon, Cyrus the Great of Persia was used to liberate them from captivity. Nevertheless, when God redeemed Israel from Nations

---

211 W. E. Vine, Merrill F. Unger, and William White Jr., *Vine's Complete Expository Dictionary of Old and New Testament Words* (Nashville, TN: T. Nelson, 1996), 515.

that had acted with malevolence and hatred against Israel, he demanded a price from the persecutors themselves, in that they paid with their very lives. (Psa. 106:10-11; Isa. 41:11-14; 49:26) When God sold his people to the pagan nations, the Israelites received nothing in return (benefits or relief), meaning that God received nothing, nor was anything given to the captors to balance out the scales. Rather, by the power of his arm, God redeemed his people, the sons of Jacob. – Psalm 77:14-15.

Isaiah 52:3-10 Updated American Standard Version (UASV)

3 For thus says Jehovah, "You were sold for nothing, and you shall be redeemed
without money." 4 For thus says Jehovah God, "My people went down at the first
into Egypt to sojourn there, and the Assyrian oppressed them without cause. 5 Now
therefore, what do I have here," declares Jehovah, "seeing that my people are taken away without cause? Their rulers wail," declares Jehovah, "and continually all the day my name is despised. 6 Therefore my people shall know my name. Therefore in that day they shall know that it is I who speak; here I am."

7 How beautiful upon the mountains
are the feet of him who brings good news,
who publishes peace, who brings good news of happiness,
who proclaims salvation,
who says to Zion, "Your God has become king!"[212]
8 Listen! your watchmen lift up their voices;
together they sing for joy;
for eye to eye they see
when Jehovah returns to Zion.
9 Break forth, sing for joy together,
you waste places of Jerusalem,
for Jehovah has comforted his people;
he has redeemed Jerusalem.
10 Jehovah has bared his holy arm
before the eyes of all the nations,
and all the ends of the earth shall see
the salvation of our God.

Therefore, the Father in his role as the *gō'ēl* included the punishing of wrongs done to his servants, ending with his sanctifying, and defending his personal name against those who used Israel's suffering as a justification to reproach him. (Psa. 78:35; Isa 59:15-20; 63:3-6, 9) As the Great Kinsman (NASB) and Redeemer of both the nation of Israel as a whole and each individual making up that nation, he pled for their cause, to satisfy justice. – Psalm 119:153-154; Jeremiah 50:33-34; Lamentations 3:58-60; See also Proverbs 23:10-11.

---

[212] Or *"Your God Reigns!"*

The man of great faith, the disease-stricken Job said, "As for me, I know that my Kinsman[213] lives, and at the last he will stand upon the earth.[214] King David sang, "Draw near to my soul, redeem me; ransom me because of my enemies!" (Psa. 69:18) He also sung at Psalm 103:4, "Who redeems your life from the pit, who crowns you with lovingkindness and mercy"? King Saul sought to kill David many times, the Philistines wanted David dead as well, as was true of others. However, God showed David loving kindness by redeeming him from the pit, i.e., the grave. – 1 Samuel 18:9-29; 19:10; 21:10-15; 23:6-29.

The Ransom of Christ Jesus

The Hebrew Old Testament Scriptures are what help us appreciate the ransom that was offered by the Son of God, Jesus Christ. It was Adam's siding with Eve in the rebellion against God's sovereignty (right to rule) that brought about the need of a ransom. Adam evidenced more love for Eve than he did for his Creator, who had given him live. Therefore, he sold his soul (life) so that he could join Eve in her transgression, sharing in her condemnation as well, losing his righteous standing before God. Therefore, he also sold any future descendants into slavery to sin and to death, as God had commanded, "from the tree of the knowledge of good and evil you shall not eat,[215] for in the day that you eat from it you shall surely die."[216] As Adam was a perfect human, who would never have become sick, or grown old, nor ever died, he sold these things for his own selfish desire of being with Eve, and he sold them for all of his progeny.

Romans 5:12-19 Updated American Standard Version (ASV)

12 Therefore, just as through one man sin entered into the world, and death
through sin, and so death spread to all men, because all sinned, 13 or until the law sin
was in the world, but sin is not imputed when there is no law. 14 Nevertheless death
reigned from Adam until Moses, even over them that had not sinned after the
likeness of Adam's transgression, who is a type of the one who is to come.

15 But the free gift is not like the trespass.[217] For if by the trespass of the one
the many died, much more did the grace of God and the gift by the grace of the one
man, Jesus Christ, abound to the many. 16 And it is not the same with the free gift as
with the way things worked through the one man who sinned. For the judgment after
one trespass was condemnation, but the gift after many trespasses was
justification.[218] 17 For if by the trespass of the one, death reigned through the one,
much more those who receive the abundance of grace and of the gift of
righteousness will reign in life through the one, Jesus Christ.

---

213 I.e., *Redeemer*

214 Lit *dust*

215 Lit *eat from it*

216 Lit., *dying you* [singular] *shall die.* Heb., moth tamuth; the first reference to death in the Scriptures

217 Lit *not as the trespass, so also the free gift*

218 Lit a declaring of righteous

[18] So, then, as through one trespass there was condemnation to all men, so too through one act of righteousness there was justification of life to all men. [19] For as through the one man's disobedience the many were made sinners, so also through the obedience of the one the many will be made righteous.

Paul, later in the same letter to the Romans, speaks on the conflict of the two natures.

Romans 7:14-25 Updated American Standard Version (UASV)

[14] For we know that the law is spiritual, but I am of the flesh, sold under sin. [15] For what I am doing, I do not understand; for I am not practicing what I would like to do, but I am doing the very thing I hate. [16] But if what I am not willing to do, this I am doing, I agree that the law is good. [17] So now I am no longer the one doing it, but sin that dwells in me. [18] For I know that nothing good dwells in me, that is, in my flesh; for the desire is present in me, but the doing of the good is not. [19] For the good that I want, I do not do, but I practice the very evil that I do not want. [20] But if what I do not want to do, this I am doing, I am no longer the one doing it, but sin which dwells in me.

[21] I find then the law in me that when I want to do right, that evil is present in me. [22] For I delight in the law of God according to the inner man, [23] but I see a different law in my members, warring against the law of my mind and taking me captive in the law of sin which is in my members. [24] Wretched man that I am! Who will deliver me from this body of death? [25] Thanks be to God through Jesus Christ our Lord! So then, I myself serve the law of God with my mind, but with my flesh, I serve the law of sin.

The law was but a shadow of the good things to come instead of the true form of these realities, as it atoned in a limited way by offering a substitute, i.e., animal sacrifices. "For it is impossible for the blood of bulls and goats to take away sins." (Heb. 10:1-4) The animal sacrifices were pictorial in yet another way, as 'when anyone offered a sacrifice of peace offerings to Jehovah to fulfill a vow or as a freewill offering from the herd or from the flock, to be accepted it must have been perfect; there was to be no blemish in it.' (Lev. 22:21) The animal sacrifices, therefore, picture, the human sacrifice that was to come, in that, he too would have to be perfect and without blemish. In this, he would actually be an equivalent, a corresponding ransom, as Adam was a perfect human, so too, the ransom to remove sin would have to be a perfect human. This enabled that human sacrifice to pay the price of redemption that would remove Adamic sin, inherited imperfection, from any human placing their trust in the human, who had made such a sacrifice.

Adam had sold his descendants into enslavement to their fallen flesh, as everyone who came after Adam is human imperfection and a slave to sin. (Rom. 7:25) By the human offering paying the price of redemption, he released Adam's offspring from sin and death. The apostle Paul wrote, "In him we have redemption through his blood, the forgiveness of our trespasses, according to the riches of his grace." (Eph. 1:7, ESV) The apostle Paul even said of himself, "For we know that the law is spiritual, but I am of the flesh, sold under sin." (Rom. 7:14) David sang,

"Behold, I was brought forth in iniquity,[219] and in sin did my mother conceive me." Therefore, God's perfect justice had to be satisfied, the one that called for a like for like, as in a "life for life, eye for eye, tooth for tooth, hand for hand, and foot for foot." – Exodus 21:23-25; Deuteronomy 19:21.

God's perfect justice does not allow humankind to provide their own redeemer. "Truly no man can ransom another, or give to God the price of his life, for the ransom of their life is costly and can never suffice." (Psa. 49:6-9, ESV) 'God showed his love for us in that while we were still sinners, he offered his Son for us.' (Rom. 5:6-8) This required the Son coming to earth, to be born as a perfect human, to be the equivalent of Adam, a corresponding ransom. Therefore, the Father, in a way we will never fully understand, placed the Son's life in the womb of Mary, a young Jewish virgin girl. (Lu 1:26-37; John 1:14) Jesus did not have a human father from which imperfection could be carried over into him. Moreover, while Mary was imperfect and could pass on sin to any offspring, in this instance, the Holy Spirit came upon her, and the power of the Most High overshadow her, protecting the baby in her womb.

Therefore, Jesus was born holy and could be called the Son of God. It is "the precious blood of Christ, like that of a lamb without blemish or spot," which redeemed humanity from sin and death. (Lu 1:35; John 1:29; 1 Pet 1:18-19) While David was born into sin (as all of humanity has been), this was not true of Jesus. However, Jesus was fully human, so he could 'sympathize with our weaknesses, and one who in every respect has been tempted as we are, yet without sin.' (Heb. 4:15) Yes, Jesus' entire human life was as a perfect human, just as Adam's had been prior to eating from the forbidden tree. Jesus' human life was 'holy, innocent, unstained, and separated from sinners.' (Heb. 7:26) Humanity had been under another Father, Satan the Devil, after Adam rejected God in the Garden of Eden. (Gen 3:1-6; John 8:44) However, through his ransom 'death, Jesus destroyed the one who has the power of death, that is, the devil, and had delivered all those who through fear of death were subject to lifelong slavery.' (Heb. 2:14-15) This is why Isaiah could refer to him prophetically as "Eternal Father." – Isaiah 9:6.

The New Testament makes it all too clear that Jesus' perfect human life was given as a price to satisfy justice and redeem humankind from sin and death. Paul tells us that we "were bought with a price." (1 Cor. 6:20; 7:23) Paul often begins his letters "Paul, a slave of Christ Jesus," as Jesus bought us from Satan the Devil, from condemnation and death, as Peter states, Jesus is the "the Master who bought" us. (Rom. 1:1; 2 Pet. 2.1) Jesus was 'slain, and by his blood, he ransomed [bought] people for God from every tribe and language and people and nation.' (Rev. 5:9, ESV) In the above texts, we find the Greek word *agorazo*, which means "literally *buy, purchase, do business in the marketplace* (MT 13.44); figuratively, as being no longer controlled by

[219] Iniquity (*awon*) "signifies an offense, intentional or not, against God's law." This meaning is also most basic to the word [*chattat*], "sin," in the Old Testament, and for this reason the words [*chattat*] and [awon] are virtually synonymous." (VCEDONTW, Volume 1, Page 122) Iniquity is anything not in harmony with God's personality, standards, ways, and will, which mars one's relationship with God.

sin *set free*; from the analogy of buying a slave's freedom for a price paid by a benefactor *redeem* (1C 6.20)."[220] The related *exagorazo* (to release by purchase) means, "*To buy up,* i.e., *ransom,* fig. *to rescue from loss*."[221] Paul said that Jesus 'redeemed [*exagorazo*][222] those who were under the law so that we might receive adoption as sons.' Paul speaks of the curse that the Jews and all of humanity was under, when he says, "Christ redeemed [*exagorazo*][223] us from the curse of the law by becoming a curse for us." (Gal. 4:5; 3:13) However, the Greek word more often used for redemption and ransoming is *lytron*, which more fully expresses the intended meaning as well.

Lytron is "the means or instrument by which release or deliverance is made possible–'means of release, ransom."[224] The *Analytical Lexicon of the Greek New Testament* says of lytron, "as a price paid for release from slavery or captivity *ransom*; figuratively, of the cost to Christ in providing deliverance from sin *price of release, ransom, means of setting free*."[225] (See Heb. 11:35) Lytron describes Christ as "the Son of Man came not to be served but to serve, and to give his soul as a ransom [*lytron*] for many." (Matt 20:28; Mark 10:45) The related word *antilytron* appears at 1 Timothy 2:6.

If we look at 1 Timothy 2:5-6, it says in part, "the man Christ Jesus, who gave himself as a ransom [*antilytron*] for all." The Greek word *antilytron* appears nowhere else in the Bible. It is related to the word that Jesus used for ransom (*lytron*) at Mark 10:45. The Greek *antilytron* broken down from *anti* means "against; in correspondence to; "instead of;" "in place of," and *lytron* means "ransom [i.e., price paid]") "The *Greek* implies not merely *ransom,* but a *substituted* or *equivalent ransom:* the *Greek* preposition, '*anti*,' implying reciprocity and vicarious substitution."[226] *The Interpreters Dictionary of the Bible* in volume 4 states: that of antilytron "The word "ransom" (lutron and antilutron) occurs only three times (Matt. 20:28=Mark 10:45; 1 Tim.2:6), but its occurrence in the first two of these passages is nevertheless of fundamental importance for understanding Jesus' own conception of his death as a redemptive act. He gives a new depth to the concept of redemption by associating with it the idea - derived from Isa. 53:5 - 6, 10 - of a substitutionary

---

[220] Timothy Friberg, Barbara Friberg, and Neva F. Miller, *Analytical Lexicon of the Greek New Testament*, Baker's Greek New Testament Library (Grand Rapids, MI: Baker Books, 2000), 33.

[221] Robert L. Thomas, *New American Standard Hebrew-Aramaic and Greek Dictionaries : Updated Edition* (Anaheim: Foundation Publications, Inc., 1998).

[222] Lit *he might by out*

[223] Lit *bought out*

[224] Johannes P. Louw and Eugene Albert Nida, *Greek-English Lexicon of the New Testament: Based on Semantic Domains* (New York: United Bible Societies, 1996), 487.

[225] Timothy Friberg, Barbara Friberg, and Neva F. Miller, *Analytical Lexicon of the Greek New Testament*, Baker's Greek New Testament Library (Grand Rapids, MI: Baker Books, 2000), 249.

[226] Robert Jamieson, A. R. Fausset, and David Brown, *Commentary Critical and Explanatory on the Whole Bible*, vol. 2 (Oak Harbor, WA: Logos Research Systems, Inc., 1997), 408.

sacrifice."[227] The reason this is the case is that we are talking about the equivalent price of one perfect human for another perfect human. Thus, this was a means for God's principal attribute justice to be satisfied.

Another related word is *lytroomai* to release or set free, with the implied analogy to the process of freeing a slave—'to set free, to liberate, to deliver, liberation, deliverance.'[228] Paul wrote to Titus that Jesus "gave himself for us to redeem [*lytroomai*] us from all lawlessness and to purify for himself a people for his own possession who are zealous for good works." (Tit 2:14, ESV) Peter states that we can know that we were ransomed from the futile ways inherited from our forefathers, not with perishable things such as silver or gold, but with the precious blood of Christ, like that of a lamb without blemish or spot." (1 Pet. 1:18-19) Another related word is *apolytrosis*, which means, "'buying back' a slave or captive, i.e. 'making free' by payment of a ransom."[229] Paul writes of Jesus, "In him we have redemption through his blood, the forgiveness of our trespasses, according to the riches of his grace." (Eph. 1:7, 14; Col. 1:14) The basic fact of both the Hebrew and Greek terms are (1) a redeeming or ransoming, i.e., deliverance, (2) brought about by a payment, (3) consisting of a corresponding equivalency.

Even though the ransom sacrifice of Jesus Christ is made available to anyone who wishes to avail himself or herself to it, not all respond to the invitation. Jesus himself said, "The one trusting[230] in the Son has eternal life, but the one who disobeys the Son will not see life, but the wrath of God remains on him." (John 3:36) The point here is that Jesus' ransom covers the Adamic inherited sin of every person and all that it entails. Everyone has the opportunity of choosing life over death, the ransom is made available, but it can be rejected. Moreover, it can be accepted and later rejected as well. "As sin reigned in death, grace also might reign through righteousness leading to eternal life through Jesus Christ our Lord." – Romans 5:21.

Hebrews 10:26-29 Updated American Standard Version (USV)

26 For if we go on sinning deliberately after receiving the knowledge of the truth, there no longer remains a sacrifice for sins, 27 but a fearful expectation of judgment, and a fury of fire that will consume the adversaries. 28 Anyone who has set aside the law of Moses dies without mercy on the evidence of two or three witnesses. 29 How much worse punishment, do you think, will be deserved by the one who has trampled underfoot the Son of God, and has profaned the blood of the covenant by which he was sanctified, and has outraged the Spirit of grace?

---

227 Dentan, R. C. *The Interpreter's Dictionary of the Bible*. Edited by George Arthur Butrick. Vol. 4. 4 vols. Nashville, TN: Abingdon Press, 1962, Volume 4, page 22.

228 Johannes P. Louw and Eugene Albert Nida, *Greek-English Lexicon of the New Testament: Based on Semantic Domains* (New York: United Bible Societies, 1996), 487.

229 William Arndt, Frederick W. Danker, and Walter Bauer, *A Greek-English Lexicon of the New Testament and Other Early Christian Literature* (Chicago: University of Chicago Press, 2000), 117.

230 The grammatical construction of pisteuo "believe" followed by eis "into" plus the accusative causing a different shade of meaning, having faith into Jesus.

Contrasted with,

Romans 5:9-10 Updated American Standard Version (ASV)

[9] Much more then, having now been justified by his blood, we shall be saved from the wrath of God through him. [10] For if while we were enemies we were reconciled to God through the death of his Son, much more, having been reconciled, we shall be saved by his life.

Just as one could not ransom a willful murderer under the Mosaic Law, Adam willfully murdered humanity with his rejection of God's sovereignty. (Rom. 5:12) Under this Scriptural point, it would seem that Adam could not be ransomed by the sacrificed life of Jesus. Nevertheless, we can be thankful that every descendant of Adam has an opportunity to be ransomed by Jesus sacrifice. Paul wrote, "So, then, as through one trespass there was condemnation to all men, so too through one act of righteousness there was justification of life to all men. For as through the one man's disobedience the many were made sinners, so also through the obedience of the one the many will be made righteous." (Rom 5:18-19) Thus, it is written, "The first man Adam became a living being"; the last Adam became a life-giving spirit. (1 Cor. 15:45) This arrangement evidences the wisdom of God and his righteously satisfying justice while at the same time showing mercy and grace, in his forgiving our sins.

Romans 3:21-26 Updated American Standard Version (UASV)

[21] But now apart from the Law the righteousness of God has been manifested, being witnessed by the Law and the Prophets, [22] even the righteousness of God through faith in Jesus Christ for all those who believe; for there is no distinction; [23] for all have sinned and fall short of the glory of God, [24] being justified as a gift by his grace through the redemption which is in Christ Jesus; [25] whom God displayed publicly as a propitiation in his blood through faith. This was to demonstrate his righteousness, because in the forbearance of God he passed over the sins previously committed; [26] it was to show his righteousness at the present time, so that he might be just and the justifier of the one who has faith in Jesus.

Universal Salvation

Universal Salvation, Christian Universalism, or simply Universalism is the doctrine that all sinful persons, who are alienated from God, because of God's great divine love and mercy, will eventually be reconciled to God. Bible Scholar Richard Bauckham outlines the history of universal salvation,

> The history of the doctrine of universal salvation (or *apokatastasis*) is a remarkable one. Until the nineteenth century, almost all Christian theologians taught the reality of eternal torment in hell. Here and there, outside the theological mainstream, were some who believed that the wicked would be finally annihilated (in its commonest form, this is the

> doctrine of 'conditional immortality').[231] Even fewer were the advocates of universal salvation, though these few included some major theologians of the early church. Eternal punishment was firmly asserted in official creeds and confessions of the churches. It must have seemed as indispensable a part of universal Christian belief as the doctrines of the Trinity and the incarnation. Since 1800 this situation has entirely changed, and no traditional Christian doctrine has been so widely abandoned as that of eternal punishment. Its advocates among theologians today must be fewer than ever before. The alternative interpretation of hell as annihilation seems to have prevailed even among many of the more conservative theologians. Among the less conservative, universal salvation, either as hope or as dogma, is now so widely accepted that many theologians assume it virtually without argument.[232]

"Modern Universalists claim that this doctrine is contained in the New Testament in the teachings of Jesus, and conforms to the laws of nature as taught by science and sanctioned by reason and philosophy."[233] One reason behind the Universalist mindset is, there dislike of the hellfire doctrine,[234] where the sinner is punished, i.e., tormented for an eternity. For the Universalist, eternal torment for one, who is born imperfect, with a natural desire toward sin, which Genesis argues is mentally bent toward wickedness, and has a heart, which is treacherous and unknowable, would be a sign of injustice, and an unloving God.

The Salvation Debate

1 Corinthians 15:25, 28 Updated American Standard Version (UASV)

25 For he must reign until he has put all his enemies under his feet. 28 When all things are subjected to him, then the Son himself also will be subjected to the One who subjected all things to him, so that God may be **all in all**.

The Good News Translations renders that last clause and prepositional phrase, "God will rule completely over all." The Universalist would say that if God were going to "be all in all or if "God will rule completely over all" he would need to reconcile **all** humans to himself eventually. Another text often used by the Universalist.

Philippians 2:10-11 Updated American Standard Version (UASV)

---

231 For details see L. E. Froom, *The Conditionalist Faith of Our Fathers* (Washington, DC: Review and Herald, 1965–1966).

232 Richard Bauckham, "Universalism: a historical survey", Themelios 4.2 (September 1978): 47–54.

233 Microsoft ® Encarta ® 2006. © 1993-2005 Microsoft Corporation. All rights reserved.

234 Please see Volume 1 of this series, *Basic Teachings of the Bible*, article titled, Is Hell a Place of eternal Torment.

[10] so that at the name of Jesus **every knee should bow**, of those who are in heaven and on earth and under the earth, [11] and **every tongue confess** that Jesus Christ is Lord, to the glory of God the Father.

Here the Universalist would argue that if "**every** knee should to bow" "and **every** tongue confess," it must follow that every human that has lived up unto the time of Christ's return will be reconciled to God in the end.

They would also point to,

Romans 5:18 Updated American Standard Version (UASV)

[18] So, then, as through one trespass there was condemnation to all men, so too through one act of righteousness there was justification of life to **all men**.

"One trespass"–"One act of righteousness"

"Condemnation"–"Justification"

"All men [in Adam]"–"All men [in Christ]"

It would seem at first that this text is a perfect balance, in that Adam's one sinful act contributed to **all** of humanity inheriting sin and imperfection, and Christ's one act as a ransom sacrifice would contribute to **all** of humanity receiving life. Before delving into a response for these verses, let us see what the Bible teaches. First, though, just know that, when we have a few Scriptures that appear to be in opposition to many Scriptures, we likely do not understand the few correctly.

The Bible Teaches

The Scriptures, which make all too clear that some will not be receiving salvation, are so abundant from Genesis to Revelation. Adam committed the most egregious sin of any human alive, as he, in essence, murdered billions of humans, by his rebellion. For this reason, Adam was told, "for you are dust, and to dust you shall return." (Gen. 3:19) Revelation 21:8 says, "But as for the cowardly, the faithless, the detestable, as for murderers, the sexually immoral, sorcerers, idolaters, and all liars, their portion will be in the lake that burns with fire and sulfur, which is the second death." There is not one verse in the Bible that speaks of redemption or a resurrection from "the second death."

Matthew 25:46 Updated American Standard Version (UASV)

[46] And these will go away into **eternal punishment**,[235] but the righteous into eternal life."

---

[235] That is eternal cutting off, from life. Lit., "lopping off; pruning."

Kolasin "akin to *kolazoo*"[236] "This means 'to cut short,' 'to lop,' 'to trim,' and figuratively a. 'to impede,' 'restrain,' and b. 'to punish,' and in the passive 'to suffer loss.'[237] The first part of the sentence is only in harmony with the second part of the sentence, if the eternal punishment is eternal death. The wicked receive eternal death and the righteous eternal life. We might note that Matthews Gospel was primarily for the Jewish Christians, and under the Mosaic Law, God would punish those who violated the law, saying they "shall be cut off [penalty of death] from Israel." (Ex 12:15; Lev 20:2-3) We need further to consider,

2 Thessalonians 1:8-9 Updated American Standard Version (UASV)

8 in flaming fire, inflicting vengeance on those who do not know God and on those who do not obey the gospel of our Lord Jesus. 9 These ones will pay the penalty of **eternal destruction**, from before the Lord[238] and from the glory of his strength,

Notice that Paul says the punishment for the wicked is "eternal destruction." Many times in talking with those that support the position of eternal torment in some hellfire, they will add a word to Matthew 25:46 in their paraphrase of the verse, '*conscious* eternal punishment.' However, Jesus does not tell us what the eternal punishment is, just that it is a punishment and it is eternal. Therefore, those who support eternal conscious fiery torment will read the verse to mean just that, while those, who hold to the position of eternal destruction, will take Matthew 25:46 to mean that. Considering that Jesus does not define what the eternal punishment is, this verse is not a proof text for either side of the hellfire argument. In addition, Matthew wrote initially in Hebrew. Under the Mosaic Law, willful sinners were to be "cut off" from the Israelite nation. – See Exodus 12:15, 19; Leviticus 7:20-21, 25, 27; many more could be listed.

Hebrews 2:14 Updated American Standard Version (UASV)

14 Therefore, since the children share in blood and flesh, he himself likewise partook of the same things, that through death he could **destroy the one** who has the power of death, that is, the devil,

Yes, Jesus' ransom sacrifice will cause the destruction of Satan the Devil. The unrighteous, also known as the wicked within the Bible are "vessels of wrath prepared for **destruction**." (Rom 9:22) Yes, "the years of the wicked are cut short." (Pro 10:27) According to Vine's Expository Dictionary of Old and New Testament Words, *olothreuo* means "'to destroy,' especially in the sense of slaying, while "*katargeo*" means, "to reduce to inactivity." In addition, *apollumi* signifies "to destroy utterly."

---

236 W. E. Vine, Merrill F. Unger, and William White Jr., *Vine's Complete Expository Dictionary of Old and New Testament Words* (Nashville, TN: T. Nelson, 1996), 498.

237 Gerhard Kittel, Gerhard Friedrich, and Geoffrey William Bromiley, *Theological Dictionary of the New Testament* (Grand Rapids, MI: W.B. Eerdmans, 1985), 451.

238 Lit *from before the face of the Lord*

The Universalist likes to stress one quality of God, taking it beyond its balanced limits, that is *mercy*. However, they ignore the other quality that mercy is balanced with, namely *justice*. God had clearly told Adam, "of the tree of the knowledge of good and evil you shall not eat, for in the day that you eat of it you shall surely die." (Gen. 2:17) The apostle Paul tells us, "The wages of sin is death." (Rom. 6:23) The prophet Ezekiel recorded God as saying, "the soul [person] who sins shall die." (Eze. 18:4, 20) God is selective in his mercy/justice, as he said, "I will be gracious to whom I will be gracious, and will show mercy on whom I will show mercy." (Ex. 33:19) God has provided the ransom sacrifice of his Son (Matt. 20:28), to cover over Adamic sin, not the willful unrepentant practicing of sin. – Hebrews 6:4; 10:26; 2 Peter 2:21.

Where did the Universalist go wrong? As they overplayed the *mercy*, while downplaying *justice*, they also overemphasize the God of love. (1 John 4:8) They are unable to wrap their mind around the God of love, who also possess the quality of justice, and even seeks vengeance on behalf of the righteous, which were treated wickedly.

However, it is also the **un**biblical doctrine of hellfire and eternal torment, which moved them emotionally into another **un**biblical doctrine, universal salvation. They would have been wiser to set aside the eternal torment in a burning hell as being **un**biblical; recognizing that punishment for one's actions that fit the offense is biblical. The position of the Annihilationist is that of eternal destruction as a punishment, which does not involve an eternal conscious torment, as it would not be compatible with the God of love, nor his justice.[239]

Exodus 21:24 Updated American Standard Version (UASV)

[24] eye for eye, tooth for tooth, hand for hand, foot for foot,

Another possibility as to why they hold to the position of universal salvation is the other **un**biblical doctrine of the immortality of all souls. This belief is that once God created a human being, bring him or her into existence, they must live forever in some fashion (physical or spiritual body), and in some place (earth, heaven, or hell). Since the Universalist arrived at the correct conclusion that God would not torture an imperfect human, who sinned for 70-80 years, by burning him forever, they just removed the place of hell (wrongly thought of as a place of eternal torment) from the equation, and accepted that all would eventually be reconciled to God. They could have simply looked at the original language words, and rightly concluded that the Hebrew *sheol* and Greek hades are not places of eternal torment, but rather the gravedom of mankind, with the punishment being eternal death.

"*Athanasia* lit., "deathlessness" (*a*, negative, *thanatos*, "death"), is rendered "immortality" in 1 Cor. 15:53, 54, of the glorified body of the believer." (Vine 1996, Volume 2, Page 321) There are no verses within the Bible, which says that every

[239] http://bible-translation.net/page/is-hell-a-place-of-eternal-torment

human has an inherent quality of immortality. Rather, as we have already seen, Adam was sentenced to death for rebelling against God, as well as God himself saying by way of his authors, "The soul that sins shall die" and "the wages of sin is death."

Romans 6:23 Updated American Standard Version (UASV)

23 For the wages of sin is death, but the free gift[240] of God is eternal life in Christ Jesus our Lord.

If every human were created with absolute eternal life within him or her; then, there would be no gift for God to give. God has given humanity free will and the right to choose. He said to the Israelites, who wanted to be his people, "I call heaven and earth to witness against you today, that I have set before you life and death, blessing and curse. Therefore choose life, that you and your offspring may live" (Deut. 30:19) In other words, man can choose to live by the righteous laws of his Creator, or he can choose to lose his life in a rebellion against his Creator. God's justice does not allow him to have wicked persons living forever among the righteous. Adam and Eve did not fully appreciate what God had done for them, such as the eternal life he set before them, a paradise garden that they were to grow until it encompassed the entire earth, and filling the earth with perfect descendants; therefore, they returned to the dust that they came from. The same exact choice is before each of us.

What about Philippians 2:10-11, "so that at the name of Jesus **every knee should bow**, of those who are in heaven and on earth and under the earth, and **every tongue confess** that Jesus Christ is Lord, to the glory of God the Father." A day is coming when all of the wicked will receive their punishment of everlasting destruction. Therefore, all who are alive on earth and in heaven will be submitting themselves to the sovereignty of God. Then, the verse will hold true, 'every knee will bow,' 'and every tongue will confess that Jesus Christ is Lord.' Thus, the knees and the tongues of the unrighteous, rebellious ones will no longer be in existence, as they will have been destroyed.

What about the argument of Romans 5:18 that Adam's one sinful act contributed to **all** of humanity inheriting sin and imperfection, and Christ one act as a ransom sacrifice would contribute to **all** of humanity receiving life. As was stated earlier, when you have a couple of verses that seem to be in conflict with many verses from Genesis to Revelation, it means that you are likely misunderstanding a couple of verses. The Scripters clearly show that only the righteous receive life. Adam was not forced to received eternal life; it was a gift from God, which was based upon his remaining faithful. Therefore, when he rejected that gift and was unfaithful, the gift of life was taken away. Thus, the same would hold true for Adam's descendants as well. – Ezekiel 18:31-32.

As you will see, "all" in Greek does not necessarily mean "all." The Greek word behind "all" is *pan*, which comes in various forms. 1 John 2:2 says that Jesus is

240 Lit *gracious gift*; Gr *kharisma*

a covering "for the sins of the **whole world**."[241] Paul says at 1 Timothy 2:6 that Jesus "gave himself as a ransom for **all** [*pantōn*, all (ones)]." Romans 5:18 says, 'Christ's one act as a ransom sacrifice would contribute to **all** [*pantas*] of humanity receiving life.' Titus 2:10 says, "For the grace of God has appeared, bringing salvation to **all** [*pasin*] men." While this seems quite clear on the surface, it is not really so. What do we do with the other verses that say only redeemable humankind will receive salvation, that is, those that repent and turnaround from their former course. (Acts 17:30, John 3:16, 1 Jn. 5:12)

Yes, not **all** is so black and white, once the interpreter looks beneath the surface. Many times the Greek word (*panta*) rendered "all" is often used in a hyperbolic sense. For example, at Luke 21:29, in speaking of a parable, it is said, "Look at the fig tree (*suke*), and **all** the trees. (*panta ta dendra*)" While the literal translation seems nonsensical, this is what pushes the reader to look deeper. The Good News Translation gives us the meaning in "Think of the fig tree and all the other trees." "Other" is not in the Greek, but English translations add words to complete the sense in the English. Regardless, the "all" in many verses, including these, is being used hyperbolically.

At Acts 2:17, Peter at Pentecost speaks of the prophecy in the Old Testament book of Joel, saying, "And in the last days it shall be, God declares, that I will pour out my Spirit on **all** [*pasan*] flesh." Was the Spirit poured out literally on **all** flesh at Pentecost? No, it was only 120 initially, and eventually a few thousand, out of millions then alive. Repeatedly when the term "all" is used in the Greek New Testament, "all" is not literally meant as "all," but rather hyperbolically to emphasize. It can have the sense of "all others," "all sorts, "all kinds," and so on. Keep in mind that God did pour his Spirit out on 'sons and daughters, young men and old men, even on my male slaves and on my female slaves.'

Another example would be at Luke 11:42, which reads, "But woe to you Pharisees! For you tithe mint and rue and every [*pan*] herb, and neglect justice and the love of God." It should be noted that both the mint and the rue are herbs. Thus, the GNT[242] renders it, "all the **other** herbs." While this author accepts the literal translations as being closest to the Word of God in English,[243] they can infer that the mint and rue are not herbs, while the dynamic equivalent translations clear it up.

Unbiblical Teaching

The universal salvation position that **all** humans will eventually be reconciled to God, receiving salvation, is unbiblical. God has given humanity free will, and as free moral persons, they have the ability to reject his sovereignty. Moreover, if

---

[241] This verses is included because it convey the same message, but it does not contain the Greek *pan*. Rather, it has *holos*, meaning "whole, complete, entirely."

[242] Good News Translation (GNT)

[243] The literal translations are the best for both Bible reading and personal Bible study, and the ambiguity of this text would be cleared up for those who research.

universal salvation were true, it would be at odds with the very reason God allowed humanity to go on after the sin of Adam, as opposed to just starting over. Satan had challenged the sovereignty of God and the integrity of humans, saying that they would not remain faithful to God, if they faced adversity. If all, were to be saved anyway (including Satan), why would God have bothered to direct Satan's attention to the integrity of Job, pointing out that humans can choose to be faithful in adverse times?

Universal salvation is a feel-good **un**biblical doctrine that our imperfect flesh wants to be true, and Satan wants us to accept as true. It allows us to not be concerned about our actions or deeds, as one will receive salvation regardless. What they are doing is removing integrity and faithfulness from the equation. However, Like Adam, who betrayed God, Like Judas Iscariot, who betrayed the Son of God, and all the rest, who have rejected God,

Hebrews 6:4-6 Updated American Standard Version (UASV)

4 For in the case of those who have once been enlightened and have tasted of the heavenly gift and have been made partakers of the Holy Spirit, 5 and have tasted the good word of God and the powers of the age to come, 6 and then have fallen away, it is impossible to renew them again to repentance, since they again crucify to themselves the Son of God and put him to public shame.

Jesus, in speaking to the Father about his disciples, said,

John 17:12 Updated American Standard Version (UASV)

12 While I was with them, I kept them in your name, which you have given me; and I guarded them and not one of them perished but the son of perdition,[244] so that the Scripture would be fulfilled.

The apostle Paul made it all too clear, as to the outcome of willful unrepentant sinners,

Hebrews 10:26-31 Updated American Standard Version (UASV)

26 For if we go on sinning deliberately after receiving the accurate knowledge[245] of the truth, there no longer remains a sacrifice for sins, 27 but a fearful expectation of judgment, and a fury of fire that will consume the adversaries. 28 Anyone who has set aside the law of Moses dies without mercy on the evidence of two or three witnesses. 29 How much worse punishment, do you think, will be deserved by the one who has trampled underfoot the Son of God, and has profaned the blood of the covenant by which he was sanctified, and has outraged the Spirit of grace? 30 For we

---

[244] Or *son of destruction*

[245] *Epignosis* is a strengthened or intensified form of *gnosis* (*epi,* meaning "additional"), meaning, "true," "real," "full," "complete" or "accurate," depending upon the context. Paul and Peter alone use *epignosis.*

know him who said, “Vengeance is mine; I will repay.”[246] And again, “The Lord will judge his people.”[247] 31 It is a fearful thing to fall into the hands of the living God.

There have been many goodhearted self-declared Christians from the second to the twenty-first century, who have held to the **un**biblical position of universal salvation. Again, this is not a biblical teaching. While it is true that “God is love” (1 John 4:8), it is just as true that he is a God of “justice” (Isa. 33:22; Ps 33:5; Job 37:23) As a God of love, he gives us free moral agents the choice between life and death, if we choose to live under his sovereignty, we receive eternal life. As a God of Justice, if we choose to reject his sovereignty, he rejects us, and we receive eternal destruction.

---

[246] Quote from Deut. 32:35

[247] Quote from Deut. 32:36

CHAPTER 7 "Once Saved, Always Saved"?

The Son of Sam, David Berkowitz

Berkowitz accused of six murders reportedly had been "saved" at a church meeting about four years before his reign of terror began.

It was 40 years ago Tuesday when "Son of Sam" killer David Berkowitz pleaded guilty to six murders during a spree that terrorized the city.

During the proceeding inside a Brooklyn courtroom on May 8, 1978, three judges — from each borough where the crimes were committed — asked Berkowitz to detail his rampage.

Berkowitz, a 24-year-old postal clerk, admitted he gunned down five young women, a young man and wounded seven.

"This plea of his is of his own choosing," Berkowitz's lawyer, Leon Stern, told the judges.

Brooklyn judge Joseph Corso wanted to make sure Berkowitz was aware of the penalty he was facing.

"Do you know what the maximum penalty is for murder in the second degree?" he asked Berkowitz, who was wearing a blue suit and striped shirt.

"Twenty-five years to life," he responded.

In a surprise moment that has largely been lost to history, Mario Merola, the Bronx District Attorney at the time, said Berkowitz also may have started up to 2,000 fires. That allegation — based on writings from Berkowitz's diaries — was never brought up in court again.

Berkowitz has said he killed young women to satisfy his neighbor's demonic dog.

"I just felt like I had no mind," Berkowitz told Larry King in 2002. "I felt something else was controlling me."

Berkowitz launched his crime spree when he fatally shot Donna Lauria, 18, and wounded her friend, Jody Valenti, 19, in the Bronx on July 29, 1976.

He used a .44-caliber Bulldog revolver.

His last victims were Stacey Moskowitz and her boyfriend Robert Violante, both 20, who were kissing in his parked car in Bath Beach, Brooklyn, on July 31, 1977.

Moskowitz died several hours later. Violante was shot in the eye and partially blinded.

Berkowitz, who had taunted cops through anonymous letters he mailed to the Daily News, was caught due to a $35 parking ticket he got before his last killing. A witness remembered seeing him lurking around the crime scene and getting a ticket for parking his Ford Galaxie in front of a hydrant.

The witness, Cacilia Davis, reached out to the NYPD four days later. Cops then cross-checked all the cars ticketed in the area that night.

Berkowitz, who lived in an apartment in Yonkers with Satanic verses painted on the walls, was one of the drivers that popped up. Cops nabbed him as he walked to his car on Aug. 10, 1977.

Berkowitz, now 64, is serving multiple life sentences. Behind bars, he has found God and now calls himself "Son of Hope." He has recently struggled with health issues and underwent emergency heart surgery in February.[248]

Berkowitz was invited to church by a former army friend, who would later relate that the new convert "came up to me grinning and laughing and saying, 'Man, I'm saved.' Then we came back that same day for the evening service and he went forward again at the invitation [to accept Christ]. He told me afterward that he just wanted to make sure it [being "saved"] took."

When a former member of the church had heard these charges against Berkowitz, another member told the news media. "I'm just thankful he was saved." Why? She declared: "The Bible says, once saved, always saved."—New York Post, August 25, 1977, p. 2.[249]

The Bible does not actually say, "Once saved, always saved" However, this has not stopped many well-intentioned, sincere Christians from believing that this is what the Bible teaches. In addition, it is true as we have seen in this book, there are Bible verses that indicate that the source for one's

---

[248] The Daily News (Retrieved Tuesday, October 30, 2018) http://www.nydailynews.com/news/crime/40-years-son-sam-berkowitz-pleaded-guilty-murders-article-1.3976835

[249] http://time.com/3949986/1977-blackout-new-york-history/

salvation is not works, but, rather, faith in Jesus Christ, together with God's "grace" and mercy.

Ephesians 2:8-9 Updated American Standard Version (UASV)

[8] For by grace you have been saved through faith; and that not of yourselves, it is the gift of God; [9] not from works, so that no man may boast.

2:8. In verse 5, Paul made the parenthetical statement, **it is by grace you have been saved**. Now, in verse 8, he picks up that idea and elaborates on it. *Grace* carries with it the idea of benevolence being bestowed on someone without that person having merited it by his actions. God was not required to offer us salvation. He would be justified in condemning all people to eternal separation from himself. In spite of the fact that our actions bring deserved judgment upon ourselves, God offered us an escape. He didn't have to, but because he loved us, he wanted to. That is *grace*, and that is what *saved* us, or delivered us, from eternal judgment. God's escape belongs to him and to his initiative alone. No part of it can be credited to you. The whole of salvation, the grace as well as the faith, is a gift of God.

He chose to make salvation possible in this way. He handed salvation to you. You did nothing but stick out a hand and accept the gift. Faith is exactly that. It is trustfully accepting from God what he has provided without totally understanding what you are receiving. Faith is giving up on being able to provide what you need for yourself and letting God give what he alone can provide.

2:9. Paul stressed this point almost redundantly. You have done absolutely nothing to earn salvation by being or doing "good." God's plan of salvation by grace places all humans on the same footing. No one may **boast** or point with pride to personal accomplishments in the realm of salvation. No person has done anything in this arena. God has done it all.[250]

2 Timothy 1:9 Updated American Standard Version (UASV)

[9] who has saved us and called us with a holy calling, not according to our works, but according to his own purpose and grace which was granted us in Christ Jesus before times eternal,

1:9. To endure, we must know the object and purpose in any enterprise. We are not called to witness and suffer just because God thinks it is a good idea. Many Christians, however, have little idea of the overarching goal of Christian living.

God has saved us ... not because of anything we have done but because of his own purpose and grace. We are delivered out of the worst of

[250] Max Anders, *Galatians-Colossians*, vol. 8, Holman New Testament Commentary (Nashville, TN: Broadman & Holman Publishers, 1999), 112.

disasters because of God's initiative toward us. It is one of the great imperatives of the Christian life that we realize the source of all our goodness and forgiveness—it is God, in Christ.

People throughout the world are consumed in the struggle to find significance and acceptance. All world religions require of their followers some method by which they attain favor with a god or acceptance and good standing in the spiritual hierarchy. Christianity alone puts all the work and effort upon God for salvation. Often, this very grace becomes the stumbling block for some people. It is hard to admit absolute need and powerlessness, yet this is what God requires of us.

But initial trust, the step into salvation, is only the beginning. God has **called us to a holy life.** This is our life purpose, the call which gives structure and substance to all our choices and everything we think, do, or say.

All this stems from God's grace, **given us in Christ Jesus before the beginning of time.** God's purposes and plan existed before creation, intended in Jesus Christ. We cannot limit what God has done or the extremity of his grace just because we do not understand how it works. How can we comprehend it or condense it to a system we can quantify and classify? We must accept with gratitude what Paul declared, keeping in mind that God's grace is undeserved.[251]

Titus 3:4-6 Updated American Standard Version (UASV)

4 But when the kindness of God our Savior and his love for mankind appeared, **5** he saved us, not by deeds of righteousness that we have done, but because of his mercy, through the washing of regeneration**[252]** and renewal by the Holy Spirit, **6** whom he poured out on us richly through Jesus Christ our Savior,

3:4. "At one time" we were enslaved to depravity (v. 3). Then Paul wrote **But when** and introduced a seismic shift. Something crucial happened through a dramatic, historical event that challenges our imprisonment to sin: **the kindness**

[251] Knute Larson, *I & II Thessalonians, I & II Timothy, Titus, Philemon*, vol. 9, Holman New Testament Commentary (Nashville, TN: Broadman & Holman Publishers, 2000), 268.

[252] **Regeneration (Rebirth), Born Again, Born of God, Born of the Spirit**: (Gr. palingenesiai; gennaō *anōthen; gennaō theos; gennaō pneuma*) This regeneration is the Holy Spirit working in his life, giving him a new nature, who repents and accepts Christ, placing him on the path to salvation. By taking in this knowledge of God's Word, we will be altering our way of thinking, which will affect our emotions and behavior, as well as our lives now and for eternity. This Word will influence our minds, making corrections in the way we think. If we are to have the Holy Spirit controlling our lives, we must 'renew our mind' (Rom. 12:2) "which is being renewed in knowledge" (Col. 3:10) of God and his will and purposes. (Matt 7:21-23; See Pro 2:1-6) All of this boils down to each individual Christian digging into the Scriptures in a meditative way, so he can 'discover the knowledge of God, receiving wisdom; from God's mouth, as well as knowledge and understanding.' (Pro. 2:5-6) As he acquires the mind that is inundated with the Word of God, he must also "be doers of the Word."–John 3:3; 6-7; 2 Corinthians 5:17; Titus 3:5; James 1:22-25.

and love of God our Savior appeared. This is the incarnation, the appearance (epiphany) of Christ among men. God's kindness and love compelled Christ's appearance at Bethlehem, his exemplary life, and his substitutionary death and resurrection.

3:5–6. Jesus, in these actual events, gained salvation for all people who believe. Rescuing us from the grip of corruption, **he saved us.**

The work of salvation comes solely from God's mercy, **not because of righteous things we had done.** As Isaiah 64:6 states, "All our righteous acts are like filthy rags." We can contrive no goodness by which to attain the favor or forgiveness of God. Salvation comes independent of human effort or desire. God initiates, acts, and pursues **because of his mercy.**

Salvation comes **through the washing of rebirth and renewal by the Holy Spirit.** These terms explain, in part, the complex activities which faith in Christ generates. The **washing of rebirth** refers to the cleansing from sin which results from trust in Jesus Christ. This purification of the sound spirit brings life. No longer living on a purely natural or physical level, believers are transformed from spirit-death to spirit-life. They count themselves "dead to sin but alive to God in Christ Jesus" (Rom. 6:11). **Renewal** carries the same idea, that a person has come into a new existence, both in this life and for eternity. The Holy Spirit participates in Salvador, establishing his presence in the soul and enabling each person to act in true righteousness.

God has **poured out** this Holy Spirit **on us generously.** God always acts in extravagance, and his gift of the Spirit to those who believe demonstrates his greatest liberality. Not only has he rescued us from the frustrations and enslavements of sin; he has assured a spiritual power and development that would lie beyond us without his personal interaction. The Spirit enables us to follow in the ways of Christ.[253]

Additionally, Jesus said,

John 3:36 Updated American Standard Version (UASV)

36 The one trusting[254] in the Son has eternal life, but the one who disobeys the Son will not see life, but the wrath of God remains on him.

---

[253] Knute Larson, *I & II Thessalonians, I & II Timothy, Titus, Philemon*, vol. 9, Holman New Testament Commentary (Nashville, TN: Broadman & Holman Publishers, 2000), 382–383.

[254] **Believe, faith, Trust in**: (Gr. *pisteuo*) If *pisteuo* is followed by the Greek preposition *eis*, ("into, in, among," accusative case), it is generally rendered "trusting in" or "trust in." (John 3:16, 36; 12:36; 14:1) The grammatical construction of the Greek verb *pisteuo* "believe" followed by the Greek preposition *eis* "into" in the accusative gives us the sense of having faith into Jesus, putting faith in, trusting in Jesus.–Matt. 21:25, 32; 27:42; John 1:7, 12; 2:23–24; 3:15–16, 36; 6:47; 11:25; 12:36; 14:1; 20:31; Acts 16:31; Rom. 4:3.

Further, the apostle John wrote,

1 John 5:13 Updated American Standard Version (UASV)

[13] These things I have written to you who believe in the name of the Son of God, in order that you may know that you have eternal life.

5:13. John clearly stated his purpose for writing the Gospel: "That you may believe that Jesus is the Christ, the Son of God, and that by believing you may have life in his name" (John 20:31). The Gospel was written to non-Christians to lead them to become Christians. In a parallel way, toward the end of his first epistle, John stated his purpose for writing it: **That you may know that you have eternal life.** First John is written to those who are Christians to give them assurance that they are saved.[255]

Some have reasoned from the above texts that if a genuine Christian has been saved if he has eternal life, it cannot be lost, or, as many Christian believe, "Once saved, always saved." However, even the Calvinists do not accept this expression. While the words themselves are not found in Scripture is the idea found there? Does "Once saved, always saved" fully express the Scriptural view of salvation and gaining eternal life? All Scriptures need to be taken into account.

Once You Are Saved, Are You Always Saved?

Jude 5 Revised Standard Version (RSV)

[5] Now I desire to remind you, though you were once for all fully informed, that he who **saved** a people out of the land of Egypt, **afterward destroyed** those who did not believe.

Here Jude is informing his readers that like the Israelites who were saved when they were brought up out of Egypt, they were later destroyed when they became unfaithful, so too, the same could happen to these born-again Christians.

Matthew 24:13 Revised Standard Version (RSV)

[13] But he who endures to the end will be saved.

[255] David Walls and Max Anders, *I & II Peter, I, II & III John, Jude*, vol. 11, Holman New Testament Commentary (Nashville, TN: Broadman & Holman Publishers, 1999), 224.

Thus, as we can see from Jesus' own words, when a person is born again, when he accepts Christ, when be puts his faith into Christ, his final salvation is not determined in those moments.

Philippians 2:12 Revised Standard Version (RSV)

12 Therefore, my beloved, as you have always obeyed, so now, not only as in my presence but much more in my absence, work out your own salvation with fear and trembling;

Paul is talking to "saints," namely, holy ones, born-again Christians as is stated in Philippians 1:1. Paul is warning them here to not be overly confident in their salvation but that they should understand that their final salvation was not assured, for they could fall away or willfully leave Christ sometime in their life, taking them off of the path of salvation.

Hebrews 10:26-27 Revised Standard Version (RSV)

26 For if we sin deliberately after receiving the knowledge of the truth, there no longer remains a sacrifice for sins, 27 but a fearful prospect of judgment, and a fury of fire which will consume the adversaries.

We have already dealt with this verse earlier, but we will reiterate that the Bible does not say that no matter what one does, what sins they commit after they are saved (really on the path of salvation), they will not lose their salvation. Rather, the Bible encourages ones to remain faithful until the end.

Hebrews 6:4-6 Revised Standard Version (RSV)

4 For it is **impossible to restore** again to **repentance** those who have once **been enlightened**, who have **tasted the heavenly gift**, and have become **partakers of the Holy Spirit**, 5 and have tasted the goodness of the word of God and the powers of the age to come, 6 if they then **commit apostasy**, since they crucify the Son of God on their own account and hold him up to contempt.

Thus, Hebrews 6:4-6, shows us that even a person who is anointed with Holy Spirit can lose his hope of salvation.

Hebrews 5:9 Revised Standard Version (RSV)

9 and being made perfect he became the source of eternal salvation to all who **obey** him,

This does not contradict the texts that state Christians are saved through faith, but rather it shows obedience is an evident demonstration that one's faith is genuine, which is the very point that James makes.

Hebrews 3:14 Revised Standard Version (RSV)

14 For we share in Christ, **if only** we hold our first confidence firm to the end.

Like Jesus words at Matthew 24:13, Paul makes it clear that those who have genuinely accepted Christ must remain faithful steadfast until the end.

Ephesians 2:8-9 Revised Standard Version (RSV)

8 For by grace you have been saved through faith; and this is not your own doing, it is the gift of God, 9 not because of works, lest any man should boast.

The provision of salvation is based on God's grace alone, which is not deserved. We all are infected with Adamic sin, inherited sin, as we are descendants of Adam, and cannot gain salvation on our own, even if our entire life was filled with works from the beginning to end. Salvation is a gift that God has given us and is only available to those who put faith in sin-atoning value of Christ, remaining steadfastly faithful until the end.

James 2:14 Revised Standard Version (RSV)

14 What does it profit, my brethren, if a man says he has faith but has not works? Can his faith save him?

James uses the term **what use is it, my brothers,** to ask a rhetorical question to highlight or emphasize his point. James asks **if someone says he has faith, but he has no works, can that faith save him?** Faith is an assurance and confidence in what is believed in based on the knowledge of that particular object. Faith is not blindly hoping for something or someone, but rather knowing and trusting with complete certainty. Rather faith is based on knowledge of something that can be known. It is putting faith **into** something or someone. The Christian faith it is not blind at all since it is in an all-powerful and holy God. Instead, Christianity is built upon the knowledge of God who is the creator of the universe and all of humanity itself.

The major issue here is in the fact that one is merely claiming to have faith. They are giving nothing more than a verbal affirmation of a belief that consists only of the framework of their mind but has not yet affected the nature of their will and produced proper actions. James makes it clear that faith is not just some head knowledge alone, but true faith is manifested in the fact that it produces appropriate actions consistent with what one claims to profess. James here asks the question for his audience to ponder and think about to come to their conclusion as he states **can such faith save him**?

Faith does not just begin and end at a mere profession of Christ. Good works in one's life then must evidence it. These works are not done as a way to earn salvation, but rather out of gratitude of a heart that has been changed by the power of Christ that made one a new creation in Christ. Good works are to be done out of the overflow of the heart that has been redeemed by the power of God through Christ. The answer to James question, as he will explain in the following verses, is faith without works is not true saving faith.

James 2:26 Revised Standard Version (RSV)

26 For as the body apart from the spirit is dead, so faith apart from works is dead.

When a person (a soul) dies (beyond clinical death), there is no longer any animating force or "spirit" within any single cell out of the body's one hundred trillion cells. Many of us have seen the animation video in science classes at school, where the cell is shown to be like a microscopic factory with an enormous amount of work taking place. Therefore, no work is taking place within the lifeless body, as all of the cells that were animated by the spirit are dead. The body is not good for anything. This is the similarity that James is trying to draw as a faith that lacks works is just as lifeless, producing no results and of no use as a corpse. The literal eye cannot see faith; however, works is an evident demonstration that faith can be seen. When one is not moved to good works, it is all too clear that this one has no real faith. Alternatively, any Christian that is motivated to good works, he possesses a genuine faith.

Acts 16:30-31 Revised Standard Version (RSV)

30 and brought them out and said, "Men, what must I do to be
saved?" 31 And they [Paul and Silas] said, "Believe in the Lord Jesus, and you
will be saved, you and your household."

If the man in the account and those of his household had been truly saved, would they not have evidenced that salvation by living their life according to their faith?

How are we supposed to reconcile what some might believe to be differences in the Scriptures over the doctrine of salvation? We know one thing for certain, there absolutely no contradictions in the Word of God. It is the interpreter who has not come to a correct understanding. For example, the apostle Paul and James are in complete harmony, simply expressing the truth of God's Word from different points of view. It is Paul who offers us the key to a correct understanding.

As both Jesus and Paul spoke of the one "who endures to the end will be saved," Paul also repeatedly likened the Christian's life to a race that must be finished if you are to receive the prize, which is a similar concept. Paul urged the Hebrew Christians, "let us also lay aside every weight and the sin which so easily entangles us, and let us **run with endurance the race** that is set before us." (Heb. 12:1) For every person **(1) seeking to enter the race**, as sinner, the Christian must take steps that are necessary for salvation. First and foremost, he must hear and accept the Word of God, place all of his trust in Jesus Christ and the ransom sacrifice, repent of all former sins and be baptized. Peter said at Pentecost, "Repent and be baptized every one of you in the name of Jesus Christ for the forgiveness of your sins, and you will receive the gift of the Holy Spirit … 'Save yourselves from this crooked generation.'" – Acts 2:37-40; 16:31-33; Romans 10:13-14.

Zondervan Illustrated Bible Backgrounds Commentary has, "**IT DOES NOT TAKE LONG EXPERIENCE** in the Christian faith to learn that maintaining a resolute commitment to Christ is not easy and demands endurance. We can find help, however, from several directions. The "cloud of witnesses" reminds us that God's people of the past have walked similar paths as the ones we are walking presently and have done so keeping faith. The exhortation of Scripture to put off those things that hinder us reminds us that the weights we embrace in life—whether unwholesome activities or attitudes of questionable value—can impede our progress in the faith. Finally, we must look to Jesus as the ultimate example of endurance. His attitude of scorning shame gives us a powerful reference point from which to evaluate the difficulties of life, especially those that come because we are committed to God's path. So too the author of Hebrews [Paul][256] challenges his readers to "strip" off everything that hinders them in the race of endurance. An ancient writer could use the term *onkos*, translated in 12:1 as [something] "that hinders," to refer to a mass, weight, or bodily fat. In the context of running, it could refer to burdensome clothing or excess bodily weight. Therefore, believers are to run the Christian race with endurance, laying aside those things that bind or weigh us down."[257]

(2) Once the person is **in the race** by now being on the track of salvation, the Christian must "take hold of that which is truly life." However, is it possible once they have a firm grip on life to lose their grip? The apostle Paul answers that question for us. "**24** Do you not know that in a race all the runners compete, but only one receives the prize? So run that you may obtain

---

[256] Who Authored the Book of Hebrews: A Defense for Pauline Authorship (retrieved Wednesday, October 31, 2018) https://christianpublishinghouse.co/2016/11/02/who-authored-the-book-of-hebrews-a-defense-for-pauline-authorship/

[257] Clinton E. Arnold, *Zondervan Illustrated Bible Backgrounds Commentary: Hebrews to Revelation.*, vol. 4 (Grand Rapids, MI: Zondervan, 2002), 75.

it. [25] Every athlete exercises self-control in all things. They do it to receive a perishable wreath, but we an imperishable. [26] Well, I do not run aimlessly, I do not box as one beating the air; [27] but I pommel my body and subdue it, lest after preaching to others I myself should be disqualified." (1 Tim. 6:19; 1 Cor. 9:24-27, RSV) Paul makes it very clear here that the only one getting the prize of life is he who finishes the race. Notice, that even the apostle Paul himself was in the race and he clearly said that he could do something that would disqualify him from the race. Again, "I pommel my body and subdue it, lest after preaching to others I myself should be disqualified."

How this could be ignored by some is beyond this author, as they would never doubt that Paul was a "saved" Christian, and even he believed he could be "disqualified" from the race. However, he knew and told us, as long as we continue throughout our lives to 'run so that we may obtain the prize,' we can remain in the race, on the track of salvation, an assurance "he who endures to the end will be saved." (Matt. 24:13) This is why those Christians who remain steadfastly in the race can be said to have "eternal life." However, if they should ever quit running or stumble to the point of no return, they would be "disqualified," losing their grip on "eternal life."

Paul follows this race analogy by warning the Christians about the danger of being too confident in their salvation. He used the example of the Israelites, who were saved by fleeing Egypt through the Red Sea. However, they stumbled while they were in the wilderness, falling into wrongdoing. He warned the Corinthians, "We ["saved" Christians] must not put the Lord to the test." Then, making his point all too clear, he stated, "let anyone who thinks that he stands take heed lest he fall." Yes, as it could happen to one of the Greatest Christians of all time, Paul, it could happen to every so-called "saved" Christian. – 1 Corinthians 10:1-12, ESV.

Now, we fully understand why Paul, throughout his fourteen letters, constantly, humbly highlighted his own need to stay in the race. For example, in speaking of his resurrection hope as a reward, like in a race,

Philippians 3:10-14 Updated American Standard Version (UASV)

[10] that I may know him and the power of his resurrection and the fellowship of his sufferings, becoming conformed to his death; [11] that by any means I may attain to the resurrection from the dead.

Reaching Forward to God's Goal

[12] Not that I have already obtained it or am already perfect, but I press on so that I may lay hold of that for which also I was laid hold of by Christ Jesus. [13] Brothers, I do not count myself as having laid hold of it: but one

thing I do, forgetting the things which are behind, and stretching forward to the things which are ahead, [14] I press on toward the goal for the prize of the upward call of God in Christ Jesus.

3:10–11. Demonstrating the lack of importance of earthly things, Paul expressed what life truly meant to him. He desired resurrection from the dead, so he sought the way that promised resurrection. The Damascus road experience transformed him. He discovered that Judaism with its traditions, regulations, and rituals could not guarantee resurrection. Only the resurrected One could. This changed Paul's aim in life. He wanted to **know Christ and the power of his resurrection**. To know Christ meant much more than knowing about him in his mind.

Knowledge is a relationship term of intimacy. Paul wanted the closest possible personal relationship with Christ, a relationship pictured in baptism as buried to the old life of sin and raised to a new life of righteousness. To know Christ in this way meant he was ready to share in Christ's sufferings, even if that meant sharing his death. Paul's longing to share with Christ comes through strongly in Galatians 2:20: "I have been crucified with Christ and I no longer live, but Christ lives in me. The life I live in the body, I live by faith in the Son of God, who loved me and gave himself for me." In everyday living, Paul maintained that his life and the lives of his readers should reflect the difference that Christ makes.

3:12. Paul's description of his desires pointed forward to a goal. He had not "arrived." Not yet mature, he was still very much in the race of the Christian life. The perfection he would have at the future resurrection was not yet attained. He still had to deal with what in Romans 7 he calls "the flesh," an innate pull to sin. He had to deal with his sinful body and was only too aware of the need for further spiritual growth. He purposes to **press on** as he had not attained the intense personal knowledge of Christ that he desired and had not become all that Christ wanted him to be. He did not press on out of personal power or will. He did so because Jesus had chosen him and on the Damascus road grabbed hold of his life. Paul always held God up as the source of every part of the salvation experience. A fact of the Christian life is that the more you mature the more you realize how much further you have to go to become like Christ.

3:13. Paul, in this verse, underlines his denial of personal power or attainment and his single-minded focus. To describe that focus, he employs the image of a runner in a race who hopes to win the prize. He cannot look back. He cannot cloud his mind with past memories. He strains every muscle in his body to achieve forward motion. Eyes focus on the finish line. Paul forgets the guilt of persecuting the church. He forgets the pain of prison and physical punishment. He forgets the frustration of disobedient church members and false teachers. He looks ahead to see the resurrection, where he will meet Jesus face-to-face.

3:14. With this focus he pursues his goal intently. His goal is **to win the prize for which God** had called him in Christ Jesus. He wants to hear God call his name and summon him to the victory stand, where he will meet Jesus face-to-face and know him in perfect intimacy. Earthly prizes do not last. Eternal prizes do. The goal can never be realized on earth. It is a goal that pulls us heavenward. Note 1 Corinthians 9:25: "Everyone who competes in the games goes into strict training. They do it to get a crown that will not last, but we do it to get a crown that will last forever." In the late 1950s, Jim Elliot, former husband of author Elisabeth Elliot, gave up his life to reach a hostile tribe in the jungles of Ecuador. His words have been immortalized: "He is not a fool who gives up what he cannot keep to gain what he cannot lose." While Paul was not spiritually where he thought he would ultimately be, he intended not to be distracted by anything as he pursued his goal (Heb. 12:1–2). Both discipline and determination are required to accomplish this objective.[258]

2 Timothy 4:6-8 Updated American Standard Version (UASV)

Fight the Fine Fight

[6] For I am already being poured out as a drink offering, and the time of my departure has come. [7] I have fought the good fight, I have finished the course, I have kept the faith. [8] Henceforth there is laid up for me the crown of righteousness, which the Lord, the righteous judge, will award to me on that day, and not only to me but also to all who have loved his appearing.

4:6. Paul had already provided Timothy with sound reasons to stay faithful to the ministry: God's certain return, the increase of falsehood and wickedness, and his own commissioning. Now Paul gave Timothy another compelling reason to stay with the hard work of ministry: **the time has come for my departure**. Paul would die soon, and Timothy must carry on the work.

Paul referred to his coming death in terms of a willing sacrifice to God, reminiscent of Romans 12:1. He stated, **I am already being poured out like a drink offering**. His imagery came from his Jewish heritage and

[258] Max Anders, *Galatians-Colossians*, vol. 8, Holman New Testament Commentary (Nashville, TN: Broadman & Holman Publishers, 1999), 244–245.

the biblical rites of devotion given to the sanctified community of faith. In Numbers 15, God defines for Israel some of the burnt offerings "made by fire … as an aroma pleasing to the Lord" (Num. 15:3). A drink offering of wine was to accompany the sacrifice of animals or grain. Just as Christ, the Lamb, was sacrificed to remove our sin guilt, so we are called to offer our lives in service as expressions of worship. Paul's offering was a literal offering of blood (often symbolized as wine) as he gave himself to the executioner's sword.

4:7–8. Paul offered three statements as a short review of his life. He meant to inspire Timothy, and all Christians, to continued faithfulness.

First, Paul declared, **I have fought the good fight**. Athletic competitions were as popular in the ancient world as in our own. Most people were familiar with the training and discipline necessary to succeed in athletic contests. Paul described his life in similar terms, except that the focus and discipline he employed were for the good fight of faith. He gave his life to the only cause worthy of devotion. He stayed with the rigors, the sacrifices, and the deprivations in order to receive the victor's reward.

Then Paul stated, **I have finished the race**. He viewed the successful completion of his life before God; he endured to the end. He remained true to the gospel despite terrible opposition. It was the very thing he asked of Timothy. Jesus gave a similar sentiment in John 17:4: "I have brought you glory on earth by completing the work you gave me to do."

There were still lepers to heal and blind people who could not see. There were many who did not believe. But both Jesus and Paul had submitted their wills to the will of God and had done what God called them to do.

This is all any of us can do. We can finish our own race. God's call upon each life is different in details and specifics, but he desires faithful endurance from all of us. We finish the race one step at a time, choosing to testify of God's goodness and grace and living rightly every day.

Paul concluded, **I have kept the faith**. This summarized what all the other phrases had described. In life and in doctrine, he had stayed the course with integrity.

4:8. As Paul awaited death, he stood on the threshold of a more glorious life to come. He knew what was ahead: **the crown of righteousness**. He knew who would confer it: **the Lord, the righteous Judge**. He knew when he would receive it: **on that day**.

> Biblical writers often used the metaphor of a crown to describe the conferring of honor or reward. Paul used this metaphor in reference to the reward of righteousness that believers will receive when Christ returns. Though an individual receives the righteousness of Christ when he trusts in him as Savior, this righteousness is not fully realized until the day of his appearing. Legally, before the holy God, we are righteous. Practically, we await Christ's return when we will experience the reward of his total righteousness.
>
> This great future urged Paul on through the persecutions, the loneliness, the disappointments. He looked ahead to the sweep of eternity, the bliss of living in God's presence, and wrote, "Though outwardly we are wasting away, yet inwardly we are being renewed day by day. For our light and momentary troubles are achieving for us an eternal glory that far outweighs them all" (2 Cor. 4:16–17).
>
> This future exists, not for Paul alone, **but also to all who have longed for his appearing**. To set our hopes on Christ's appearing qualifies us as children of God. The unbeliever cannot look forward to the day of Christ's return. It means nothing to him. But to those who have staked their lives upon his coming, that day promises a uniting with the Lord. There is joy in anticipation of seeing him.[259]

It was only after Paul neared the end of his life that he wrote: "I have fought the good fight, I have finished the course, I have kept the faith." At this point in Paul's life, he could finally say with confidence: "Henceforth there is laid up for me the crown of righteousness, which the Lord, the righteous judge, will award to me on that day." Therefore, the inspired, fully inerrant words of Paul are completely consistent Jesus words, "he who endures to the end will be saved." (Matt. 24:13) This is why Paul constantly pleaded with fellow Christians to be on guard. Their eternal life was at risk all the way up unto the end, namely, Jesus return or their falling asleep in death. Yes, if you are truly appreciative of the salvation you have been given through the ransom sacrifice of Jesus Christ, you will not be overconfident. You will remain in the race without stumbling out of it or leaving the race. You will strive to remain steadfastly faith to Jesus Christ like the apostle Paul and other early Christians. Yes, the ones Paul encouraged to "work out your salvation with fear and trembling."

[259] Knute Larson, *I & II Thessalonians, I & II Timothy, Titus, Philemon*, vol. 9, Holman New Testament Commentary (Nashville, TN: Broadman & Holman Publishers, 2000), 321–322.

CHAPTER 8 Are the Five Points of Calvinism Biblical?

Is Total Depravity Biblical?

Total depravity (also called radical corruption or pervasive depravity) is a Protestant theological doctrine derived from the concept of original sin. It teaches that, as a consequence of man's fall, every person born into the world is enslaved to the service of sin as a result of their fallen nature and, apart from the efficacious (irresistible) or prevenient (enabling) grace of God, is completely unable to choose by themselves to follow God, refrain from evil, or accept the gift of salvation as it is offered.

Roger Olson quotes Arminius saying:

> "In this state, the Free Will of man towards the True Good is not only wounded, maimed, infirm, bent and weakened [*attenuatum*]; but it is also imprisoned [*captivatum*], destroyed, and lost: And its powers are not only debilitated and useless they be assisted by grace, but it has no powers whatsoever except such as are excited by Divine grace."

Olson continues, "This Arminian statement alone should put to rest the all-too-common misconception that Arminius and Arminians believe the human free will survived the Fall intact. Leading Reformed scholar Robert Letham perpetuates this myth in his article 'Arminianism' in *The Westminster Handbook to Reformed Theology*. Describing Arminius' theology he writes, 'Moreover, [for him] the fallen will remains free.' This is, of course, simply not true."

Millard J. Erickson,

Depravity Sinfulness, corruption, or pollution of one's nature. **Depravity, Total** The idea that sinfulness affects the whole of one's nature and colors all that one does; it does not necessarily mean that one is as sinful as one can possibly be.[260]

The Bible does teach that fallen man (Genesis 3:6) every part of him: his mind, will, emotions and flesh, are been corrupted by sin (missing the mark of perfection). Isaiah 64:6 tells us, We have all become like one who is

[260] Millard J. Erickson, *The Concise Dictionary of Christian Theology* (Wheaton, IL: Crossway Books, 2001), 49.

unclean, and all our righteous deeds are like a polluted garment. We all fade like a leaf, and our errors, like the wind, take us away." Jesus tells us, "So, every healthy tree bears good fruit, but the diseased tree bears bad fruit. A healthy tree cannot bear bad fruit, nor can a diseased tree bear good fruit." – Matthew 7:17-18.

What does the Bible says about total depravity (sinfulness, corruption, or pollution of one's nature)? Jeremiah 17:9 says, "The heart is deceitful above all things, and desperately sick; who can understand it?" The Bible says that man was was brought forth in error, and in sin was conceived and is dead in the trespasses and sins. (Psalm 51:5, Psalm 58:3, Ephesians 2:1-5) Genesis 6:5; 8:21 tells us that fallen man is mentally bent toward evil, not that he is evil. The Bible further teaches that fallen man has loved the darkness rather than the light because their works were evil. (John 3:19; John 8:34) It is written: "None is righteous, no, not one; no one understands; no one seeks for God." (Romans 3:10-11) The aostle Paul's words at 1 Corinthians 2:14 are often misinterpretated, taken to mean that man cannot understand the things of God. 2:14 reads, "But the natural man does not accept the things of the Spirit of God, for they are foolishness to him, and he is **not able to understand** them, because they are **examined spiritually**." Roy B. Zuck writes, "The Greek word *ginosko* ("to understand") does not mean comprehend intellectually; it means know by experience. The unsaved obviously do not experience God's Word because they do not welcome it. Only the regenerate has the capacity to welcome and experience the Scriptures, by means of the Holy Spirit." (Zuck 1991, 23)

Hundreds of millions of Christians use this verse as support that without the "Holy Spirit," we can fully understand God's Word. They would argue that without the "Spirit" the Bible is nothing more than foolish nonsense to the reader. What we need to do before, arriving at the correct meaning of what Paul meant, is grasp what he meant by his use of the word "understand," as to what is 'foolish.' In short, "the things of the Spirit of God" are the "Spirit" inspired Word of God. The natural man sees the inspired Word of God as foolish, and "he is not able to understand them."

Paul wrote, "But the natural man does not accept the things of the Spirit of God, for they are foolishness to him." What did Paul mean by this statement? Did he mean that if the Bible reader did not have the "Spirit" helping him, he would not be able to grasp the correct meaning of the text? Are we to understand Paul as saying that without the "Spirit," the Bible and its teachings are beyond our understanding?

We can gain a measure of understanding as to what Paul meant, by observing how he uses the term "foolishness" elsewhere in the very same letter. At 1 Corinthians 3:19, it is used in the following way, "For the wisdom of this world is foolishness with God." This verse helps us to arrive at the use in two stages: (1) the verse states that human wisdom is foolishness with God, (2) and we know that the use of foolishness here does not mean that God cannot understand (or grasp) human wisdom. The use is that He sees human wisdom as 'foolish' and rejects it as such.

Therefore, the term "foolishness" of 1 Corinthians 3:19 is not in reference to not "understanding," but as to one's view of the text, its significance, or better yet, lack of significance, or lack of value. We certainly know that God can understand the wisdom of the world, but condemns it as being 'foolish.' The same holds true of 1 Corinthians 1:20, where the verbal form of foolishness is used, "Has not God made foolish the wisdom of the world?" Thus, we have the term "foolishness" being used before and after 1 Corinthians 2:14, (1:20; 3:19). In all three cases, we are dealing with the significance, the value being attributed to something.

Thus, it seems obvious that we should attribute the same meaning to our text in question, 1 Corinthians 2:14. In other words, the Apostle Paul, by his use of the term "foolishness," is not saying that the unbeliever is unable to understand, to grasp the Word of God. If this were the case, why would we ever share the Word of God, the gospel message with an unbeliever? Unbelievers can understand the Word of God; however, unbelievers see it as foolish, having no value or significance. The resultant meaning of chapters 1-3 of 1 Corinthians is that the unbelieving world of mankind can understand the Word of God. However, they view it as foolish (missing value or significance). God, on the other hand, understands the wisdom of the world of mankind but views it foolish (missing value or significance). Therefore, in both cases, the information is understood or grasped; however, it is rejected because of the party considering it, they believe it lacks value or significance.

We pray for the guidance of the Holy Spirit, and our spirit, or mental disposition, needs to be attuned to God and His Spirit through study and application. Now, if our mental disposition is not in tune with the Spirit, we will not come away with the right answer. As Ephesians shows, we can grieve the Spirit.

Paul tells us "For the wrath of God is revealed from heaven against all ungodliness and unrighteousness of men, who by their unrighteousness suppress the truth." The choose to suppress the truth, it is not hidden from them. That was the lie that Satan told Eve, that God is withholding the truth (knowledge) from man. Genesis 3:5 says, "For God knows that when you eat of it your eyes will be opened, and you will be like God, knowing good and evil." They knew good and evil as it was good to not eat from the tree and evil to eat from it. This speaks of challemging God's sovereigny, their choosing for themselves what is good and evil. Proverbs 14:12 says, "here is a way that seems right to a man, but its end is the way of death." What did Solomon mean?

Making choices that are wise and having a flourishing, successful life no doubt demands the knowledge, good sense, and life skills to recognize what is right from what is wrong. However, the Bible warns:

There is a way that seems right to a man: **way; road; journey**: (דֶּרֶךְ derek) is literally a way, path, route, road, highway to be able to get from one place to another. (Gen. 16:7) It also refers to the **journey** that has a known destination, going from one place to another, with the route in mind. In addition, *derek* also refers to the **way**, that is, a course of conduct, behavior, way of life, what is done, the **way** you conduct yourself on this journey filled with life-choices that you make in this imperfect age of Satan's world. The father is giving the son the **way** to go by way of wisdom. **Seems right**, infers a moral character, a way of behaving. We can imagine a journey wherein the traveler thinks he is headed in the right direction and that he has laid out his path correctly that will get him toward his destination. But he realizes in the last moment that the path he has chosen leads to death. Man is of course a masculine reference, but this also applies to the life of a woman as well.

but its end is the way of death: Of course, here, **its end** is referring to "the end of the journey," "the end of the path," "the end of the road," "the end of his life." And, undoubtedly, **the way of death** is referring to the "way," "path," "route," "road" that ends in death.

Therefore, we must learn how to distinguish between what is actually the right way and what may seem like the right way. The expression **the way of death** is telling us that there are going to be many false, ambiguous, unreliable, illusory **ways**. Every major or significant decision that we make in like either keeps us on the right way or can divert us off the right way. Our human foresight is limited, so we must have a deep grasp of God's Word to guide us. We must avoid the way of the fool, the way of excessive pleasure, and putting our way over the way of God. Sadly, as Jesus tells us, the way of death belongs to a great many self-deluded souls. (Matt. 7:21-23) These ones believe that they are doing the will of God, when, in reality, they are doing the will of themselves

Their **way** is of stupidity and disregard, the **way** of the world of man that is alienated from God and earthly mindedness as opposed to the mind of Christ, the way of emotionalism, and pleasing the flesh, seems to be the right way to those who walk in them. They have a blind zeal that leads only their **way**, not the **way** of God. They imagine this will lead them to eternal life. Furthermore, they glorify themselves in their own eyes, imagining that all will be well at in the end. Jesus said, "Not everyone who says to me, 'Lord, Lord,' will enter the kingdom of heaven, but the one who does the will of my Father who is in heaven. On that day many will say to me, 'Lord, Lord, did we not prophesy in your name, and cast out demons in your name, and do many mighty works in your name?' And then will I declare to them, 'I never knew you; depart from me, you workers of lawlessness.'" (Matt. 7:21-23) Their **end** is very terrifying, and even more so as they near the end of the **way**: the **way of death**, eternal destruction; their error in judgment will certainly be their destruction, and they will die because they chose to lie to themselves. Self-delusion will in the end be a case of self-destroyer.

Romans 3:9-18 Updated American Standard Version (UASV)

Both Jews and Greeks are Under Sin

9 What then? Are we better than they? Not at all, for we have already charged that both Jews and Greeks are all under sin; 10 as it is written,

"None is righteous, not even one;
11 there is no one who understands;
there is no one who seeks for God.
12 All have turned aside; together they have become worthless;
there is none who does good,
there is not even one."[261]
13 "Their throat is an open grave;
with their tongues they keep deceiving."
"The venom of asps is under their lips."[262]
14 "Whose mouth is full of cursing and bitterness;"[263]
15 "Their feet are swift to shed blood;
16 destruction and misery are in their paths,

[261] Verses 10–12 are a quotation from Ps 14:1–3

[262] A quotation from Ps 5:9 and Ps 140:3

[263] A quotation from Ps 10:7

[17] and the way of peace they have not known."[264]
[18] "There is no fear of God before their eyes."[265]

If total depravity **does not mean** that fallen man is as wicked or as sinful as he can be, or that he lacks a conscience, nor has any sense of right or wrong, or that he is unable to do things that are good, or that he cannot understand the Scriptures; but rather means "the idea that sinfulness affects the whole of one's nature and colors all that one does; it does not necessarily mean that one is as sinful as one can possibly be" as Erickson puts it; then biblically it is acceptable.

Is Unconditional Election Biblical?

Unconditional election (also called sovereign election or unconditional grace) is a Calvinist doctrine relating to predestination that describes the actions and motives of God prior to his creation of the world, when he predestined some people to receive salvation, the elect, and the rest he left to continue in their sins and receive the just punishment, eternal damnation, for their transgressions of God's law as outlined in the Old and New Testaments of the Bible. God made these choices according to his own purposes apart from any conditions or qualities related to those persons.The counter-view to unconditional election is the Arminian view of conditional election, the belief that God chooses for eternal salvation those who he foreknows will exercise their free will to respond to God's prevenient grace with faith in Christ.

Ephesians 1:3-6 Updated American Standard Version (UASV)

Spiritual Blessings

[3] Blessed be the God and Father[266] of our Lord Jesus Christ, who has blessed us with every spiritual blessing in the heavenly places in Christ, [4] even as he chose us in him before the foundation of the world, that we should be holy and blameless before him.[267] In love [5] he foreordained[268] us to adoption[269] as sons through Jesus Christ to himself, according to the good

[264] Verses 15–17 are a quotation from Isa 59:7–8

[265] A quotation from Ps 36:1

[266] Or *God and the Father*

[267] Or h*im, having in love foreordained us*

[268] That is, *decided beforehand*

[269] **Adoption:** (υἱοθεσία huiothesia) The Greek noun is a legal term that literally means "adoption as a son," which means to take or accept a son or daughter who is not naturally such by relationship, including full inheritance rights. The apostle Paul mentions adoption several times about those with a new status as called and chosen by God. These ones were born as offspring of the imperfect Adam, were formerly in slavery to sin. Through purchase through Jesus' life as a ransom, many have received the

pleasure of his will 6 to the praise of the glory of his grace, which he freely bestowed on us[270] in the Beloved.

Blessed be the God and Father of our Lord Jesus Christ, who has blessed us with every spiritual blessing in the heavenly places in Christ, (1:3)

Blessed be the God and Father of our Lord Jesus Christ. The Greek word (εὐλογητός eulogētos) rendered **blessed** pertains to being worthy of praise or commendation. The meaning here is that we owe our gratitude to God for all that he has done for us. The reason for our gratitude is given in the verses that follow. God "chose us in him before the foundation of the world." God foreknew that Adam and Eve were going to sin, which is not a case of predestination, as predestination is unbiblical. See the answer to this under Chapter 1 Bible Difficulties below. Paul is very much concerned with carrying out his original eternal will and purpose of eternal life for man, and now the salvation of man. Because of the inspired Word of God, man is now aware of the plan that God had in place even before the foundation of the world, so all glory and exaltation belongs to God.

Who has blessed us with every spiritual blessing.

The love of God is seen in the creation of heavenly spiritual creatures and human creatures. It is God's nature to bestow divine favor and goodness on his creation. Here these blessings are described as **spiritual**, and the likely meaning refers to the spiritual life of God's human creatures. "It is also possible to interpret πνευματικός in Eph 1:3 as referring to 'the Holy Spirit,' that is to say, these blessings would be those which come from the Spirit of God (see 12.21)."[271] We note that "riches" is mentioned five times throughout Ephesians (1:7, 18; 2:7; 3:8, 16), which is used strictly in a spiritual sense. But we also have peace, redemption, and adoption, which are the work of the Holy Spirit mentioned in the following verses. These are undoubtedly blessings that *genuine Christians* appreciate.

In the heavenly places in Christ. The Greek phrase **in heavenly places** (ἐν τοῖς ἐπουρανίοις en tois epouraniois) found here occurs in four other places in Ephesians. (1:20; 2:6; 3:10; 6:12) The context shows that Christians who are going to be with Christ are viewed so by God because they 'obtained an inheritance' with his Son. Even though some of these are

---

adoption as sons and daughters becoming heirs with the only-begotten Son of God, Jesus Christ. – Rom. 8:15, 23; 9:4; Gal. 4:5; Eph. 1:5.

[270] Or *wherewith he endued us*

[271] Johannes P. Louw and Eugene Albert Nida, *Greek-English Lexicon of the New Testament: Based on Semantic Domains* (New York: United Bible Societies, 1996), 322–323.

still on earth, it is as though they have already been "raised up with him and seated us with him in the heavenly places in Christ Jesus." (Eph 1:11, 18-20; 2:4-7, 22.) Paul tells us elsewhere, "If then you have been raised up with Christ, keep seeking the things above, where Christ is, seated at the right hand of God." (Col. 3:3) And the apostle John tells us, "Beloved ones, now we are children of God, and it has not appeared as yet what we will be. We know that when he appears, we will be like him, because we will see him just as he is." – 1 John 3:2.

even as he chose us in him before the foundation of the world, that we should be holy and blameless before him. (1:4)

Even as he chose us. Are some chosen (predestined) to eternal salvation and others to eternal condemnation? The 16th-century Reformer John Calvin wrote: "We define predestination as the eternal design of God, whereby he determined what he wanted to do with each man. For he did not create them all in the same condition but foreordains some to everlasting life and others to eternal damnation." Does God really ordain each of us individually ahead of time as to what our actions and our final destiny are going to be? What does the Bible really teach?

We know that God can foretell the future. He describes himself as "declaring the end from the beginning and from ancient times things not yet done, saying, 'My counsel shall stand, and I will accomplish all my purpose.'" (Isaiah 46:10) There are many examples of God having used his foreknowledge to foretell events before they were to take place in the Scriptures. In many cases, this was centuries before they were to take place. (Daniel 8:20, 21; Micah 5:2)And they came true just as he had prophesied. God had chosen the Israelite nation and Christians before the founding of the earth as his chosen ones. In ancient times Israel became the typical holy nation, for to it, Jehovah said: "And you shall be to me a kingdom of priests and a holy nation. These are the words that you shall speak to the sons of Israel. For you are a holy people to Jehovah your God: Jehovah your God has chosen you to be a people for his own possession, out of all the peoples that are on the face of the earth." (Ex. 19:6; Deut. 7:6) When we look at the Greek New Testament, it speaks of predestination or foreordination relative to those who will receive eternal life and those who will receive eternal destruction.

The words generally translated as "foreknow," "foreknowledge," and "foreordain" (i.e., predestine) are found in the Greek New Testament; the same basic views are conveyed in the Hebrew Scriptures. God indeed has the power of predestination and the faculty of foreknowledge. However, we need to understand foreknowledge and foreordination as they relate to God, grasping certain aspects. There are certain situations and events that take place because God has foreordained that they will (no creature in the universe can hinder these things), but it is not the case that **every event** must take place as it does because God has predetermined it; removing all free will. What God foreknows is because of the infallibility of his power of perception into the future, as though it were a timeline (more on this later). However, as we will see, this in no way violates our free will. In most cases, predestination has to do with groups like the Israelites and events, like the Exodus from Egypt, without foreordaining the specific individuals who will be involved in these groups or events. On the other hand, God's foreknowledge is not limited to groups and events, as he can see the future of every living creature.

God knows in advance what choice people will freely make. The free decisions of human beings determine what foreknowledge God has of them, as opposed to the reverse. The foreknowledge does not determine the free decision; it is the free decisions that determine the foreknowledge. Judas Iscariot betraying Jesus does not happen because God foreknows it, but God foreknows the event because it will happen. The event is logically prior to the foreknowledge, so he foreknows it because it will happen, even though the foreknowledge is chronologically before the event. We can see foreknowledge in this as the foreshadowing of something. When you see the shadow of someone coming around the corner of the building, you see his or her shadow on the ground before you see the person. You know that person is about to come around the corner because of their shadow, but the shadow does not determine the person; the person determines the shadow. God's foreknowledge is like the foreshadowing of a future event. By seeing this foreshadowing, you know the events will happen, But the shadow does not determine the reality; the reality determines the shadow. Therefore, we should think of God's foreknowledge as the foreshadowing of things to come. Therefore, just because God will know something will happen, this does not prejudice or remove the freedom of that happening. Thus, those who believe that God's foreknowledge removes the freedom of the person are mistaken. They posit a constraint upon human choices, which is really quite unintelligible.

God can step into the timeline and tweak anything to create a different outcome if he chooses to do so, which will then alter many future events because it will create a ripple effect in the timeline. If God were to alter anything that was already going to happen, making different choices outside of what was already going to occur in the present, it would have a ripple effect on future events. Let us use Willian Tyndale, which I believe God did step in to the timeline to protect Tyndale from the Catholic Church that was hunting him down for translating the Bible from the original languages of Hebrew

(OT) and Greek (NT) into English. Let us say that God did step in to alter things, allowing Tyndale to survive to the point of bringing us the first printed translation in 1526; it would have had an impact on all English translations that lay ahead in the future: the Coverdale translation of 1535, the Matthew's Bible of 1537, The Great Bible of 1539, Cranmer's Bible of 1540, the Geneva Bible of 1560, and, of course, the King James Version of 1611, and all other down to the Revised Version of 1881, the 1801 American Standard Version, the 1952 Revised Standard Version, the 1960-1995 New American Standard Bible, the 2001 English Standard Version, and 2022 Updated American Standard Version. Think of the impact of the English translations had the Catholic Church executed Tyndale in 1523.

Earlier, we said that those who believe that God's foreknowledge removes a person's freedom are mistaken. They posit a constraint upon human choices, which is really quite unintelligible. How so? Those who God chose must persevere if they are to receive the reward of eternal life. In fact, Jesus said, "the one who endures to the end will be saved." (Matt. 24:13) Why are we told this if the ones chosen thousands of years ago were final? "God created man in his own image." (Genesis 1:27) When creating man, free will was imperative if he was to love and honor God, serving him faithfully. God did not create robots with every moment predetermined beforehand. Our free-willed love is how God can refute Satan's false accusations. God says: "Be wise, my son, and make my heart glad, that I may return a word to my reproacher." (Proverbs 27:11) That is, 'that I may reply to him who reproaches me.'

If God's foreknowledge **does** determine our free decisions, those chosen by God would note freely love God; their love for their Creator could never be genuine. This is why Satan called man's love for God into question in the book of Job. Also, the Bible says that God is impartial, but how can that be so if foreknowledge determines those who are chosen for salvation irrespective of their individual merits? In addition, if these ones are receiving such privileged and favored positions, while others are fated to eternal punishment, how could anyone expect genuine and heartfelt feelings of appreciation and thankfulness in the "elect," or "chosen ones." – Genesis 1:27; Job 1:8; Acts 10:34-35.

The greatest difficulty is the Great Commission that Jesus Christ gave to his "elect" or "chosen ones." He said, "this gospel of the kingdom will be proclaimed throughout the whole world as a testimony to all nations, and then the end will come." (Matt. 24:14) Why, this would be pointless work because some are supposedly predestined to eternal salvation, and others to eternal condemnation. Jesus later said, "Go therefore and **make disciples** of all nations, baptizing them … teaching them …" Why if some are supposedly predestined to eternal salvation and others to eternal condemnation. Jesus said before his ascension back to heaven, "you will be my witnesses in Jerusalem and in all Judea and Samaria, and to the end of the earth." If God's foreknowledge does determine their free decisions, the preaching work essentially pointless? Persuading, persuading, and persuasion, as well as explaining, proving, and defending, are used in reference to Paul's preaching work many times. Notice the meaning of persuasion and how it is meaningless when the outcome is already predetermined.

Persuasion: (Gr. πεισμονή peismonē, πείθω peithō) The Greek word literally means to **1.) persuade**, convince (Matt. 27:20; Ac 12:20; 18:4; 19:8, 26; 23:28; 26:28). It means "to be assured of" or "to be convinced and certain of the truth of something." Through the art of persuasion, one can cause another to adopt a certain position, view, belief, or course of action. Someone convinces or persuades another by bringing about a change of mind by means of sound, logical reasoning. Someone convinces or persuades another to adopt a new belief and to act on that belief. It also means to **2.) trust**, rely (Lu 11:22; 2 Cor. 1:9); **3.) be assured** (1 John 3:19); **4.) obey** (Heb. 13:17); **5.) be a follower**, be a disciple (Ac 5:36, 37); **6.) be certain**, be sure (Heb. 13:18).

Predestine? Paul told the Christians in Rome, "For those whom he **foreknew** he also **predestined** to be conformed to the image of his Son, in order that he might be the firstborn among many brothers. And those whom he predestined he also called, and those whom he called he also justified, and those whom he justified he also glorified." (Romans 8:29-30, ESV, CSB, LEB, NASB, similar) How should we understand the term "predestined" used by Paul? The Greek word (προορίζω proorizō) has the sense of **predetermining**, which means to **determine** something ahead of time or before its occurrence, **decide beforehand**, predestine (Ac 4:28; Ro 8:29, 30; 1Co 2:7; Eph 1:5, 11) Paul's words here cannot be used as a dogmatic argument for individual predetermined predestination. If we are going to understand this in context, we must look at the last two verses Romans 8:38-39, "For I am sure that neither death nor life, nor angels nor rulers, nor things present nor things to come, nor powers, nor height nor depth, nor anything else in all creation, **will be able to separate us from the love of God** in Christ Jesus our Lord." *Nothing* can separate the believer from God's love. This does not mean that a believer cannot choose to abandon the love of God.

Jude 5 Updated American Standard Version (UASV)

[5] Now I want to remind you, though you know all things once for all, that the Lord, after saving a people out of the land of Egypt, *afterward destroyed* those who did not believe.

Matthew 24:13 Updated American Standard Version (UASV)

[13] But the one who endures to the end will be saved.

Here, Jesus clearly states that a person's salvation is not guaranteed at the moment that they accept him, have faith in him, and dedicate their lives to him.

Philippians 2:12 Updated American Standard Version (UASV)

[12] So then, my beloved, just as you have always obeyed, not as in my presence only, but now much more in my absence, work out your own salvation with fear and trembling;

Paul, here was writing to born-again Christians, "the saints" or "holy ones" at Philippi, for Philippians 1:1 state, "Paul and Timothy, servants pledged to Christ Jesus, to all the holy ones in Christ Jesus that are in Philippi …" Paul in 2:12 is urging them not to be overly confident, as their final salvation was not assured as Jesus had stated, only those who survived to the end. (Matthew 24:13) True, God is at work in us, enabling us to carry out his will and purposes, but we must cooperate with the Holy Spirit by, as Paul said, working out our salvation.

Hebrews 6:4-6 Updated American Standard Version (UASV)

[4] For in the case of **those who have** once been enlightened and have tasted of the heavenly gift and have been made partakers of the Holy Spirit, [5] and have tasted the good word of God and the powers of the age to come, [6] **and then** [after that] have **fallen away**, it is impossible to **renew** them again to repentance, since they again crucify to themselves the Son of God and put him to public shame.

Fall Away, Forsake, or Turn Away: (Gr. *parapiptō*) The sense of *parapiptō* is to fall away or forsake the truth.–Heb. 6:6.

Renew, Restore, or Bring Back: (Gr. *anakainizō*) The sense of *anakainizō* is to cause change to a previous state, to start anew.–Heb. 6:6.

On this text M. R. De Haan in *Studies in Hebrews* correctly observes,

If that is not a description of true, born-again believers, then language means nothing, and we cannot understand anything in the Word of God any more. Five marks of the believer are given:

1. They were once enlightened.
2. They had tasted the heavenly gift.
3. They were partakers of the Holy Ghost.
4. They had tasted the good Word of God.
5. They had knowledge of prophecy.[272]

Hebrews 10:26-27 Updated American Standard Version (UASV)

[26] For if **we** [Paul and the born-again Jewish Christians] **go on sinning** deliberately **after receiving** the **accurate knowledge** of the truth, there no longer remains a sacrifice for sins, [27] but a fearful expectation of judgment, and a fury of fire that will consume the adversaries.

This clearly states that one can lose salvation. Paul says "we," meaning that he includes himself and the born again Jewish Christians that he is writing to, both needing to remain faithful, which suggests that they have the free will to be unfaithful.

2 Peter 2:20-21 Updated American Standard Version (UASV)

[20] For if, after they **[born-again believers]** have escaped the defilements of the world by the accurate knowledge of the Lord and Savior Jesus Christ, **they are again entangled in them and are overcome**, the last state has become worse for them than the first. [21] For it would have been **better for them never to have known** the way of righteousness than after knowing it to **turn back from the holy** commandment delivered to them.

If the born-again believer who has been made righteous through "the accurate knowledge the Lord and Savior Jesus Christ" cannot lose their salvation, why are there so many warnings about their **falling away** or **turning back**? Again, many Bible verses show that those who have been saved; are still obligated to endure faithfully. (Matthew 24:13; Hebrews 10:36; 12:2, 3; Revelation 2:10) The Christians in the First-century showed joy when they saw that fellow born-again believers were enduring in their faith. (1 Thessalonians 1:2, 3; 3 John 3-4) So, does it seem logical that God, through the Bible, would emphasize **faithful endurance** and warn of **falling away** (leaving the faith, leaving Christ) if those who did not endure and fell away would be saved anyway?

---

[272] M. R. De Haan, *Studies in Hebrews* (Grand Rapids, MI: Kregel Publications, 1996), 104–105.

Ephesians 2:8-9 Updated American Standard Version (UASV) [8] For by grace you have been **saved through faith**; and that not of yourselves, it is the gift of God; [9] not from works, so that no man may boast.

The complete provision for salvation for a born-again Christian is God's grace. There is no way that any human can gain salvation on their own, regardless of how man good Christian works they may do. Salvation is an undeserved gift from God to all who put faith in the sin-atoning sacrifice of Jesus Christ. Let's look a little deeper at Ephesians 2:8-9.

For by grace, you have been saved – By an undeserved gift from God. It is not by your Own merit; it is not because we have any claim.

Through faith – Grace bestowed the underserved gift of salvation through faith or with believing **into** Jesus Christ.

And that not of yourselves – Salvation does not proceed from yourself. The word rendered "that" - τοῦτο touto - is in the neuter gender, and the word "faith" - πίστις pistis - is in the feminine. Therefore, the word "that," does not refer particularly to faith as being the gift of God but to "the salvation by grace" of which he had been speaking.

It is the gift of God – Salvation by grace is his gift. It is not of merit; it is wholly by favor.

Not from works – The entire provision for salvation is an expression of God's undeserved kindness. There is no way that a descendant of Adam can gain salvation on his own, no matter how noble his works are. Salvation is a gift from God given to those who put faith in the sin-atoning value of the ransom sacrifice of the Son, Jesus Christ.

James 2:14-26 is no contradiction with Paul here in Ephesians 2:8-9, it is a compliment. James makes it clear that faith is not just some head knowledge alone, but true faith is manifested in producing appropriate actions consistent with what one claims to profess. James here asks the question for his audience to ponder and think about to come to their conclusion as he states, **can such faith save him**?

Faith does not just begin and end at a mere profession of Christ. Good works in one's life then must evidence it. These works are not done as a way to earn salvation but rather out of gratitude for a heart that has been changed by the power of Christ that made one a new creation in Christ. Good works are to be done out of the overflow of the heart that the power of God has redeemed through Christ. As he explains in verses 15-26, the answer to James' question is that faith without works is not true saving faith.

Therefore, the fact that one does not act according to his words proves his words to be dead and false. It is dead in itself to just claim to have faith but have no works. The word that James uses for dead is *nekros* which means "*inactive, inoperative.*" (Vine 1996, 148) This believer's mere lip service to faith without the outward expression of faith through works is inactive. James is making it clear that without works, his faith is dormant and dead and, therefore, proves that he truly does not have faith. Jesus himself said that many would be judged for the supposed claim of faith without works on judgment day with the parable of the sheep and the goats. – Matthew 25:31-46.

For the body apart from the spirit is dead, so also faith apart from works is dead. (James 2:26)

For the body apart from the spirit is dead. The Greek word (πνεῦμα pneuma) is commonly used to denote *spirit*, *wind*, *breath*, and *life force*. The meaning here is the obvious one, that the body is animated or kept alive by the presence of the (spirit) life force and that when that is withdrawn, hope departs. The body has no life independent of the presence of the spirit. The Greek *pneuma* represents the life force from God that was given to Adam and Eve, which is introduced into every child thereafter, and animates the human soul or person. As James 2:26 states: "The body apart from the spirit [*pneumatos*] is dead."

So also, faith without works is dead. It is just as essential that faith and that works should be animated by faith as there is that the body and spirit should be united to form a living man. If good works do not result from faith, there is no true faith. No justification does not put a person on the path to salvation. There is no being declared righteous by God. If faith does not generate works, a truly Christian life, it is dead. It has no power, and it is worthless. James was not making some argument against real and genuine faith. In addition, he was not making an argument against its significance in justification. He was arguing against the idea Christians only needed faith alone to be on the path of salvation, and it need not come with good works. James argues that if there is genuine faith, it will always follow that good works are there. Just as you cannot have a body without the breath of life, you cannot have faith without works. It is *only* faith that can justify and save. But if that faith does not have works, it is not really faith. It is pseudo-faith, so there is no justification, no salvation. If the faith does not result in genuine Christian life, it is like the body without the spirit (breath of life). It is meaningless.

James and Paul are not at odds with each other, as they both agree that the person needs true faith to be justified, declared righteous, and enter the path of salvation. Both James and Paul agree that to have genuine faith; one must have works as well that evidence a holy Christian life. Both believe the opposite of that is true too. If a Christian does not have a holy life, their faith is a mere facade. The entire New Testament makes these things clear. If we do not believe in Jesus Christ, we cannot be justified before God, and if our faith is not genuine, it is impossible to lead a holy life. Claiming that no works are necessary for having faith is like saying a dead body of a living man. It is just ridiculous.

When a person (a soul) dies (beyond clinical death), there is no longer any animating force or "spirit" within any single cell out of the body's one hundred trillion cells. Many of us have seen the animation video in science classes at school, where the cell is shown to be like a microscopic factory with an enormous amount of work taking place. Therefore, no work is taking place within the lifeless body, as all of the cells animated by the spirit are dead. The body is not good for anything. This is the similarity that James is trying to draw our attention to, as a faith that lacks works is just as lifeless, producing no results and of no use as a corpse. The literal eye cannot see faith; however, works demonstrate that faith can be seen. When one is not moved to good works, it is clear that this one has no real faith. Alternatively, any Christian that is motivated to do good works, possesses a genuine faith.

We have spoken about works for many pages now. So, the next question is, what are some examples of works that should be evident in Christian life? The works are the fruitage of the Spirit (Gal. 5:22-23), the will of the Father (Matt. 7:21-23), and the Great Commission (Matt. 24:14; 28;19-20; Acts 1:8), as well as obeying such things as love your neighbor, helping those who need it if it is within your power, living a holy life, etc.

What about the Following Bible Verse?

John 6:37, 39 Updated American Standard Version (UASV)

37 All that the Father gives me will come to me, and the one who comes to me I will never cast out. 39 And this is the will of him who sent me, that I should **lose nothing of all that he has given me**, but raise it up on the last day.

This verse does nothing to undo the fact that born-again Christians have free will and can choose to reject Jesus Christ. It only says, Jesus will never cast the born-again believer out and that he will not lose any believers but it does not say that believers are unable to exercise their free will, choosing to leave him.

The argument that some make is that true born-again believers in Christ cannot lose their salvation. Their argument is that if anyone professing Christian rejects Jesus Christ, he simply was not truly a born-again believer in the first place. Their verse to support this is,

1 John 2:19 Updated American Standard Version (UASV)

19 They went out from us, but **they were not of us**; for if they had been of us, they would have continued with us; but they went out, so that they would be revealed that they all are not of us.

This is not dealing with born-again believers as to whether they can lose their salvation or not; it is dealing with the antichrist.

1 John 2:18 Updated American Standard Version (UASV)

18 Little children, it is the last hour; and just as you heard that antichrist is coming, even now many antichrists have arisen; whereby we know that it is the last hour.

The context for 1 John 2;19 is 1 John 2:8, which talks about the antichrist, not whether true believers can or cannot lose their salvation. It is not about whether believers were really believers at all; it is about the antichrist.[273]

Before the foundation of the world. We will turn to Christian apologist William Lane Craig. Significantly, certain New Testament passages also seem to affirm a beginning of time. For example, we read in Jude 25, "to the only God, our Savior through Jesus Christ our Lord, be glory, majesty, dominion, and authority, *before all time* and *now* and *forever*" (*pro pantos tou aionos kai nun kai eis pantas tous aionas).* The passage contemplates an everlasting future duration but affirms a beginning to past time and implies God's existence, using an almost inevitable *façon de parler,* "before" time began. Similar expressions are found in two intriguing passages in the pastoral epistles. In Titus 1.2-3, in a passage laden with temporal language, we read of those chosen by God "in hope of eternal life (*zoes aioniou*) which God, who never lies, promised before age-long time (*pro chronon aionion*) but manifested

---

[273] **Antichrist**: (ἀντίχριστος antichristos) The term "Antichrist," occurs in the NT five times. From those five times, we gather this entity is "against" (i.e., denies Christ) or "instead of" (i.e., false Christs) Jesus Christ. *Many antichrists* began back in the apostle John's day and will continue up unto Jesus' second coming. (1 John 2:18) The antichrist is referred to as a number of individuals taken together, i.e., collectively. (2 John 1;7) Persons who deny Jesus Christ are the antichrist. (1 John 2:22) All who deny the divinity of Jesus Christ as the One and Only Son of God is the antichrist. (1 John 2:22; John 10:36; Lu 9:35) Some antichrists are apostates who left the faith and are now in opposition to the truth. (1 John 2:18-19) Those who oppose the true followers of Jesus are the antichrist. (John 15:20-21) Antichrists are individuals or nations opposing Jesus or trying to supplant his kingly authority. – Ps. 2:2; Matt. 24:24; Rev. 17:3, 12-14; 19:11-21.

at the proper time (*kairois idiois*)." And in II Timothy 1.9 we read of God's "purpose and grace, which were given to us in Christ Jesus before age-long time (*pro chronon aionion*), but now (*nun*) manifested by the appearing of our Savior Christ Jesus." Arndt and Gingrich render *pro chronon aionion* as "before time began."[274] Similarly, in I Corinthians 2.7 Paul speaks of a secret, hidden wisdom of God "which God decreed before the ages (*pro ton aionon)* for our glorification." Such expressions are in line with the Septuagint, which describes God as "the one who exists before the ages (*ho hyparchon pro ton aionon*)" (LXX Psalm 54.20 [Ps 55.19]). That such *pro-* constructions are to be taken seriously and not merely as idioms connoting "for long ages" (cf. Romans 16.25: *chronois aioniois*) is confirmed by the many similar expressions concerning God and His decrees "before the foundation of the world" (*pro kataboles kosmou*) (John 17.24; Ephesians 1.4; I Peter 1.20; cf. Revelation 13.8). Evidently it was a common understanding of the creation described in Genesis 1.1 that the beginning of the world was coincident with the beginning of time or the ages; but since God did not begin to exist at the moment of creation, it therefore followed that He existed "before" the beginning of time. God, at least "before" creation, must therefore be atemporal. *Alternatively is there any Scriptural reason to believe that since creation God is limited by time (i.e. not "simultaneously" in the past, present and future)?* Yes, indeed! The biblical writers typically portray God as engaged in temporal activities, including foreknowing the future and remembering the past, and when they speak directly of God's eternal existence they do so in terms of beginningless and endless temporal duration: "Before the mountains were brought forth, or ever thou hadst formed the earth and the world, from everlasting to everlasting thou art God" (Psalm 90.2). "Holy, holy, holy is the Lord God Almighty, who was and is and is to come!" (Revelation 4.8b). Only in the context of the doctrine of creation do the biblical authors provide any inkling that God is not literally in time. *What about heaven as the permanent abode of God (from where Jesus is ruling on the right hand of the Father)?* I see no reason to think that heaven is timeless. On the contrary, the fact that Christ can ascend there shows that it is not, for there was a time there when he had not yet ascended and time after which he had. *How does "a thousand years like one day" (2 Pet.3:8) fit into things?* This verse is neutral on the issue, meaning only that for a beginningless and endless being, whatever the mode of His existence, the duration of time on Earth is trivial. *Is there only a difference between the perception of time by God and us, or an actual difference between heaven and the physical world/earth?* Just a difference of perception; the amount of time is an irrelevancy for an eternal being. So although Scriptural authors usually speak

---

[274] *A Greek-English Lexicon of the New Testament,* by W. Bauer, trans. and ed. W. F. Arndt and F. W. Gingrich, s.v. "aionios."

of God as temporal and everlasting, there is some evidence, at least, that when God is considered in relation to creation He must be thought of as the transcendent Creator of time and the ages and therefore as existing beyond time. It may well be the case that in the context of the doctrine of creation the biblical writers were led to reflect on God's relationship to time and chose to affirm His transcendence. Still the evidence is not clear, and we seem forced to conclude with Barr that "if such a thing as a Christian doctrine of time has to be developed, the work of discussing it and developing it must belong not to biblical but to philosophical theology."[275]

That we should be holy and blameless before him. The Greek word (Heb. קֹדֶשׁ qodesh; Gr. ἅγιος hagios) rendered holy refers to ones who have the characteristics of moral purity; **holy**, pure (1Pe 1:15–16) **Blameless**: (Heb. תָּם tam; תָּמִים tamim; Gr. ἄμωμος amōmos; ἀμώμητος amōmētos; ἀπρόσκοπος aproskopos) means, "perfect, blameless, sincerity, entire, whole, complete, and full." Of course, Noah, Jacob, and Job were not literally perfect. When used for imperfect humans, the terms are relative, not absolute. However, if one is *fully* committed to following a life course based on God's will and purposes, fully living by his laws, and repents when he falls short, God will credit his righteousness. – Gen. 6:6; 25:27; Job 9:20-221 Ps. 119:1; Pro. 11:20; Phil 2:15; 1 Thess. 5:23.

In love he foreordained us to adoption as sons through Jesus Christ to himself, according to the good pleasure of his will (1:5)

In love he foreordained us. The Greek word here is (προορίζω proorizō). It literally means "foreknow," to know something ahead of time before it occurs. The context will help us determine precisely what Paul meant here. These do not mean anything like "select" or "choose in advance." It simply means "to know" ahead of time before it occurs.

Foreknowledge: (πρόγνωσις prognōsis) The Greek noun simply means to plan in advance, **have knowledge beforehand**, **what is known beforehand**, that which is known ahead of time or before a particular temporal reference. (Acts 2:23; 1 Pet. 1:2) If we accept the equation that foreknowledge equals foreordain, sin is the result, not the result of Adam's choice, but of God's choosing, which should make us feel uncomfortable. Foreknowledge does not equal foreordain. It is better to understand that God knows in advance what choice people will freely make. The free decisions of human beings determine what foreknowledge God has of them, as opposed to the reverse. The foreknowledge does not determine the free decision; it is the free decisions that determine the foreknowledge. In this, we can

[275] Barr, *Biblical Words for Time*, p. 149.

distinguish what we might call **Chronological Priority and Logical Priority**. Chronological priority would mean that Event "A" [God's knowledge], as it relates to time, would come before Event "B" [the event God foreknows]. Thus, God's knowledge is chronologically prior to the event that he foreknows. However, logically speaking, the event is prior to God's foreknowledge. In other words, the event does not happen because God foreknows it, but God foreknows the event because it will happen. The event is logically prior to the foreknowledge, so he foreknows it because it will happen, even though the foreknowledge is chronologically prior to the event. We can see foreknowledge in this as the foreshadowing of something. When you see the shadow of someone coming around the corner of the building, you see their shadow on the ground before you see the person. You know that person is about to come around the corner because of their shadow, but the shadow does not determine the person; the person determines the shadow. God's foreknowledge is like the foreshadowing of a future event. By seeing this foreshadowing, you know the events will happen, But the shadow does not determine the reality; the reality determines the shadow. Therefore, we should think of God's foreknowledge as the foreshadowing of things to come. Therefore, just because God will know something will happen, this does not prejudice or remove the freedom of that happening. In fact, if the events were to happen differently, God's foreknowledge would be different as well. An illustration of this is as an infallible barometer of the weather. Whatever the barometer says, you know what the weather will be like because it is infallible. However, the barometer does not determine the temperature; the weather determines the barometer's findings. Thus, God's foreknowledge is like an infallible barometer of the future. It lets him know what the future will be, but it does not constrain the future in any way. The future will happen anyway the free moral agent wants it to happen. However, the barometer will track whatever direction the future will take. Suppose this is the timeline . . . . Let us place an event "**E**" on the timeline, i.e., Judas' betrayal of Jesus. Let us suppose **God** is back here in time, and by his foreknowledge (the dotted line), he knows that "**E**" will happen (Judas will betray Jesus). How does God's knowledge about "E" constrain "E" from happening? How can God's knowing "**E**" will occur make "**E**" occur?

If you were to erase the line and say **God** does not have foreknowledge of the future, how has anything changed? How would "**E**" (Judas' betrayal) be affected if you erased God's foreknowledge of it? "**E**" (Judas' betrayal) would occur just the same; it would not affect anything at all. Therefore, the presence of God's foreknowledge really does not prejudice anything about whether "**E**" will occur or not. What we need to understand is this, if Judas

(**"E"**) were not to betray Jesus, then God would **not** have foreknown Judas' betrayal **("E")** of Jesus because it would not have been on the timeline. In addition, as long as that statement is true, "**E**" being able to occur and not occur, God's foreknowledge does not prejudice anything concerning "**E**'s" occurrence. – **Attribution**: Much of this information is borrowed from a Dr. William Lane Craig video.

To adoption as sons through Jesus Christ to himself, according to the good pleasure of his will. In the Greek New Testament, the apostle Paul, on several occasions, mentions adoption concerning the new status of those who God has chosen. These were born into sin as descendants of the imperfect Adam, and they were slaves to sin and did not have the natural sonship of God. Through the ransom sacrifice, they were adopted as sons through Jesus Christ to himself. They were not born into such sonship, but rather only by God's choosing them according to the good pleasure of his will were they adopted as sons.

Adoption: (υἱοθεσία huiothesia) The Greek noun is a legal term that literally means "adoption as a son," which means to take or accept a son or daughter who is not naturally such by relationship, including full inheritance rights. The apostle Paul mentions adoption several times about those with a new status as called and chosen by God. Born as offspring of the imperfect Adam, these were formerly in slavery to sin. Through purchase through Jesus' life as a ransom, many have received the adoption as sons and daughters becoming heirs with the only-begotten Son of God, Jesus Christ. – Rom. 8:15, 23; 9:4; Gal. 4:5; Eph. 1:5.

to the praise of the glory of his grace, which he freely bestowed on us in the Beloved. (1:6)

To the praise of the glory of his grace.

The expression here *To the praise* (ἔπαινος epainos) is an exhortation, an obligation. Many times the Hebrew term (כָּבוֹד kabod) is a **manifestation of power** and glory to his people (Ex 16:7; Nu 14:22); his **glorious presence**, formally, glory. (Ex 29:43; 1Sa 4:21) And the Greek term (δόξα doxa) rendered **glory** also refers to the manifestation of God's **saving presence** and his **redemptive power** with his people. **Grace, Undeserved Kindness** is a Greek word (χάρις charis) with the sense of good that God freely gives; especially to the benefit of the recipient, which is a kindness that is not deserved. The free and unmerited favor, generous love, and kindness of God manifested in the salvation of sinners and the bestowal of blessings. It is given even though it is unearned and unmerited, driven exclusively by the generosity of God. – 2Co 6:1; Eph 1:7.

Which he freely bestowed on us in the Beloved. The Greek verb (χαριτόω charitoō), which is rendered **freely bestowed**, is only found here and in Luke 1:28. It means God's bestowing favorable goodwill upon his people, to **show kindness**, graciously give, and freely give.

When we think about the love behind God creating the billions of universes and Adam and Eve, with the intention of a perfect human family filling the earth, it is amazing that one of God's angels would challenge God's sovereignty and that Adam and Eve would betray him. That Satan suggested, God's human creation was imperfect, unsound, weak faulty, that if they faced any kind of difficulty, they too would revel against God's right to rule. He implied that man does not love God; he only obeys him because of what God does for them. (Job 1:7-12; 2:2-5) In the face of all of those false accusations, God's glorious grace evidences his confidence in his creation by choosing us in him before the foundation of the world for adoption to himself as sons through Jesus Christ.

God is INDIRECTLY responsible for SOME things and DIRECTLY responsible for OTHER things

Romans 8:28 Updated American Standard Version (UASV)

28 And we know that all things work together for good for those who love God, for those who are called according to his purpose.

We need to understand Roman's 8:28 better, as it is often misused. Many read into Paul's words that God causes everything to happen, both good or bad. This is certainly one reason that the subject of suffering and evil is often misunderstood. It is true that nothing happens outside of God's plan for our good. God is responsible for everything, but not always directly. If he started the human race, and we end up with what we now have, in essence, he is responsible. Just as parents, who have a child are similarly responsible for the child committing murder 21 years into his life because they procreated and gave birth to the child. The mother and father are indirectly responsible. King David commits adultery with Bathsheba and has her husband Uriah killed to cover things up, and impregnates Bathsheba, but the adulterine child, who remains nameless, died. Is God responsible for the death of that child? We can answer yes and no to that question. He is responsible in two ways: **(1)** He created humankind so there would have been no affair, murder, adulterine child if he had not. **(2)** He did not step in and save the child when he had the power to do so. However, he is not **directly** responsible, because he did not make King David and Bathsheba commit the acts that led to the child being born, nor did he bring an illness on the adulterine child, he just did not move in to protect the child, in a time that had a high rate of infant deaths.

God is INDIRECTLY responsible for ALL things and DIRECTLY responsible for SOME things. When we attribute things to God we need to qualify (i.e., explain) them. Without explaining the directly or indirectly part of God being responsible, we would be saying God brought about Vlad Dracula, Joseph Stalin, and Adolf Hitler for our good. God is **indirectly** responsible for all events in human history because he allowed sin to enter the world, as opposed to just destroying Satan, Adam, and Eve and starting over. God is directly responsible for many human events because he directly stepped in miraculously and used a group, person, organization, or country to carry out his will and purposes. God is indirectly responsible for Joseph Stalin and Adolf Hitler. God is directly responsible for Babylon conquering Jerusalem. God is directly responsible for helping William Tyndale bring us the first printed English translation of the Bible. We can only know afterward (sometimes) if God is directly or indirectly responsible, and then, it is still an educated guess. Overly attributing everything to God without explaining whether he is directly or indirectly responsible is why unbelievers sometimes see Christians as illogical and irrational. A four-year-old child was rescued from a surging river by a priest in 1894. If the child were rescued in the same manner today, the media would quote Christian leaders as saying God used the priest to save the child. However, only afterward do we know that this is not true. Why? Because that four-year-old child, who nearly drowned in that river in 1894 was Adolf Hitler. Hitler being saved by the priest can be indirectly attributed to God not directly.

The reason people think that God does not care about us is the words of some religious leaders, which have made them, feel this way. When tragedy strikes, what do some pastors and Bible scholars often say? When 9/11 took place, with thousands dying in the twin towers of New York, many ministers said: "It was God's will. God must have had some good reason for doing this." When religious leaders make such comments or similar ones, they are actually blaming God for the bad things that happened. Yet, the disciple James wrote, "Let no one say when he is tempted, 'I am being tempted by God,' for God cannot be tempted with evil, and he himself tempts no one." (James 1:13) God never directly causes what is bad. Indeed, "far be it from God that he should do wickedness, and from the Almighty that he should do wrong." (Job 34:10 God has **allowed** sin, old age, wickedness, suffering, and death to enter humanity after the rebellion by Satan, Adam, and Eve. He did not **cause** Satan to rebel, Eve to eat of the forbidden tree, or Adam to join that rebellion but God had allowed them to exercise the free will that he gave them.

God allowed these things as an object lesson for his creation. What has this object lesson proven? God does not cause evil and suffering. (Rom. 9:14)

The fact that God has allowed evil, pain, and suffering have shown that independence from God has not brought about a better world. (Jer. 8:5-6, 9) God's permission of evil, pain, and suffering has also proved that Satan has not been able to turn all humans away from God. (Ex. 9:16; 1 Sam. 12:22; Heb. 12:1) The fact that God has permitted evil, pain, and suffering to continue has provided proof that only God, the Creator, has the capability and the right to rule over humankind for their eternal blessing and happiness. (Eccl. 8:9) Satan has been the god of this world since the sin in Eden (over 6,000 years), and how has that worked out for man, and what has been the result of man's course of independence from God and his rule? – Matthew 4:8-9; John 16:11; 2 Corinthians 4:3-4; 1 John 5:19; Psalm 127:1.

Is Limited Atonement Biblical?

Limited atonement (also called **definite atonement** or **particular redemption**) is a doctrine accepted in some Christian theological traditions. It is particularly associated with the Reformed tradition and is one of the five points of Calvinism. The doctrine states that though the death of Jesus Christ is sufficient to atone for the sins of the whole world, it was the intention of God the Father that the atonement of Christ's death would work itself out in only the elect, thereby leading them without fail to salvation. According to Limited Atonement, Christ died for the sins of the elect alone, and no atonement was provided for the reprobate. This is in contrast to a belief that God's **prevenient grace**[276] (or "enabling grace") enables all to respond to the salvation offered by God in Jesus Christ (Acts 2:21) so that it is each person's decision and response to God's grace that determines whether Christ's atonement will be effective to that individual. A modified form of the doctrine also exists in **Molinism**.[277]

Millard J. Erickson,

"**Atonement** The aspect of the work of Christ, and particularly his death, that makes possible the restoration of fellowship between individual believers and God."[278] If Limited Atonement is limited in the sense that atonement is available to all but only applicable to the redeemable who

[276] Prevenient grace (or enabling grace) is a Christian theological concept rooted in Arminian theology, though it appeared earlier in Catholic theologies. It is divine grace that precedes human decisions.

[277] Molinism, named after 16th-century Spanish Jesuit priest and Roman Catholic theologian Luis de Molina, is the thesis that God has middle knowledge. It seeks to reconcile the apparent tension of divine providence and human free will.:20 Prominent contemporary Molinists include William Lane Craig, Alfred Freddoso, Thomas Flint, Kenneth Keathley, and Dave Armstrong.

[278] Millard J. Erickson, *The Concise Dictionary of Christian Theology* (Wheaton, IL: Crossway Books, 2001), 17.

choose to accept the ransom sacrifice, to the receptive hearts, to those who accept Jesus Christ; then, Christ's atonement will be effective to that individual, and Limited Atonement would be biblical.

Does the Bible Teach Universal Salvation?

The history of the doctrine of universal salvation (or *apokatastasis*) is a remarkable one. Until the nineteenth century, almost all Christian theologians taught the reality of eternal torment in hell. Here and there, outside the theological mainstream, were some who believed that the wicked would be finally annihilated (in its commonest form, this is the doctrine of 'conditional immortality').[279] Even fewer were the advocates of universal salvation, though these few included some major theologians of the early church. Eternal punishment was firmly asserted in official creeds and confessions of the churches. It must have seemed as indispensable a part of universal Christian belief as the doctrines of the Trinity and the incarnation. Since 1800 this situation has entirely changed, and no traditional Christian doctrine has been so widely abandoned as that of eternal punishment. Its advocates among theologians today must be fewer than ever before. The alternative interpretation of hell as annihilation seems to have prevailed even among many of the more conservative theologians. Among the less conservative, universal salvation, either as hope or as dogma, is now so widely accepted that many theologians assume it virtually without argument.[280]

"Modern Universalists claim that this doctrine is contained in the New Testament in the teachings of Jesus, and conforms to the laws of nature as taught by science and sanctioned by reason and philosophy."[281] One reason behind the Universalist mindset is, their dislike of the hellfire doctrine,[282] where the sinner is punished, i.e., tormented for an eternity. For the Universalist, eternal torment for one, who is born imperfect, with a natural desire toward sin, which Genesis argues is mentally bent toward wickedness, and has a heart, which is treacherous and unknowable, would be a sign of injustice, and an unloving God.

The Salvation Debate

1 Corinthians 15:25, 28 Updated American Standard Version (UASV)

---

[279] For details see L. E. Froom, *The Conditionalist Faith of Our Fathers* (Washington, DC: Review and Herald, 1965–1966).

[280] Richard Bauckham, "Universalism: a historical survey", Themelios 4.2 (September 1978): 47–54.

[281] Microsoft ® Encarta ® 2006. © 1993-2005 Microsoft Corporation. All rights reserved.

[282] Please see WHAT WILL HAPPEN If YOU DIE?: Should You Be Afraid of Death or of People Who Have Died? **ISBN-13:** 978-1945757839

25 For he must reign until he has put all his enemies under his feet.
28 When all things are subjected to him, then the Son himself also will be subjected to the One who subjected all things to him, so that God may **be all in all**.

The Good News Translations renders that last clause and prepositional phrase, "God will rule completely over all." The Universalist would say that if God were going to "be all in all or if "God will rule completely over all" he would need to reconcile **all** humans to himself eventually. Another text often used by the Universalist.

Philippians 2:10-11 Updated American Standard Version (UASV)

10 so that at the name of Jesus **every knee should bow**, of those who are in heaven and on earth and under the earth,
11 and **every tongue confess** that Jesus Christ is Lord, to the glory of God the Father.

Here the Universalist would argue that if "**every** knee should to bow" "and **every** tongue confess," it must follow that every human that has lived up unto the time of Christ's return will be reconciled to God in the end.

They would also point to,

Romans 5:18 Updated American Standard Version (UASV)

18 So, then, as through one trespass there was condemnation to all men, so too through one act of righteousness there was justification of life **to all men**.

"One trespass"–"One act of righteousness"

"Condemnation"–"Justification"

"All men [in Adam]"–"All men [in Christ]"

It would seem at first that this text is a perfect balance, in that Adam's one sinful act contributed to **all** of humanity inheriting sin and imperfection, and Christ one act as a ransom sacrifice would contribute to **all** of humanity receiving life. Before delving into a response to these verses, let us see what the Bible teaches. First, though, just know that, when you have a few Scriptures that appear to be in opposition to many Scriptures, you likely do not understand the few correctly.

The Bible Teaches

The Scriptures, which make all too clear that some will not be receiving salvation, are so abundant from Genesis to Revelation. Adam committed the most egregious sin of any human alive, as he, in essence, murdered billions of humans, by his rebellion. For this reason, Adam was told, "for you are dust, and to dust you shall return." (Gen. 3:19) Revelation 21:8 says, "But as for the cowardly, the faithless, the detestable, as for murderers, the sexually immoral, sorcerers, idolaters, and all liars, their portion will be in the lake that burns with fire and sulfur, which is the second death." There is not one verse in the Bible that speaks of redemption or a resurrection from "the second death."

Matthew 25:46 Updated American Standard Version (UASV)

46 And these [unrighteous] will go away into **eternal punishment** [*Kolasin*, lopping off, cutting off], but the righteous into eternal life."

Kolasin "akin to *kolazoo*"[283] "This means 'to cut short,' 'to lop,' 'to trim,' and figuratively a. 'to impede,' 'restrain,' and b. 'to punish,' and in the passive 'to suffer loss.'[284] The first part of the sentence is only in harmony with the second part of the sentence, if the eternal punishment is eternal death. The wicked receive eternal death and the righteous eternal life. We might note that Matthews Gospel was primarily for the Jewish Christians, and under the Mosaic Law, God would punish those who violated the law, saying they "shall be cut off [penalty of death] from Israel." (Ex 12:15; Lev 20:2-3) We need further to consider,

2 Thessalonians 1:8-9 Updated American Standard Version (UASV)

8 in flaming fire, inflicting vengeance on those who do not know God and on those who do not obey the gospel of our Lord Jesus. 9 These ones will pay the penalty of **eternal destruction**, from before the Lord and from the glory of his strength,

Notice that Paul says, the punishment for the wicked is "eternal destruction." Many times in talking with those that support the position of eternal torment in some hellfire, they will add a word to Matthew 25:46 in their paraphrase of the verse, '*conscious* eternal punishment.' However, Jesus does not tell us what the eternal punishment is, just that it is a punishment, and it is eternal. Therefore, those who support eternal conscious fiery torment will read the verse to mean just that, while those, who hold to the position of eternal destruction, will take Matthew 25:46 to mean that. Considering that Jesus does not define what the eternal punishment is, this verse is not a proof text for either side of the hellfire argument.

---

[283] W. E. Vine, Merrill F. Unger, and William White Jr., *Vine's Complete Expository Dictionary of Old and New Testament Words* (Nashville, TN: T. Nelson, 1996), 498.

[284] Gerhard Kittel, Gerhard Friedrich, and Geoffrey William Bromiley, *Theological Dictionary of the New Testament* (Grand Rapids, MI: W.B. Eerdmans, 1985), 451.

Hebrews 2:14 Updated American Standard Version (UASV)

14 Therefore, since the children share in blood and flesh, he himself likewise partook of the same things, that through death he could **destroy the one** who has the power of death, that is, the devil,

Yes, Jesus' ransom sacrifice will cause the destruction of Satan, the Devil. The unrighteous, also known as the wicked within the Bible are "vessels of wrath prepared for **destruction**." (Rom 9:22) Yes, "the years of the wicked are cut short." (Pro 10:27) According to Vine's Expository Dictionary of Old and New Testament Words, *olothreuo* means "'to destroy,' especially in the sense of slaying, while "*katargeo*" means, "to reduce to inactivity." In addition, *apollumi* signifies "to destroy utterly."

The Universalist likes to stress one quality of God, taking it beyond its balanced limits, that is *mercy*. However, they ignore the other quality that mercy is balanced with, namely *justice*. God had clearly told Adam, "of the tree of the knowledge of good and evil you shall not eat, for in the day that you eat of it you shall surely die." (Gen. 2:17) The apostle Paul tells us, "The wages of sin is death." (Rom. 6:23) The prophet Ezekiel recorded God as saying, "the soul [person] who sins shall die." (Eze. 18:4, 20) God is selective in his mercy/justice, as he said, "I will be gracious to whom I will be gracious, and will show mercy on whom I will show mercy." (Ex 33:19) God has provided the ransom sacrifice of his Son (Matt 20:28), to cover over Adamic sin, not the willful unrepentant practicing of sin. (Heb. 6:4; 10:26; 2 Pet 2:21)

Where did the Universalist go wrong? As they overplayed the *mercy*, while downplaying *justice*, they also overemphasize the God of love. (1 John 4:8) They are unable to wrap their mind around the God of love, who also possess the quality of justice, and even seeks vengeance on behalf of the righteous, which were treated wickedly.

However, it is also the **un**biblical doctrine of hellfire and eternal torment, which moved them emotionally into another **un**biblical doctrine, universal salvation. They would have been wiser to set aside the eternal torment in a burning hell as being **un**biblical; recognizing that punishment for one's actions that fit the offense is biblical. The position of the Annihilationist is that of eternal destruction as a punishment, which does not involve an eternal conscious torment, as it would not be compatible with the God of love, nor his justice.

Exodus 21:24 Updated American Standard Version (UASV)

24 eye for eye, tooth for tooth, hand for hand, foot for foot,

Another possibility as to why they hold to the position of universal salvation is the other **un**biblical doctrine of immortality of all souls. This belief is that once God created a human being, bring him or her into existence, they must live forever in some fashion (physical or spiritual body), and in some place (earth, heaven, or hell). Since the Universalist arrived at the correct conclusion that God would not torture an imperfect human, who sinned for 70-80 years, by burning him forever, they just removed the place of hell (wrongly thought of as a place of eternal torment) from the equation, and accepted that all would eventually be reconciled to God. They could have simply looked at the original language words, and rightly concluded that the Hebrew *sheol* and Greek hades are not places of eternal torment, but rather the gravedom of mankind, with the punishment being eternal death.

"*Athanasia* lit., "deathlessness" (*a*, negative, *thanatos*, "death"), is rendered "immortality" in 1 Cor. 15:53, 54, of the glorified body of the believer." (Vine 1996, Volume 2, Page 321) There are no verses within the Bible, which says that every human has an inherent quality of immortality. Rather, as we have already seen, Adam was sentenced to death for rebelling against God, as well as God himself saying by way of his authors, "The soul that sins shall die" and "the wages of sin is death."

Romans 6:23 Updated American Standard Version (UASV)

23 For the wages of sin is death, but the free gift[48] of God is eternal life in Christ Jesus our Lord.

If every human were created with absolute eternal life within him or her; then, there would be no gift for God to give. God has given humanity free will and the right to choose. He said to the Israelites, who wanted to be his people, "I call heaven and earth to witness against you today, that I have set before you life and death, blessing and curse. Therefore choose life, that you and your offspring may live" (Deut. 30:19) In other words, man can choose to live by the righteous laws of his Creator, or he can choose to lose his life in a rebellion against his Creator. God's justice does not allow him to have wicked persons living forever among the righteous. Adam and Eve did not fully appreciate what God had done for them, such as the eternal life he set before them, a paradise garden that they were to grow until it encompassed the entire earth, and filling the earth with perfect descendants; therefore, they returned to the dust that they came from. The same exact choice is before each of us.

What about Philippians 2:10-11, "so that at the name of Jesus **every knee should bow**, of those who are in heaven and on earth and under the earth, and **every tongue confess** that Jesus Christ is Lord, to the glory of

God the Father." A day is coming when all of the wicked will receive their punishment of everlasting destruction. Therefore, all who are alive on earth and in heaven will be submitting themselves to the sovereignty of God. Then, the verse will hold true, 'every knee will bow,' 'and every tongue will confess that Jesus Christ is Lord.' Thus, the knees and the tongues of the unrighteous, rebellious ones will no longer be in existence, as they will have been destroyed.

What about the argument of Romans 5:18 that Adam's one sinful act contributed to **all** of humanity inheriting sin and imperfection, and Christ's one act as a ransom sacrifice would contribute to **all** of humanity receiving life. As was stated earlier, when you have a couple of verses that seem to be in conflict with many verses from Genesis to Revelation, it means that you are likely misunderstanding a couple of verses. The Scripters clearly show that only the righteous receive life. Adam was not forced to receive eternal life; it was a gift from God, which was based upon his remaining faithful. Therefore, when he rejected that gift and was unfaithful, the gift of life was taken away. Thus, the same would hold true for Adam's descendants as well.– Ezekiel 18:31-32

As you will see, "all" in Greek does not necessarily mean "all." The Greek word behind "all" is *pan*, which comes in various forms. 1 John 2:2 says that Jesus is a covering "for the sins of the **whole world**."[285] Paul says at 1 Timothy 2:6 that Jesus "gave himself as a ransom for **all** [*pantōn*, all (ones)]." Romans 5:18 says, 'Christ's one act as a ransom sacrifice would contribute to **all** [*pantas*] of humanity receiving life.' Titus 2:10 says, "For the grace of God has appeared, bringing salvation to **all** [*pasin*] men." While this seems quite clear on the surface, it is not really so. What do we do with the other verses that say only redeemable humankind will receive salvation, that is, those that repent and turnaround from their former course. (Acts 17:30, John 3:16, 1 Jn. 5:12)

Yes, not **all** is so black and white, once the interpreter looks beneath the surface. Many times the Greek word (*panta*) rendered "all" is often used in a hyperbolic sense. For example, at Luke 21:29, in speaking of a parable, it is said, "Look at the fig tree (*suke*), and **all** the trees. (*panta ta dendra*)" While the literal translation seems nonsensical, this is what pushes the reader to look deeper. The Good News Translation gives us the meaning in "Think of the fig tree and all the other trees." "Other" is not in the Greek, but English

[285] his verses is included because it convey the same message, but it does not contain the Greek *pan*. Rather, it has *holos*, meaning "whole, complete, entirely."

translations add words to complete the sense in the English. Regardless, the "all" in many verses, including these, is being used hyperbolically.

In Acts 2:17, Peter at Pentecost speaks of the prophecy in the Old Testament book of Joel, saying, "And in the last days it shall be, God declares, that I will pour out my Spirit on **all** [*pasan*] flesh." Was the Spirit poured out literally on **all** flesh at Pentecost? No, it was only 120 initially, and eventually a few thousand, out of millions then alive. Repeatedly when the term "all" is used in the Greek New Testament, "all" is not literally meant as "all," but rather hyperbolically to emphasize. It can have the sense of "all others," "all sorts, "all kinds," and so on. Keep in mind that God did pour his Spirit out on 'sons and daughters, young men and old men, even on my male slaves and on my female slaves.'

Another example would be in Luke 11:42, which reads, "But woe to you Pharisees! For you tithe mint and rue and every [*pan*] herb, and neglect justice and the love of God." It should be noted that both the mint and the rue are herbs. Thus, the GNT renders it, "all the **other** herbs." While this author accepts the literal translations as being closest to the Word of God in English, they can infer that the mint and rue are not herbs, while the dynamic equivalent translations clear it up.

Unbiblical Teaching

The universal salvation position that **all** humans will eventually be reconciled to God, receiving salvation, is unbiblical. God has given humanity free will, and as free moral persons, they have the ability to reject his sovereignty. Moreover, if universal salvation were true, it would be at odds with the very reason God allowed humanity to go on after the sin of Adam, as opposed to just starting over. Satan had challenged the sovereignty of God and the integrity of humans, saying that they would not remain faithful to God, if they faced adversity. If all, were to be saved anyway (including Satan), why would God have bothered to direct Satan's attention to the integrity of Job, pointing out that humans can choose to be faithful in adverse times?

Universal salvation is a feel-good **un**biblical doctrine that our imperfect flesh wants to be true, and Satan wants us to accept as true. It allows us to not be concerned about our actions or deeds, as one will receive salvation regardless. What they are doing is removing integrity and faithfulness from the equation. However, Like Adam, who betrayed God, Like Judas Iscariot, who betrayed the Son of God, and all the rest, who have rejected God,

Hebrews 6:4-6 Updated American Standard Version (UASV)

4 For in the case of those who have once been enlightened and have tasted of the heavenly gift and have been made partakers of the Holy Spirit, 5 and have tasted the good word of God and the powers of the age to come, 6 and then have fallen away,[286] it is impossible to renew[287] them again to repentance, since they again crucify to themselves the Son of God and put him to public shame.

Jesus, in speaking to the Father about his disciples, said,

John 17:12 Updated American Standard Version (UASV)

12 While I was with them, I kept them in your name, which you have given me. I have guarded them, and not one of them has been lost except the son of destruction, that the Scripture might be fulfilled.

The apostle Paul made it all too clear, as to the outcome of willful unrepentant sinners,

Hebrews 10:26-31 Updated American Standard Version (UASV)

26 For if we go on sinning deliberately after receiving the accurate knowledge[288] of the truth, there no longer remains a sacrifice for sins, 27 but a fearful expectation of judgment, and a fury of fire that will consume the adversaries. 28 Anyone who has set aside the Law of Moses dies without mercy on the evidence of two or three witnesses. 29 How much worse punishment, do you think, will be deserved by the one who has trampled underfoot the Son of God, and has profaned the blood of the covenant by which he was sanctified, and has outraged the Spirit of grace? 30 For we know him who said, "Vengeance is mine; I will repay."[289] And again, "The Lord

---

[286] **Fall Away, Forsake, or Turn Away**: (παραπίπτω parapiptō) The sense of *parapiptō* is to fall away or forsake the truth. – Heb. 6:6.

[287] **Renew, Restore, or Bring Back**: (ἀνακαινίζω anakainizō) The sense of *anakainizō* is to cause change to a previous state, to start anew. – Heb. 6:6.

[288] **Accurate Knowledge**: (ἐπίγνωσις epignōsis) This is a strengthened or intensified form of *gnosis* (*epi,* meaning "additional"), meaning "true," "real," "full," "complete" or "accurate," depending upon the context. It is a personal recognition where one understands something clearly and distinctly or as true and valid. Paul and Peter alone use *epignosis.* Paul uses the term 15 times, while Peter uses it four times. Paul wrote about some who were "always learning and yet never able to come to accurate knowledge of truth." (2Ti 3:6-7) He also prayed for those in the Colossian church, who clearly had some knowledge of the will and purposes of the Father, for they had become Christians, "that [they] may be filled with the accurate knowledge of his will in all spiritual wisdom and understanding." (Col 1:9) All Christians should desire to obtain or achieve accurate knowledge of God's Word. (Eph 1:15-17; Php 1:9; 1Ti 2:3-4), It is crucial in one's effort at putting on the new person that Paul spoke of, and in gaining peace. – Rom. 1:28; Eph. 1:17; Phil. 1:9; Col. 1:9-10; 3:10; 1 Tim 2:4; 2Pe 1:2.

[289] Quote from Deut. 32:35

will judge his people."[290] [31] It is a fearful thing to fall into the hands of the living God.

There have been many goodhearted self-declared Christians from the second to the twenty-first century, who have held to the **un**biblical position of universal salvation. Again, this is not a biblical teaching. While it is true that "God is love" (1 John 4:8), it is just as true that he is a God of "justice" (Isa. 33:22; Ps 33:5; Job 37:23) As a God of love, he gives us free moral agents the choice between life and death, if we choose to live under his sovereignty, we receive eternal life. As a God of Justice, if we choose to reject his sovereignty, he rejects us, and we receive eternal destruction.

Revelation 3:11 Updated American Standard Version (UASV)

[11] I am coming quickly; hold fast what you have, so that no one will take your crown.

Matthew 24:13 Updated American Standard Version (UASV)

[13] But the one who endures to the end will be saved.

Many do not want to accept it, and it is not works versus grace or faith alone but we need to have a righteous standing with God at all times, or at best at the time of Jesus' return. (Ezekiel 33:12-16) This is why we are called on to 'work out our salvation.' We do this with a **healthy fear and trembling** of falling short. It is not some dreadful fear that is all consuming all the time, it is a reverential fear of falling short with our greatest love, God.

The original Greek word (**κατεργάζομαι katergazomai**) rendered 'work out' here means bringing something to completion. Therefore, there is not one true or genuine Christian who is doomed to fail or to quit. God is absolutely confident that all true Christians can 'work out their salvation' that he has given them, that is obedience to his will and purposes (Matt. 7:21-23), the working out that leads to their salvation, or He would not have inspired the apostle Paul to have written such a statement. So, how do we stay on the path or journey to salvation? It is not in our own strength. If the strength to stay on the path to salvation was ours alone; then, there would be no need for "fear and trembling." Rather, God 'acts within us,' the Holy Spirit working in our mind and heart by way of the Spirit-inspired Scriptures, helping us "to will and to act." With the loving help of the Heavenly Father, there is no reason why any true or genuine Christians should not make the right choices in life and live by them? – Luke 11:13.

[290] Quote from Deut. 32:36

Work out your own salvation - This important command was first addressed to Christians, but there is no reason why the same command should not be regarded as addressed to all - for it is equally applicable to all. The duty of doing this is enjoined here; the reason for making the effort, or the encouragement for the effort, is stated in Philippians 2:13. In regard to the command here, it is natural to inquire why it is a duty; and what is necessary to be done in order to comply with it? On the first of these inquiries, it may be observed that it is a duty to make a personal effort to secure salvation or to work out our salvation.

Philippians 2:13 Updated American Standard Version (UASV)

13 for it is God who works in you, both **to will and to act**, on behalf of his good pleasure.

(1) Because God commands it. There is no command more frequently repeated in the Scriptures, than the command to make to ourselves a new heart; to strive to enter in at the strait gate; to break off from sin, and to repent.

(2) It is a duty because it is our own personal interest that is at stake. No one else has, or can have, as much interest in our salvation as we have. Every person has the duty to be as happy as possible here and to be prepared for eternal happiness in the future world. No person has a right either to throw away his life or his soul. He has no more right to do the one than the other; and if it is a person's duty to endeavor to save his life when in danger of drowning, it is no less his duty to endeavor to save his soul when in danger of hell.

(3) Our earthly friends cannot save us. No effort of theirs can deliver us from eternal death without our own exertion. Great as may be their solicitude for us, and much as they may do, there is a point where their efforts must stop - and that point is always short of our salvation unless we are roused to seek salvation. They may pray, and weep, and plead, but they cannot save us. There is work to be done on our own hearts which they cannot do.

(4) It is a duty because the salvation of the soul will not take care of itself without an effort on our part. There is no more reason to suppose this than that health and life will take care of themselves without our own exertion. And yet many live as if they supposed that somehow all would yet be well; that the matter of salvation need not give them any concern, for that things will so arrange themselves that they will be saved. Why should they suppose this anymore in regard to religion than in regard to anything else?

(5) It is a duty, because there is no reason to expect the divine interposition without our own effort. No such interposition is promised to any man, and why should he expect it? In the case of all who have been saved, they have made an effort - and why should we expect that God will favor us more than he did them? "God helps them who help themselves;" and what reason has any man to suppose that he will interfere in his case and save him if he will put forth no effort to "work out his own salvation?" In regard to the other inquiry - What does the command imply; or what is necessary to be done in order to comply with it? We may observe, that it does not mean:

(a) That we are to attempt to deserve salvation on the ground of merit. That is out of the question; for what can man do that shall be an equivalent for eternal happiness in heaven? Nor,

(b) Does it mean that we are to endeavor to make atonement for past sins. That would be equally impossible, and it is, besides, unnecessary. That work has been done by the great Redeemer. But it means:

(i) That we are to make an honest effort to be saved in the way which God has appointed;

(ii) That we are to break off from our sins by true repentance;

(iii) That we are to believe in the Saviour, and honestly to put our trust in him;

(iv) That we are to give up all that we have to God;

(v) That we are to break away from all evil companions and evil plans of life; and,

(vi) That we are to resist all the allurements of the world and all the temptations which may assail us that would lead us back from God, and are to persevere unto the end. The great difficulty in working out salvation is in forming a purpose to begin at once. When that purpose is formed, salvation is easy.

With fear and trembling - That is, with that kind of anxiety which one has who feels that he has an important interest at stake, and that he is in danger of losing it. The reason or the ground for "fear" in this case is in general this: there is danger of losing the soul.

(1) So many persons make shipwreck of all hope and perish, that there is danger that we may also.

(2) There are so many temptations and allurements in the world, and so many things that lead us to defer attention to religion, that there is danger that we may be lost.

(3) There is danger that if the present opportunity passes, another may not occur. Death may soon overtake us. No one has a moment to lose. No one can designate one single moment of his life, and say, "I may safely lose that moment. I may safely spend it in the neglect of my soul."

(4) It should be done with the most earnest concern, front the immensity of the interest at stake. If the soul is lost, all is lost. And who is there that can estimate the value of that soul which is thus in danger of being lost forever?

Philippians 2:13 Updated American Standard Version (UASV)

13 for it is God who works in you, both to will and to act, on behalf of his good pleasure.

For it is God who works in you - This is given as a reason for making an effort to be saved, or for working out our salvation. It is often thought to be the very reverse, and people often feel that if God works "in us to will and to do," there can be no need of our making an effort and that there would be no use in it. If God does all the work, say they, why should we not patiently sit still, and wait until He puts forth His power and accomplishes in us what He wills? It is of importance, therefore, to understand what this declaration of the apostle means, in order to see whether this objection is valid, or whether the fact that God "works in us" is to be regarded as a reason why we should make no effort. The word rendered "worketh" - ἐνεργῶν energōn - working - is from a verb meaning to work, to be active to produce effect - and is that from which we have derived the word "energetic." The meaning is, that God "produces a certain effect in us;" he exerts such an influence over us as to lead to a certain result in our minds - to wit, "to will and to do." Nothing is said of the mode in which this is done, but logic and reason dictates that we are led by way of the inspired, inerrant Scriptures. In regard to the divine agency here referred to, however, certain things, though of a negative character, are clear:

(1) It is not God who acts for us. He leads us to "will and to do." It is not said that he wills and does for us, and it cannot be. It is man that "wills and does" - though God so influences him that he does it.

(2) He does not compel or force us against our will. He leads us to will as well as to do. The will cannot be forced; and the meaning here must be

that God exerts such an influence as to make us willing to obey Him; compare Psa. 110:3.

(3) It is not a physical force, but it must be a moral influence. A physical power cannot act on the will. You may chain a man, incarcerate him in the deepest dungeon, starve him, scourge him, apply red-hot tongs to his flesh, or place on him the thumb-screw, but the will is still free. You cannot bend that or control it, or make him believe otherwise than as he chooses to believe. The declaration here, therefore, cannot mean that God compels us, or that we are anything else but free agents still, though He "works in us to will and to do." It must mean merely that he exerts such an influence as to secure this result.

Both to will and to act, on behalf of his good pleasure - Not to will and to do everything, but "His good pleasure." The extent of the divine agency here referred to, is limited to that, and no man should adduce this passage to prove that God "works" in him to lead him to commit sin. This passage teaches no such doctrine. It refers here to Christians and means that he works in their hearts that which is agreeable to him, or leads them to "will and to do" that which is in accordance with his own will. The word rendered "good pleasure" - εὐδοκία eudokia - means "delight, good-will, favor;" then "good pleasure, purpose, will;" see Eph. 1:5; 2Th. 1:11. Here it means that which would be agreeable to him; and the idea is, that he exerts such an influence as to lead people to will and to do that which is in accordance with his will. Paul regarded this fact as a reason why we should work out our salvation with fear and trembling. It is with that view that he urges it, and not with any idea that it will embarrass our efforts, or be a hindrance to us in seeking salvation. The question then is, how this fact can be a motive to us to make an effort? In regard to this we may observe:

(1) That the work of our salvation is such that we need help, and such help as God only can impart. We need it to enable us to overcome our sins; to give us such a view of them as to produce true penitence; to break away from our evil companions; to give up our plans of evil, and to resolve to lead different lives. We need help that our minds may be enlightened; that we may be led in the way of truth; that we may be saved from the danger of error, and that we may not be suffered to fall back into the ways of transgression. Such help we should welcome from any quarter; and any assistance furnished on these points will not interfere with our freedom.

(2) The influence which God exerts on the mind is in the way of help or aid. What He does will not embarrass or hinder us. It will prevent no effort which we make to be saved; it will throw no hindrance or obstacle in the way. When we speak of Gods working "in us to will and to do," people often seem

to suppose that His agency will hinder us, or throw some obstacle in our way, or exert some evil influence on our minds, or make it more difficult for us to work out our salvation than it would be without His agency. But this cannot be. We may be sure that all the influence which God exerts over our minds, will be to aid us in the work of salvation, not to embarrass us; will be to enable us to overcome our spiritual enemies and our sins, and not to put additional weapons into their hands or to confer on them new power. Why should people ever dread the influence of God on their hearts, as if he would hinder their efforts for their own good?

(3) The fact that God works is an encouragement for us to work. When a man is about to set out a peach or an apple tree, it is an encouragement for him to reflect that the agency of God is around him and that he can cause the tree to produce blossoms, and leaves, and fruit. When he is about to plow and sow his farm, it is an encouragement, not a hindrance, to reflect that God works and that he can quicken the grain that is sown, and produce an abundant harvest. What encouragement of a higher order can man ask? And what farmer is afraid of the agency of God in the case, or supposes that the fact that God exerts an agency is a reason why he should not plow and plant his field or set out his orchard? Poor encouragement would a man have in these things if God did not exert any agency in the world, and could not be expected to make the tree grow or to cause the grain to spring up; and equally poor would be all the encouragement in religion without his aid.

Biblical Passages that clarify Limited Atonement:

- Jesus promises that whosoever believes in him has everlasting life. John 3:16
- Peter proclaims that everyone who calls upon Jesus will be saved. Acts 2:21
- God calls all people everywhere to repent. Acts 17:30, 2 Peter 3:9
- God desires all people to be saved. 1 Timothy 2:4
- Jesus is a ransom for all. 1 Timothy 2:6
- Jesus is the propitiation "for our sins, and not for ours only but also for the sins of the whole world." 1 John 2:2

Atonement The aspect of the work of Christ, and particularly his death, that makes possible the restoration of fellowship between individual believers and God.[291] If Limited Atonement is limited in the sense that atonement is

[291] Millard J. Erickson, *The Concise Dictionary of Christian Theology* (Wheaton, IL: Crossway Books, 2001), 17.

available to all but only applicable to the redeemable who choose to accept the ransom sacrifice, to the receptive hearts, to those who accept Jesus Christ; then, Christ's atonement will be effective to that individual, and Limited Atonement would be biblical.

Is Irresistible Grace Biblical?

Irresistible grace (also called **effectual grace**, **effectual calling**, or **efficacious grace**) is a doctrine in Christian theology particularly associated with Calvinism, which teaches that the saving grace of God is effectually applied to those whom he has determined to save (the elect) and, in God's timing, overcomes their resistance to obeying the call of the gospel, bringing them to faith in Christ. It is to be distinguished from prevenient grace, particularly associated with Arminianism, which teaches that the offer of salvation through grace does not act irresistibly in a purely cause-effect, deterministic method, but rather in an influence-and-response fashion that can be both freely accepted and freely denied.

Grace, Efficacious A reference to the fact that those whom God has chosen for eternal life will unfailingly come to belief and salvation. Some use the term *irresistible grace*, but that is a more negative concept.[292]

The Doctrine

Some claim that fourth-century Church Father Augustine of Hippo taught that God grants those whom he chooses for salvation the gift of persevering grace, and that they could not conceivably fall away.[citation needed] This doctrine gave rise to the doctrine of irresistible grace (gratia irresistibilis), though the term was not used during Augustine's lifetime.

According to Calvinism, those who obtain salvation do so, not by their own "free" will, but because of the sovereign grace of God. That is, men yield to grace, not finally because their consciences were more tender or their faith more tenacious than that of other men. Rather, the willingness and ability to do God's will are evidence of God's own faithfulness to save men from the power and the penalty of sin, and since man is dead in sin and a slave to it, he cannot decide or be wooed to follow after God: God must powerfully intervene by giving him life and drawing the sinner to himself. In short, Calvinism argues that regeneration must precede faith. In contrast, Arminianism argues that God's grace through Jesus Christ stirs up a

---

[292] Millard J. Erickson, *The Concise Dictionary of Christian Theology* (Wheaton, IL: Crossway Books, 2001), 82.

willingness to know God and respond to the gospel before regeneration; it is how God intervenes that separates Calvinism from Arminianism.

Calvin says of this intervention that "it is not violent, so as to compel men by external force; but still it is a powerful impulse of the Holy Spirit, which makes men willing who formerly were unwilling and reluctant." Despite the denial within Calvin and within the Calvinist confessions John Gill says that "this act of drawing is an act of power, yet not of force; God in drawing of unwilling, makes willing in the day of His power: He enlightens the understanding, bends the will, gives an heart of flesh, sweetly allures by the power of His grace, and engages the soul to come to Christ, and give up itself to Him; he draws with the bands of love. Drawing, though it supposes power and influence, yet not always coaction and force: music draws the ear, love the heart, and pleasure the mind."

Lutheran

Like Calvinists, Lutherans view the work of salvation as monergistic in which an unconverted or unrepentant person always resists and rejects God and his ways. Even during conversion, the Formula of Concord says, humans resist "the Word and will of God, until God awakens him from the death of sin, enlightens and renews him." Furthermore, they both see the preaching of the gospel as a means of grace by which God offers salvation.

Calvinists distinguish between a resistible, outward call to salvation given to all who hear the free offer of the gospel, and an efficacious, inward work by the Holy Spirit. Every person is unwilling to follow the outward call to salvation until, as the Westminster Confession puts it, "being quickened and renewed by the Holy Spirit, he is thereby enabled to answer this call, and to embrace the grace offered and conveyed by it." Once inwardly renewed, every person freely follows God and his ways as "not only the obligatory but the preferable good," and hence that special renewing grace is always effective.

Contrary to the Calvinist position, Lutherans hold that whenever the Holy Spirit works outwardly through the Word and sacraments, he always acts inwardly through them as well. Unlike Calvinists, Lutherans believe the Holy Spirit always works efficaciously. The Word heard by those that resist it is just as efficacious as the Word preached to those that convert. The Formula of Concord teaches that when humans reject the calling of the Holy Spirit, it is not a result of the Word being less efficacious. Instead, contempt for the means of grace is the result of "the perverse will of man, which rejects or perverts the means and instrument of the Holy Spirit, which God offers him through the call, and resists the Holy Ghost, who wishes to be efficacious, and works through the Word..."

Lutherans are certain that the work of the Holy Spirit does not occur merely alongside the means of grace to regenerate, but instead is an integral part of them, always working through them wherever they are found. Lutherans teach that the Holy Spirit limits himself to working only through the means of grace and nowhere else, so that those who reject the means of grace are simultaneously resisting and rejecting the Holy Spirit and the grace he brings.

Biblical Passages Related to the Doctrine

The statement of St. Paul is said to confirm that those whom God effectually calls necessarily come to full salvation: "(T)hose whom (God) predestined He also called, and those whom He called He also justified, and those whom He justified He also glorified" (Romans 8:28,30). Of course, this confirmation depends upon the belief that when God elected certain individuals for salvation, He either did not know or did not consider who would respond and obey, though the Apostle Peter refers to the "Elect according to the foreknowledge of God the Father, through sanctification of the Spirit, unto obedience and sprinkling of the blood of Jesus Christ". 1 Peter 1:2

Calvinists also rely upon several verses from the sixth chapter of the Gospel of John, which contains a record of Jesus' teaching on humanity's abilities and God's activities in salvation, as the central proof text for the Calvinist doctrine:

John 6:37, 39: "All that the Father gives me will come to me.... And this is the will of him who sent me, that I should lose nothing of all that He has given me, but raise it up on the last day." Those who come to Jesus can expect relief, help, assistance and guidance in in their walk through this life, with hope of eternal life ahead.

John 6:44–45: "No one can come to me unless the Father who sent me draws him.... Everyone who has heard and learned from the Father comes to me." God the Father personally cares for every individual. He draws each person who is receptve to his Son by reaching them individually through the the great commission to make disciples and by helping them to grasp and apply God's Word by means of the Holy Spirit.

John 6:65: "(N)o one can come to me unless it is granted him by the Father." God can read hearts and minds, and he had foreknowledge, so he knows those who will respond favorably to his love even though they have yet come to know him.

Proponents of Arminianism argue that the word "draw" (Greek: ἕλκω, helkô) as used in John 6:44 does not require the sense of "drag," though Calvinists teach this is the word's usual meaning (as in Jn. 18:10; 21:6; 21:11; Acts 16:19; 21:30; James 2:6). They point to John 12:32 as an example: "And I, when I am lifted up from the earth, will draw all people to myself." Many Arminians interpret this to mean that Jesus draws all people to Himself, but the draw only enables people to come to Him, since, if the call was truly irresistible, then all must come to Christ and be saved. They may also note that in the Septuagint version of Jeremiah 38:13, when Jeremiah is lifted out of the pit where he was left to die, this Greek verb is used for the action which his rescuers performed after he voluntarily secured the ropes under his armpits, and that this rescue was certainly performed in cooperation with Jeremiah's wishes and would have failed if he did not cooperate. Therefore, they may argue, even if the semantics of "draw" are understood in the usual sense, this should only be taken to indicate the source of the power, not the question of whether the person being drawn responds to the drawing, or to indicate that the drawing is done irrespective of their will.

Calvinists argue that (1) the word "draw" should be understood according to its usual semantics in both John 6:44 and 12:32; (2) the word "all" (translated "all people" in v. 12:32) should be taken in the sense of "all kinds of people" rather than "every individual"' and thus (3) the former verse refers to an irresistible internal call to salvation and the latter to the opening of the Kingdom of God to the Gentiles, not a universal, resistible internal call. Of course, that argument requires acceptance of either the doctrine of Limited Atonement or universalism, since John 12:32 clearly states that "Jesus will draw all." Some have asserted on this basis that the text of John 6:44 can entail either universalism or Calvinism (inclusive of Limited Atonement), but not Arminianism.

Arminian William Barclay argues that "man's resistance can defeat the pull of God" mentioned in John 6:44, but commentator Leon Morris contends that "(n)ot one of (Barclay's) examples of the verb ('draw') shows the resistance as successful. Indeed we can go further. There is not one example in the New Testament of the use of this verb where the resistance is successful. Always the drawing power is triumphant, as here." Such arguments invite the criticism that Calvinists teach salvation by decree of God rather than justification by faith alone, that they "so zealously sought to guard the free grace of God in salvation that they denied faith any involvement at all in the actual justification of sinners." But even if the drawing power is always triumphant, the ability to resist does not depend upon the meaning of the word “draw” in John 12:32, but on the question what the "draw" is intended to accomplish. Calvinism assumes that persons who Jesus "draws" will be regenerated. Arminianism states that all are drawn to Jesus to be given an enabling grace. “Jesus does not define what 'his drawing' will accomplish in John 12, only that He will do it.” Even if the semantics of “draw” are understood in the manner Calvinist's urge, this should only be taken to indicate the sufficiency of the power to draw (they were “not able to draw” as in John 21:6, or they were able to do so as in John 21:11), rather than to define what God does to those he draws. Arminians reject the Calvinist teaching that God draws for the purpose of forced regeneration irrespective of their wishes. Rather Arminians believe God draws all persons to provide all with an ability or enabling to believe, as prevenient grace teaches.

Objections to the Doctrine

Christians associated with Arminianism, such as John Wesley and part of the Methodist movement, reject this Calvinist doctrine. They believe that as Adam and Eve were free to choose between right and wrong, humanity is able, as a result of the prevenient or preceding grace of God through Jesus Christ, to choose to turn from sin to righteousness and believe on Jesus Christ who draws all of humanity to himself. And I, if I be lifted up from the earth, will draw all men unto me. John 12:32. In this view, (1) after God's universal dispensation of grace to mankind, the will of man, which was formerly adverse to God and unable to obey, can now choose to obey through the work of Christ; and (2) although God's grace is a strong initial catalyst to effect salvation, it is not irresistible but may be ultimately resisted and rejected by a human being.

Both Calvinism and Arminianism agree that the question of the resistibility of grace is inexorably bound up with the theological system's view of the sovereignty of God. The fundamental question is whether God can allow individuals to accept or reject his grace and yet remain sovereign. If so, then grace can be resistible. If not, then grace must be irresistible. This different understanding of sovereignty is often attributed to an improper understanding of total depravity. However, both Calvin and Arminius taught total depravity. Total depravity is expressly affirmed in Article III of the Five articles of Remonstrance. Nevertheless, Calvinist Charles Hodge says, “The (Arminian) and (Roman Catholic) doctrine is true, if the other parts of their doctrinal system are true; and it is false if that system be erroneous. If the (Calvinistic) doctrine concerning the natural state of man since the fall, and the sovereignty of God in election, be Scriptural, then it is certain that sufficient grace does not become efficacious from the cooperation of the human will." Hodge's argument follows Calvinist teaching which denies that the work of Jesus Christ empowers humanity to respond to the gospel before regeneration.

Calvinism's rejection of prevenient grace leaves humanity in a state of Total Depravity which requires regeneration of an individual before that individual is capable to believe or repent. John the Baptist called all to his baptism for the remission of sins Mark 1:4 and multitudes responded without regeneration Mark 1:5. The New Testament regularly calls individuals to repent and believe with no indication that they had been previously regenerated. The Apostle Peter called the Jews to repent and be converted Acts 3:19. Jesus promised that the Holy Spirit would convict the world of sin John 16:8. Calvinism's response is found in Limited Atonement. So as a result of the Calvinist understanding of God's sovereignty, one must conclude that God's election does not depend upon any human response, necessitating a belief in (1) both Total Depravity and Unconditional Election, (2) Irresistible Grace rather than Prevenient Grace, and (3) Limited Atonement; if any of these beliefs are rejected, this logic fails.[293]

Is Perseverance of the Saints Biblical?

Perseverance, Doctrine of The teaching that those who are genuine believers will endure in the faith to the end.[294]

Perseverance of the saints (also called preservation of the saints) is a Christian teaching that asserts that once a person is truly "born of God" or "regenerated" by the indwelling of the Holy Spirit, they will continue doing good works and believing in God until the end of their life.

Sometimes this position is held in conjunction with Reformed Christian confessions of faith in traditional Calvinist doctrine, which argues that all men are "dead in trespasses and sins", and so apart from being resurrected from spiritual death to spiritual life, no-one chooses salvation alone. However, it must be distinguished from Arminianism, which also teaches that all men are "dead in trespasses and sins," and could not respond to the gospel if God did not enable individuals to do so by His prevenient grace.

alvinists maintain that God selected certain individuals for salvation, before the world began, and that he subsequently irresistably draws only these

[293] **Attribution**: This article incorporates some text from the public domain: Wikipedia, the free encyclopedia, and Edward D. Andrews

[294] Millard J. Erickson, *The Concise Dictionary of Christian Theology* (Wheaton, IL: Crossway Books, 2001), 153.

selected individuals to faith in him and his son, Jesus. In support of this, they interpret John 6:44 as a statement that only those pre-ordained for belief in god are drawn to him, with an irresistable grace, as opposed to the Arminian interpretation that all are drawn to him by his prevenient grace, which individuals may resist. Calvinists also use their interpretation of Ephesians 1:4 and Philippians 1:4 in the writings of the apostle Paul as indication that God chose believers in Christ before the world was created, not based upon foreseen faith, but based upon his sovereign decision to save whomever he pleased to save.

The doctrine of Perseverance of the Saints is distinct from the doctrine of Assurance, which describes how a person may first be sure that they have obtained salvation and an inheritance in the promises of the Bible including eternal life. The Westminster Confession of Faith covers Perseverance of the Saints in chapter 17, and Assurance of Grace and Salvation in chapter 18. Perseverance of the Saints is also distinct from the related doctrine of eternal security, the former indicating security of sanctification/condition while the latter indicates security of (forensic) justification/salvation.

Reformed Doctrine

The Reformed tradition has consistently seen the doctrine of perseverance as a natural consequence to predestination. According to Calvinists, since God has drawn the elect to faith in Christ by regenerating their hearts and convincing them of their sins, and thus saving their souls by his own work and power, it naturally follows that they will be kept by the same power to the end. Since God has made satisfaction for the sins of the elect, they can no longer be condemned for them, and through the help of the Holy Spirit, they must necessarily persevere as Christians and in the end be saved. Calvinists believe this is what Peter is teaching in 1 Peter 1:5 when he says that true believers are "kept by the power of God through faith unto salvation." Outside Calvinist denominations, this doctrine is widely considered to be flawed.

Calvinists also believe that all who are born again and justified before God necessarily and inexorably proceed to sanctification. Failure to proceed to sanctification in their view is considered by some as evidence that the person in question was never truly saved to begin with. Proponents of this doctrine distinguish between an action and the consequences of an action, and suggest that after God has regenerated someone, the person's will has been changed, that "old things pass away" and "all things are become new," as it is written in the Bible, and he or she will as a consequence persevere in the faith.

The Westminster Confession of Faith defined perseverance as follows:

> They whom God hath accepted in His Beloved, effectually called and sanctified by his Spirit, can neither totally nor finally fall away from the state of grace; but shall certainly persevere therein to the end, and be eternally saved. —Westminster Confession of Faith (chap. 17, sec. 1).

This definition does not deny the possibility of failings in one's Christian experience, because the Confession also says:

> Nevertheless [believers] may, through the temptations of Satan and of the world, the prevalency of corruption remaining in them, and the neglect of the means of their preservation, fall into grievous sins; and for a time continue therein; whereby they incur God's displeasure, and grieve his Holy Spirit: come to be deprived of some measure of their graces and comforts; have their hearts hardened, and their consciences wounded; hurt and scandalize others, and bring temporal judgments upon themselves (sec. 3).

Theologian Charles Hodge summarizes the thrust of the Calvinist doctrine:

> Perseverance…is due to the purpose of God [in saving men and thereby bringing glory to his name], to the work of Christ [in canceling men's debt and earning their righteousness], to the indwelling of the Holy Spirit [in sealing men in salvation and leading them in God's ways], and to the primal source of all, the infinite, mysterious, and immutable love of God.

On a practical level, Calvinists do not claim to know who is elect and who is not, and the only guide they have is the verbal testimony and good works (or "fruit") of each individual. Any who "fall away" are assumed not to have been truly converted to begin with, though Calvinists do not claim to know with certainty who did and who did not persevere.

Essentially, Reformed doctrine believes that the same God whose power justified the Christian believer is also at work in the continued sanctification of that believer. As Philippians 2:13 says, "It is God who is at work in you, both to will and work for his good pleasure;" thus, all who are truly born again are kept by God the Father for Jesus Christ, and can neither totally nor finally fall from the state of grace, but will persevere in their faith to the end, and be eternally saved. While Reformed theologians acknowledge that true believers at times will fall into sin, they maintain that a real believer in Jesus Christ cannot abandon one's own personal faith to the dominion of sin, basing their understanding on key scriptural passages such as Christ's words, "By their fruit you will know them" (Mt 7:16,20) and "He that endures to the end will be saved." (Mt 24:13) Similarly, a passage in 1 John says, "This is how we know who the children of God are and who the children of the devil are: Anyone who does not do what is right is not a child of God." (1Jn 3:7-9) The person who has truly been made righteous in Jesus Christ did not simply have faith at some point in life, but continues to live in that faith. (Rom 1:17) This view understands that the security of believers is inseparable from their perseverance in the faith.

Passages That Cannot Be Overlooked

Romans 11:22: 22 Note then the kindness and the severity of God: severity toward those who have fallen, but God's kindness to you, provided you continue in his kindness. Otherwise you too will be cut off.

1 Corinthians 9:25-27: 25 Every athlete exercises self-control in all things. They do it to receive a perishable wreath, but we an imperishable. 26 So I do not run aimlessly; I do not box as one beating the air. 27 But I discipline my body and keep it under control,[a] lest after preaching to others I myself should be disqualified.

1 Corinthians 10:12: 12 Therefore let anyone who thinks that he stands take heed lest he fall.

Galatians 5:4: 4 You are severed from Christ, you who would be justified by the law; you have fallen away from grace.

2 Peter 2:20: 20 For if, after they have escaped the defilements of the world through the knowledge of our Lord and Savior Jesus Christ, they are again entangled in them and overcome, the last state has become worse for them than the first.

Colossians 1:21-23: 21 And you, who once were alienated and hostile in mind, doing evil deeds, 22 he has now reconciled in his body of flesh by his death, in order to present you holy and blameless and above reproach before him, 23 if indeed you continue in the faith, stable and steadfast, not shifting from the hope of the gospel that you heard, which has been proclaimed in all creation[a] under heaven, and of which I, Paul, became a minister.

Hebrews 3:12-14: 12 Take care, brothers, lest there be in any of you an evil, unbelieving heart, leading you to fall away from the living God. 13 But exhort one another every day, as long as it is called "today," that none of you may be hardened by the deceitfulness of sin. 14 For we have come to share in Christ, if indeed we hold our original confidence firm to the end.

Revelation 3:2-5: [2] Wake up, and strengthen what remains and is about to die, for I have not found your works complete in the sight of my God. [3] Remember, then, what you received and heard. Keep it, and repent. If you will not wake up, I will come like a thief, and you will not know at what hour I will come against you. [4] Yet you have still a few names in Sardis, people who have not soiled their garments, and they will walk with me in white, for they are worthy. [5] The one who conquers will be clothed thus in white garments, and I will never blot his name out of the book of life. I will confess his name before my Father and before his angels.

Jude 5: [5] Now I want to remind you, although you once fully knew it, that Jesus, who *saved* a people out of the land of Egypt, *afterward destroyed* those who did not believe. [Italics added]

Matt. 24:13: [13] But the one who endures to the end will be saved.

Phil. 2:12: [12] Therefore, my beloved, as you have always obeyed, so now, not only as in my presence but much more in my absence, work out your own salvation with fear and trembling,

Heb. 10:26-27: [26] For if we go on sinning deliberately after receiving the knowledge of the truth, there no longer remains a sacrifice for sins, [27] but a fearful expectation of judgment, and a fury of fire that will consume the adversaries.

Eph. 2:8-9: [8] For by grace you have been saved through faith. And this is not your own doing; it is the gift of God, [9] not a result of works, so that no one may boast.

Heb. 5:9: [9] And being made perfect, he became the source of eternal salvation to all who *obey* him, (Italics added.)

Jas. 2:14, 26: [14] What good is it, my brothers, if someone says he has faith but does not have works? Can that faith save him? [26] For as the body apart from the spirit is dead, so also faith apart from works is dead.

Acts 16:30-31: "'Men, what must I do to be saved?' And they [Paul and Silas] said, 'Believe in the Lord Jesus, and you will be saved, you and your household.'"

Digging Deeper

Jude 5 Updated American Standard Version (UASV)

[5] Now I want to remind you, though you know all things once for all, that the Lord, after saving a people out of the land of Egypt, *afterward destroyed* those who did not believe.

Matthew 24:13 Updated American Standard Version (UASV)

13 But the one who endures to the end will be saved.

Here, Jesus clearly states that a person's salvation is not guaranteed at the moment that they accept him, have faith in him, and dedicate their lives to him.

Philippians 2:12 Updated American Standard Version (UASV)

12 So then, my beloved, just as you have always obeyed, not as in my presence only, but now much more in my absence, work out your own salvation with fear and trembling;

Paul, here was writing to born-again Christians, "the saints" or "holy ones" at Philippi, for Philippians 1:1 state, "Paul and Timothy, servants pledged to Christ Jesus, to all the holy ones in Christ Jesus that are in Philippi …" Paul in 2:12 is urging them not to be overly confident, as their final salvation was not assured as Jesus had stated, only those who survived to the end. (Matthew 24:13) True, God is at work in us, enabling us to carry out his will and purposes, but we must cooperate with the Holy Spirit by, as Paul said, working out our salvation.

Hebrews 6:4-6 Updated American Standard Version (UASV)

4 For in the case of **those who have** once been enlightened and have tasted of the heavenly gift and have been made partakers of the Holy Spirit, 5 and have tasted the good word of God and the powers of the age to come, 6 **and then** [after that] have **fallen away,** it is impossible to **renew** them again to repentance, since they again crucify to themselves the Son of God and put him to public shame.

Fall Away, Forsake, or Turn Away: (Gr. *parapiptō*) The sense of *parapiptō* is to fall away or forsake the truth.–Heb. 6:6.

Renew, Restore, or Bring Back: (Gr. *anakainizō*) The sense of *anakainizō* is to cause change to a previous state, to start anew.–Heb. 6:6.

On this text M. R. De Haan in *Studies in Hebrews* correctly observes,

If that is not a description of true, born-again believers, then language means nothing, and we cannot understand anything in the Word of God anymore. Five marks of the believer are given:

1. They were once enlightened.
2. They had tasted the heavenly gift.
3. They were partakers of the Holy Ghost.

4. They had tasted the good Word of God.
5. They had knowledge of prophecy.[295]

Hebrews 10:26-27 Updated American Standard Version (UASV)

26 For if **we** [Paul and the born-again Jewish Christians] **go on sinning** deliberately **after receiving** the **accurate knowledge** of the truth, there no longer remains a sacrifice for sins, 27 but a fearful expectation of judgment, and a fury of fire that will consume the adversaries.

This clearly states that one can lose salvation. Paul says "we," meaning that he includes himself and the born again Jewish Christians that he is writing to, both needing to remain faithful, which suggests that they have the free will to be unfaithful.

2 Peter 2:20-21 Updated American Standard Version (UASV)

20 For if, after they **[born-again believers]** have escaped the defilements of the world by the accurate knowledge of the Lord and Savior Jesus Christ, **they are again entangled in them and are overcome**, the last state has become worse for them than the first. 21 For it would have been **better for them never to have known** the way of righteousness than after knowing it to **turn back from the holy** commandment delivered to them.

If the born-again believer who has been made righteous through "the accurate knowledge the Lord and Savior Jesus Christ" cannot lose their salvation, why are there so many warnings about their **falling away** or **turning back**? Again, many Bible verses show that those who have been saved; are still obligated to endure faithfully. (Matthew 24:13; Hebrews 10:36; 12:2, 3; Revelation 2:10) The Christians in the First-century showed joy when they saw that fellow born-again believers were enduring in their faith. (1 Thessalonians 1:2, 3; 3 John 3-4) So, does it seem logical that God, through the Bible, would emphasize **faithful endurance** and warn of **falling away** (leaving the faith, leaving Christ) if those who did not endure and fell away would be saved anyway?

Ephesians 2:8-9 Updated American Standard Version (UASV) 8 For by grace you have been **saved through faith**; and that not of yourselves, it is the gift of God; 9 not from works, so that no man may boast.

The complete provision for salvation for a born-again Christian is God's grace. There is no way that any human can gain salvation on their own, regardless of how man good Christian works they may do. Salvation is an

295 M. R. De Haan, *Studies in Hebrews* (Grand Rapids, MI: Kregel Publications, 1996), 104–105.

undeserved gift from God to all who put faith in the sin-atoning sacrifice of Jesus Christ. Let's look a little deeper at Ephesians 2:8-9.

For by grace, you have been saved – By an undeserved gift from God. It is not by your Own merit; it is not because we have any claim.

Through faith – Grace bestowed the underserved gift of salvation through faith or with believing **into** Jesus Christ.

And that not of yourselves – Salvation does not proceed from yourself. The word rendered "that" - τοῦτο touto - is in the neuter gender, and the word "faith" - πίστις pistis - is in the feminine. Therefore, the word "that," does not refer particularly to faith as being the gift of God but to "the salvation by grace" of which he had been speaking.

It is the gift of God – Salvation by grace is his gift. It is not of merit; it is wholly by favor.

Not from works – The entire provision for salvation is an expression of God's undeserved kindness. There is no way that a descendant of Adam can gain salvation on his own, no matter how noble his works are. Salvation is a gift from God given to those who put faith in the sin-atoning value of the ransom sacrifice of the Son, Jesus Christ.

James 2:14-26 is no contradiction with Paul here in Ephesians 2:8-9, it is a compliment. James makes it clear that faith is not just some head knowledge alone, but true faith is manifested in producing appropriate actions consistent with what one claims to profess. James here asks the question for his audience to ponder and think about to come to their conclusion as he states, **can such faith save him**?

Faith does not just begin and end at a mere profession of Christ. Good works in one's life then must evidence it. These works are not done as a way to earn salvation but rather out of gratitude for a heart that has been changed by the power of Christ that made one a new creation in Christ. Good works are to be done out of the overflow of the heart that the power of God has redeemed through Christ. As he explains in verses 15-26, the answer to James' question is that faith without works is not true saving faith.

Therefore, the fact that one does not act according to his words proves his words to be dead and false. It is dead in itself to just claim to have faith but have no works. The word that James uses for dead is *nekros* which means "*inactive, inoperative*." (Vine 1996, 148) This believer's mere lip service to faith without the outward expression of faith through works is inactive. James is making it clear that without works, his faith is dormant and dead and, therefore, proves that he truly does not have faith. Jesus himself said that many would be judged for the supposed claim of faith without works on judgment day with the parable of the sheep and the goats. – Matthew 25:31-46.

For the body apart from the spirit is dead, so also faith apart from works is dead. (James 2:26)

For the body apart from the spirit is dead. The Greek word (πνεῦμα pneuma) is commonly used to denote *spirit*, *wind*, *breath*, and *life force*. The meaning here is the obvious one, that the body is animated or kept alive by the presence of the (spirit) life force and that when that is withdrawn, hope departs. The body has no life independent of the presence of the spirit. The Greek *pneuma* represents the life force from God that was given to Adam and Eve, which is introduced into every child thereafter, and animates the human soul or person. As James 2:26 states: "The body apart from the spirit [*pneumatos*] is dead."

So also, faith without works is dead. It is just as essential that faith and that works should be animated by faith as there is that the body and spirit should be united to form a living man. If good works do not result from faith, there is no true faith. No justification does not put a person on the path to salvation. There is no being declared righteous by God. If faith does not generate works, a truly Christian life, it is dead. It has no power, and it is worthless. James was not making some argument against real and genuine faith. In addition, he was not making an argument against its significance in justification. He was arguing against the idea Christians only needed faith alone to be on the path of salvation, and it need not come with good works. James argues that if there is genuine faith, it will always follow that good works are there. Just as you cannot have a body without the breath of life, you cannot have faith without works. It is *only* faith that can justify and save. But if that faith does not have works, it is not really faith. It is pseudo-faith, so there is no justification, no salvation. If the faith does not result in genuine Christian life, it is like the body without the spirit (breath of life). It is meaningless.

James and Paul are not at odds with each other, as they both agree that the person needs true faith to be justified, declared righteous, and enter the path of salvation. Both James and Paul agree that to have genuine faith; one must have works as well that evidence a holy Christian life. Both believe the opposite of that is true too. If a Christian does not have a holy life, their faith is a mere facade. The entire New Testament makes these things clear. If we do not believe in Jesus Christ, we cannot be justified before God, and if our faith is not genuine, it is impossible to lead a holy life. Claiming that no works are necessary for having faith is like saying a dead body of a living man. It is just ridiculous.

When a person (a soul) dies (beyond clinical death), there is no longer any animating force or "spirit" within any single cell out of the body's one hundred trillion cells. Many of us have seen the animation video in science classes at school, where the cell is shown to be like a microscopic factory with an enormous amount of work taking place. Therefore, no work is taking place within the lifeless body, as all of the cells animated by the spirit are dead. The body is not good for anything. This is the similarity that James is trying to draw our attention to, as a faith that lacks works is just as lifeless, producing no results and of no use as a corpse. The literal eye cannot see faith; however, works demonstrate that faith can be seen. When one is not moved to good works, it is clear that this one has no real faith. Alternatively, any Christian that is motivated to do good works, possesses a genuine faith.

We have spoken about works for many pages now. So, the next question is, what are some examples of works that should be evident in Christian life? The works are the fruitage of the Spirit (Gal. 5:22-23), the will of the Father (Matt. 7:21-23), and the Great Commission (Matt. 24:14; 28;19-20; Acts 1:8), as well as obeying such things as love your neighbor, helping those who need it if it is within your power, living a holy life, etc.

What about the Following Bible Verse?

John 6:37, 39 Updated American Standard Version (UASV)

37 All that the Father gives me will come to me, and the one who comes to me I will never cast out. 39 And this is the will of him who sent me, that I should **lose nothing of all that he has given me**, but raise it up on the last day.

This verse does nothing to undo the fact that born-again Christians have free will and can choose to reject Jesus Christ. It only says, Jesus will never cast the born-again believer out and that he will not lose any believers but it does not say that believers are unable to exercise their free will, choosing to leave him.

The argument that some make is that true born-again believers in Christ cannot lose their salvation. Their argument is that if anyone professing Christian rejects Jesus Christ, he simply was not truly a born-again believer in the first place. Their verse to support this is,

1 John 2:19 Updated American Standard Version (UASV)

19 They went out from us, but **they were not of us**; for if they had been of us, they would have continued with us; but they went out, so that they would be revealed that they all are not of us.

This is not dealing with born-again believers as to whether they can lose their salvation or not; it is dealing with the antichrist.

1 John 2:18 Updated American Standard Version (UASV)

18 Little children, it is the last hour; and just as you heard that antichrist is coming, even now many antichrists have arisen; whereby we know that it is the last hour.

The context for 1 John 2;19 is 1 John 2:8, which talks about the antichrist, not whether true believers can or cannot lose their salvation. It is not about whether believers were really believers at all; it is about the antichrist.[296]

In general, proponents of the doctrine of perseverance interpret such passages, which urge the church community to persevere in the faith but seem to indicate that some members of the community might fall away, as encouragement to persevere rather than divine warnings. That is, they view the prophets and apostles as writing "from the human perspective", in which the members of the elect are unknowable and all should "work out [their] own salvation" (Phil 2:12) and "make [their] calling and election sure," (2Pet 1:10) rather than "from the divine perspective", in which those who will persevere, according to Calvinism, are well known. The primary objection to this Calvinist approach is that it might equally be said that these difficult passages are intended to be divine warnings to believers who do not persevere, rather than a revealing of God's perpetual grace towards believers.

Interpretations of **Hebrews 6:4–6**

4 For it is impossible, in the case of those who have once been enlightened, who have tasted the heavenly gift, and have shared in the Holy Spirit, 5 and have tasted the goodness of the word of God and the powers of the age to come, 6 and then have fallen away, to restore them again to

[296] **Antichrist**: (ἀντίχριστος antichristos) The term "Antichrist," occurs in the NT five times. From those five times, we gather this entity is "against" (i.e., denies Christ) or "instead of" (i.e., false Christs) Jesus Christ. *Many antichrists* began back in the apostle John's day and will continue up unto Jesus' second coming. (1 John 2:18) The antichrist is referred to as a number of individuals taken together, i.e., collectively. (2 John 1;7) Persons who deny Jesus Christ are the antichrist. (1 John 2:22) All who deny the divinity of Jesus Christ as the One and Only Son of God is the antichrist. (1 John 2:22; John 10:36; Lu 9:35) Some antichrists are apostates who left the faith and are now in opposition to the truth. (1 John 2:18-19) Those who oppose the true followers of Jesus are the antichrist. (John 15:20-21) Antichrists are individuals or nations opposing Jesus or trying to supplant his kingly authority. – Ps. 2:2; Matt. 24:24; Rev. 17:3, 12-14; 19:11-21.

repentance, since they are crucifying once again the Son of God to their own harm and holding him up to contempt.

Hebrews 6:4-6 is said by some to be one of the Bible's most difficult passages to interpret, and may present the most difficulty for proponents of the Eternal Security of the Believer. The passage is understood by some to mean that "falling away" from an active commitment to Christ may cause one to lose their salvation, after they have attained salvation either according to the Reformed or Free Grace theology. However, numerous conservative Bible scholars do not believe the passage refers to a Christian losing genuinely attained salvation.

For it is impossible, in the case of those who have once been enlightened, who have tasted the heavenly gift, and have shared in the Holy Spirit, and have tasted the goodness of the word of God and the powers of the age to come, and then have fallen away, to restore them again to repentance, since they are crucifying once again the Son of God to their own harm and holding him up to contempt. For land that has drunk the rain that often falls on it, and produces a crop useful to those for whose sake it is cultivated, receives a blessing from God. But if it bears thorns and thistles, it is worthless and near to being cursed, and its end is to be burned.

— Hebrews 6:4-8

One interpretation holds that this passage is written not about Christians but about unbelievers who are convinced of the basic truths of the gospel but who have not placed their faith in Jesus Christ as Savior. They are intellectually persuaded but spiritually uncommitted. The phrase "once enlightened" (6:4) may refer to some level of instruction in biblical truth. "…have tasted the good word of God and the powers of the age to come, and then have fallen away…" could be a reference to those who have tasted the truth about Jesus but, not having come all the way to faith, fall away from even the revelation they have been given. The tasting of truth is not enough to keep them from falling away from it. They must come all the way to Christ in complete repentance and faith.

A second interpretation holds that this passage is written about Christians, and that the phrases "partakers of the Holy Ghost", "enlightened", and "tasted of the heavenly gift" are all descriptions of true believers. Some passages, including Hebrews 6:4-6 and 10:23-31, are taken by some to suggest that a 'saved' person can lose their salvation. Others see them as severe warnings which do not include the loss of salvation, but in many cases fiery judgment for those who were never saved and only playing at Christianity.

A third interpretation maintains that Hebrews 6:4-8 describes only those who temporarily backslide in their faith, and does not address the issue of the loss of salvation. This interpretation is well presented in an exegetical outline of the book of Hebrews found on the website of Ariel Ministries, a Messianic-Jewish organization founded by Arnold Fruchtenbaum in 1971. Some advocates of this position claim that the passage says that those who experience the five spiritual privileges mentioned in verses 4 and 5 cannot lose their salvation and then be saved again later (i.e. be "restore[d]... again to repentance") because that would require a recrucifixion of Christ (v. 6), thus rendering ineffectual his initial propitiatory death, putting Him to open shame. This position maintains that the Greek word used for "repentance" in verse 6 refers to "salvation repentance" rather than "repentance to restore fellowship." Supporters of this interpretation also cite the overall context of chapters 5 and 6 as evidence for their position: chapter 5 concludes with a rebuke to the recipients of the epistle for wasting time, dawdling in spiritual infancy, while chapter 6 begins with an exhortation not to continue wasting time as spiritual infants, but to "press on to maturity."

Biblical theologian David DeSilva writes that "Many interpreters are driven to treat this passage as either a 'problem passage' or crux for a specific theological or ideological conviction." DeSilva agrees that the passage cannot refer to "saved" individuals since the author of Hebrews views salvation as the deliverance and reward that awaits the faithful at the return of Christ. Those who have trusted God's promise and Jesus' mediation are "those who are about to inherit salvation' which comes at Christ's second coming.[Heb 9:28] He argues that the passage refers to unbelievers who have received God's gifts and have benefited from God's grace, yet still remained skeptics.

Biblical theologian B. J. Oropeza suggests that those who read and listened to this letter had experienced persecutions in the past, and the author of Hebrews acknowledges that some church members had become apostates. The several terms in Hebrews 6:1–6 are to stress that these former apostates had experienced conversion-initiation; there is no place in the New Testament, for example, where unbelievers or fake Christians explicitly share in the Holy Spirit as did these former members. The author of Hebrews thus rhetorically stresses that despite all these benefits and experiences that confirmed their conversion, they fell away; and now he warns the hearers of this message that in their present state of malaise and neglecting church gatherings, the same thing could happen to them. The consequences of apostasy without restoration are portrayed as dire (Hebrews 6:7–8; Hebrews 10:26–29; Hebrews 12:15-17).

Objections Perseverance of the Saints

The primary objection put against Perseverance of the Saints is that its teaching may lead believers to sin freely, if they know they can never lose their salvation, without fear of eternal consequences. Traditional Calvinists see this charge as being justly leveled against the Free Grace doctrine, which does not see sanctification as a necessary component of salvation, and in the controversy over Lordship salvation, traditional Calvinists argued against the proponents of the Free Grace doctrine. Traditional Calvinists, and many other non-Calvinist evangelicals, posit that a truly converted heart will necessarily follow after God and live in accordance with his precepts, though perfection is not achievable, struggles with sin will continue, and some temporary "backsliding" may occur.

Arminian view

The central tenet of the Arminian view is that although believers are preserved from all external forces that might attempt to separate them from God, they have the free will to separate themselves from God. Although God will not change his mind about a believer's salvation, a believer can willingly repudiate faith (either by express denial of faith or by continued sinful activity combined with an unwillingness to repent). In this manner, salvation is conditional, not unconditional as Calvinism teaches.

Traditional Calvinists do not dispute that salvation requires faithfulness. However, Calvinists contend that God is sovereign and cannot permit a true believer to depart from faith. Arminians argue that God is sufficiently sovereign and omnipotent to embed free will into humanity, so that true Christians may exercise free will and fall away from the saving grace they once possessed.[297]

Comparison Among Protestants

This table summarizes the views of three different Protestant beliefs.

Calvinism	Lutheranism	Arminianism
Perseverance of the saints: the eternally elect in Christ will certainly persevere in faith.	Falling away is possible, but God gives gospel assurance.	Preservation is conditional upon continued faith in Christ; with the possibility of a final apostasy.

[297] **Attribution**: This article incorporates some text from the public domain: Wikipedia, the free encyclopedia, and Edward D. Andrews

CHAPTER 9 Determinism, Fatalism, Predestination, and Foreknowledge

Arminian View of the Free Will

I. *Definitions.*—1. Mind is one and indivisible. For convenience in language, the phenomena of mind are generalized, and names given to the powers by which phenomena become possible and to which phenomena are referred. Those powers of mind which are immediately concerned in the acquisition, retention, and classification of knowledge are classed together and generalized so that the generic name of the *intellect* is made to include them all, or, more briefly, the mind's power to know is called the *intellect.* In like manner, the susceptibility of *feeling* is called the *sensibility*, and the power to put forth action is called the *will.* Not that there are three distinct entities, for evidently it is the same one and indivisible mind that perceives, judges, remembers, imagines, is pleased or displeased, loves or hates, chooses, resolves, determines, acts. Perhaps it would be quite as scientific as is the usual method of statement to say that mind, considered as an entity, is one, simple, indivisible, and ultimate; that the same one mind, considered as a power to know, is called the intellect; considered as a power of feeling, is called the sensibility; and considered as a power of action, is called the *will.*

2. Edwards defines will as "the power to choose." This is unscientific and inadequate, because there are evidently other phenomena of mind as distinctly active, and as clearly distinguished from knowledge and from feeling, as is choice.

Tappan's definition of will is "the mind's causality." This is not objectionable, unless it be said that it is too general and does not enable the thinker to form a definite conception.

Whedon says the will is "that power of the mind by which it becomes the conscious author of an intentional act." This is more specific, and is correct so far as it goes; but it may be asked, Is not will sometimes active when there is no intention or purpose cognized in consciousness? Does not the mind put forth acts of will unconsciously?

Haven says, "I understand by the will that power which the mind has of determining or deciding what it will do and of putting forth volitions accordingly."

Upham says "the will may properly enough be defined the mental power or susceptibility by which we put forth volitions." These are both defective, because they require a knowledge of what is meant by the term volitions.

Manifestly mind is so perfectly one, and its phenomena are so thoroughly interpenetrated, each and all being mutually conditioned one upon the other, that accurate and exhaustive definition is extremely difficult, if not impossible. In the present state of mental science, perhaps we say the best thing possible, and all that is requisite for practical purposes, when we say that to know, to feel, and to act is an exhaustive category of mental phenomena, and the mind's power to act is what is expressed by the term "the will."

3. In general use, all acts of will are called *volitions*. Some writers, however, distinguish them as "choices" and "volitions;" but no reason is apparent for varying from the general usage, as the distinction sought may be easily made when necessary by simply noting one class as volitions in choice, and the other as volitions in the executive *nisus*. To make a choice, to form a purpose, to seek an end, to indulge an intention, to resolve to do, with other terms of similar import, express acts of mind which are different from the mental *nisus* that moves the mind or body, or both, to do the thing intended. As between idleness and employment, as between one form of occupation and another, and as between several books lying before me, I determine to take up a particular book and give attention to the reading of the same, and the study of the topic on which it treats. These selections and the determination formed are acts of will—are choices, volitions in choice; but no one of them alone, nor all of them together, have as yet stirred a muscle. Another act of will is requisite to move the body and do the work intended: this may be called volition in the executive nisus.

The executive power of will is exerted both upon the mind and upon the body—upon the mind as in all acts whereby attention is confined to any particular topics; upon the body as in all cases of intended muscular movement.

The above, in a matter so well understood, may suffice as a sort of index pointing towards, rather than accurately defining, what is intended by the terms "will," "choice," "volition," and their synonyms; and we now proceed to the discussion of the question which, more than all others connected herewith, is of vital importance, namely—

II. *The Freedom of the Will.*—Fatalism is a denial of the existence of free-will in any sense in which the term may be used. What *is* is, because it could not *not be;* and what is *not* is not, because it *could* not be. The actual is equal to the possible, and the non-existent is equal to the impossible. Eternal fate governs all existences and events. Of course atheists are universally fatalists. Materialism, when it asserts that nothing exists but matter, is inseparably associated with fatalism, and in any of the forms which it assumes it is logically fatalistic. Dualism and pantheism always lead in the same direction, though dualists and pantheists are not all professed fatalists. One form of professed theism is confessedly fatalistic, namely, that species of theism which affirms that God acts from the necessities of his nature, so that he does all he can do, and what he does he cannot avoid doing, the actual being, by the necessity of God's nature, the measure of the possible. All that it is deemed needful to say of fatalism in this connection is that it contradicts the universal convictions of the human mind. All men, fatalists themselves included, have an ineradicable conviction that many things might be different from what they are. All men irresistibly conceive an essential difference between a man and a machine, and conceive that that difference is found chiefly in the fact that man chooses his ends and the means of their accomplishment, and the machine does not. Fatalism, if true, cannot be proved, for to admit the possibility of its truth long enough for the consideration of an argument is to admit that human thought is a necessary falsehood; and arguments against fatalism are evidently futile, for the fatalist is by his own profession compelled to ignore all confidence in his own thinkings. Rejecting as he does ultimate principles, denying intuitive truths, there is no foundation for an argument.

The antagonism between fatalism and freedom may be found in their answer to the question, Is mind subject to the law of necessity in every direction, and in the same sense that matter is subject to that law? The fatalist affirms and the freedomist denies. For all that is apparent, the antagonists must stand face to face forever—the one affirming and the other denying—with nothing for either to say that will be of any service to the other.

Among antifatalists there is great diversity of opinion, and here controversy begins. All are agreed in affirming the doctrine of human liberty, or technically in asserting the doctrine of free-will; but they instantly begin to differ by giving different and opposite definitions of the terms "liberty," "freedom," "certainty," "necessity," etc. This controversy may be as explicitly stated, and the arguments pro and con, as perspicuously presented, with some advantage as to brevity, as in any other method, by making the whole discussion consist in an answer to the sole question, Is there existent such a thing as "power to the contrary?" It may be said that this question does not cover the whole ground of controversy, since some allow that "the power to the contrary" is essential to a probation, and that the first man possessed it; affirming only that the posterity of the first pair, by reason of their relation to the first sin, do not possess it. This is true; but it is also true that all, or well-nigh all, arguments adduced to prove the non-existence of a power to the contrary in the posterity of Adam prove, if they prove anything, not the non-existence, but the impossibility, of such a power. The question may be stated in other terms—Is mind a power competent for either of several different results? When the mind chooses A, could it at the same time and under the same circumstances have chosen B instead? Is mind, or is it not, an either-causal power? Is it, or is it not, in respect to any event, a first cause? The parties to this controversy have been called *Freedomists* and *Necessitarians*. We adopt these terms not only for convenience, but because they explicitly characterize the opinions held by each.

1. Freedomists affirm that the power to the contrary is not only conceivable, but actual; that it is involved in all intuitive conceptions of infinite power; that at any moment in infinite duration God can create or refrain from creating; that, creating a world, he can place its centre in any one given point in space or in any one of an infinite number of other points; that this power in God is absolutely free from all constraint, either from anything external to himself or from anything pertaining to his own nature. They further affirm that God created man in this feature of his image, so that to deprive man of it entirely would be to dehumanize him—would be to reduce him to the character and condition of a brute, or perhaps worse, to mere machinery. They still further affirm that the possession of this power is fundamental and essential in the make-up of a moral being. Necessitarians deny the power to the contrary. They affirm—stating it in the mildest terms they choose to adopt—an invariable antecedency in all events, psychical as well as physical. All phenomena are uniform, equally so whether pertaining to matter or to mind. External objects determine perception, perception determines emotion, emotion determines desire, desire determines volition in choice, volition in choice determines volition in the executive nisus, and this determines the external muscular action. The chain is unbreakable; the connection between choice and desire is as uniform, as impossible to be otherwise, as is the connection between external object and perception. Every cause is potent only for one sole effect; every antecedent is followed, and must be followed, by one sole consequent. As Edwards puts it, the law of necessity governs all events; it is absurd to suppose the possibility of the opposite of what is. Discussions on this subject among theologians have primary and chief respect to the power for good. Pelagians affirm that the power for good is as essential to human nature as any other power. Of course it was not lost by the fall, and all men come into personal consciousness as fully possessed of power to choose the good as they are possessed of power to choose the evil. Augustinians and Arminians affirm that power to choose

the good was lost by the first sin; that man became enslaved, and that the race have inherited the enslavement. Augustinians further affirm that the lost power is never restored; that if man wills a good, it is by a divine efficiency causing him thus to will—in other words, the power to the contrary does not exist in the human mind, has not since the first sin, and never will. Arminians agree with Pelagians in affirming that the power to the contrary is essential to a moral nature, to a being morally responsible, but differ from them when they deny that the power to good was lost by sin. Arminians agree with Augustinians in affirming that the posterity of the first pair have inherited an enslaved nature, but they differ from them when they assert that this enslavement is perpetual. Arminians affirm that the race, except the first pair, come into personal consciousness under grace; that the unconditioned benefits of atonement include not only personal existence, but also all the requisites of a fair probation, among which the power to refuse the evil and choose the good is chief, is fundamental and essential. These differences among theologians deserve mention in this connection; but its is not needful that they be kept in mind, for the discussion is the same, whether they be considered or left out of the account.

(1.) Freedomism is sustained by an appeal to *universal consciousness.* It is affirmed that every man does, every day of his life, many things with a consciousness while doing these things that he has power to do otherwise. It is objected to this appeal by opponents that consciousness testifies to the *acts* of mind, and not to its *powers.* This objection is an assumption which all psychologist do not admit, and it cannot be denied that man is, in some sense, conscious of his powers. But allowing the objection to stand for what it is worth, it is still averred that the consciousness of a conviction so universal as is the conviction that very many things we do, we do with the same ability to do otherwise that we have to do as we do, is as determinative as any conviction ever existing in consciousness. If consciousness can be relied upon in any testimony that it gives respecting human nature, or if a conviction existing in universal consciousness is any evidence that that conviction is true, then man is free in the sense of the freedomists; he possesses power, or, more accurately, he is himself a power for either of several results.

(2.) Freedomists affirm that the power to the contrary is essential to *moral obligation;* that a conviction of its existence arises necessarily from a consciousness of moral responsibility. It is affirmed that it is impossible for any one to feel responsible for any event, unless he also feels that that event is under his control. If one feels obligated to choose the good, he must also feel that he has power to do so; if he feels condemned for choosing the evil, he must also feel that he might have chosen the good. These convictions are in perfect accordance with what, in abstract science, must be judged as just, honorable, and right. Wherever obligation and responsibility exist, alternatively must be coexistent. In justice and in honor, punishment cannot be awarded for the unavoidable; if but one way be possible, moral desert is impossible. Necessitarians attempt to avoid these manifest inferences by affirming that not a power to contrary, but voluntariness, is the basis of obligation and responsibility; voluntariness, they say, is self-motion in the absence of constraint. It is said if a man choose evil unconstrained by anything extraneous to himself, he is responsible; though being what he is it were impossible for him to choose otherwise. Moreover, it is said that it is no matter how he came to be what he is, whether his depravity be concreated, infused, or self-imposed, if his acts are his own and not another's, he is responsible. Is this so? If without any fault or agency of my own I am a slave to evil desires, so that I have no power or ability to choose good, am I responsible for the evil I do? Let the common sense of mankind answer.

(3.) Freedomists aver that a denial of power to the contrary, if not itself identical with fatalism, is logically its equivalent, since absence of power to be otherwise equals necessity. The term necessity cannot be more accurately defined than by the term absence of power to the contrary. In reply, necessitarians make a distinction between a physical and a moral necessity; the former being found in the connection between a physical cause and its effect, and the latter between a mental state and its consequent. Edwards says the necessity he contends for is "the full and fixed connection between the thing signified by the subject and predicate of a proposition which affirms something to be true." The rejoinder of the freedomist is that necessity is always the same, whatever be the subject to which it applies, and is always impossibility of the opposite. No distinction founded on an irrelevant matter, nor the obscurity of Edwards's definition, avails to avert the force of the evident affirmation that absence of power to be otherwise is necessity, fate; and necessitarianism equals fatalism.

(4.) Freedomists affirm that to deny the power to the contrary is to deny human liberty fully and totally. If man cannot do otherwise than he does, he is not free. To avoid this affirmation, vicious definitions are given of the terms liberty, freedom, etc. Liberty is power to do as you will, to will as you choose, to do as you are pleased, etc. To do as you will defines physical liberty, the freedom of the body, and has no relation whatever to mental freedom. To will as you choose is without significance, because choosing is willing, and liberty, if anywhere, is found in the choice itself, and not in the accordance with it of any subsequent act either of body or mind. To will as you are pleased admits the inseparable connection between choice and antecedent pleasure or desire, and may reject the possibility of the opposite, and this is precisely that for which the definition is constructed. When used for this purpose, the outcome is simply a statement of the issue; the definition, and all that depends upon it, avails nothing in averting the affirmation that the denial of a possible opposite is a denial of the possibility of freedom fully and totally. Liberty does not exist, fixed fate governs all things.

(5.) As a corollary of the above, freedomists affirm that necessitarianism must, if consistent with itself, equally with fatalism, deny all moral distinctions and regard the idea of a moral government as chimerical.

2. The principal arguments adduced in support of necessitarianism are as follows:

(1.) *Causality.*—Volitions are effects, and must have a cause; the cause being what it is, the effect cannot be otherwise than it is. This is regarded by opponents as a plain begging of the question, for it assumes that all causes are potent only for one sole effect, when the question under discussion is whether or not mind is a cause equally potent for each of several different effects. If it be asked, What causes the mind to cause as it does? the answer is, Nothing causes it; it is itself first cause of its own volitions, and is by its nature an adequate cause of all its volitions, both general and particular.

(2.) Edwards's *reductio ad absurdum.* If the mind be self-determined, it must determine itself in any given volition by an antecedent volition; but if this antecedent volition be self-determined, it also must be determined by another antecedent volition, and so on *ad infinitum.* But to suppose such an infinite series of volitions is absurd; therefore mind is not self-determined. All the force of this argument comes from the unfortunate use of the term self-determined. Mind is not determin*ed*, it is itself determin*er*. The supposed antecedent volition is useless, and the series is stopped at its beginning.

(3.) *Utility.*—The question is asked, "What is the use of a power that is never used?" The events that do occur are produced each by a power adequate to its production; if there be a power adequate for the production of an opposite event, it is never used, is useless, and therefore need not be. The fallacy here consists in the assumption that the doctrine of freedom supposes two powers—one to do, and another not to do. Whereas the assertors of a power to the contrary affirm that the same one power is fully adequate to the production of either of several different results. Mind is such a cause that when it produces effect A, it is fully adequate to produce effect B instead.

(4.) *Motivity.*—It is said mind cannot act without a motive. In a conflict of motives the strongest must prevail, therefore volitions always are as the strongest motive. The fallacy of this argument comes from the materialistic idea conveyed by the term "strongest." There is no analogy between mental and material phenomena that admits of such argumentation. The strength of a motive cannot be represented by the weights of a balance; to infer prevalence from strength in mental the same as in physical phenomena is vicious. If, however, the term strongest motive must be used, it is indispensable that it be distinctly stated in what the strength of a motive consists; the term strength must be clearly defined. "The so-called strength of a motive," says Whedon, "may be defined the degree of probability that the will will choose in accordance with it, or on account of it." This definition being admitted, the argument is closed, for beyond all controversy it is evident that great improbabilities do sometimes occur; an improbability, however great, is not the equivalent even of a certainty, much less of a necessity.

But, again, the argument assumes that mind never acts but in view of motives, and that it cannot act without a motive. This is not admitted. Every active man, every day of his life, in a thousand indifferent and unimportant movements, both of mind and body, acts in the total absence from consciousness of any motive or reasons for doing as he does; and, again, in an equilibrium of conflicting motives, clearly cognized in consciousness, man can make a choice. This is not a supposed case, but is of actual and frequent occurrence. Men frequently with strong motives for action find themselves without any motive whatever for action in one way rather than another, and yet in these circumstances they put forth volitions as readily and as easily as when a strong preponderance is obvious. The argument from the strength of motives is not determinative.

(5.) *Divine Prescience.*—Infinite wisdom must include a perfect knowledge from eternity of all existences and events. A complete history of the universe through all time must have always been perfectly cognized by the Divine Mind. God's foreknowledge can never be disappointed. All existences and events will be as God has from eternity foreknown them; therefore the opposite to what is, and the different from it, could not be; the power to the contrary does not exist. Let it be distinctly noted that the inference here is not merely the non-existence of a power to the contrary, but its impossibility; and if the argument proves an impossibility in human affairs, it also proves the same as to divine affairs—indeed, as to all events from eternity to eternity—and God himself is forever shut up to one sole and necessary history; the actual equals the possible; eternal fate governs God and all that is not God.

The premises are unquestionable, but the conclusion is a *non-sequitur*. A future event may be certain, may be known as certain, and its opposite be possible notwithstanding; *will be* is not the same as *must be*. The argument would be equally forcible if the foreknowledge of God were eliminated. Knowledge is not causative; the knowledge of an event has nothing to do with its production. All that the divine prescience of future events does in this argument is to prove their certainty. But this must be admitted without such proof: all things will be as they will be, whether God knows them or not. The history of the universe will be in one way, and not two; objective certainty is self-evident. But certainty is not necessity; it does not exclude the possibility of an opposite. Prescience neither helps nor hurts this case at all. If a man can see no difference between certainty and necessity, he cannot admit contingency; he is logically shut up to invincible fate. If one does apprehend a clear difference between will be and must be, he may affirm both prescience and contingency. Between these two parties thus cognizing these ultimate ideas there must be a perpetual difference of opinion on the question under discussion. Further controversy is useless; they have reached the ultimate of the question; they must stand face to face, one affirming contingency, and the other necessity, without the possibility of an argument from either that will be of any service to the other.

(6.) *Divine Sovereignty.*—God governs the world in accordance with a plan. No existence or event can be permitted to contravene his plan; all existences and events must be included in the plan, and each must form a constituent part thereof. To suppose anything contingent upon the human will is to take that thing from the purview of the divine sovereignty, subject it to human caprice, to uncertainty, to chance. Therefore nothing can be possible which is different from what is.

All the strength of this argument lies in one or the other, or both, of two conceptions. One of these conceptions is that a perfect government implies an absolute control, a determining efficiency; the other is that contingency is the equivalent of uncertainty, no cause, chance. The one conception is that the divine sovereignty cannot be complete and perfect unless all that is not God be reduced to the condition of machinery. The antagonist of this idea is the conception of a government of beings endowed with alternative powers. The idea that a contingency is an uncertainty is antagonized by the conception that contingency and certainty may both be predicated of the same event; it may be certain that a thing will be, and yet, at the same time, be possible that it may not be. These antagonizing conceptions are ultimate; and two parties, the one entertaining one and the other the other, must forever be at variance. Controversy closes, the one party affirming and the other denying. If God cannot know how his creatures will conduct themselves when endowed with alternative power, when left to determine their conduct by their own free will; if he cannot govern the world when much of its history is within the power of his creatures, when much that is, is determined and enacted by the free volitions of men, then freedomism must quit the field, and, as we see it, fatalism is triumphant. There are innumerable possibilities which never become actual; if the actual be the measure of the possible, then fate governs all things.[298]

Calvin's Predestination

Predestination, a doctrine upon which great division of opinion prevails among Christians.

I. *Definition.*—The word predestinate properly signifies to *destine* (i.e. to set apart, or devote to a particular use, condition, or end) *beforehand.* It therefore denotes a mere act of the will and should be carefully distinguished from that exercise of power by which volitions are actualized or carried into effect. Etymologically it would be proper to say that God before the foundation of the world predestinated the sun to be luminous, the loadstone to attract, the atmosphere to perform its varied ministries. In theological language, however, God would be said to have "foreordained" or "decreed" these things, the term "predestinate" being restricted to God's supposed determinations respecting the destinies of men in the future world. The early Lutheran divines generally distinguished *prædestinatio stricte dicta*, or predestination in its narrower sense, and *prædestinatio late dicta*, or predestination in its wider signification. The former was God's decree to save all persevering believers in Christ; the latter was that original redemptive volition in which he "will have all man to be saved" (1 Tim. 2:4). In the Reformed Church the word has sometimes been employed as synonymous with election (q. v.), sometimes as covering both election and reprobation (q. v.). Arminius, in his 15*th Pub. Disputation*, seems to prefer the former usage as more scriptural, but he is not followed in this respect by his remonstrant successors. Calvin and most of his followers employ the term as applying to the reprobative decrees of God as much as to the elective (see this point discussed under Calvinism in vol. ii, p. 43, col. 2).

II. *Is Predestination Absolute or Conditional?*—The cardinal point of the predestination controversy has always been this question: Are the decrees by

---

[298] M. Raymond, "Will, Arminian View of The," *Cyclopædia of Biblical, Theological, and Ecclesiastical Literature* (New York: Harper & Brothers, Publishers, 1881), 989–992.

which certain individuals are elected to eternal life and other individuals doomed to everlasting misery *respective* or *irrespective*—that is, were these decrees based upon God's foreknowledge (q. v.) of the different use individuals would make of their moral agency, or were they not? The Arminian takes the affirmative, the Calvinist the negative. The former reasons in this wise: Divine predestination in its widest sense is God's free and perfect foreplanning of creation and providence. It was antecedent to the production of the first created thing. So viewed, it must be evident to any rational theist that predestination was objectively absolute but subjectively conditioned—*absolute objectively* because there existed nothing extraneous to the divine mind to limit its action; *conditioned subjectively* because the essential perfections of God demand that his will should always act in strict conformity with the dictates of his own infinite wisdom, justice, and benevolence. But though predestination, regarded as the complete, all-embracing plan of God, was objectively absolute, it is obvious that the various individual decrees which are conceived of as components of that plan must mutually limit and condition each other. Thus the divine determination that "while the earth remaineth seed-time and harvest shall not cease" was not an absolute decree, but one conditioned upon the divine determination, antecedent to it in the order of nature, that there should be an earth with planetary motion, etc. Were not each decree adjusted to every other they could not conspire to the attainment of a common end. Instead of being integrating elements of one wise and self-consistent plan, some might be found superfluous, some perhaps in direct collision. Hence no individual decree can be regarded as irrespective or unconditioned; each is conditioned on the one hand by the perfections of God, on the other by the whole system of divine pre-volitions of which it forms a part. Now an absolute, irreversible decree, continues the Arminian, either electing an individual to eternal life or dooming him to everlasting death, fails to answer to either of these essential conditions or characteristics of a divine decree. It would be palpably inconsistent with the divine perfections on the one hand, and absolutely irreconcilable with known determinations of God on the other. Such an elective decree would be incompatible with God's rationality and impartiality, while such a reprobative one would directly conflict not only with his benevolence, but even with his justice. Both would be at open war with the known design of the Creator that men should enjoy the endowment of moral agency and shape their own eternal destinies. Hence an unconditional, irrespective election of some unto life, and an unconditional, irrespective reprobation of others unto death, cannot be maintained. If any are individually elected or reprobated, they must have been elected or reprobated with reference to the foreseen use they would make of their moral agency, for only on this principle can any theory of predestination be constructed which shall not compromise the divine character or conflict with known determinations respecting man.

So just and conclusive is this reasoning that the long task of the absolute predestinarians has been to devise some expedient by which unconditional election and reprobation may be shown to be compatible with the divine attributes and with all known divine decrees. Several have been tried. (1.) Perhaps the most legitimate of them all is that adopted by those divines who consider the divine will the ground of all rational and moral qualities and distinctions. If, as these divines affirm, nothing is rational or irrational, just or unjust, right or wrong, except that for the time being it is God's will that it should be so, then evidently an arbitrary damnation of innocent beings may be just as right and proper an act as any other. If he wills it to be right, then it is right, however it may seem to us. Hence, on this scheme, we have only to suppose that God wills an act to be right to render it perfectly proper and consistent for him to perform it. Only on this hypothesis can irrespective predestination be successfully defended. (2.) Another class of divines, unable to adopt this bold principle (according to which God is able to abrogate the moral law as easily as the old ceremonial one of the Jews), yet forced to mitigate in some way the revolting horrors of an irrespective reprobation, have sought relief in the following scheme: Men, considered *in puris naturalibus*, in themselves only, were incapable of anything supernatural. Only by the aid of supernatural and divine grace could their nature be confirmed and strengthened if it should remain in its integrity, or restored if it should become corrupt. To illustrate his grace, God determined by an immutable decree to elect certain men, so viewed, to participancy in his grace and glory. To show his sovereign freedom, he determined to pass by the remainder (*præterition*), and not communicate to them that divine aid requisite to keep them from sin; then, when the persons passed by become sinners, he proposes to demonstrate his justice by their damnation. How much real relief this device affords may be seen by consulting Arminius, *Declaration of Sentiments*, or Watson, *Institutes*, pt. ii, ch. xxviii. (3.) Another expedient sometimes employed in the construction of a predestinarian theodicy is to regard sin as a mere negation. As brought forward by Dr. Chalmers (*Institutes*, pt. iii, ch. v), it might be viewed as a modification of the last-mentioned. Both fail to vindicate even the justice of God, since in each case the finally damned are damned solely for failing to do what they have no ability, natural or vouchsafed, to perform. (4.) A fourth scheme is called *sublapsarianism.* In this the fall of man was antecedent in the order of the divine decrees to election and reprobation. All men are viewed as personally guilty of Adam's sin and justly obnoxious with him to eternal death. From this mass God sovereignly and graciously elected some unto life for a demonstration of his mercy; the rest he reprobated to everlasting woe for a demonstration of his justice. In all this it is claimed that there was nothing inconsistent with God's character, since all might justly have been damned. It happens, however, that few are ready to acquiesce in this all-important premise, to wit, that all the descendants of Adam are justly obnoxious to eternal death on account of his sin, hence the conclusion avails nothing to most men. Failing in all these ingenious contrivances to harmonize unconditional predestination with God's known attributes and principles of administration as moral governor, the abettors of the doctrine usually come finally (5) to bare assertion. They maintain the unconditionality of election and reprobation on the one hand, and on the other the perfect justice and benevolence of God and adequate agency of man, without attempting to reconcile the two. They resolve the palpable contradiction into a mere "mystery," and imperiously shut every opponent's mouth with the misemployed Scripture, "Who art thou that repliest against God?"

As our limits do not admit of a methodical examination of the various passages of Scripture in which Calvinists find their doctrine asserted or assumed, we shall be obliged to refer the reader to Watson, and to those commentators who have not devoted themselves to Biblical interpretation merely as an advantageous polemical agency. We only remark, in passing, that no fact is more striking or significant in the whole history of Scripture exegesis than the steady gravitation of all sound expositors to the exegetical views of the early Remonstrants. Tholuck gratefully acknowledges his obligation to them, and even Prof. Stuart quite as often follows Grotius as Calvin. Indeed, he confesses that he cannot find irrespective election in Rom. 8:28–30, nor can he see "how it is to be made out" on rational grounds (*Com. Excursus*, x, 477). In like manner he adopts the interpretation of Rom. 7:5–25, which it cost Arminius so much to establish, and believes the time is coming "when there will be but one opinion among intelligent Christians about the passage in question, as there was but one before the dispute of Augustine with Pelagius" (*Excursus*, vii).

III. *History of the Doctrine.*—The unanimous and unquestioned doctrine of the Church on this point for more than four hundred years was, so far as developed into distinctness, precisely identical with that which owes its scientific form and name to Arminius (q. v.). The early fathers often expressed themselves unguardedly, and, in so doing, sometimes laid themselves open to the charge of a leaning towards the erroneous views afterwards systematized by Pelagius (q. v.) and his coadjutors, [see Pelagianism]; but their general sentiment was soundly evangelical and capable of an enunciation entirely free from every suspicion of consanguinity with that heresy. "In respect to predestination," says Wiggers, "the fathers before

Augustine differed entirely from him.... They founded predestination upon prescience.... Hence the Massilians were entirely right when they maintained that Augustine's doctrine of predestination was contrary to the opinion of the fathers and the sense of the Church" (*Augustinism and Pelagianism*, transl. by Prof. Emerson). Justin Martyr, Irenæus, Clement of Alexandria, Origen, and Chrysostom—all in clear and decisive statements—gave their adherence to the theory of conditional predestination, rejecting the opposite as false, dangerous, and utterly subversive of the divine glory. It is evident that they did not investigate the subject to the depth to which it is requisite for the full discussion of it to go, and that various questions, which must be put before it can be brought completely before us, they either did not put or hastily regarded as of very little moment; but it is enough to dwell upon the fact that they did employ their thoughts upon it, and have so expressed themselves as to leave no doubt of the light in which it was contemplated by them. Justin, in his dialogue with Trypho, remarks, that "they who were foreknown as to become wicked, whether angels or men, did so not from any fault of God. αἰτίᾳ τοῦ Θεοῦ, but from their own blame;" by which observation he shows that it was his opinion that God foresaw in what manner his intelligent creatures would act, but that this did not affect their liberty, and did not diminish their guilt. A little after he says more fully that "God created angels and men free to the practice of righteousness, having planted in them reason, through which they knew by whom they were created and through whom they existed, when before they were not, and prescribed to them a law by which they were to be judged, if they acted contrary to right reason. Wherefore we, angels and men, are through ourselves convicted as being wicked, if we do not lay hold of repentance. But it the Logos of God foretells that some angels and men would go to be punished, he does so because he foreknew that they would certainly become wicked; by no means, however, because God made them such." Justin thus admits that man is wholly dependent upon God, deriving existence and everything which he has from the Almighty; but he is persuaded that we were perfectly able to retain our integrity, and that, although it was foreseen that we should not do so, this did not abridge our moral power, or fix any imputation on the Deity in consequence of our transgression. Tatian, in his oration against the Greeks—an excellent work, which, although composed after the death of Justin, was written, in all probability, before its author had adopted the wild opinions which he defended towards the conclusion of his life—expresses very much the same sentiments avowed by Justin. He says, "Both men and angels were created free, so that man becoming wicked through his own fault may be deservedly punished, while a good man, who, from the right exercise of his free will, does not transgress the law of God, is entitled to praise; that the power of the divine Logos, having in himself the knowledge of what was to happen, not through fate or unavoidable necessity, but from free choice, predicted future things, condemning the wicked and praising the righteous." Irenæus, in the third book of his work against heresies, has taken an opportunity to state his notions about the origin of evil. The seventy-first chapter of that book is entitled, "A proof that man is free, and has power to this extent, that of himself he can choose what is good or the contrary." In illustration of this he remarks, "God gave to man the power of election, as he did to the angels. They, therefore, who do not obey are justly not found with the good, and receive deserved punishment, because God, having given them what was good, they did not keep it, but despised the riches of the divine mercy." The next chapter is entitled, "A proof that some men are not good by nature and others wicked, and that what is good is within the choice of man." In treating on this subject, Irenæus observes that "if the reverse were the case, the good would not merit praise nor the wicked blame, because, being merely what, without any will of theirs, they had been made, they could not be considered as voluntary agents. But," he adds, "since all have the same nature, and are able to retain and to do what is good, and may, on the other hand, lose it and not do it, some are, even in the sight of men, and much more in that of God deservedly praised and others blamed." In support of this he introduces a great variety of passages from Scripture. It appears, however, that the real difficulty attending the subject had suggested itself to his mind, for he inquires in the seventy-third chapter why God had not from the beginning made man perfect, all things being possible to him. He gives to this question a metaphysical and unsatisfactory answer, but it so far satisfied himself as to convince him that there could not, on this ground, be any imputation justly cast on the perfections of the Almighty, and that, consequently, a sufficient explanation of the origin of evil and of the justice of punishing it was to be found in the nature of man as a free agent, or in the abuse of that liberty with which man had been endowed (see Irenæus, iv, 392; Justin, *c. Trypho*, c. 140).

In the Western Church all the early theologians and teachers were equally unanimous. While the Alexandrian theologians laid special stress on *free will*, those of the West dwelt more on *human depravity* and on the necessity of *grace*. On the last-named point all agreed. It was conceded that it was conditioned by *free will*. Unconditional predestination they all denied. This stage of Church doctrine is represented by Hilary of Poitiers and Ambrose of Milan, as well as by Tertullian (*Adv. Marcion*, ii, 6), who, much as he sometimes needed the doctrine of irresistible grace, would never so much as adopt an unconditional election, much less an unconditional reprobation. Tertullian had also speculated upon the moral condition of man, and has recorded his sentiments with respect to it. He explicitly asserts the freedom of the will; lays down the position that, if this be denied, there can be neither reward nor punishment; and in answer to an objection that since free will has been productive of such melancholy consequences it would have been better that it had not been bestowed, he enters into a formal vindication of this part of our constitution. In reply to another suggestion that God might have interposed to prevent the choice which was to be productive of sin and misery, he maintains that this could not have been done without destroying that admirable constitution by which alone the interests of virtue can be really promoted. He thus thought that sin was to be imputed wholly to man, and that it is perfectly consistent with the attributes of God, or rather illustrates these attributes, that there should be a system under which sin was possible, because without this possibility there could have been no accountable agents. From what has been stated on this subject, it seems unquestionable that the apostolic fathers did not at all enter upon the subject of the origin of evil; that the writers by whom they were succeeded were satisfied that, in the sense in which the term is now most commonly used, there was no such thing as predestination; that they uniformly represented the destiny of man as regulated by the use or abuse of his free will; that, with the exception of Irenæus, they did not attempt to explain why such a creature as man, who was to fall into sin, was created by a Being of infinite goodness; that the sole objection to their doctrine seemed to them to be that prescience was incompatible with liberty, and that, when they answered this, they considered that nothing more was requisite for receiving, without hesitation, the view of man upon which they often and fondly dwelt, as a free and accountable agent, who might have held fast his integrity, and whose fall from that integrity was to be ascribed solely to himself, as it did not at all result from any appointment of the Supreme Being. So Hilary of Poitiers declares that the decree of election was not *indiscretus*, and emphatically asserts the harmonious connection between grace and free will, the powerlessness of the latter, and yet its importance as a condition of the operation of divine grace. "As the organs of the human body," he says (*De Trinit.* ii, 35), "cannot act without the addition of moving causes, so the human soul has indeed the capacity for knowing God, but if it does not receive through faith the gift of the Holy Spirit it will not attain to that knowledge. Yet the gift of Christ stands open to all, and that which all want is given to every one as far as he will accept it." "It is the greatest folly," he says in another passage (*Psa.* 51, § 20), "not to perceive that we live in dependence on and through God, when we imagine that in things which men undertake and hope for they may venture to depend on their own strength. What we have, we have from God; on him must all our hope be placed." Accordingly he did not admit an unconditional predestination; he did not find it in the passages in Rom. 9 commonly adduced in favor of it respecting the election of Esau, but only a predestination conditioned by the divine foreknowledge of his determination of will; otherwise every man would be born under a necessity of sinning (*Psa.* 57, § 3). Neander, in portraying his system, says: "Hilary considered it very important to set forth distinctly that all the operations of divine grace are conditioned on man's free will, to repel everything which might serve to favor the notion of a natural necessity, or of an unconditional divine predestination" (2:562). So Ambrose, who lived a little later, and even Jerome, who exhibited such zeal in behalf of Augustinism, declares, without reservation, that divine election is based upon foreknowledge. True, Augustine cites two passages (*De Dono Perseverantiæ*, 19) from Ambrose as favoring his scheme, but all commentators upon this father assure us that these passages by no means give ground for attributing to him the Augustinian view of election. Ambrose carries the approximation to Augustine a step further. He says (*Apol. David*, ii, § 76): "We have all sinned in the first man, and by the propagation of nature the propagation of guilt has also passed from one to all; in him human nature has sinned." A transfer of Adam's guilt may seem to be here expressed, but in other expressions it is disowned (*Psa.* 48, § 9). Ambrose admitted neither irresistible grace nor unconditional predestination; he made predestination to depend on prescience (*De Fide*, lib. v, § 83). In other places, however, his language approaches more nearly to that of Augustine (see Hase, *Dogmatik*, § 162; Gieseler, *Dogmengesch.* § 39; Neander, *History of Dogmas*, i, 343, 344). To quote Neander again: "Although the freedom of the divine election and the creative agency of grace are made particularly prominent in these passages, still they do not imply any necessary exclusion of the state of recipiency in the individual as a condition, and accordingly this assertion of Ambrose admits of being easily reconciled with the assertion first quoted. In another place, at least (*De Fide*, lib. v, § 83), he expressly supposes that predestination is conditioned by foreknowledge (*ibid.* ii, 564)." The substantial doctrines of the fathers as to the extent of grace before Augustine was that Christ died, not for an elect portion of mankind, but for all men, and that if men are not saved the guilt and the fault are their own (Gieseler, *Dogmengeschichte*, § 72).

Thus we see that for more than four hundred years not a single voice was heard, either in the Eastern or Western Church, in advocacy of the notion of an unconditional divine predestination. At this point Augustine, already in very advanced old age, and under controversial pressure, took the first step towards Calvinism by pronouncing the decree of *election* unconditional. In explaining the relation between man's activity and decisive influence, Pelagius had denied human depravity, and maintained that, although God gives man the power to do good, the will and the act are man's. He denied that there was any divine energy in grace that could impair the operations of free will. Augustine, on the other hand, maintained that grace is an internal operation of God upon those whom he designs to save, imparting not only the power, but also the will to do good. The fact that some are saved and others lost he attributed to the will of God. Hence his doctrines of unconditional predestination, of particular redemption, and of special and irresistible grace. *Reprobation*, he granted, was based upon foreseen guilt, but apparently unconscious of the inconsistency, he denied the applicability of the same principle to election. In 529 the system of Augustine was established as Church doctrine by the Council of Arausio (Orange), but the reaction against the strictly logical yet essentially immoral nature of his dogma has been perpetually manifested. See Augustine.

Four hundred years more passed away before a man could be found bold enough to complete Augustine's theory by declaring that, as God has sovereignly and immutably elected whomsoever he has pleased unto life, without any foresight of faith and obedience, so he has of his own good pleasure freely and unchangeably predestinated whomsoever he has pleased unto everlasting misery, without any reference to foreknown sin and guilt on their part. This anticipator of Calvin was a Saxon monk named Gottschalk (Godeschalcus). His novel view brought down upon him not merely ecclesiastical censure, but even persecution. His doctrine was condemned by a council which archbishop Rabanus Maurus had called at Mayence, A.D. 848 (Mansi, *Concil.* xiv, 914), and Gottschalk, who was then travelling, was sent to his metropolitan, archbishop Hincmar of Rheims, who called another council at Quiercy in 849. Here he was defended by Ratramnus, the opponent of Paschasius Radbertus in the Eucharistic controversy, and also by Remigius, afterwards archbishop of Lyons; but notwithstanding these powerful supporters, he was condemned a second time, and ordered to undergo the penalty of flogging, which the rule of St. Benedict imposed upon monks who troubled the Church. After this condemnation he was imprisoned in the monastery of Hautvillers, where he died, without having recanted his opinions, about the year 868. See Gottschalk.

While the friends of Gottschalk were endeavoring to obtain his absolution and release, Hincmar put forward Johannes Scotus Erigena (q. v.) to answer his predestination theory, which Erigena did in 851, in his treatise *De Prædestinatione*, in which he raised up a cloud of adversaries by the freedom with which he contradicted the established doctrines of the Church as to the nature of good and evil. Further controversy being thus aroused, Hincmar summoned a second council at Quiercy in 853, which confirmed the decision as to the real doctrine of the Church arrived at by the previous council (Mansi, *Concil.* xiv, 995). A rival council was called by the opposite party from the provinces of Lyons, Vienne, and Arles, which met at Valence in 855. But instead of fully confirming the opinion of Gottschalk, this council considerably modified it by declaring that although sin is foreknown by God, it is not so predestined as to make it inevitably necessary that it should be committed (*ibid.* xv, 1). Hincmar now wrote two works on the subject, one of which is not extant; the other is entitled *De Prædestinatione Dei et Libero Arbitrio adversus Gottschalcum et cæteros Prædestinatianos.* Having thus explained his views at length, they were substantially accepted, in the form of six doctrinal canons, by the Synod of Langres, and by that of Toul (A.D. 859), held at Savonières a few days afterwards (Mansi, *Concil.* xv, 525–27), and thus the controversy terminated. See Manguin, *Collect. auctor. de Prædest. et Gratia* (1650); Ussher, *Gotteschalci et Prædest. Controv. Hist.*; Cellot, *Hist. Gotteschalci Prædest.* (1655).

No authoritative or influential teacher appeared to support Gottschalk's views for seven hundred years. The most conspicuous of those who did so was Thomas Bradwardine (A.D. 1290–1349), warden of Merton College, and afterwards archbishop of Canterbury. His work on the subject is entitled *De Causa Dei contra Pelagium et de Virtute causarum ad suos Mertonenses*, and in this he gave free will so low a place that he may be almost called a necessitarian. Thomas Aquinas, who flourished during the 13th century, wrote largely upon the nature of grace and predestination. His opinions upon these subjects were nearly the same with those of Augustine; and so much, indeed, was he conceived to resemble in genius and understanding that distinguished prelate, that it was asserted the soul of Augustine had been sent into the body of Aquinas. He taught that God from all eternity, and without any regard to their works, predestinated a certain number to life and happiness; but he found great delight in endeavoring to reconcile this position with the freedom of the human will. His celebrated antagonist, John Duns Scotus, an inhabitant of Britain, surnamed, from the acuteness and bent of his mind, the Subtile Doctor, also directed his attention in the following century to the same thorny speculations, but he took a different view of them from Aquinas; and we find in the works of these two brilliant lights of the schoolmen all that the most learned in the dark ages thought upon this question.

In the midst of the ferment of the Reformation, the subject of predestination was revived by a controversy between Erasmus and Luther, the former writing an able *Diatribe de Libero Arbitrio* in 1524, and Luther following it up with his halting treatise *De Servo Arbitrio*, in which he went so near to the predestinarians as to deny that any free will can exist in man before he has received the gift of faith. But at this stage stepped forth John Calvin (q. v.) as the champion of predestinarianism. He found the Reformed churches in a perfectly chaotic state as respects doctrines. They possessed no coherent creed or system. They were held together by agreement in mere negations. They needed nothing so much as a positive system. Calvin, a stripling of twenty-five, gave them one. It answered all the essential conditions. It was anti-popish, anti-Lutheran, anti-Socinian. In the pressing exigency it was seized upon, and Calvin became the dictator of all the Reformed churches. Scotland sent her young men to him to be educated, so also did Holland, the Puritans of England, and the Protestants of France. Among the Romanists, the Molinists (q. v.), and Jansenists (q. v.), in their controversy on the subject of free will, carried on with great acrimony, the opinions of Gottschalk were discussed anew, but without lessening the majority of the Arminianists (see Sismondi, *Hist. Prædest.* in Zacharius's *Thesaur. Theol.* ii, 199).

In the Church of England the later Low-Church party have tempered down the opinions of their Puritan predecessors, and are not often disposed to go beyond the doctrine of "predestination to life" as stated in the seventeenth of the Thirty-Nine Articles of Religion, which carefully excludes the double predestination of Gottschalk and the predestinarians. This article of the Church of England is often adduced by Calvinists as favorable to their peculiar views of absolute predestination; but such a representation of it is rendered plausible only by adding to its various clauses qualifying expressions to suit that purpose. In our articles Church of England, Confessions, and Calvinism, have been exhibited the just and liberal views of Cranmer and the principal English reformers on this subject, the sources from which they drew the Articles of Religion and the public formularies of devotion, and some of the futile attempts of the high predestinarians in the Church to inoculate the public creed with their dogmas. Cartwright and his followers, in their second "Admonition to Parliament" in 1572, complained that the Articles speak dangerously of "falling from grace;" and in 1587 they preferred a similar complaint. The labors of the Westminster Assembly at a subsequent period, and their abortive result, in relation to this subject, are well known. Long before Arminius had turned his thoughts to the consideration of general redemption, a great number of the English clergy had publicly taught and defended the same doctrine. It was about 1571 that Dr. Peter Baroe, "a zealous anti-Calvinian," was made Margaret professor of divinity in the University of Cambridge, and he went on teaching in his lectures, preaching in his sermons, determining in the schools, and printing in several books, diverse points contrary to Calvinism. And this he did for several years, without any manner of disturbance or interruption. The heads of the university, in a letter to lord Burleigh, dated March 8, 1595, say he had done it for fourteen or fifteen years preceding, and they might have said twenty; for he printed some of his lectures in 1574, and the prosecution he was at last under, which will be considered hereafter, was not till 1595. In 1584 Mr.

Harsnet, afterwards archbishop of York, preached against absolute reprobation at St. Paul's Cross, the greatest audience then in the kingdom; as did the judicious Mr. Hooker at the Temple in the year following. In the year 1594 Mr. Barret preached at St. Mary's in Cambridge against Calvinism, with very smart reflections upon Calvin himself, Beza, Zanchi, and several others of the most noted writers in that scheme. In the same year Dr. Baroe preached at the same place to the same purpose. By this time Calvinism had gained considerable ground, being much promoted by the learned Whitaker and Mr. Perkins; and several of the heads of the university being in that scheme, they complained of the two sermons above mentioned to lord Burleigh their chancellor. Their determination was to bring Barret to a retraction. He modified his statements, but it may reasonably be doubted whether he ever submitted according to the form they drew up. When the matter was laid before archbishop Whitgift, he was offended at their proceedings, and wrote to lord Burleigh that some of the points which the heads had enjoined Barret to retract were such as the most learned Protestants then living varied in judgment upon, and that the most ancient and best divines in the land were in the chiefest points in opinion against the heads and their resolutions. Another letter he sent to the heads themselves, telling them that they had enjoined Barret to affirm that which was contrary to the doctrine held and expressed by many sound and learned divines in the Church of England, and in other churches likewise men of best account; and that which for his own part he thought to be false and contrary to the Scriptures; for the Scriptures are plain that God by his absolute will did not hate and reject any man. There might be impiety in believing the one, there could be none in believing the other; neither was it contrary to any article of religion established by authority in this Church of England, but rather agreeable thereto. This testimony of the archbishop is very remarkable; and though he afterwards countenanced the Lambeth Articles, that is of little or no weight in the case. The question is not about any man's private opinion, but about the doctrine of the Church; and supposing the archbishop to be a Calvinist, as he seems to have been at least in some points, this only adds the greater weight to his testimony, that the English Church has nowhere declared in favor of that scheme. The archbishop descended to the particulars charged against Barret, asking the heads what article of the Church was contradicted by this or that notion of his; and Whitaker in his reply does not appeal to one of the articles as against Barret, but forms his plea upon the doctrines which then generally obtained in pulpits. His words are, "We are fully persuaded that Mr. Barret hath taught untruth, if not against the articles, yet against the religion of our Church, publicly received, and always held in her majesty's reign, and maintained in all sermons, disputations, and lectures." But even this pretence of his, weak as it would have been though true, is utterly false, directly contrary, not only to what has been already shown to be the facts of the case, but also to what the archbishop affirmed, and that too, as must be supposed, upon his own knowledge. As to Dr. Baroe, he met with many friends who espoused his cause. Mr. Strype particularly mentions four—Mr. Overal, Dr. Clayton, Mr. Harsnet, Dr. Andrews—all of them great and learned men, men of renown, and famous in their generation. How many more there were nobody can tell. The heads in their letter to lord Burleigh do not pretend that the preaching against Calvinism gave a general offence, but that it offended many—which implies that there were many others on the opposite side; and they expressly say there were divers in the anti-Calvinistic scheme, whom they represent as maintaining it with great boldness. But what put a stop to this prosecution against Baroe was a reprimand from their chancellor, the lord Burleigh, who wrote to the heads that as good and as ancient were of another judgment, and that they might punish him, but it would be for well-doing." But Dr. Whitaker, regius professor of divinity in Cambridge, could not endure the further prevalence of the doctrines of general redemption in that university; he therefore, in 1595, drew up nine affirmations, elucidatory of his views of predestination, and obtained for them the sanction of several Calvinian heads of houses, with whom he repaired to archbishop Whitgift. Having heard their *ex parte* statement, his grace summoned bishops Flecher and Vaughan, and Dr. Tyndal, dean of Ely, to meet Dr. Whitaker and the Cambridge deputation at his palace in Lambeth, on Nov. 10, 1595; where, after much polishing and altering, they produced Whitaker's affirmation, called the "Lambeth Articles" (q. v.). Dr. Whitaker died a few days after his return from Lambeth with the nine articles to which he had procured the patronage of the primate. After his demise, two competitors appeared for the vacant king's professorship—Dr. Wotton, of King's College, a professed Calvinist, and Dr. Overal of Trinity College, "almost as far," says Heylin, "from the Calvinian doctrine in the main platform of predestination as Baroe, Harsnet, or Barret are conceived to be. But when it came to the vote of the university, the place was carried for Overal by the major part; which plainly shows that though the doctrines of Calvin were so hotly stickled here by most of the heads, yet the greater part of the learned body entertained them not." "The Lambeth Articles," it is well observed, "are no part of the doctrine of the Church of England, having never had any of the least sanction either from the parliament or the convocation. They were drawn up by Prof. Whitaker; and though they were afterwards approved by archbishop Whitgift, and six or eight of the inferior clergy, in a meeting they had at Lambeth, yet this meeting was only in a private manner, and without any authority from the queen; who was so far from approving of their proceedings that she not only ordered the articles to be suppressed, but was resolutely bent for some time to bring the archbishop and his associates under a *præmunire*, for presuming to make them without any warrant or legal authority." Such, in brief, was the origin and such the fate of the Lambeth Articles, without the countenance of which the defenders of Calvinism in the Church of England could find no semblance of support for their manifold affirmations on predestination and its kindred topics. At the census of 1851 two congregations calling themselves "Predestinarians" were returned.

Through the Puritans the Calvinistic notions were spread all over New England, and by the Reformed Dutch and other Presbyterisn bodies carried through most of the Middle and Western States of America. In some quarters they have been either outgrown [See Oberlin Theology], or so modified by outside Arminian influences as to be scarcely discernible; still, in the creeds and standards of several large denominations of the world the peculiar doctrines of Calvinism are unequivocally enunciated. From that celebrated synod known as the Westminster Assembly came forth the Calvinistic Confession and its catechisms, and its form of Church government. These wonderful documents have been preserved unchanged to the present time. The formulas of the Presbyterian Church of America at this time are essentially the same that were promulgated by the Westminster Assembly of Divines more than to hundred years ago. These forms of doctrine must be assented to, at least tacitly, by all the members of that Church. They must be distinctly professed by all its ministers and office-bearers. They are taught from the chairs of its theological schools, and they are elaborately systematized and ably defended in its noble "bodies of divinity"—of which the best and ablest, by Dr. Hodge, of Princeton, has recently been issued. That these teach the doctrines of predestination nobody denies; that to unsophisticated minds they exalt the divine sovereignty at the expense of his justice and his grace has seemed to be the case to Arminianists, who hold that, to make them agree with the language of Holy Scripture, entirely illegitimate methods of accommodation have had to be resorted to. See Arminianism; Calvinism.

IV. *Connection of Predestination with other Doctrines.*—Much confusion and obscurity has arisen in the progress of the predestinarian controversy from failing to keep the real issue always distinctly in view. The point in controversy is not whether or not God had a plan when he entered upon creation. See Foreknowledge; Providence. Neither is it whether or not that plan embraced a positive preappointment of every individual event in the whole range of futurity. Nor yet is it whether or not an exercise of divine energy is inseparably connected with any or all of God's predeterminations so that they are "effectual" decrees. See Calling; Grace. The real question is: Has God by an immutable and eternal decree predestinated some of the human family unto eternal life, and all the others unto everlasting perdition, without any reference whatever to the use they may make of their moral agency? This the Calvinist affirms, usually basing his affirmation solely on what he regards as Scripture authority, and often admitting that the human mind cannot reconcile it with the character of God or the dictates of human reason. Among the deniers, some have repudiated the supposition of any "decrees" at all respecting *individual* salvation, maintaining only the general ones, "He that believeth shall be saved, he that believeth not," etc. Others allow an individual or personal election, but, like Watson, understand by it "an act of God done in time, subsequent even to the administration of the means of salvation" (*Inst.* ii, 338). Others, as the older Arminians generally, suppose that specific individuals were eternally predestinated to life and death, but strictly according to their foreknown obedience or disobedience to the Gospel.[299]

IS THE FOREKNOWLEDGE OF GOD COMPATIBLE WITH FREE WILL?

How do Predestination and Foreknowledge Differ?

First, we will offer how the secular sources would define the words, which is really what the populace believes. Second, we will see what the Scriptures say about the original language words and how they are to be understood as to groups (e.g., the Israelites) and individuals (e.g., Samson, Jeremiah, Cyrus, Esau and Jacob, John the Baptist, and Judas Iscariot). When it comes to individuals, we **need not** look at every case, but rather just Judas Iscariot, who will be representative of them all. Below are how the world views predestination and foreknowledge and like most things, it has some aspects correct and others not so much.

The 16th-century Reformer John Calvin wrote: "We define predestination as the eternal design of God, whereby he determined what he wanted to do with each man. For he did not create them all in the same condition but foreordains some to everlasting life and others to eternal damnation."

---

[299] John M'Clintock and James Strong, "Predestination," *Cyclopædia of Biblical, Theological, and Ecclesiastical Literature* (New York: Harper & Brothers, Publishers, 1894), 496–502.

Does God really ordain each of us individually ahead of time as to what our actions and our final destiny are going to be? What does the Bible really teach?

The Secular Definition of Predestination and Foreknowledge

PREDESTINATION: (1) *The advance decision by God about events*: in some religious beliefs, the doctrine that God, a deity, or fate has established in advance everything that is going to happen and that nothing can change this. (2) *God's decision of who goes to Heaven*: in some religious beliefs, the doctrine that God decided at the beginning of time who would go to heaven after death and who would not. (3) *Act of foreordaining*: the human or supposedly divine act of deciding the fate of people or things beforehand.

FOREKNOWLEDGE: *knowledge of something before it happens*: knowledge or awareness that something is going to happen, either from information that has been acquired or by paranormal means.

The Biblical Definition of Predestination and Foreknowledge

The words generally translated as "foreknow," "foreknowledge," and "foreordain" (i.e., predestine) are found in the Greek New Testament, the same basic views are conveyed in the Hebrew Scriptures. It is true that God has the power of predestination and the faculty of foreknowledge. However, we need to understand foreknowledge and foreordination as they relate to God, grasping certain aspects. There are certain situations and events that take place because God has foreordained that they will (no creature in the universe can hinder these things), but it is not the case that **every event** must take place as it does because God has predetermined it, removing all free will. What God foreknows is because of the infallibility of his power of perception into the future, as though it were a timeline (more on this later). However, as we will see, this in no way violates our free will. In most cases, predestination has to do with groups like the Israelites and events, like the Exodus from Egypt, without foreordaining the specific individuals who will be involved in these groups or events. On the other hand, God's foreknowledge is not limited to groups and events, as he can see the future of every living creature.

DETERMINE, DETERMINATE

1. *krino* (κρίνω, 2919), primarily "to separate," hence, "to be of opinion, approve, esteem," Rom. 14:5, also "to determine, resolve, decree," is used in this sense in Acts 3:13; 20:16; 25:25; 27:1; 1 Cor. 2:2; 2 Cor. 2:1; Titus 3:12.

2. *horizo* (ὁρίζω, 3724) denotes "to bound, to set a boundary" (Eng., "horizon"); hence, "to mark out definitely, determine"; it is

translated "to determine" in Luke 22:22, of the foreordained pathway of Christ; Acts 11:29, of a "determination" to send relief; 17:26, where it is used of fixing the bounds of seasons. In Acts 2:23 the verb is translated "determinate," with reference to counsel. Here the verbal form might have been adhered to by the translation "determined"; that is to say, in the sense of "settled."

In Romans 1:4 it is translated "declared," where the meaning is that Christ was marked out as the Son of God by His resurrection and that of others (see under declare). In Acts 10:42 and 17:31 it has its other meaning of "ordain," that is, "to appoint by determined counsel." In Heb. 4.7, it is translated "limiteth," but preferably in the RV, "defineth," with reference to a certain period; here again it approaches its primary meaning of marking out the bounds of.

3. *proorizo* (προορίζω, 4309), *pro*, "beforehand," and No. 2, denotes "to mark out beforehand, to determine before, foreordain"; in Acts 4:28, KJV, "determined before," RV, "foreordained"; so the RV in 1 Cor. 2:7, KJV, "ordained", in Rom. 8:29-30 and Eph. 1:5, 11, KJV, "predestinate," RV, "foreordain."

4. *epiluo* (ἐπιλύω, 1956), lit., "to loosen upon," denotes "to solve, expound," Mark 4:34; "to settle," as of a controversy, Acts 19:39, KJV, "it shall be determined," RV, "it shall be settled."

5. *diaginosko* (διαγινώσκω, 1231), besides its meaning "to ascertain exactly," Acts 23:15, was an Athenian law term signifying "to determine," so used in 24:22, RV, "determine"; KJV, "know the uttermost of."[300]

FOREKNOW, FOREKNOWLEDGE

1. **Verb.**

proginosko (προγινώσκω, 4267), "to know before" (*pro*, "before," *ginosko*, "to know"), is used (a) of divine knowledge, concerning (1) Christ, 1 Pet. 1:20, RV, "foreknown" (KJV, "foreordained"); (2) Israel as God's earthly people, Rom. 11:2; (3) believers, Rom. 8:29; "the foreknowledge" of God is the basis of His foreordaining counsels; (b) of human knowledge, (1) of persons, Acts 26:5; (2) of facts, 2 Pet. 3:17.¶

1. **Noun.**

---

[300] W. E. Vine, Merrill F. Unger, and William White Jr., *Vine's Complete Expository Dictionary of Old and New Testament Words* (Nashville, TN: T. Nelson, 1996), 165–166.

prognosis (πρόγνωσις, 4268), "a foreknowledge" (akin to A.), is used only of divine "foreknowledge," Acts 2:23; 1 Pet. 1:2. "Foreknowledge" is one aspect of omniscience; it is implied in God's warnings, promises, and predictions. See Acts 15:18. God's "foreknowledge" involves His electing grace, but this does not preclude human will. He "foreknows" the exercise of faith, which brings salvation. The apostle Paul stresses especially the actual purposes of God rather than the ground of the purposes, see, e.g., Gal. 1:16; Eph. 1:5, 11. The divine counsels will ever be unthwartable.[301]

"Foreknowledge" translates the Greek prognōsis (from pro, before, and gnosis, knowledge). (Ac 2:23; 1 Pet 1:2) It means that God knows something before it happens, or that he has given the knowledge of this to a prophet, who now knows as well. The related Greek verb proginōskō is used two times with regard to humans. (Ac 26:4-5; 2 Pet. 3:17) It also means that someone has knowledge of something before it occurs. In Paul's statement that all the Jews had "known for a long time" (Gr. knowing before) with him (i.e., knew him before he became a Christian), and in Peter's reference to the "knowing this beforehand" (about false teachers who are twisting the Scriptures) had by those addressed in his second letter.

Judas, though imperfect, had lived in intimate association with Jesus Christ, the Son of God, while he was initially faithful, he turned traitor; Jesus referring to him as "the son of destruction." (Joh. 17:12) The apostate "man of lawlessness" is also called "the son of destruction." (2Thess. 2:3) When Jesus' referred to Judas as "the son of destruction," he indicated that when Judas died, there was no hope of his returning in some future resurrection. Judas would not live on in God's memory. Here we have the Greek verb *apōleto* for "perish" and the Greek noun *apōleias* for "destruction," "waste" "annihilation," and "ruin." Clinton E. Arnold writes, "The expression ["son of destruction"] can refer either to Judas's character[302] or his destiny.[303] The NIV rendering "doomed to destruction" suggests the latter, though, of course, both are true. The noun 'destruction' (*apōleia*) commonly refers in the New Testament to final condemnation. … This suggests that "son of destruction" labels Judas Iscariot as part of a typology of evil personages across the sweep of salvation history seeking to thwart God's sovereign purposes."[304]

---

301 IBID, 249.

302 E.g., Heb. "children of unrighteousness" becomes "children of perdition" in Isa. 57:4 LXX; the same phrase is found in Jub. 10:3.

303 Heb. "the people I have totally destroyed" becomes "the people of perdition" in Isa. 34:5 LXX.

304 Clinton E. Arnold, *Zondervan Illustrated Bible Backgrounds Commentary: John, Acts.*, vol. 2 (Grand Rapids, MI: Zondervan, 2002), 154.

John 17:12 Updated American Standard Version (UASV)

12 While I was with them, I kept them in your name, which you have given me; and I guarded them and not one of them perished but the son of destruction,[*] so that the Scripture would be fulfilled.

[*] Or *son of perdition*

Let it be made clear that God did not predestine Judas Iscariot or coerce him to act against his own free will. How do we correctly understand Judas' freedom as it relates to God's foreknowledge? Because God has the power to exercise his foreknowledge of everything in advance, some have suggested that it was fated prior to Judas' birth that he would betray Jesus. In short, yes, God foresaw that Judas would betray him; however, Judas had the free will choice to change his mind at any point of such an idea entering it. If Judas had changed his mind, God would have foreseen something else. However, we must keep in mind that God is able to also foresee heart condition, heart attitude, not just events. Therefore, God would have not only foreseen the decision Judas made but also his unreceptive heart.

Let us deal with this very important issue of God's foreknowledge, as it is, a Bible difficulty, which Christians have struggled to answer. What lies below is largely based on the work of the apologist world-renowned Dr. William Lane Craig.

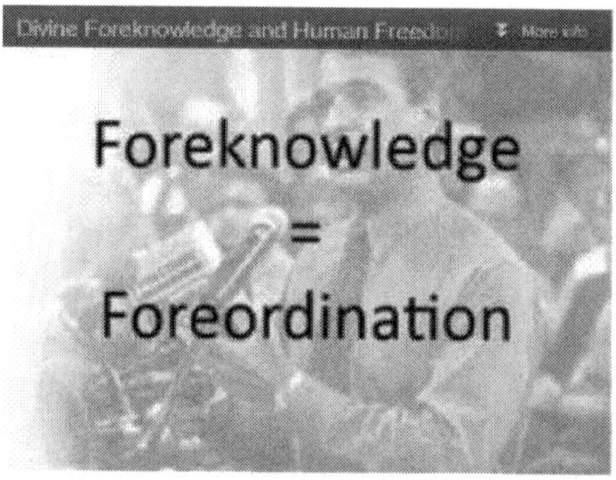

Many Bible critics say, by knowing that Judas will betray Jesus hundreds of years in advance, that makes it foreordained to happen. As a result, human freedom is removed. Based on this reasoning, God foreordained even the sin of Adam and Eve, and thus they never had the free will to do otherwise. The Bible says that God is not the author of sin, but this would argue otherwise, contradicting Scripture. However, with this equation, sin is the result, not the result of Adam's choice, but of God's choosing, which should make us feel uncomfortable.

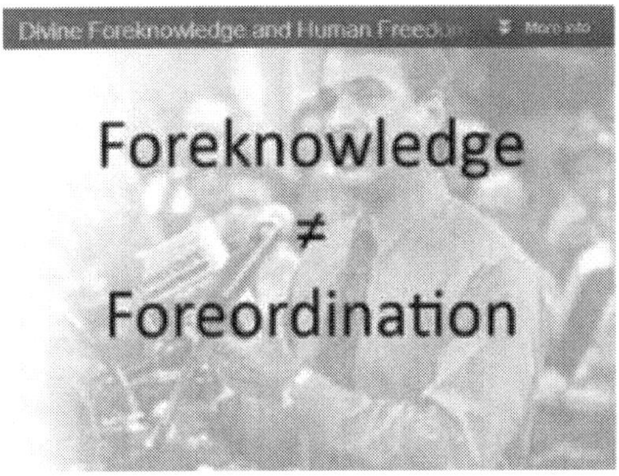

The best solution to this problem is to deny this equivalence, saying that foreknowledge does not equal foreordination.

FOREKNOWLEDGE

Does Not =

FOREORDINATION

It is better to understand it that God knows in advance what choice people will freely make. It is the free decisions of human beings that determine what foreknowledge God has of them, as opposed to the reverse.

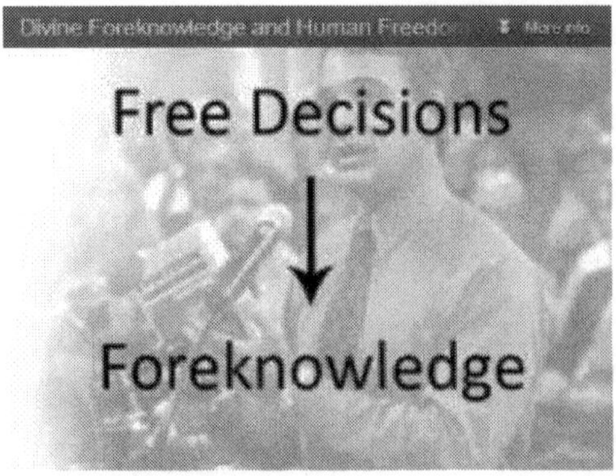

FOREKNOWLEDGE

Determine

FREE DECISIONS

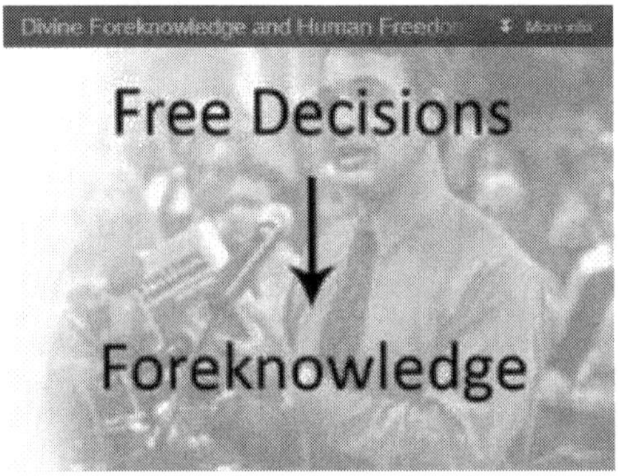

FREE DECISIONS

Determine

FOREKNOWLEDGE

The foreknowledge does not determine the free decision; it is the free decisions that determine the foreknowledge. In this, we can distinguish what we might call **Chronological Priority and Logical Priority**.

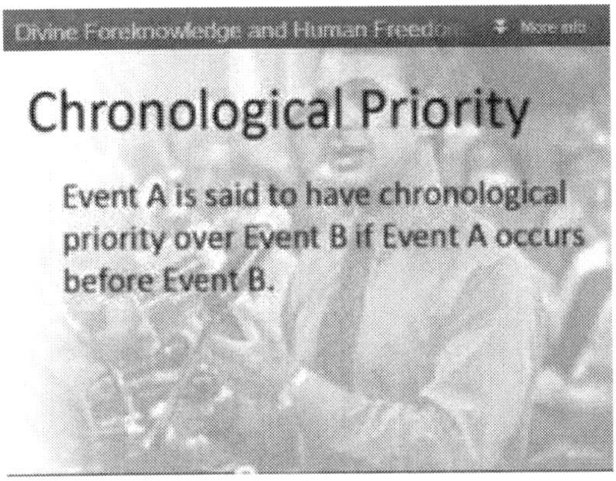

Chronological priority would mean that Event "A" [God's knowledge], as it relates to time, would come before Event "B" [the event God foreknows]. Thus, God's knowledge is chronologically prior to the event that he foreknows.

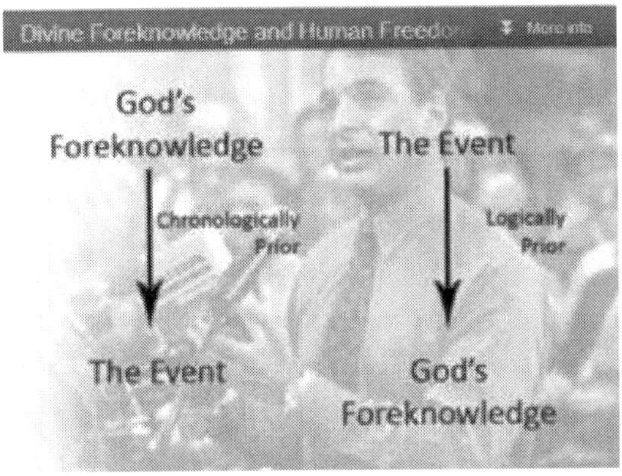

CHRONOLOGICAL PRIORITY

God's foreknowledge

Prior to Event

However, logically speaking, the event is prior to God's foreknowledge.

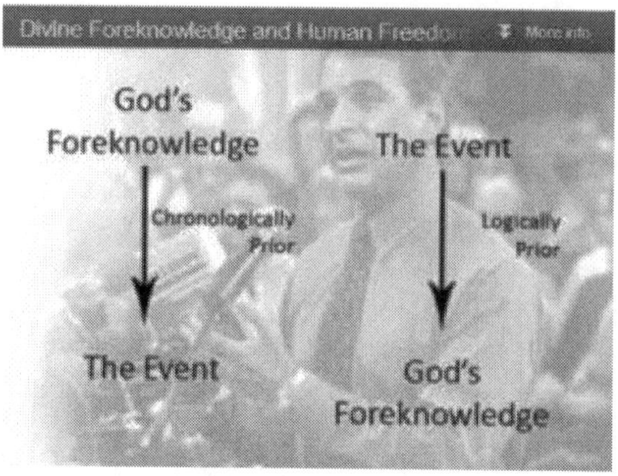

LOGICAL PRIORITY

Event

Prior to

God's foreknowledge

In other words, the event does not happen because God foreknows it, but God foreknows the event because it will happen. The event is logically prior to the foreknowledge, so he foreknows it because it will happen, even though the foreknowledge is chronologically prior to the event.

We can see foreknowledge on this, as the foreshadowing of something. When you see the shadow of someone coming around the corner of the building, you see his or her shadow on the ground before you see the person. You know that person is about to come around the corner because of their shadow but the shadow does not determine the person, the person determines the shadow.

God's foreknowledge is like the foreshadowing of a future event. By seeing this foreshadowing, you know the events will happen, But the shadow does not determine the reality, the reality determines the shadow. Therefore, we should think of God's foreknowledge as the foreshadowing of things to come. Therefore, just because God will know something will happen, this does not prejudice or remove the freedom of that happening.

In fact, if the events were to happen differently, God's foreknowledge would be different as well. An illustration of this is, like an infallible barometer of the weather. Whatever the barometer says, because it is infallible, you know what the weather will be like. However, the barometer does not determine the weather; the weather determines the barometer's findings. Thus, God's foreknowledge is like an infallible barometer of the future. It lets him know what the future is going to be, but it does not constrain the future in any way. The future is going to happen anyway the free moral agent wants it to happen. However, the barometer is going to track whatever direction the future will take.

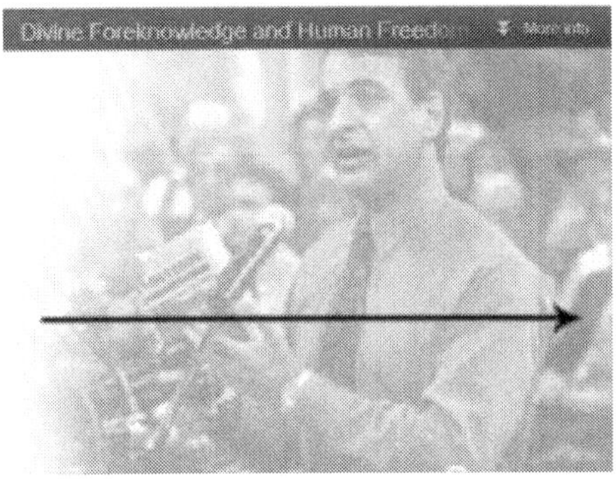

Thus, those who believe that God's foreknowledge removes the freedom of the person are mistaken. They posit a constraint upon human choices, which is really quite unintelligible. Let us use another illustration.

Suppose this is the timeline . . .

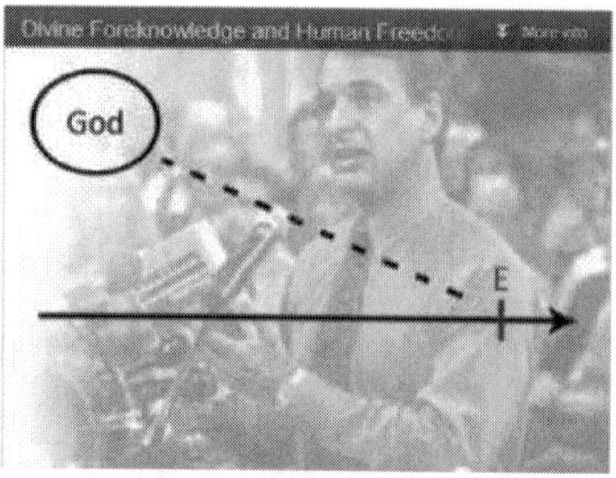

Let us place an event "**E**" on the timeline, i.e., Judas' betrayal of Jesus.

Let us suppose **God** is back here in time and by his foreknowledge (the dotted line); he knows that "**E**" will happen (Judas will betray Jesus). How does God's knowledge about "E" constrain "E" from happening? How can God's knowing "**E**" will occur make "**E**" occur?

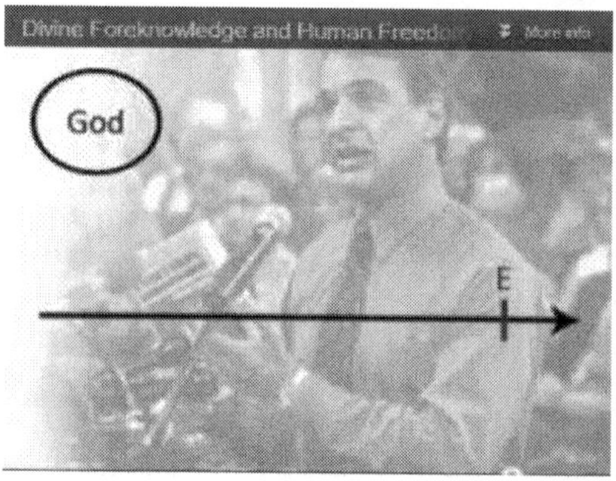

If you were to erase the line and say **God** does not have foreknowledge of the future, how has anything changed? How would "**E**" (Judas' betrayal) be affected if you erased God's foreknowledge of it? "**E**" (Judas' betrayal) would occur just the same, it would not affect anything at all.

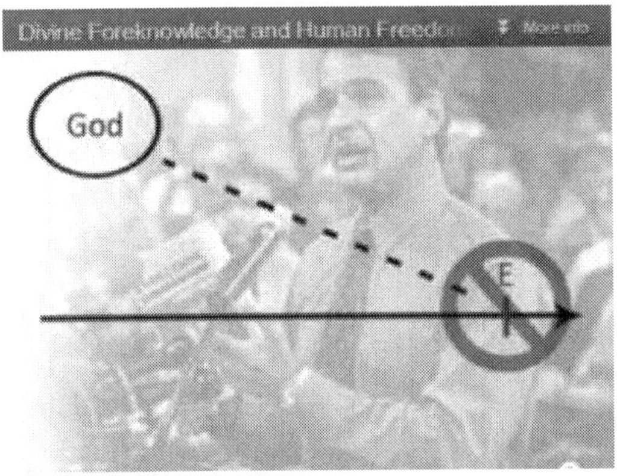

Therefore, the presence of God's foreknowledge really does not prejudice anything about whether "**E**" will occur or not. Therefore, those who think that foreknowledge is incompatible with freedom are simply quite mistaken.

What we need to understand is this, if Judas ("**E**") were not to betray Jesus; then, God would **not** have foreknown Judas' betrayal **("E")** of Jesus because it would not have been on the timeline. In addition, as long as that statement is true, "**E**" being able to occur and not occur, God's foreknowledge does not prejudice anything with respect to "**E**'s" occurrence.

Let us review without the "E" getting in our way of thinking it through. God can see the timeline similar to the way that a man in a helicopter looking down on a parade. Just as the man in the helicopter can see things before they get to the spectators, so too, God can see down the timeline to things that have not taken place yet. God knew way back in Genesis 3:15 when it was prophesied that the serpent (Satan) was to bruise Jesus and that Satan's agent for doing so was going to be Judas Iscariot.

Just because God has the ability to see down the timeline, this does not affect Judas' free will choice that he would come to make. On this, Andreas J. Köstenberger writes, "This does not alter the fact that Judas made his decision as a responsible agent and that he will be held accountable and judged for his evil act (see Mark 14:21 = Matt. 26:24)"[305] If we look at the diagram below, it gives us a visual aid of what God can see. Let us take persons such as myself, one who struggles with understanding deep scientific information. Just because I cannot fully understand the scientific areas of astronomy (the scientific study of the universe), this does not mean that an

[305] Andreas J. Köstenberger, *John*, Baker Exegetical Commentary on the New Testament (Grand Rapids, MI: Baker Academic, 2004), 494.

astronomer's in-depth explanation of the motions, positions, sizes, composition, and behavior of astronomical objects is any less true because I am baffled. When he or she goes into an in-depth discussion of how these objects are studied and interpreted from the radiation they emit and from data gathered by interplanetary probes, I cannot just blurt out, "you are wrong" because I do not understand the how of things. However, some in science would do just that to a far more intelligent person than all of them combined, namely, God.

God has the ability to step into the timeline and tweak anything, to create a different outcome if he chooses to do so, which will then alter many future events because it will create a ripple effect in the timeline. If God were to alter anything that was already going to happen, making different choices outside of what was already going to occur in the present, it would have a ripple effect on future events. Let us use Willian Tyndale, which I believe God did step into the timeline to protect Tyndale from the Catholic Church that was hunting him down for translating the Bible from the original languages of Hebrew (OT) and Greek (NT) into English. Let us say that God did step in to alter things, allowing Tyndale to survive to the point of bringing us the first printed translation in 1526, it would have had an impact on all English translations that lied ahead in the future: the Coverdale translation of 1535, the Matthew's Bible of 1537, The Great Bible of 1539, Cranmer's Bible of 1540, the Geneva Bible of 1560, and, of course, the King James Version of 1611, and all other down to the Revised Version of 1881, the 1801 American Standard Version, the 1952 Revised Standard Version, the 1960-1995 New American Standard Bible, and the 2001 English Standard Version. Think of the impact of the English translations had the Catholic Church executed Tyndale in 1523.

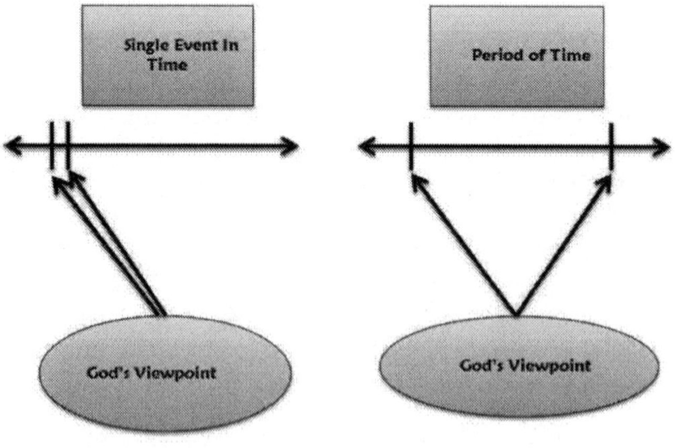

Bibliography

Akin, D. L. (2001). *The New American Commentary: 1, 2, 3 John.* Nashville, TN: Broadman & Holman .

Akin, D. L., Nelson, D. P., & Peter R. Schemm, J. (2007). *A Theology for the Church.* Nashville: B & H Publishing.

Anders, M. (1999). *Holman New Testament Commentary: vol. 8, Galatians-Colossians* . Nashville, TN: Broadman & Holman Publishers.

Anders, M., & Butler, T. (2002). *Holman Old Testament Commentary: Isaiah.* Nashville, TN: B&H Publishing.

Anders, M., & McIntosh, D. (2009). *Holman Old Testament Commentary - Deuteronomy.* Nashville: B&H Publishing.

Anders, M., & McIntosh, D. (2009). *Holman Old Testament Commentary - Deuteronomy (pp. 359-360).* . Nashville: B&H Publishing.

Andrews, S. J., & Bergen, R. D. (2009). *Holman Old Testament Commentary: 1-2 Samuel.* Nashville: Broadman & Holman.

Arnold, C. E. (2002). *Zondervan Illustrated Bible Backgrounds Commentary Volume 2: John, Acts.* . Grand Rapids, MI: Zondervan.

Arnold, C. E. (2002). *Zondervan Illustrated Bible Backgrounds Commentary Volume 3: Romans to Philemon.* Grand Rapids: Zondervan.

Arnold, C. E. (2002). *Zondervan Illustrated Bible Backgrounds Commentary Volume 4: Hebrews to Revelation.* Grand Rapids, MI: Zondervan.

Arnold, C. E. (2002). *Zondervan Illustrated Bible Backgrounds Commentary: Matthew, Mark, Luke, vol. 1.* Grand Rapids, MI: Zondervan.

Barker, K. L., & Bailey, W. (2001). *The New American Commentary: vol. 20, Micah, Nahum, Habakkuk, Zephaniah.* Nashville, TN: Broadman & Holman Publishers.

Benner, D. G., & Hill, P. C. (1985, 1999). *Baker Encyclopedia of Psychology and Counseling (Second Edition).* Grand Rapids: Baker Books.

Bercot, D. W. (1998). *A Dictionary of Early Christian Beliefs.* Peabody: Hendrickson.

Blomberg, C. (1992). *The New American Commentary: Matthew.* Nashville, TN: Broadman & Holman Publishers.

Boa, K., & Kruidenier, W. (2000). *Holman New Testament Commentary: Romans.* Nashville: Broadman & Holman.

Boles, K. L. (1993). *The College Press NIV commentary: Galatians & Ephesians.* Joplin, MO: College Press.

Borchert, G. L. (2001). *The New American Commentary: John 1-11* . Nashville, TN: Broadman & Holman Publishers.

Borchert, G. L. (2002). *The New American Commentary vol. 25B, John 12–21.* Nashville: Broadman & Holman Publishers.

Boyd, G. A., & Eddy, P. R. (2002, 2009). *Across the Spectrum [Secon Edition].* Grand Rapids: Baker Academic.

Brand, C., Draper, C., & Archie, E. (2003). *Holman Illustrated Bible Dictionary: Revised, Updated and Expanded.* Nashville, TN: Holman.

Bratcher, R. G., & Hatton, H. (1993). *A Handbook on the Revelation to John.* New York: United Bible Societies.

Bromiley, G. W. (1986). *The International Standard Bible Encyclopedia (Vol. 1-4).* Grand Rapids, MI: William B. Eerdmans Publishing Co.

Bromiley, G. W., & Friedrich, G. (1964-). *Theological Dictionary of the New Testament, ed. Gerhard Kittel, vol. 4.* Grand Rapids, MI: Eerdmans.

Brooks, J. A. (1992). *The New American Commentary: Mark (Volume 23).* Nashville: Broadman & Holman Publishers.

Bullinger, E. W. (1898). *Figures of Speech Used in the Bible.* London; New York: E. & J. B. Young & Co.

Butler, T. C. (2000). *Holman New Testament Commentary: Luke.* Nashville, TN: Broadman & Holman Publishers.

Butler, T. C. (2005). *Holman Old Testament Commentary - Hosea, Joel, Amos, Obadiah, Jonah, Micah* . Nashville: Broadman & Holman Publishers.

Cooper, R. (2000). *Holman New Testament Commentary: Mark.* Nashville: Broadman & Holman Publishers.

Easley, K. H. (1998). *Revelation, vol. 12, Holman New Testament Commentary.* Nashville, TN:: Broadman & Holman Publishers.

Elwell, W. A. (2001). *Evangelical Dictionary of Theology (Second Edition).* Grand Rapids: Baker Academic.

Elwell, W. A. (2001). *Evangelical Dictionary of Theology (Second Edition).* Grand Rapids: Baker Academic.

Elwell, W. A., & Beitzel, B. J. (1988). *Baker Encyclopedia of the Bible.* Grand Rapids, MI: Baker Book House.

Elwell, W. A., & Comfort, P. W. (2001). *Tyndale Bible Dictionary.* Wheaton: Tyndale House Publishers.

Enns, P. P. (1997). *The Moody Handbook of Theology.* Chicago: Moody Press.

Erickson, M. J. (1998). *Christian Theology.* Grand Rapids, MI: Baker Academic.

Erickson, M. J. (2013). *Christian Theology (Third Edition).* Grand Rapids, MI: Baker Academic.

Ferguson, E. (2009). *Baptism in the Early Church: History, Theology, and Liturgy in the First Five Centuries* . Grand Rapids, MI: Eerdmans.

Friberg, T., Friberg, B., & Miller, N. F. (2000). *Analytical Lexicon of the Greek New Testament.* Grand Rapids: Baker Books.

Friberg, T., Friberg, B., & Miller, N. F. (2000). *Analytical Lexicon of the Greek New Testament, Baker's Greek New Testament Library.* Grand Rapids, MI: Baker Books.

Gangel, K. O. (1998). *Holman New Testament Commentary: Acts.* Nashville, TN: Broadman & Holman Publishers.

Gangel, K. O. (2000). *Holman New Testament Commentary, vol. 4, John* . Nashville, TN: Broadman & Holman Publishers.

Gangel, K. O. (2001). *Holman Old Testament Commentary: Daniel.* Nashville: Broadman & Holman Publishers.

Garrett, D. A. (1993). *The New American Commentary: Vol. 14 (Proverbs, Ecclesiastes, Song of Songs).* Nashville: Broadman & Holman Publishers.

Geisler, N. L. (2011). *Systematic Theology in One Volume.* Minneapolis, MN: Bethany House.

George, T. (2001). *The New American Commentary: Galatians* . Nashville, TN: Broadman & Holman Publishers.

Grudem, W. (2011). *Making Sense of the Bible: One of Seven Parts from Grudem's Systematic Theology (Making Sense of Series).* Grand Rapids: Zondervan.

Gruden, W. (2011). *Are Miraculous Gifts for Today?: 4 Views (Counterpoints: Bible and Theology).* Grand Rapids: Zondervan.

Harris, R. L., Archer, G. L., & Waltke, B. K. (1999, c1980). *Theological Wordbook of the Old Testament.* Chicago: Moody Press.

Hill, J. (2006). *Zondervan Handbook to the History of Christianity.* Oxford: Lion.

Keener, C. S. (1993). *The IVP Bible Background Commentary: New Testament.* Downer Groves, IL: InterVarsity Press.

Kittel, G., Friedrich, G., & Bromiley, G. W. (1995, c1985). *Theological Dictionary of the New Testament.* Grand Rapids: Eerdmans.

Knight, G. W. (1992). *The Pastoral Epistles: A Commentary on the Greek Text, New International Greek Testament Commentary.* Grand Rapids, MI; Carlisle, England: W.B. Eerdmans; Paternoster Press.

Larson, K. (2000). *Holman New Testament Commentary, vol. 9, I & II Thessalonians, I & II Timothy, Titus, Philemon.* Nashville, TN: Broadman & Holman Publishers.

Lea, T. D. (1999). *Holman New Testament Commentary: Vol. 10, Hebrews, James.* Nashville, TN: Broadman & Holman Publishers.

Lea, T. D., & Griffin, H. P. (1992). *The New American Commentary, vol. 34, 1, 2 Timothy, Titus.* Nashville: Broadman & Holman Publishers.

Martin, D. M. (2001, c1995). *The New American Commentary 33 1, 2 Thessalonians* . Nashville, TN: Broadman & Holman.

Martin, G. S. (2002). *Holman Old Testament Commentary: Numbers.* Nashville: Broadman & Holman Publishers.

Mathews, K. A. (2001). *The New American Commentary vol. 1A, Genesis 1-11:26* . Nashville: Broadman & Holman Publishers.

Matthews, K. A. (2001). *The New American Commentary Vol. 1B, Genesis 11:27-50:26.* Nashville: Broadman and Holman Publishers.

McMinn, M. R. (2010). *Psychology, Theology, and Spirituality in Christian Counseling (AACC Library).* Carol Stream, IL: Tyndale House Publishers.

McReynolds, P. R. (1999). *Word Study: Greek-English.* Carol Stream: Tyndale House Publishers.

Melick, R. R. (2001). *The New American Commentary: vol. 32, Philippians, Colissians, Philemon.* Nashville, TN : Broadman & Holman Publishers.

Miller, S. R. (1994). *Daniel, vol. 18, The New American Commentary.* Nashville:: Broadman & Holman Publishers.

Moo, D. (2000). *The Letter of James: Pillar New Testament Commentary.* Grand Rapids: William B. Eerdman's Publishing Company.

Morris, L. (1992). *The Gospel According to Matthew, The Pillar New Testament Commentary*. Grand Rapids, MI(; Leicester, England: W.B. Eerdmans; Inter-Varsity Press,.

Mounce, R. H. (2001). *The New American Commentary: Vol. 27 Romans.* Nashville, TN: Broadman & Holman Publishers.

Mounce, W. D. (2006). *Mounce's Complete Expository Dictionary of Old & New Testament Words.* Grand Rapids, MI: Zondervan.

Polhill, J. B. (2001). *The New American Commentary 26: Acts.* Nashville: Broadman & Holman Publishers.

Pratt Jr, R. L. (2000). *Holman New Testament Commentary: I & II Corinthians, vol. 7.* Nashville: Broadman & Holman Publishers.

Ramsey, B. (. (2006). *Manichean Debate (Works of Saint Augustine).* New City Press: Hyde Park.

Richardson, K. (1997). *The New American Commentary Vol. 36 James.* Nashville: Broadman & Holman Publishers.

Robertson, P. E. (Spring 1998). Theology of the Healthy Church. *The Theological Educator: A Journal of Theology and Ministry*, 45-52.

Rooker, M. F. (2000). *The New American Commentary, vol. 3A, Leviticus.* Nashville: Broadman & Holman Publishers.

Rooker, M. F. (2005). *Holman Old Testament Commentary: Ezekiel.* Nashville: Broadman & Holman Publishers.

Schreiner, T. R. (2003). *The New American Commentary: 1, 2 Peter, Jude.* Nashville: Broadman & Holman.

Stein, R. H. (1994). *A Basic Guide to Interpreting the Bible: Playing by the Rules.* Grand Rapids: Baker Books.

Stein, R. H. (2001, c1992). *The New American Commentary: Luke.* Nashville, TN: Broadman & Holman .

Stuart, D. K. (2006). *The New American Commentary: An Exegetical Theological Exposition of Holy Scripture EXODUS.* Nashville: Broadman & Holman.

Swanson, J. (1997). *Dictionary of Biblical Languages with Semantic Domains: Greek (New Testament).* Oak Harbor: Logos Research Systems.

Swanson, J. (1997). *Dictionary of Biblical Languages with Semantic Domains: Hebrew (Old Testament).* Oak Harbor: Logos Research Systems.

Swindoll, C. R., & Zuck, R. B. (2003). *Understanding Christian Theology.* Nashville, TN: Thomas Nelson Publishers.

Taylor, R. A., & Clendenen, R. E. (2007). *The New American Commentary: Haggai, Malachi, , vol. 21A* . Nashville, TN: Broadman & Holman Publishers.

Terry, M. S. (1883). *Biblical Hermeneutics: A Treatise on the Interpretation of the Old and New Testaments.* Grand Rapids: Zondervan.

Thomas, R. L. (1992). *Revelation 1-7: An Exegetical Commentary* . Chicago, IL: Moody Publishers.

Thomas, R. L. (1995). *Revelation 8-22: An Exegetical Commentary* . Chicago, IL: Moody Publishers.

Thomas, R. L. (1998, 1981). *New American Standard Hebrew-Aramaic and Greek Dictionaries: Updated Edition.* Anaheim: Foundation Publications, Inc.

Towns, E. L. (2002). *Theology for Today.* Belmont: Wadsworth Group.

Towns, E. L. (2006). *Concise Bible Dictrines: Clear, Simple, and Easy-to-Understand Explanations of Bible Doctrines.* Chattanooga: AMG Publishers.

Vine, W. E. (1996). *Vine's Expository Dictionary of Old and New Testament Words.* Nashville: Thomas Nelson.

Vunderink, R. W., & Bromiley, G. W. (1979–1988). *The International Standard Bible Encyclopedia, Revised (,* . Grand Rapids, MI: Wm. B. Eerdmans.

Walls, D., & Anders, M. (1996). *Holman New Testament Commentary: I & II Peter, I, II & III John, Jude.* Nashville: Broadman & Holman Publishers.

Walton, J. H. (2009). *Zondervan Illustrated Bible Backgrounds Commentary (Old Testament) Volume 1: Genesis, Exodus, Leviticus, Numbers, Deuteronomy.* Grand Rapids, MI: Zondervan.

Walton, J. H. (2009). *Zondervan Illustrated Bible Backgrounds Commentary (Old Testament) Volume 3: 1 & 2 Kings, 1 & 2 Chronicles, Ezra, Nehemiah, Esthe.* Grand Rapids, MI: Zondervan.

Walton, J. H. (2009). *Zondervan Illustrated Bible Backgrounds Commentary (Old Testament) Volume 5: The Minor Prophets, Job, Psalms, Proverbs, Ecclesiastes, Song of Songs.* Grand Rapids, M: Zondervan.

Watson, R. (1832). *A Biblical and Theological Dictionary: Explanatory of the History, Manners and Customs of the Jews.* New York: Waugh and T. Mason.

Weber, S. K. (2000). *Holman New Testament Commentary, vol. 1, Matthew.* Nashville, TN: Broadman & Holman Publishers.

Wood, D. R. (1996). *New Bible Dictionary (Third Edition).* Downers Grove: InterVarsity Press.

Zodhiates, S. (2000, c1992, c1993). *The Complete Word Study Dictionary: New Testament.* Chattanooga: AMG Publishers.

Zuck, R. B. (1991). *Basic Bible Interpretation: A Prafctical Guide to Discovering Biblical Truth.* Colorado Springs: David C. Cook.

Zweig, S. (1936). *Castellio gegen Calvin oder Ein Gewissen gegen die Gewalt [Castellio against Calvin or a conscience against violence].* Herbert Reichner: H. Reichner.

Zweig, S. (1951). *Erasmus; The Right to Heresy: Castellio against Calvin.* . London: Cassell.

Made in the USA
Middletown, DE
14 March 2024

51495738R00170